Opposing Viewpoints in American History

SECOND EDITION

Volume 2: From Reconstruction to the Present

Opposing Viewpoints in American History

VOLUME 2
FROM RECONSTRUCTION TO THE PRESENT

William Dudley
VOLUME EDITOR

John C. Chalberg
CONSULTING EDITOR

GREENHAVEN PRESS
An imprint of Thomson Gale, a part of The Thomson Corporation

Detroit • New York • San Francisco • New Haven, Conn. • Waterville, Maine • London

Opposing Viewpoints in American History
Volume 2: From Reconstruction to the Present

William Dudley, volume editor, and John C. Chalberg, consulting editor

LIBRARY OF CONGRESS CATALOGING-IN-PUBLICATION DATA

Opposing viewpoints in American history / William Dudley, volume editor; John C. Chalberg, consulting editor.
    v. cm.
    Includes bibliographical references and index.
    Contents: v. 1. From colonial times to Reconstruction – v. 2. From Reconstruction to the present.
    Audience: Grades 9–12.
    ISBN-13: 978-0-7377-3184-2 (v. 1 : lib. alk. paper) --
    ISBN-10: 0-7377-3184-2 (v. 1 : lib. alk. paper) --
    ISBN-13: 978-0-7377-3185-9 (v. 1 pbk. : alk. paper) --
    ISBN-10: 0-7377-3185-0 (v. 1 pbk. : alk. paper) --
    [etc.]
    1. United States -- History -- Sources -- Juvenile literature. I. Dudley, William, 1964–. II. Chalberg, John.
    E173.O7 2007
    973–dc22
                                                                 2006024673

ISBN-13:

978-0-7377-3184-2
  (v. 1 : lib. alk. paper)
978-0-7377-3185-9
  (v. 1 : pbk. : alk. paper)

978-0-7377-3186-6
  (v. 2 : lib. alk. paper)
978-0-7377-3187-3
  (v. 2 : pbk. : alk. paper)

ISBN-10:

0-7377-3184-2
  (v. 1 : lib. alk. paper)
0-7377-3185-0
  (v. 1 : pbk. : alk. paper)

0-7377-3186-9
  (v. 2 : lib. : alk. paper)
0-7377-3187-7
  (v. 2 : pbk. : alk. paper)

Printed in the United States of America
10 9 8 7 6 5 4 3 2 1

Contents

Contents

OPPOSING VIEWPOINTS IN AMERICAN HISTORY

Contents

Foreword

Educators have long sought ways to engage and interest students in American history. They have also tried to sharpen their students' critical thinking skills by teaching them how to effectively analyze and evaluate the material they read. *Opposing Viewpoints in American History* has been designed with both these objectives in mind.

Opposing Viewpoints in American History is an anthology of primary documents—the speeches, letters, articles, and other writings that are the raw material from which historians seek to understand and reconstruct the past. Assembled in two volumes (*Volume 1: From Colonial Times to Reconstruction* and *Volume 2: From Reconstruction to the Present*), these viewpoints trace American social, political, and diplomatic history from the time of the earliest European contact to the twenty-first century. The excerpts represent a wide spectrum of American voices, both the famous and the unfamiliar, expressing opinions on the critical issues of their times.

To help sustain student interest and stimulate critical thinking, primary documents in *Opposing Viewpoints in American History* are paired in a running debate format. This arrangement allows readers to compare and contrast opposing viewpoints on an issue. For example, readers can evaluate Thomas Paine's stirring call for American independence in *Common Sense* by comparing it with the tightly reasoned arguments of Loyalist Charles Inglis. Within these two volumes, early English settlers provide opposing views of life in the new colonies; Supreme Court justices clash over whether to extend civil rights to blacks and, over a hundred years later, debate the same issue in regard to World War II Japanese American internees. Franklin D. Roosevelt's call for a New Deal is complemented by Herbert Hoover's dire warnings about the harms of government meddling. A U.S. president and peace studies academic differ on how America should respond to the September 11, 2001, terrorist attacks. The paired structuring of sources found in *Opposing Viewpoints in American History* also reflects the important reality that American history itself has been a story of conflict and controversy. The birth of the nation was the result of a hotly debated decision to break from Great Britain, and Americans have continued to debate the meaning and direction of their nation ever since.

Along with primary documents, *Opposing Viewpoints in American History* includes several supplementary features intended to enhance the reader's understanding. Introductions and timelines supply basic historical background for each section of the two volumes. In addition, for each viewpoint the editors have provided essential biographical information about the author; a brief overview of the issue being debated; and questions designed to stimulate interest, reinforce comprehension, and encourage critical thinking. The combination of primary texts and background information make *Opposing Viewpoints in American History*, by itself or in conjunction with other American history textbooks, an effective way to teach and engage students in American history.

This second edition of *Opposing Viewpoints in American History* includes key viewpoints regarding the September 11 terrorist attacks and the Iraq War. In addition, bibliographies that accompany each pair of opposing viewpoints have been updated to include newly published material.

Thomas Jefferson once said that "difference of opinion leads to inquiry, and inquiry to truth"—a statement as valid today as in Jefferson's time. It is the editors' hope that this volume will challenge students to actively inquire into the "difference of opinion" found on the pages of America's history in order to better understand the nation's past.

Part 1
REBUILDING AFTER THE CIVIL WAR (1865–1895)

CHRONOLOGY

1865

March 3 Freedman's Bureau established.

April 9 Robert E. Lee surrenders to Ulysses S. Grant, ending Civil War.

April 14 President Abraham Lincoln assassinated.

November Mississippi enacts Black Code.

December 18 Thirteenth Amendment, banning slavery, ratified.

December 24 Ku Klux Klan founded in Tennessee.

1866

April 9 Congress passes Civil Rights Act over President Andrew Johnson's veto, nullifying state Black Codes.

July 24 Congress readmits the state of Tennessee to the Union.

July 30 Race riot in New Orleans results in 200 casualties.

1867

March 1 Nebraska enters the Union.

March 30 United States purchases Alaska from Russia.

1868

May President Andrew Johnson avoids impeachment by one vote.

June 22–24 Arkansas, Alabama, Florida, Louisiana, South Carolina, and North Carolina are readmitted to the Union.

July 21 Fourteenth Amendment, guaranteeing black civil rights, ratified.

November 3 Ulysses S. Grant elected president.

December 25 President Johnson grants amnesty for all Confederate leaders.

1869

March 15 Woman suffrage amendment to the Constitution proposed in Congress.

May 10 Nation's first transcontinental railroad completed.

November 6 First intercollegiate football game played.

December 10 Wyoming Territory grants women the right to vote.

1870

January 10 Standard Oil Company incorporated in Cleveland, Ohio.

January 20 Virginia readmitted to the Union.

February 23 Mississippi readmitted to the Union.

February 25 Hiram R. Revels of Mississippi become nation's first black senator.

March 30 Fifteenth Amendment, forbidding racial restrictions on suffrage, ratified.

1871

March 3 Congress nullifies past treaties and makes Indians wards of the federal government.

April 20 Ku Klux Klan Act passed by Congress.

October 8–11 Great Chicago fire destroys much of the city of Chicago.

1872

March 1 Yellowstone National Park established by Congress.

June 19 Freedman's Bureau abolished.

November 28 Susan B. Anthony arrested while attempting to vote.

November 5 Grant reelected president.

1873

March 3 Comstock law bars obscenity (including birth control information) from the federal mails.

September Wall Street Panic of 1873 occurs.

1875

March 1 Civil Rights Act of 1875 forbids racial segregation in public places.

1876

February 2 National League of baseball teams organized.

March Alexander Graham Bell invents the telephone.

May–November Centennial Exposition occurs at Philadelphia.

August 1 Colorado admitted to the Union.

1877

March 2 Rutherford B. Hayes declared winner of close and controversial presidential election.

April Remaining federal troops are withdrawn from the South.

June–October Nez Percé War occurs.

July Railway workers stage first national strike.

1878

August 21 American Bar Association founded.

1879

Winter *Progress and Poverty* by Henry George published.

February 15 Act of Congress permits women to argue cases before the U.S. Supreme Court.

October 21 Thomas Edison invents the first practical incandescent light.

1880

November 2 James A. Garfield elected president.

1881

February 19 Kansas adopts statewide prohibition.

May 21 American Red Cross founded.

July 2 President Garfield shot.

July 4 Booker T. Washington founds the Tuskegee Institute.

September 19 Garfield dies; Vice President Chester A. Arthur becomes president.

1882

January 2 Standard Oil Trust founded.

May 6 Chinese Exclusion Act passed.

1883

January 16 Pendleton Act sets up Civil Service Commission.

May 24 Brooklyn Bridge opens.

July 4 Debut of "Buffalo Bill's Wild West Show."

October 15 Supreme Court in *Civil Rights Cases* declares Civil Rights Act of 1875 unconstitutional.

November 18 Standard railway time zones adopted in United States.

1884

December *Adventures of Huckleberry Finn* by Mark Twain published.

November 4 Grover Cleveland elected president.

1886

February 7 Anti-Chinese riots engulf Seattle.

May Haymarket Square bombing and riot occurs.

September 4 Apache chief Geronimo captured, ending last major Indian war.

October 28 Statue of Liberty dedicated.

December 8 American Federation of Labor formed.

1887

February 4 Interstate Commerce Commission established by Congress.

February 8 Dawes Severalty Act converts Indian tribal lands to individual ownership.

1888

February First use of secret ballot in the United States public election occurs in Louisville, Kentucky.

November 6 Benjamin Harrison elected president.

1889

June Andrew Carnegie's "Gospel of Wealth" article published.

November North Dakota, South Dakota, and Montana reach statehood.

1890

November Census Bureau declares the end of the frontier.

July Idaho and Wyoming made states.

July 2 Passage of Sherman Antitrust Act outlawing monopolies.

September 25 Yosemite National Park established.

December 29 146 Sioux Indians killed by U.S. troops at the Wounded Knee massacre.

1891

December Basketball invented by James Naismith.

May 19 Populist Party launched in Cincinnati, Ohio.

1892

January 1 Immigration receiving station in New York City transferred to Ellis Island.

July–November Homestead strike by steelworkers against the Carnegie Steel Company.

September First successful gas-powered automobile made in the U.S.

November 8 Grover Cleveland elected president.

1893

January 17 Queen Liliuokalani of Hawaii overthrown.

June 27 Crash of New York stock market begins four years of depression.

November 7 Women's suffrage adopted in Colorado by popular vote.

1894

July 2 President Cleveland sends in federal troops to enforce injunction against Pullman railway strike.

August 27 Nation's first graduated income tax law passed by Congress.

1895

May 20 Supreme Court in *Pollack v. Farmer's Loan and Trust* declares federal income tax unconstitutional.

September 18 Booker T. Washington speaks at the Atlanta Exposition.

PREFACE

The Civil War had profound and lasting repercussions on the United States. No change was more dramatic than the death of the defining institution of the defeated Confederacy—slavery—which was abolished by constitutional amendment eight months after Robert E. Lee surrendered to Ulysses S. Grant at Appomattox in April 1865. Other significant changes took longer to materialize. For example, the military demands of war propelled advances in technology that laid the foundation for an explosion of industrial development in the victorious North. Still other transformations stemmed from wartime efforts by Congress to bind the far-flung nation together. Both the 1862 Homestead Act and the decision the same year to sponsor construction of a transcontinental railroad helped spur postwar westward migration—a development that transformed the western regions of the country.

The changes America underwent during the three decades following the war's end did not proceed without controversies and debates, as the following selection of opposing viewpoints illustrates. Some of the issues presented here were of special concern to specific regions of the country. Americans were frequently at odds over matters pertaining to the reconstruction of the South, the industrialization of the North, and the settlement of the West. Other issues, such as labor/management relations and immigration, were national in scope. But all of these disagreements took place in the context of a nation that was growing rapidly in population, wealth, and power.

THE SOUTH AND RECONSTRUCTION

Reconstruction (1865–1877) was dominated by two fundamental questions. One question concerned the manner in which the former Confederate states should be reintegrated into the Union. At issue was whether they should be permitted to regain their status as states quickly, as President Abraham Lincoln proposed before his April 1865 assassination, or whether they should be held as conquered provinces, as Radical Republicans in Congress argued. Closely related to this dilemma was a second question: How should the 4 million former slaves be reintegrated into what was no longer a slave society? Should they be granted the right to vote and otherwise participate in the political process? Or should their political and social rights be restricted, as many whites in both the North and the South believed? Radical Republicans insisted on federal control of Confederate states to ensure that the ex-slaves would soon be given political equality, economic opportunity, and full civil rights. Opponents of the Radical Republicans generally opposed federal control of state governments, in large part because they wanted to pass state laws that would limit the rights and powers of blacks (as many Southern states did after the Civil War by enacting special "Black Codes").

The Radical Republicans achieved mixed success in their goals. They passed federal laws that were designed to achieve a measure of integration throughout the South. Through the Fourteenth and Fifteenth Amendments, respectively, black Americans were granted citizenship and black men received the right to vote. But by 1877 all federal troops had been withdrawn from the former Confederate states, all eleven states had been readmitted to the Union, and political leadership in the South had returned to conservative whites. Three-quarters of the southern black population became sharecroppers, many of whom were so poor that their material welfare was not much better than it had been under slavery. During the 1880s southern writers and political leaders hailed the rise of a "New South" based on industrial renaissance and postwar reconciliation. But critics, both white and black, argued that whether the issue was race relations or economic development, the region still had a long way to go.

IMMIGRATION, MIGRATION, AND THE AMERICAN FRONTIER

The South was not the only region of the country divided along racial and ethnic lines. Blacks faced racial prejudice and discrimination in other parts of the nation. Moreover, the fears of some Americans were directed not only at blacks (who then constituted a relatively small portion of the population outside the South), but also at other minorities, including newly arrived immigrants and American Indians.

Between 1860 and 1890 more than 10 million people immigrated to the United States. A large number of them came from Asia and southern and eastern Europe, areas that were previously not a major source of immigrants. While some settled in rural areas, many instead formed ethnic enclaves within America's cities. Some Americans encouraged immigration and praised immigrants' contributions to America, but others looked at the unfamiliar newcomers with suspicion. Some feared that immigrants would take jobs from native-born Americans or that the presence of large numbers of low-wage immigrant laborers in the workforce would depress wages. In California and other western states, Chinese immigrants and other minorities were often the victims of racial prejudice—and sometimes violence. On the local and national levels, debates began on whether the traditional American policy of open immigration should be abandoned.

Far away from America's cities and coastal regions, the areas affected by immigration, conflict arose between the Native American inhabitants of the western regions and the cowboys, pioneers, farmers, and other newcomers who sought Indian land. Conflicts between settlers and Indians often turned violent. In the 1870s and 1880s, partly in response to attacks by Native Americans and partly to secure the plains for settlement, the U.S. government launched numerous military campaigns to remove Native Americans to reservations. Many reformers argued that the reservations would provide Indians with a better, more secure way of life. They believed that Native Americans would benefit from learning modern agricultural methods, whites' social practices, and Christian religious beliefs. Although some whites decried the forced relocations, which they perceived as government abuses against American Indians, few advocated returning land to the Indian tribes or preserving Native American culture.

In addition to the Indian wars, the settlement of the West brought with it the destruction of the buffalo herds, the rise and fall of the open-range cattle system, and the joining of the East and the West by railroad. Between 1870 and 1890 the non-Indian population west of the Mississippi River grew from 7 million to 17 million. By 1890 the U.S. Census Bureau declared that the frontier, in the form of an unbroken line delineating an unsettled region, had all but disappeared. The prairies formerly populated by herds of buffalo and nomadic tribes of American Indians were now populated with farmers trying to earn a living from the land.

AGRARIAN PROTEST

The millions of people drawn west by the prospect of land to homestead faced a harsh life with numerous obstacles to success. Drought, locusts, and other natural disasters were a setback for some, but many farmers came to believe that their problems were the result of social inequities and faceless enemies, including banks, railroads, and corporations.

Previous generations of American farmers and settlers had been largely self-sufficient. They obtained their food, clothing, simple tools, and other necessities of life directly from their own land and toil or by trade in local markets. But in the years following the Civil War, farmers increasingly concentrated on raising cash crops, such as wheat, corn, or cotton. These crops were then shipped by rail to distant markets. Over time farmers grew dependent on railroad companies to market their products and on banks for working capital to buy needed land and farm machinery. Many farmers failed to break even due to the expensive shipping rates charged by railroads and the high interest rates of banks. The steady drop of prices for staple crops in the years following the Civil War, especially during the 1880s, worsened farmers' already bleak prospects.

Some farmers responded to economic distress by organizing among themselves. Their political efforts led to the formation of the Grange movement of the 1870s, the Farmers' Alliance network of the 1880s, and the Populist Party of the 1890s. All these movements called for greater regulation of banks and railroads; the Populist Party demanded outright government ownership of the railroads.

THE INDUSTRIAL NORTH

While the frontier was being settled and the South was struggling to recover from the Civil War, the northern states led the nation in the most significant economic development of the era: the rapid rise and supremacy of industry, which by the 1890s had exceeded agriculture as a source of income for Americans. Advances in technology were a key factor in this industrial growth. Between 1860 and 1890, 440,000 patents were issued by the U.S. Patent Office. Among the inventions of the era were the telegraph, telephone, typewriter, and adding machine. The manufacture of steel, essential for railroad rails and skyscrapers, became a major American industry. With the growth of industry came controversies over the distribution of the wealth it produced.

RICH AND POOR

The industrial age created an unprecedented gap between the rich and the poor. A few Americans were able to obtain great fortunes for themselves. The number of millionaires rose from around twenty in 1850 to more than three thousand in 1900. Tycoons such as Andrew Carnegie (steel), John D. Rockefeller (oil), and J. Pierpont Morgan (banking and railroads) became dominant figures of the era, overshadowing in fame and power even presidents of the United States. Some praised these entrepreneurs as geniuses of business organization who helped to harness natural resources and to provide industrial products for American businesses and consumers. Others criticized them for using unethical methods to destroy competitors, for having little or no regard for the public good, and for underpaying and mistreating their workers.

At the other end of the economic scale were those who labored in the nation's factories, on the nation's rails, and in the nation's mines. These laborers typically worked at least sixty hours a week for low wages, often in hazardous conditions. The percentage of self-employed workers in America fell from about half of the workforce in 1860 to one-third by 1900; consequently, more workers than ever before were dependent on wages for a living. Their dependency on wages, combined with the fact that they could be laid off or fired at any time, created a perilous economic situation for many workers and their families. Some workers responded by forming labor unions and engaging in strikes. However, while they laid foundations for future labor movement successes, most of these efforts failed in the face of intense business and legal opposition.

The expansion of industry in these years had some positive results for American workers. The general decline in prices, while harmful for farmers dependent on crop sales, meant that workers with steady jobs enjoyed rising real incomes to help them purchase the increasing variety of consumer goods. The industrial revolution supported a growing middle class, provided work opportunities for America's immigrants, and allowed more women to find wage jobs outside the home. Many Americans viewed the growth of the middle class and the ascent of such figures as Carnegie, who rose from an impoverished immigrant to a steel magnate, as proof that in America anyone who worked hard could succeed and become rich. However, as the century drew to a close, some people were concerned that America's industrialization was not helping the nation as a whole, and that the widening divide between rich and poor Americans threatened national ideals of freedom and equality. These questions continued to be part of the American dialogue as the nation approached the twentieth century.

RECONSTRUCTION AND THE NEW SOCIAL ORDER IN THE SOUTH

Viewpoint 1A

Reconstruction Should Be Harsh (1865)

William Mason Grosvenor (1835–1900)

INTRODUCTION *William Mason Grosvenor, an abolitionist prior to the Civil War, commanded one of the first units of black soldiers organized to fight for the North in that conflict. During the war he observed firsthand the relatively lenient reconstruction process by which the state government of Louisiana was re-created under Northern military occupation, with little change in the political or economic status of blacks beyond the abolition of slavery. In an article published in the* New Englander *magazine in 1865, excerpted here, Grosvenor criticizes the state and local government established during the Civil War. He also takes issue with the "abeyance" theory of reconstruction—the idea that the Confederate states, whose secession did not have legal validity, still possessed all their constitutional prerogatives as member states of America, and should be restored these temporarily suspended rights as speedily as possible.*

On what foundation does the North have the right to dictate social changes in the South, according to Grosvenor? What problem does he have with the Confederate states retaining their original constitutions?

It is fortunate that the political victory achieved in the re-election of President Lincoln is generally received, not with noisy exultation, but with calm and thoughtful thankfulness. It gives ground for hope that in rejoicing over triumphs gained and dangers escaped, the nation will not be blind to the severer trial yet to be met, and the fearful responsibilities that will attend it. . . .

There remains the . . . most serious test of all—the trial of wisdom and statesmanship. This is not merely a rebellion or a political contest with which we have to deal: it is a revolution. Our task is to obey and execute a fiat of the Almighty, written on the face of the Western hemisphere in the course of the Mississippi river. "There

From William Mason Grosvenor, "The Law of Conquest to True Basis of Reconstruction," *New Englander*, vol, 29, January 1865.

shall be, upon this broad domain, one nation and but one." The shock of arms revealed the fact that we had never been one people, and that a true nationality, embracing all States and sections, had never existed. Heterogeneous populations, hostile systems, and irreconcilable ideas had only been placed in contact, and held to bare juxta-position by a constitutional compact. No chemical union had ever taken place; for that the white-hot crucible of civil war was found necessary. To keep up the fire until antagonistic elements are refined away and a perfect union is effected is needful, and is the deliberate purpose of the nation, expressed in the late election; but that is not all. To direct the process of amalgamation, to determine the time for each step, and to give shape to the new substance, will demand the most exalted statesmanship. A single error may cause a flaw that shall send the whole work back to the furnace. . . .

But whether the future nationality shall be equal to the glorious possibilities of free government, whether the harmony of forces and homogeneity of elements shall be complete, will depend upon the measure of statesmanship that may guide the work now close at hand. Already a great constitutional reform is demanded; and we are but dull scholars if we have not learned through all the severe experiences of this war, that no work of human device is perfect, and that nations, like children, will outgrow their clothes. Already the financial problem calls for something more than temporary expedients. Already questions of a standing army, of a permanent revenue, and of tariff or direct taxation, require reexamination by the light of new events and needs. Already the problem of the future of the negro race assumes the gravest importance, and can be deferred but a little longer. Questions of amnesty or punishment of public enemies already engage the attention of rulers and people. Behind these there throng in the anteroom whole troops of problems new and strange—of interests needing protection and claims clamoring for adjustment. The offing is full of questions, fast anchored once, but now cast adrift by the storm. The change to which we are called is radical. It is the new-birth of nation. . . .

THE PROPER MODE OF RECONSTRUCTION

Of all the unsolved problems the most important, and the one that demands most urgently thorough examination and final settlement, is that which concerns the present status of the rebellious States and the proper mode of reconstruction. It is too momentous a subject to be left to chance. . . . The question is one of no little difficulty; it goes deeper than all our statutes and deeper than the Constitution itself, and makes all precedents as useless as the trilobites. The very multitude of theories darkens counsel, and rarely, if ever, has the question been stripped of all extraneous matter and clearly stated. It has nothing to do with slavery or confiscation. It is simply this: "Do the civil rights under our government, once vested in certain States and the citizens of those States, still exist, and, if so, in whom are they vested?" To discuss particular measures of reconstruction and attempt partial reorganizations, without first giving to this question a final and formal answer, is to put up a frame and finish off a wing before the shape of the building is fixed or the foundation laid....

---■---

Punishment... shall be severe enough to prevent for all future time the recurrence of a crime so terribly destructive.

---■---

It would surely be not a little to the credit of the nation to sweep away... all those paltry *simulacra* of elections and organizations which have hitherto started up like mushrooms in the track of our armies.... Have we not seen enough of these manufactured organizations, which "live, move and have their being" in the baggage wagons of our army? They afford excellent chances for political chicanery; nice honors and fat offices are recovered from "abeyance" by men whose surprising merit had not been discovered in times of peace; but is the Union cause materially helped or do the Union loving people of the South thereby obtain any substantial protection? Is it not time to ask if these sickly plants do not cost more than it is worth to rear them, and to look with favor on a theory, which, by removing all pretext for such premature growths, sweeps away the whole system of political jugglery so engendered?

PUNISHING TREASON

Another consideration seems worthy of especial attention. Our law of treason is less effective or severe than that of other civilized nations. To the framers of the Constitution treason seemed a crime strangely horrid and improbable, and there doubtless appeared to be greater danger from an over rigorous loyalty, which, in times of excitement, might mistake reasonable freedom of thought and speech for hostility to the government.... But, were the South to lay down her arms to-day, and resume the rights which the abeyance theory concedes, there is no security that even these leaders would not find absolute immunity from punishment. Even the most notorious traitor could exercise every right of citizenship until he had been tried and convicted by a jury from his own State, and nothing in the laws of that State would exclude any other notorious traitor from the jury-box. What punishment would [Jefferson] Davis fear from a jury of Mississippians, of

whom perhaps half had just laid aside smoking muskets and dripping swords to enter the panel? To place such immunity within the reach of rebels, who may abandon the contest whenever they find it hopeless, is to put a premium on treason. We are cramped by no legal forms of constitutional obligations, unless we choose, in punishing this rebellion. Rising to the proportions of a civil war, it has placed in the hands of the nation not only the remedial agencies of the courts, but the torch and sword of the conqueror. Rebels are now not rebels only, but public enemies; Gettysburg's slaughter and Sherman's march have a broader sweep than any enacted penalties; and the right of conquest cuts deeper than any conceivable measure of confiscation. The law of war becomes supreme, and of that law *"Vae Victis"* ["Woe to the vanquished"] is the epitome. We have only to apply the principles of the decision above quoted to the work of reconstruction, to make sure that the punishment, for leaders at least, shall be severe enough to prevent for all future time the recurrence of a crime so terribly destructive to the national prosperity and the national honor....

Schemes of reconstruction which make possible immunity for the great conspirators, or instant return to all political privileges for traitors as well as loyalists, will not be such as the people will approve or the nation can safely adopt. Nor will it answer, in overflowing leniency for past offenses, to neglect security for healthy political action in the future. Men who have deliberately betrayed trusts guarded by all the sanctity of an oath are not safely to be trusted as loyal and true citizens, whenever they may choose to renew an obligation once violated. But the state constitutions only can effectually debar any from suffrage, office, or trust; under the abeyance theory each State can demand recognition with her old constitution and laws; nor is it easy to find authority for requiring particular changes as conditions of recognition. Instead of retaining these old constitutions, redolent of the slave-pen, defiled in every part by the use of traitors, and infested in every joint and crevice by claims that loyal men must loathe but can never wholly extirpate, the erection and admission of new States demolishes all these relies of a shameful past, and secures new and spotless constitutions, each in harmony in every part with the spirit of the new era, and instinct and vital with freedom and loyalty.

Viewpoint 1B

Reconstruction Should Be Lenient (1866)

Herman Melville (1819–1891)

INTRODUCTION *Northern-born writer Herman Melville, most famous for his novels including* Moby Dick, *wrote a short collection of poems inspired by the Civil War that was published in 1866. In a companion essay to the poetry collection, excerpted here, the antislavery and antiwar Melville argues for a humane and revenge-free reconstruction policy toward the defeated Confederate states.*

Why should Southern rebels not be viewed as traitors, according to Melville? How does he believe the nation should approach the status of black ex-slaves?

There seems no reason why patriotism and narrowness should go together, or why intellectual impartiality should be confounded with political trimming, or why serviceable truth should keep cloistered because not partisan. Yet the work of reconstruction, if admitted to be feasible at all, demands little but common sense and Christian charity. Little but these? These are much.

SOUTHERN PENITENCE

Some of us are concerned because as yet the South shows no penitence. But what exactly do we mean by this? Since down to the close of the war she never confessed any for braving it, the only penitence now left her is that which springs solely from the sense of discomfiture; and since this evidently would be a contrition hypocritical, it would be unworthy in us to demand it. Certain it is that penitence, in the sense of voluntary humiliation, will never be displayed. Nor does this afford just ground for unreserved condemnation. It is enough, for all practical purposes, if the South have been taught by the terrors of civil war to feel that secession, like slavery, is against destiny; that both now lie buried in one grave; that her fate is linked with ours; and that together we comprise the nation. . . .

Patriotism is not baseness, neither is it inhumanity. The mourners who this summer bear flowers to the mounds of the Virginian and Georgian dead are, in their domestic bereavement and proud affection, as sacred in the eye of heaven as are those who go with similar offerings of tender grief and love into the cemeteries of our Northern martyrs. And yet, in one aspect, how needless to point the contrast. . . .

There were excesses which marked the conflict, most of which are perhaps inseparable from a civil strife so intense and prolonged, and involving warfare in some border countries new and imperfectly civilized. Barbarities also there were, for which the Southern people collectively can hardly be held responsible, though perpetrated by ruffians in their name. But surely other qualities—exalted ones—courage and fortitude matchless, were likewise displayed, and largely; and justly may these be held the characteristic traits, and not the former.

In this view, what Northern writer, however patriotic, but must revolt from acting on paper a part anyway akin to that of the live dog to the dead lion; and yet it is right to rejoice for our triumph, so far as it may justly imply an advance for our whole country and for humanity.

From Herman Melville, *Battle-Pieces and Aspects of War.* (New York, 1866).

Let it be held no reproach to anyone that he pleads for reasonable consideration for our late enemies, now stricken down and unavoidably debarred, for the time, from speaking through authorized agencies for themselves. Nothing has been urged here in the foolish hope of conciliating those men—few in number, we trust—who have resolved never to be reconciled to the Union. On such hearts everything is thrown away except it be religious commiseration, and the sincerest. Yet let them call to mind that unhappy secessionist [Edmund Ruffin], not a military man, who, with impious alacrity, fired the first shot of the Civil War at Sumter, and a little more than four years afterward fired the last one into his own heart at Richmond.

Noble was the gesture into which patriotic passion surprised the people in a utilitarian time and country; yet the glory of the war falls short of its pathos—a pathos which now at last ought to disarm all animosity. . . .

As frankly let us own—what it would be unbecoming to parade were foreigners concerned—that our triumph was won not more by skill and bravery than by superior resources and crushing numbers; that it was a triumph, too, over a people for years politically misled by designing men, and also by some honestly erring men, who, from their position, could not have been otherwise than broadly influential; a people who, though, indeed, they sought to perpetuate the curse of slavery, and even extend it; were not the authors of it but (less fortunate, not less righteous than we) were the fated inheritors; a people who, having a like origin with ourselves, share essentially in whatever worthy qualities we may possess. No one can add to the lasting reproach which hopeless defeat has now cast upon secession by withholding the recognition of these verities.

Surely we ought to take it to heart that the kind of pacification, based upon principles operating equally all over the land, which lovers of their country yearn for, and which our arms, though signally triumphant, did not bring about, and which lawmaking, however anxious or energetic or repressive, never by itself can achieve, may yet be largely aided by generosity of sentiment public and private. Some revisionary legislation and adaptive is indispensable; but with this should harmoniously work another kind of prudence, not unallied with entire magnanimity. Benevolence and policy—Christianity and Machiavelli—dissuade from penal severities toward the subdued. Abstinence here is as obligatory as considerate care for our unfortunate fellowmen late in bonds, and, if observed, would equally prove to be wise forecast. The great qualities of the South, those attested in the war, we can perilously alienate, or we may make them nationally available at need.

THE PLACE OF BLACKS

The blacks, in their infant pupilage to freedom, appeal to the sympathies of every humane mind. The paternal guardianship which, for the interval government exercises over them was prompted equally by duty and benevolence. Yet such kindliness should not be allowed to exclude kindliness to communities who stand nearer to us in nature. For the future of the freed slaves we may well be concerned; but the future of the whole country, involving the future of the blacks, urges a paramount claim upon our anxiety. Effective benignity, like the Nile, is not narrow in its bounty, and true policy is always broad.

To be sure, it is vain to seek to glide, with molded words, over the difficulties of the situation. And for them who are neither partisans, nor enthusiasts, nor theorists, nor cynics, there are some doubts not readily to be solved. And there are fears. Why is not the cessation of war now at length attended with the settled calm of peace? Wherefore in a clear sky do we still turn our eyes toward the South, as the Neapolitan, months after the eruption, turns his toward Vesuvius? Do we dread lest the repose may be deceptive? In the recent convulsion has the crater but shifted?

No consideration should tempt us to pervert the national victory into oppression for the vanquished.

Let us revere that sacred uncertainty which forever impends over men and nations. Those of us who always abhorred slavery as an atheistical iniquity, gladly we join in the exulting chorus of humanity over its downfall. But we should remember that emancipation was accomplished not by deliberate legislation; only through agonized violence could so mighty a result be effected. In our natural solicitude to confirm the benefit of liberty to the blacks, let us forbear from measures of dubious constitutional rightfulness toward our white countrymen—measures of a nature to provoke, among other of the last evils, exterminating hatred of race toward race.

In imagination let us place ourselves in the unprecedented position of the Southerners—their position as regards the millions of ignorant manumitted slaves in their midst, for whom some of us now claim the suffrage. Let us be Christians toward our fellow whites, as well as philanthropists toward the blacks, our fellowmen. In all things and toward all, we are enjoined to do as we would be done by. Nor should we forget that benevolent desires, after passing a certain point, cannot undertake their own fulfillment without incurring the risk of evils beyond those sought to be remedied. Something may well be left to the graduated care of future legislation, and to Heaven....

But, so far as immediate measures looking toward permanent reestablishment are concerned, no consideration should tempt us to pervert the national victory into oppression for the vanquished. Should plausible promise of eventual good, or a deceptive or spurious sense of duty, lead us to essay this, count we must on serious consequences, not the least of which would be divisions among the Northern adherents of the Union....

Let us pray that the terrible historic tragedy of our time may not have been enacted without instructing our whole beloved country through terror and pity; and may fulfillment verify in the end those expectations which kindle the bards of progress and humanity.

FOR FURTHER READING

Dan T. Carter, *When the War Was Over: The Failure of Self-Reconstruction in the South.* Baton Rouge: Louisiana State University Press, 1985.

LaWanda Cox and John H. Cox, *Politics, Principle, and Prejudice, 1865–1866: Dilemma of Reconstruction America.* Glencoe, IL: Free Press, 1963.

Eric Foner, *Reconstruction: America's Unfinished Revolution, 1863–1877.* New York: Harper & Row, 1988.

Stanton Garner, *The Civil War World of Herman Melville.* Lawrence: University Press of Kansas, 1993.

Harold M. Hyman, *A More Perfect Union: The Impact of the Civil War and Reconstruction Upon the Constitution.* New York: Knopf, 1973.

Viewpoint 2A

The Ku Klux Klan Is a Terrorist Organization (1870)

Albion W. Tourgee (1838–1905)

INTRODUCTION *Following the Civil War a group of white Northerners settled in the former Confederate states and became involved in local politics. Albion W. Tourgee, a lawyer and Civil War veteran, was one of these so-called "carpetbaggers." He helped rewrite North Carolina's state constitution in 1868 and served six years as a state judge. He later wrote several novels based on his experiences in the South.*

The efforts of Tourgee and others to reconstruct Southern society and assist the region's ex-slave population met local resistance that was sometimes carried out by secretive and violent groups. The Ku Klux Klan, founded in Tennessee in 1866, was the most famous of these secret societies. In an 1870 letter to North Carolina's Republican senator Joseph C. Abbott, Tourgee describes how Republican officeholders and supporters—and blacks in general—were being met with violent and murderous attacks by the Ku Klux Klan. Victims had no recourse in local government or law enforcement, Tourgee reports. He calls for more action from the federal government to restore law and order in the South. The letter, excerpted here, was published in the New York Tribune.

What examples of Ku Klux Klan violence does Tourgee describe? What effects has the Civil War had on public tolerance of violence? What steps does he argue the federal government should take?

There have been twelve murders in five counties of the district during the past eighteen months, by bands of disguised villains. In addition to this, from the best information I can derive, I am of the opinion that in this district alone there have been 1,000 outrages of a less serious nature perpetrated by the same masked fiends. Of course this estimate is not made from any absolute record, nor is it possible to ascertain with accuracy the entire number of beatings and other outrages which have been perpetrated. The uselessness, the utter futility of complaint from the lack of ability in the laws to punish is fully known to all. The danger of making such complaint is also well understood. It is therefore not unfrequently by accident that the outrage is found out, and unquestionably it is frequently absolutely concealed. Thus, a respectable, hard working white carpenter was working for a neighbor, when accidentally his shirt was torn, and disclosed his back scarred and beaten. The poor fellow begged for the sake of his wife and children that nothing might be said about it, in the Ku-Klux had threatened to kill him if he disclosed how he had been outraged. Hundreds of cases have come to my notice and that of my solicitor. . . .

■

There is sometimes a fiendish malignity and cunning displayed in the form and character of the outrages.

■

CRIMES OF THE KLAN

Men and women come scarred, mangled, and bruised, and say: "The Ku-Klux came to my house last night and beat me almost to death, and my old woman right smart, and shot into the house, 'bust' the door down, and told me they would kill me if I made complaint;" and the bloody mangled forms attest the truth of their declarations. On being asked if any one knew any of the party it will be ascertained that there was no recognition, or only the most uncertain and doubtful one. In such cases as these nothing can be done by the court. We have not been accustomed to enter them on record. A man of the best standing in Chatham told me that

Albion W. Tourgee, *Some of the Outrages—Letter from Judge Tourgee to Senator Abbott*, Greensboro, NC, May 24, 1870.

he could count up 200 and upward in that county. In Alamance County, a citizen in conversation one evening enumerated upward of 50 cases which had occurred within his own knowledge, and in one section of the county. He gave it as his opinion that there had been 200 cases in that county. I have no idea that he exceeded the proper estimate. That was six months ago, and I am satisfied that another hundred would not cover the work done in that time.

These crimes have been of every character imaginable. Perhaps the most usual has been the dragging of men and women from their beds, and beating their naked bodies with hickory switches, or as witnesses in an examination the other day said, "sticks" between a "switch" and a "club." From 50 to 100 blows is the usual allowance, sometimes 200 and 300 blows are administered. Occasionally an instrument of torture is owned. Thus in one case two women, one 74 years old, were taken out, stripped naked, and beaten with a paddle, with several holes bored through it. The paddle was about 30 inches long, 3 or 4 inches wide, and 1/4 of an inch thick, of oak. Their bodies were so bruised and beaten that they were sickening to behold. They were white women and of good character until the younger was seduced, and swore her child to its father. Previous to that and so far as others were concerned her character was good.

Again, there is sometimes a fiendish malignity and cunning displayed in the form and character of the outrages. For instance, a colored man was placed astride of a log, and an iron staple driven through his person into the log. In another case, after a band of them had in turn violated a young negro girl, she was forced into bed with a colored man, their bodies were bound together face to face, and the fire from the hearth piled upon them. The K.K.K. rode off and left them, with shouts of laughter. Of course the bed was soon in flames, and somehow they managed to crawl out, though terribly burned and scarred. The house was burned.

I could give other incidents of cruelty, such as hanging up a boy of nine years old until he was nearly dead, to make him tell where his father was hidden, and beating an old negress of 103 years old with garden pallings because she would not own that she was afraid of the Ku-Klux. But it is unnecessary to go into further detail. In this district I estimate their offenses as follows, in the past ten months: Twelve murders, 9 rapes, 11 arsons, 7 mutilations, ascertained and most of them on record. In some no identification could be made. . . .

THE GOVERNMENT SLEEPS

And yet the Government sleeps. The poor disarmed nurses of the Republican party—those men by whose ballots the Republican party holds power—who took their lives in their hands when they cast their ballots for U.S. Grant and other officials—all of us who happen to be beyond the pale of the Governmental regard—must be sacrificed, murdered, scourged, mangled, because some contemptible party scheme might be foiled by doing us justice. I could stand it very well to fight for Uncle Sam, and was never known to refuse an invitation on such an occasion; but this lying down, tied hand and foot with the shackles of the law, to be killed by the very dregs of the rebellion, the scum of the earth, and not allowed either the consolation of fighting or the satisfaction that our "fall" will be noted by the Government, and protection given to others thereby, is somewhat too hard. I am ashamed of the nation that will let its citizens be slain by scores, and scourged by thousands, and offer no remedy or protection. I am ashamed of a State which has not sufficient strength to protect its own officers in the discharge of their duties, nor guarantee the safety of any man's domicile throughout its length and breadth. I am ashamed of a party which, with the reins of power in its hands, has not nerve or decision enough to arm its own adherents, or to protect them from assassinations at the hands of their opponents. A General who in time of war would permit 2,000 or 3,000 of his men to be bushwhacked and destroyed by private treachery even in an enemy's country without any one being punished for it would be worthy of universal execration, and would get it, too. How much more worthy of detestation is a Government which in time of peace will permit such wholesale slaughter of its citizens? It is simple cowardice, inertness, and wholesale demoralization. The wholesale slaughter of the war has dulled our Nation's sense of horror at the shedding of blood, and the habit of regarding the South as simply a laboratory, where every demagogue may carry on his reconstructionary experiments at will, and not as an integral party of the Nation itself, has led our Government to shut its eyes to the atrocities of these times. Unless these evils are speedily remedied, I tell you, General, the Republican party has signed its death warrant. It is a party of cowards or idiots—I don't care which alternative is chosen. The remedy is in our hands, and we are afraid or too dull to bestir ourselves and use it.

But you will tell me that Congress is ready and willing to act if it only knew what to do. Like the old Irish woman it wrings its hands and cries, "O Lawk, O Lawk; if I only knew which way." And yet this same Congress has the control of the militia and can organize its own force in every county in the United States, and arm more or less of it. This same Congress has the undoubted right to guarantee and provide a republican government, and protect every citizen in "life, liberty, and the pursuit of happiness," as well as the power conferred

by the XVth Amendment. And yet we suffer and die in peace and murderers walk abroad with the blood yet fresh upon their garments, unharmed, unquestioned and unchecked. Fifty thousand dollars given to good detectives would secure, if well used, a complete knowledge of all this gigantic organization of murderers. In connection with an organized and armed militia, it would result in the apprehension of any number of these Thugs *en masque* and with blood on their hands. What then is the remedy? *First*: Let Congress give to the U.S. Courts, or to Courts of the States under its own laws, cognizance of this class of crimes, as crimes against the nation, and let it provide that this legislation be enforced. Why not, for instance, make going armed and masked or disguised, or masked or disguised in the night time, an act of insurrection or sedition? *Second*: Organize militia, National—State militia is a nuisance—and arm as many as may be necessary in each county to enforce its laws. *Third*: Put detectives at work to get hold of this whole organization. Its ultimate aim is unquestionably to revolutionize the Government. If we have not pluck enough for this, why then let us just offer our throats to the knife, emasculate ourselves, and be a nation of self-subjugated slaves at once.

Viewpoint 2B

The Ku Klux Klan Is a Peacekeeping Organization (1872)

John Brown Gordon (1823–1904)

INTRODUCTION *In 1871 the U.S. Congress established a special committee to investigate the rise of white secret societies in the South, such as the Ku Klux Klan, that used vigilante violence and terrorism to keep the newly enfranchised blacks in "their place." The following viewpoint is drawn from testimony by John Brown Gordon, one of the people questioned by the committee. Gordon had been a general in the Confederate army; after federal troops were withdrawn from the South in 1877 he entered Georgia politics and eventually reached both the governorship and the U.S. Senate. In response to questions by the committee, Gordon denies specific knowledge about the Ku Klux Klan, but argues that white groups are being formed in the South for the purposes of peacekeeping and self-protection against the threat of black violence. He specifically cites the Union League, a political group organized by northern Republicans, as being possibly responsible for black-on-white violence.*

What evidences does Gordon use to argue that blacks were threatening whites? What criticisms does he make about "radicals"? Ralph Lowell Eckert and other historians have concluded that Gordon was in fact a member of the Georgia Klan; how does this revelation affect the credibility of his testimony?

Question. What do you know of any combinations in Georgia, known as Ku-Klux, or by any other name, who have been violating the law?

Answer. I do not know anything about any Ku Klux organization, as the papers talk about it. I have never heard of anything of that sort except in the papers and by general report; but I do know that an organization did exist in Georgia at one time. I know that in 1868—I think that was the time—I was approached and asked to attach myself to a secret organization in Georgia. I was approached by some of the very best citizens of the State—some of the most peaceable, law-abiding men, men of large property, who had large interests in the State. The object of this organization was explained to me at the time by these parties; and I want to say that I approved of it most heartily. I would approve again of a similar organization, under the same state of circumstances.

---◼---

This society was purely a police organization to keep the peace, to prevent disturbances in our State.

---◼---

Question. Tell us about what that organization was.

Answer. The organization was simply this—nothing more and nothing less: it was an organization, a brotherhood of the property-holders, the peaceable, law-abiding citizens of the State, for self-protection. The instinct of self-protection prompted that organization; the sense of insecurity and danger, particularly in those neighborhoods where the negro population largely predominated. The reasons which led to this organization were three or four. The first and main reason was the organization of the Union League, as they called it, about which we knew nothing more than this: that the negroes would desert the plantations, and go off at night in large numbers; and on being asked where they had been, would reply, sometimes, "We have been to the muster"; sometimes, "We have been to the lodge"; sometimes, "We have been to the meeting." Those things were observed for a great length of time. We knew that the "carpet-baggers," as the people of Georgia called these men who came from a distance and had no interest at all with us; who were unknown to us entirely; who from all we could learn about them did not have any very exalted position at their homes—these men were organizing the colored people. We knew that beyond all question. We knew of certain instances where great crimes had been committed;

John Brown Gordon, from *Testimony Taken by the Joint Select Committee to Inquire into the Condition of Affairs in the Late Insurrectionary States: Alabama*, vol. 1, Washington DC: Government Printing Office, 1872.

where overseers had been driven from plantations, and the negroes had asserted their right to hold the property for their own benefit. Apprehension took possession of the entire public mind of the State. Men were in many instances afraid to go away from their homes and leave their wives and children, for fear of outrage. Rapes were already being committed in the country. There was this general organization of the black race on the one hand, and an entire disorganization of the white race on the other hand. We were afraid to have a public organization; because we supposed it would be construed at once, by the authorities at Washington, as an organization antagonistic to the Government of the United States. It was therefore necessary, in order to protect our families from outrage and preserve our own lives, to have something that we could regard as a brotherhood—a combination of the best men of the country, to act purely in self-defense, to repel the attack in case we should be attacked by these people. That was the whole object of this organization. I never heard of any disguises connected with it; we had none, very certainly. This organization, I think, extended nearly all over the State. It was, as I say, an organization purely for self-defense. It had no more politics in it than the organization of the Masons. I never heard the idea of politics suggested in connection with it.

A PEACE POLICE ORGANIZATION

Question. Did it have any antagonism toward either the State or the Federal Government?

Answer. None on earth—not a particle. On the contrary, it was purely a peace police organization, and I do know of some instances where it did prevent bloodshed on a large scale. I know of one case in Albany, Georgia, where, but for the instrumentality of this organization, there would have been, beyond all doubt, a conflict, growing out of a personal difficulty between a black man and a white man. The two races gathered on each side, but this organization quelled the trouble easily and restored peace, without any violence to anybody, and without a particle of difficulty with either the black race or the white. They stopped one just as much as they did the other. This society was purely a police organization to keep the peace, to prevent disturbances in our State. That was the motive that actuated me in going into it, and that was the whole object of the organization, as explained to me by these persons who approached me. I approved of the object.

Question. You had no riding about at nights?

Answer. None on earth. I have no doubt that such things have occurred in Georgia. It is notoriously stated—I have no personal knowledge of anything of the kind, but I have reason to believe it—that disguised parties have committed outrages in Georgia; but we have discovered in some cases that these disguised parties did not belong to any particular party. . . . The truth is simply this: that individuals in Georgia of all parties and all colors have, I suppose, committed outrage; but such affairs have been purely personal, just as they are when they occur anywhere else in the United States. I do not believe any more crimes have been committed in Georgia than in any other community of the same number anywhere else in the country. That is my honest conviction. I do not believe that any crime has ever been committed by this organization of which I have spoken, and of which I was a member. I believe it was purely a peace police—a law-abiding concern. That was its whole object, and it never would have existed but for the apprehension in the minds of our people of a conflict in which we would have had no sympathy and no protection. We apprehended that the sympathy of the entire Government would be against us; and nothing in the world but the instinct of self-protection prompted that organization. We felt that we must at any cost protect ourselves, our homes, our wives and children from outrage. We would have preferred death rather than to have submitted to what we supposed was coming upon us. At this time I do not believe any such organization exists, or has existed for a long time. I have not heard of it for two years, I am certain.

SELF-PROTECTION IS NO LONGER NEEDED

Question. Why did it cease to exist; why did it pass away?

Answer. Well, sir, it just dissolved because the courts became generally established; and though the courts were in the hands of the opposite party, our people believed they were trying to do justice; that a general protection was extended over us. Our people thought we could get justice at the hands of these judges; though they were of the opposite party, and though negroes were on the juries, we were satisfied that in the existing condition of things we were safe. . . .

You must remember that we were in a state of anarchy there for a long time. We had no law but drum-head courts-martial. Our people were entirely powerless to do anything. We always felt that if the Federal troops were kept in our midst we would be protected. I want to state that with great emphasis. Our people have always felt that if the white troops of the Federal Army could have been stationed in our midst in those negro belts we would have been safe. But the troops were perhaps two hundred miles away; and before they could have been brought to our relief the whole neighborhood might have been slaughtered. We then believed that such a thing might occur on almost any night. Such was the condition of things in Georgia at that time. I do not believe that it exists now, or has existed for two years. To my certain knowledge this organization never

did exist as a political organization. I do not know what may have been the case elsewhere; but very certainly there was no politics in this thing in Georgia, so far as I had anything to do with it; and I think that the organization was of the same character all over the State—probably over the South wherever it existed. We never called it Ku-Klux, and therefore I do not know anything about Ku-Klux.

FOR FURTHER READING

Ralph Lowell Eckert, *John Brown Gordon: Soldier, Southerner, American.* Baton Rouge: Louisiana State University Press, 1989.

Glenn M. Linden, *Voices from the Reconstruction Years, 1865–1877.* Fort Worth, TX: Harcourt Brace College Publishers, 1999.

George Rable, *But There Was No Peace: The Role of Violence in the Politics of Reconstruction.* Athens: University of Georgia Press, 1984.

Allan W. Trelease, *White Terror: The Ku Klux Klan Conspiracy and Southern Reconstruction.* New York: Harper & Row, 1971.

THE GILDED AGE: INDUS-TRIALIZATION AND LABOR CONFLICTS

Viewpoint 3A

Concentrations of Wealth Harm America (1883)

Henry George (1839–1897)

INTRODUCTION *Henry George was a social reformer and prolific writer on American social and economic conditions. A printer, seaman, and self-taught political economist (his schooling stopped at the seventh grade), George's writings, especially his 1879 book* Progress and Poverty, *gained him nationwide fame. In the following selection from his 1883 book* Social Problems, *George condemns the growing inequality between the wealthy few and the impoverished many as one of the harmful developments of America's new industrial age.*

What does George consider to be the true sources of the great business fortunes being created at that time? How do his views on the attainment of wealth differ from those of Andrew Carnegie, author of the opposing viewpoint?

There is in all the past nothing to compare with the rapid changes now going on in the civilized world. It seems as though in the European race, and in the nineteenth century, man was just beginning to live—just grasping his tools and becoming conscious of his powers. The snail's pace of crawling ages has suddenly become the headlong rush of the locomotive, speeding faster and faster. This rapid progress is primarily in industrial methods and material powers. But industrial changes imply

From Henry George, *Social Problems* (New York, 1883).

social changes and necessitate political changes. Progressive societies outgrow institutions as children outgrow clothes. Social progress always requires greater intelligence in the management of public affairs; but this the more as progress is rapid and change quicker....

Great aggregations of wealth ... tend to corrupt government and take it out of the control of the masses of the people.

INDUSTRIALIZATION AND WEALTH

The tendency of steam and of machinery is to the division of labor, to the concentration of wealth and power. Workmen are becoming massed by hundreds and thousands in the employ of single individuals and firms; small storekeepers and merchants are becoming the clerks and salesmen of great business houses; we have already corporations whose revenues and pay rolls belittle those of the greatest States. And with this concentration grows the facility of combination among these great business interests. How readily the railroad companies; the coal operators, the steel producers, even the match manufacturers, combine, either to regulate prices or to use the powers of government! The tendency in all branches of industry is to the formation of rings against which the individual is helpless, and which exert their power upon government whenever their interests may thus be served.

It is not merely positively, but negatively, that great aggregations of wealth, whether individual or corporate, tend to corrupt government and take it out of the control of the masses of the people. "Nothing is more timorous than a million dollars—except two million dollars." Great wealth always supports the party in power, no matter how corrupt it may be. It never exerts itself for reform, for it instinctively fears change. It never struggles against misgovernment. When threatened by the holders of political power it does not agitate, nor appeal to the people; it buys them off. It is in this way, no less than by its direct interference, that aggregated wealth corrupts government, and helps to make politics a trade. Our organized lobbies, both legislative and Congressional, rely as much upon the fears as upon the hopes of moneyed interests. When "business" is dull, their resource is to get up a bill which some moneyed interest will pay them to beat. So, too, these large moneyed interests will subscribe to political funds, on the principle of keeping on the right side of those in power, just as the railroad companies deadhead [transport for free] President [Chester A.] Arthur when he goes to Florida to fish.

The more corrupt a government the easier wealth can use it. Where legislation is to be bought, the rich make the laws; where justice is to be purchased, the rich have the ear of the courts. And if, for this reason, great wealth does not absolutely prefer corrupt government to pure government, it becomes none the less a corrupting influence. A community composed of very rich and very poor falls an easy prey to whoever can seize power. The very poor have not spirit and intelligence enough to resist; the very rich have too much at stake....

CAN ANYONE BE RICH?

The comfortable theory that it is in the nature of things that some should be poor and some should be rich, and that the gross and constantly increasing inequalities in the distribution of wealth imply no fault in our institutions, pervades our literature, and is taught in the press, in the church, in school and in college.

This is a free country, we are told—every man has a vote and every man has a chance. The laborer's son may become President; poor boys of to-day will be millionaires thirty or forty years from now, and the millionaire's grandchildren will probably be poor. What more can be asked? If a man has energy, industry, prudence and foresight, he may win his way to great wealth. If he has not the ability to do this he must not complain of those who have. If some enjoy much and do little, it is because they, or their parents, possessed superior qualities which enabled them to "acquire property" or "make money." If others must work hard and get little, it is because they have not yet got their start, because they are ignorant, shiftless, unwilling to practise that economy necessary for the first accumulation of capital; or because their fathers were wanting in these respects. The inequalities in condition result from the inequalities of human nature, from the difference in the powers and capacities of different men. If one has to toil ten or twelve hours a day for a few hundred dollars a year, while another, doing little or no hard work, gets an income of many thousands, it is because all that the former contributes to the augmentation of the common stock of wealth is little more than the mere force of his muscles. He can expect little more than the animal, because he brings into play little more than animal powers. He is but a private in the ranks of the great army of industry, who has but to stand still or march, as he is bid. The other is the organizer, the general, who guides and wields the whole great machine, who must think, plan and provide; and his larger income is only commensurate with the far higher and rarer powers which he exercises, and the far greater importance of the function he fulfils. Shall not education have its reward, and skill its payment? What incentive would there be to the toil needed to learn to do anything well were great prizes not to be gained by those who learn to excel? It would not merely be gross injustice to refuse a Raphael or a Rubens more than a house-painter, but it would prevent the development of great painters. To destroy inequalities in condition would be to destroy the incentive to progress. To quarrel with them is to quarrel with the laws of nature. We might as well rail against the length of the days or the phases of the moon; complain that there are valleys and mountains; zones of tropical heat and regions of eternal ice. And were we by violent measures to divide wealth equally, we should accomplish nothing but harm; in a little while there would be inequalities as great as before.

This, in substance, is the teaching which we constantly hear. It is accepted by some because it is flattering to their vanity, in accordance with their interests or pleasing to their hope; by others, because it is dinned into their ears. Like all false theories that obtain wide acceptance, it contains much truth. But it is truth isolated from other truth or alloyed with falsehood.

To try to pump out a ship with a hole in her hull would be hopeless; but that is not to say that leaks may not be stopped and ships pumped dry. It is undeniable that, under present conditions, inequalities in fortune would tend to reassert themselves even if arbitrarily leveled for a moment; but that does not prove that the conditions from which this tendency to inequality springs may not be altered. Nor because there are differences in human qualities and powers does it follow that existing inequalities of fortune are thus accounted for. I have seen very fast compositors and very slow compositors, but the fastest I ever saw could not set twice as much type as the slowest, and I doubt if in other trades the variations are greater. Between normal men the difference of a sixth or seventh is a great difference in height—the tallest giant ever known was scarcely more than four times as tall as the smallest dwarf ever known, and I doubt if any good observer will say that the mental differences of men are greater than the physical differences. Yet we already have men hundreds of millions of times richer than other men.

That he who produces should have, that he who saves should enjoy, is consistent with human reason and with the natural order. But existing inequalities of wealth cannot be justified on this ground. As a matter of fact, how many great fortunes can be truthfully said to have been fairly earned? How many of them represent wealth produced by their possessors or those from whom their present possessors derived them? Did there not go to the formation of all of them something more than superior industry and skill? Such qualities may give the first start, but when fortunes begin to roll up into millions there will always be found some element of monopoly, some appropriation of wealth produced by others. Often there is a total absence of superior industry,

skill or self-denial, and merely better luck or greater unscrupulousness.

SOURCES OF GREAT WEALTH

An acquaintance of mine died in San Francisco recently, leaving $4,000,000, which will go to heirs to be looked up in England. I have known many men more industrious, more skilful, more temperate than he—men who did not or who will not leave a cent. This man did not get his wealth by his industry, skill or temperance. He no more produced it than did those lucky relations in England who may now do nothing for the rest of their lives. He became rich by getting hold of a piece of land in the early days, which, as San Francisco grew, became very valuable. His wealth represented not what he had earned, but what the monopoly of this bit of the earth's surface enabled him to appropriate of the earnings of others.

A man died in Pittsburgh, the other day, leaving $3,000,000. He may or may not have been particularly industrious, skilful and economical, but it was not by virtue of these qualifies that he got so rich. It was because he went to Washington and helped lobby through a bill which, by way of "protecting American workmen against the pauper labor of Europe," gave him the advantage of a sixty-per-cent tariff. To the day of his death he was a stanch protectionist, and said free trade would ruin our "infant industries." Evidently the $3,000,000 which he was enabled to lay by from his own little cherub of an "infant industry" did not represent what he had added to production. It was the advantage given him by the tariff that enabled him to scoop it up from other people's earnings.

This element of monopoly, of appropriation and spoliation will, when we come to analyze them, be found largely to account for all great fortunes....

Take the great Vanderbilt fortune. The first Vanderbilt was a boatman who earned money by hard work and saved it. But it was not working and saving that enabled him to leave such an enormous fortune. It was spoliation and monopoly. As soon as he got money enough he used it as a club to extort from others their earnings. He ran off opposition lines and monopolized routes of steamboat travel. Then he went into railroads, pursuing the same tactics. The Vanderbilt fortune no more comes from working and saving than did the fortune that Captain Kidd buried.

Or take the great Gould fortune. Mr. Gould might have got his first little start by superior industry and superior self-denial. But it is not that which has made him the master of a hundred millions. It was by wrecking railroads, buying judges, corrupting legislatures, getting up rings and pools and combinations to raise or depress stock values and transportation rates.

So, likewise, of the great fortunes which the Pacific railroads have created. They have been made by lobbying through profligate donations of lands, bonds and subsidies, by the operations of Crédit Mobilier and Contract and Finance Companies, by monopolizing and gouging. And so of fortunes made by such combinations as the Standard Oil Company, the Bessemer Steel Ring, the Whisky Tax Ring, the Lucifer Match Ring, and the various rings for the "protection of the American workman from the pauper labor of Europe."...

Through all great fortunes, and, in fact, through nearly all acquisitions that in these days can fairly be termed fortunes, these elements of monopoly, of spoliation, of gambling run. The head of one of the largest manufacturing firms in the United States said to me recently, "It is not on our ordinary business that we make our money; it is where we can get a monopoly." And this, I think, is generally true....

I am not denouncing the rich, nor seeking, by speaking of these things, to excite envy and hatred; but if we would get a clear understanding of social problems, we must recognize the fact that it is due to monopolies which we permit and create, to advantages which we give one man over another, to methods of extortion sanctioned by law and by public opinion, that some men are enabled to get so enormously rich while others remain so miserably poor. If we look around us and note the elements of monopoly, extortion and spoliation which go to the building up of all, or nearly all, fortunes, we see on the one hand how disingenuous are those who preach to us that there is nothing wrong in social relations and that the inequalities in the distribution of wealth spring from the inequalities of human nature; and on the other hand, we see how wild are those who talk as though capital were a public enemy, and propose plans for arbitrarily restricting the acquisition of wealth. Capital is a good; the capitalist is a helper, if he is not also a monopolist. We can safely let any one get as rich as he can if he will not despoil others in doing so.

There are deep wrongs in the present constitution of society, but they are not wrongs inherent in the constitution of man nor in those social laws which are as truly the laws of the Creator as are the laws of the physical universe. They are wrongs resulting from bad adjustments which it is within our power to amend. The ideal social state is not that in which each gets an equal amount of wealth, but in which each gets in proportion to his contribution to the general stock. And in such a social state there would not be less incentive to exertion than now; there would be far more incentive. Men will be more industrious and more moral, better workmen and better citizens, if each takes his earnings and carries them home to his family, than where they put their earnings in a "pot" and gamble for them until some have far more than they could have earned, and others have little or nothing.

Viewpoint 3B
Concentrations of Wealth Help America (1889)

Andrew Carnegie (1835–1919)

INTRODUCTION *Andrew Carnegie was one of the leading industrialists of the Gilded Age. His business ventures in railroads and steel enabled this immigrant from a poor Scottish family to amass a fortune estimated at one point to be over half a billion dollars. Unlike most of his business peers, Carnegie was a frequent commentator on social and economic issues; he contributed articles to various journals and wrote several books. One of the most famous of his articles first appeared in the June 1889 issue of the* North American Review. *Carnegie defends the creation of large fortunes such as his own as an inevitable and necessary part of industrial progress. He also prescribes how affluent people should use their riches. The essay, excerpted here, became popularly known as "The Gospel of Wealth."*

Do Carnegie and Henry George, author of the opposing viewpoint, have similar or incompatible views on the effects of America's industrialization? Why might Carnegie's opinions expressed here have drawn criticism from both the right and the left of the political spectrum.

The problem of our age is the proper administration of wealth, that the ties of brotherhood may still bind together the rich and poor in harmonious relationship. The conditions of human life have not only been changed, but revolutionized, within the past few hundred years. In former days there was little difference between the dwelling, dress, food, and environment of the chief and those of his retainers. The Indians are today where civilized man then was. When visiting the Sioux, I was led to the wigwam of the chief. It was like the others in external appearance, and even within the difference was trifling between it and those of the poorest of his braves. The contrast between the palace of the millionaire and the cottage of the laborer with us today measures the change which has come with civilization. This change, however, is not to be deplored, but welcomed as highly beneficial. It is well, nay, essential, for the progress of the race that the houses of some should be homes for all that is highest and best in literature and the arts, and for all the refinements of civilization, rather than that none should be so. Much better this great irregularity than universal squalor. Without wealth there can be no Maecenas [a generous patron of the arts]. The "good old times" were not good old times. Neither master nor servant was as well situated then as today. A relapse to old conditions would be disastrous to both—not the least so to him who serves—and would sweep away civilization with it.

From Andrew Carnegie, "Wealth," *North American Review*, June 1889.

But whether the change be for good or ill, it is upon us, beyond our power to alter, and, therefore, to be accepted and made the best of. It is a waste of time to criticize the inevitable.

It is easy to see how the change has come. One illustration will serve for almost every phase of the cause. In the manufacture of products we have the whole story. It applies to all combinations of human industry, as stimulated and enlarged by the inventions of this scientific age. Formerly, articles were manufactured at the domestic hearth, or in small shops which formed part of the household. The master and his apprentices worked side by side, the latter living with the master, and therefore subject to the same conditions. When these apprentices rose to be masters, there was little or no change in their mode of life, and they, in turn, educated succeeding apprentices in the same routine. There was, substantially, social equality, and even political equality, for those engaged in industrial pursuits had then little or no voice in the State.

The inevitable result of such a mode of manufacture was crude articles at high prices. Today the world obtains commodities of excellent quality at prices which even the preceding generation would have deemed incredible. In the commercial world similar causes have produced similar results, and the race is benefited thereby. The poor enjoy what the rich could not before afford. What were the luxuries have become the necessaries of life. The laborer has now more comforts than the farmer had a few generations ago. The farmer has more luxuries than the landlord had, and is more richly clad and better housed. The landlord has books and pictures rarer and appointments more artistic than the king could then obtain.

The price we pay for this salutary change is, no doubt, great. We assemble thousands of operatives in the factory, and in the mine, of whom the employer can know little or nothing, and to whom he is little better than a myth. All intercourse between them is at an end. Rigid castes are formed, and, as usual, mutual ignorance breeds mutual distrust. Each caste is without sympathy with the other, and ready to credit anything disparaging in regard to it. Under the law of competition, the employer of thousands is forced into the strictest economies, among which the rates paid to labor figure prominently, and often there is friction between the employer and the employed, between capital and labor, between rich and poor. Human society loses homogeneity.

Not evil, but good, has come to the race from the accumulation of wealth by those who have had the ability and energy to produce it.

CONCENTRATIONS OF WEALTH ARE ESSENTIAL

The price which society pays for the law of competition, like the price it pays for cheap comforts and luxuries, is also great; but the advantages of this law are also greater still than its cost—for it is to this law that we owe our wonderful material development, which brings improved conditions in its train. But, whether the law be benign or not, we must say of it, as we say of the change in the conditions of men to which we have referred: It is here; we cannot evade it; no substitutes for it have been found; and while the law may be sometimes hard for the individual, it is best for the race, because it insures the survival of the fittest in every department. We accept and welcome, therefore, as conditions to which we must accommodate ourselves, great inequality of environment; the concentration of business, industrial and commercial, in the hands of a few; and the law of competition between these, as being not only beneficial, but essential to the future progress of the race. . . .

Objections to the foundations upon which society is based are not in order, because the condition of the race is better with these than it has been with any other which has been tried. Of the effect of any new substitutes proposed we cannot be sure. The Socialist or Anarchist who seeks to overturn present conditions is to be regarded as attacking the foundation upon which civilization itself rests, for civilization took its start from the day when the capable, industrious workman said to his incompetent and lazy fellow, "If thou dost not sow, thou shalt not reap," and thus ended primitive Communism by separating the drones from the bees. One who studies this subject will soon be brought face to face with the conclusion that upon the sacredness of property civilization itself depends—the right of the laborer to his hundred dollars in the savings-bank, and equally the legal right of the millionaire to his millions. Every man must be allowed "to sit under his own vine and fig-tree, with none to make afraid," if human society is to advance, or even to remain so far advanced as it is. To those who propose to substitute Communism for this intense Individualism, the answer therefore is: The race has tried that. All progress from that barbarous day to the present time has resulted from its displacement. Not evil, but good, has come to the race from the accumulation of wealth by those who have had the ability and energy to produce it. . . .

We start, then, with a condition of affairs under which the best interests of the race are promoted, but which inevitably gives wealth to the few. Thus far, accepting conditions as they exist, the situation can be surveyed and pronounced good. The question then arises—and if the foregoing be correct, it is the only question with which we have to deal—What is the proper mode of administering wealth after the laws upon which civilization is founded have thrown it into the hands of the few? And it is of this great question that I believe I offer the true solution. . . .

DISPOSING OF SURPLUS WEALTH

There are but three modes in which surplus wealth can be disposed of. It can be left to the families of the decedents; or it can be bequeathed for public purposes; or, finally, it can be administered by its possessors during their lives. Under the first and second modes most of the wealth of the world that has reached the few has hitherto been applied. Let us in turn consider each of these modes. The first is, the most injudicious. . . . The question which forces itself upon thoughtful men in all lands is, Why should men leave great fortunes to their children? If this is done from affection, is it not misguided affection? Observation teaches that, generally speaking, it is not well for the children that they should be so burdened. Neither is it well for the State. Beyond providing for the wife and daughters moderate sources of income, and very moderate allowances indeed, if any, for the sons, men may well hesitate; for it is no longer questionable that great sums bequeathed often work more for the injury than for the good of the recipients. Wise men will soon conclude that, for the best interests of the members of their families, and of the State, such bequests are an improper use of their means. . . .

As to the second mode, that of leaving wealth at death for public uses, it may be said that this is only a means for the disposal of wealth, provided a man is content to wait until he is dead before he becomes of much good in the world. Knowledge of the results of legacies bequeathed is not calculated to inspire the brightest hopes of much posthumous good being accomplished by them. The cases are not few in which the real object sought by the testator is not attained, nor are they few in which his real wishes are thwarted. . . . Besides this, it may fairly be said that no man is to be extolled for doing what he cannot help doing, nor is he to be thanked by the community to which he only leaves wealth at death. Men who leave vast sums in this way may fairly be thought men who would not have left it at all had they been able to take it with them. The memories of such cannot be held in grateful remembrance, for there is no grace in their gifts. It is not to be wondered at that such bequests seem so generally to lack the blessing.

The growing disposition to tax more and more heavily large estates left at death is a cheering indication of the growth of a salutary change in public opinion. The State of Pennsylvania now takes—subject to some exceptions—one tenth of the property left by its citizens. The budget presented in the British Parliament the other day proposes to increase the death duties; and, most significant of all, the new tax is to be a graduated one. Of all forms of taxation this seems the wisest. Men who continue

hoarding great sums all their lives, the proper use of which for public ends would work good to the community from which it chiefly came, should be made to feel that the community, in the form of the State, cannot thus be deprived of its proper share. By taxing estates heavily at death the State marks its condemnation of the selfish millionaire's unworthy life. . . .

THE SOLUTION

There remains, then, only one mode of using great fortunes; but in this we have the true antidote for the temporary unequal distribution of wealth, the reconciliation of the rich and the poor—a reign of harmony, another ideal, differing, indeed, from that of the Communist in requiring only the further evolution of existing conditions, not the total overthrow of our civilization. It is founded upon the present most intense Individualism, and the race is prepared to put it in practice by degrees whenever it pleases. Under its sway we shall have an ideal State, in which the surplus wealth of the few will become, in the best sense, the property of the many, because administered for the common good; and this wealth, passing through the hands of the few, can be made a much more potent force for the elevation of our race than if distributed in small sums to the people themselves. Even the poorest can be made to see this, and to agree that great sums gathered by some of their fellow-citizens and spent for public purposes, from which the masses reap the principal benefit, are more valuable to them than if scattered among themselves in trifling amounts through the course of many years.

If we consider the results which flow from the Cooper Institute [an adult education institute founded by industrialist and philanthropist Peter Cooper], for instance, to the best portion of the race in New York not possessed of means, and compare these with those which would have ensued for the good of the masses from an equal sum distributed by Mr. Cooper in his lifetime in the form of wages, which is the highest form of distribution, being for work done and not for charity, we can form some estimate of the possibilities for the improvement of the race which lie embedded in the present law of the accumulation of wealth. Much of this sum, if distributed in small quantities among the people, would have been wasted in the indulgence of appetite, some of it in excess, and it may be doubted whether even the part put to the best use, that of adding to the comforts of the home, would have yielded results for the race, as a race, at all comparable to those which are flowing and are to flow from the Cooper Institute from generation to generation. Let the advocate of violent or radical change ponder well this thought. . . .

This, then, is held to be the duty of the man of wealth: To set an example of modest, unostentatious living, shunning display or extravagance; to provide moderately for the legitimate wants of those dependent upon him; and, after doing so, to consider all surplus revenues which come to him simply as trust funds, which he is called upon to administer, and strictly bound as a matter of duty to administer in the manner which, in his judgment, is best calculated to produce the most beneficial results for the community—the man of wealth thus becoming the mere trustee and agent for his poorer brethren, bringing to their service his superior wisdom, experience, and ability to administer, doing for them better than they would or could do for themselves....

In bestowing charity, the main consideration should be to help those who will help themselves; to provide part of the means by which those who desire to improve may do so; to give those who desire to rise the aids by which they may rise; to assist, but rarely or never to do all. Neither the individual nor the race is improved by alms-giving. Those worthy of assistance, except in rare cases, seldom require assistance.

The rich man is thus almost restricted to following the examples of Peter Cooper, Enoch Pratt of Baltimore, and others, who know that the best means of benefiting the community is to place within its reach the ladders upon which the aspiring can rise—free libraries, parks, and means of recreation, by which men are helped in body and mind; works of art, certain to give pleasure and improve the public taste; and public institutions of various kinds, which will improve the general condition of the people; in this manner returning their surplus wealth to the mass of their fellows in the forms best calculated to do them lasting good.

Thus is the problem of rich and poor to be solved. The laws of accumulation will be left free, the laws of distribution free. Individualism will continue, but the millionaire will be but a trustee for the poor, intrusted for a season with a great part of the increased wealth of the community, for administering it for the community far better than it could or would have done for itself. The best minds will thus have reached a stage in the development of the race in which it is clearly seen that there is no mode of disposing of surplus wealth creditable to thoughtful and earnest men into whose hands it flows, save by using it year by year for the general good. This day already dawns. Men may die without incurring the pity of their fellows, still sharers in great business enterprises from which their capital cannot be or has not been withdrawn, and which is left chiefly at death for public uses; yet the day is not far distant when the man who dies leaving behind him millions of available wealth, which was free for him to administer during life, will pass away "unwept, unhonored, and unsung," no matter to what uses he leaves the dross which he cannot take with him. Of such as these the public verdict will then be "The man who dies thus rich dies disgraced."

Such, in my opinion, is the true gospel concerning wealth, obedience to which is destined some day to solve the problem of the rich and the poor, and to bring "Peace on earth, among men good will."

FOR FURTHER READING

Andrew C. Livesay, *Andrew Carnegie and the Rise of Big Business.* Boston: Little, Brown, 1975.

John L. Thomas, *Alternative America: Henry George, Edward Bellamy, Henry Demarest Lloyd and the Adversary Tradition.* Cambridge, MA: Belknap Press, 1983.

John Ord Tipple, *Andrew Carnegie/Henry George: The Problem of Progress.* Cleveland, OH: H. Allen, 1960.

Joseph Frazier Wall, ed., *The Andrew Carnegie Reader.* Pittsburgh: University of Pittsburgh Press, 1992.

Viewpoint 4A
The Organizing of Labor into Unions Is Dangerous (1886)

Henry Clews (1834–1923)

INTRODUCTION *Henry Clews was a leading financier during and after the Civil War, and served as an economic adviser to President Ulysses S. Grant. In the following viewpoint, excerpted from an 1886 article in the* North American Review, *Clews denounces what he sees as a clear danger to America—the growth of unionism in the American labor force. He specifically attacks the Knights of Labor, the leading U.S. national organization of workers during the 1880s. Clews argues that American workers are treated much better than in other countries and argues that striking workers can be readily replaced by immigrants from Europe.*

What individual rights does Clews emphasize? Why does he believe that laborers have "no ground for complaint"?

The Knights of Labor have undertaken to test, upon a large scale, the application of compulsion as a means of enforcing their demands. The point to be determined is whether capital or labor shall, in future, determine the terms upon which the invested resources of the nation are to be employed.

———◼———

The demands of the Knights and their Sympathizers...are...completely subversive of the social order.

———◼———

To the employer, it is a question whether his individual rights as to the control of his property shall be so far overborne as to not only deprive him of his freedom but

Henry Clews, "The Folly of Organized Labor," *North American Review,* June 1886.

also expose him to interferences seriously impairing the value of his capital. To the employees, it is a question whether, by the force of coercion, they can wrest, to their own profit, powers and control which, in every civilized community, are secured as the most sacred and inalienable rights of the employer.

This issue is so absolutely revolutionary of the normal relations between labor and capital, that it has naturally produced a partial paralysis of business, especially among industries whose operations involve contracts extending into the future. There has been at no time any serious apprehension that such an utterly anarchical movement could succeed so long as American citizens have a clear perception of their rights and their true interests; but it has been distinctly perceived that this war could not fail to create a divided if not hostile feeling between the two great classes of society; that it must hold in check not only a large extent of ordinary business operations but also the undertaking of those new enterprises which contribute to our national progress, and that the commercial markets must be subjected to serious embarrassments.

From the nature of the case, however, this labor disease must soon end one way or another; and there is not much difficulty in foreseeing what its termination will be. The demands of the Knights and their sympathizers, whether openly expressed or temporarily concealed, are so utterly revolutionary of the inalienable rights of the citizen and so completely subversive of social order that the whole community has come to a firm conclusion that these pretensions must be resisted to the last extremity of endurance and authority; and that the present is the best opportunity for meeting the issue firmly and upon its merits.

LOST SYMPATHY

The organizations have sacrificed the sympathy which lately was entertained for them on account of inequities existing in certain employments; they stand discredited and distrusted before the community at large as impracticable, unjust, and reckless; and, occupying this attitude before the public, their cause is gone and their organization doomed to failure. They have opened the floodgates to the immigration of foreign labor, which is already pouring in by the thousands; and they have set a premium on nonunion labor, which will be more sought for than ever, and will not be slow to secure superior earnings by making arrangements with employers upon such terms and for such hours as may best suit their interests. Thus, one great advantage will incidentally come out of this crisis beneficial to the workingman, who, by standing aloof from the dead-level system of the unions, will be enabled to earn according to his capacity and thereby maintain his chances for rising from the rank of the employee to that of the employer.

This result cannot be long delayed; because not only is loss and suffering following close upon the heels of the strikers, but the imprudences of their leaders are breeding dissatisfaction among the rank and file of the organizations, which, if much further protracted, will gravely threaten their cohesion. It is by no means certain that we may not see a yet further spread of strikes, and possibly with even worse forms of violence than we have yet witnessed; but, so long as a way to the end is seen, with a chance of that end demonstrating to the organizations that their aspirations to control capital are impossible dreams, the temporary evils will be borne with equanimity....

LABOR AND IMMIGRATION

There have been numerous vacancies created by the strikers voluntarily resigning. There has been no difficulty in filling these vacancies by those that are equally capable, if not more so, from other countries flocking to our shores. The steam ferry which connects this country and Europe has demonstrated this by the steamer that arrived in six days and ten hours' time from European shores to our own. As the interval between the downtrodden and oppressed operatives of the Old World and America is thus reduced to hours, Europe will quickly send to us all the labor we need to meet the emergency.... Strikes may have been justifiable in other nations but they are not justifiable in our country, and there is where the mistake was in organizing such a movement. The Almighty has made this country for the oppressed of other nations, and therefore this is the land of refuge for the oppressed, and the hand of the laboring man should not be raised against it.

The laboring man in this bounteous and hospitable country has no ground for complaint. His vote is potential and he is elevated thereby to the position of man. Elsewhere he is a creature of circumstance, which is that of abject depression. Under the government of this nation, the effort is to elevate the standard of the human race and not to degrade it. In all other nations it is the reverse. What, therefore, has the laborer to complain of in America? By inciting strikes and encouraging discontent, he stands in the way of the elevation of his race and of mankind.

The tide of emigration to this country, now so large, makes peaceful strikes perfectly harmless in themselves, because the places of those who vacate good situations are easily filled by the newcomers. When disturbances occur under the cloak of strikes, it is a different matter, as law and order are then set at defiance. The recent disturbances in Chicago, which resulted in the assassination of a number of valiant policemen through some cowardly Polish nihilist firing a bomb of dynamite in their midst, was the worst thing that could have been done for the cause of the present labor agitation, as it alienates all sympathy from them. It is much to the credit, however, of Americans and Irishmen that, during the recent uprising of the labor classes, none of them have taken part in any violent measures whatsoever, nor have they shown any sympathy with such a policy.

Viewpoint 4B

Labor Unions Are Essential (1894)

Samuel Gompers (1850–1924)

INTRODUCTION *Samuel Gompers, one of America's most prominent labor leaders, began his labor career as head of a union of cigar makers. In 1886 he cofounded the American Federation of Labor (AFL)—an association of trade unions—and served as the AFL's president almost continuously thereafter until his death.*

The following viewpoint is taken from an 1894 open letter to Peter Grosscup, a judge in the U.S. District Court of Illinois. Grosscup was presiding over the indictment of American Railway Union president Eugene V. Debs for violating a court injunction against strikes (such injunctions were frequently issued by the government to curb work stoppages). In his charge to the jury Grosscup claimed that union organizing constituted a harmful and illegal activity. Gompers, in his letter, rejects this then-common argument and defends the right and necessity of workers to organize and bargain collectively.

What might Gompers find most objectionable about the arguments of Henry Clews, author of the opposing viewpoint? What role does Gompers see for government in helping the working class?

You say that, as you stated in your charge to the grand jury, you believe in labor organizations within such lawful and reasonable limits as will make them a service to the laboring man and not a menace to the lawful institutions of the country. I have had the pleasure of reading your charge to the grand jury, and have only partially been able to discover how far you believe in labor organizations.

WHAT WORKERS CAN DISCUSS

You would certainly have no objection officially or personally to workingmen organizing, and in their meetings discuss perhaps "the origin of man," benignly smiling upon each other and declaring that all existing things are right, going to their wretched homes to find some freedom in sleep from gnawing hunger. You would have them extol the virtues of monopolists and wreckers of the people's welfare. You would not have them consider seriously the fact that more than 2 million of their

fellows are unemployed, and though willing and able, cannot find the opportunity to work in order that they may sustain themselves, their wives, and their children. You would not have them consider seriously the fact that [George] Pullman who has grown so rich from the toil of his workmen that he can riot in luxury, while he heartlessly turns these very workmen out of their tenements into the streets and leave to the tender mercies of corporate greed. Nor would you have them ponder upon the hundreds of other Pullmans of different names.

You know, or ought to know, that the introduction of machinery, is turning into idleness thousands faster than new industries are founded, and yet, machinery certainly should not be either destroyed or hampered in its full development. The laborer is a man, he is made warm by the same sun and made cold—yes, colder—by the same winter as you are. He has a heart and brain, and feels and knows the human and paternal instinct for those depending upon him as keenly as do you.

What shall the workers do? Sit idly by and see the vast resources of nature and the human mind be utilized and monopolized for the benefit of the comparative few? No. The laborers must learn to think and act, and soon, too, that only by the power of organization and common concert of action can either their manhood be maintained, their rights to life (work to sustain it) be recognized, and liberty and rights secured.

Since you say that you favor labor organizations within certain limits, will you kindly give to thousands of your anxious fellow citizens what you believe the workers could and should do in their organizations to solve this great problem? Not what they should not do. You have told us that....

PROGRESS AND POVERTY

One becomes enraptured in reading the beauty of your description of modern progress. Could you have had in mind the miners of Spring Valley or Pennsylvania, or the clothing workers of the sweatshops of New York or Chicago when you grandiloquently dilate,

> Who is not rich today when compared with his ancestors of a century ago? The steamboat and the railroad bring to his breakfast table the coffees of Java and Brazil, the fruits from Florida and California, and the steaks from the plains. The loom arrays him in garments and the factories furnish him with a dwelling that the richest contemporaries of his grandfather would have envied. With health and industry he is a prince.

Probably you have not read within the past year of babes dying of starvation at their mothers' breasts. More than likely the thousands of men lying upon the bare stones night after night in the City Hall of Chicago last winter escaped your notice. You may not have heard

From a letter of Samuel Gompers, reprinted in the *American Federationist*, vol. 1, September 1894.

of the cry for bread that was sounded through this land of plenty by thousands of honest men and women. But should these and many other painful incidents have passed you by unnoticed, I am fearful that you may learn of them with keener thoughts with the coming sleets and blasts of winter.

You say that "labor cannot afford to attack capital." Let me remind you that labor has no quarrel with capital, as such. It is merely the possessors of capital who refuse to accord to labor the recognition, the right, the justice which is the laborers' due with whom we contend.

See what is implied by your contemptuous reference to the laborer when you ask, "Will the conqueror destroy his trophy?" Who ever heard of a conqueror marching unitedly with his *trophy*, as you would have them? But if by your comparison you mean that the conqueror is the corporation, the trust, the capitalist class, and ask then whether they would destroy their *trophy*, I would have you ask the widows and orphans of the thousands of men killed annually through the avarice of railroad corporations refusing to avail themselves of modern appliances in coupling and other improvements on their railroads.

Inquire from the thousands of women and children whose husbands or fathers were suffocated or crushed in the mines through the rapacious greed of stockholders clamoring for more dividends. Investigate the sweating dens of the large cities. Go to the mills, factories, through the country. Visit the modern tenement houses or hovels in which thousands of workers are compelled to eke out an existence. Ask these whether the conqueror (monopoly) cares whether his trophy (the laborers) is destroyed or preserved. Ascertain from employers whether the laborer is not regarded the same as a machine, thrown out as soon as all the work possible has been squeezed out of him.

LABOR LEGISLATION

Are you aware that all the legislation ever secured for the ventilation or safety of mines, factory, or workshop is the result of the efforts of organized labor? Do you know that the trade unions were the shield for the seven-year-old children from being the conqueror's trophy until they become somewhat older? And that the reformatory laws now on the statute books protecting or defending the trophies of both sexes, young and old from the fond care of the conquerors were wrested from congresses, legislatures, and parliaments despite the Pullmans, the Jeffries, the Ricks, the Tafts, the Williams, the Woods, or the Grosscups.

———————■———————

The labor movement as represented by the trades unions stand for right, for justice, for liberty.

———————■———————

By what right, sir, do you assume that the labor organizations do not conduct their affairs within lawful limits, or that they are a menace to the lawful institutions of the country? Is it because some thoughtless or overzealous member at a time of great excitement and smarting under a wrong may violate under a law or commit an improper act? Would you apply the same rule to the churches, the other moral agencies and organizations that you do to the organizations of labor? If you did, the greatest moral force of life today, the trade unions, would certainly stand out the clearest, brightest, and purest. Because a certain class (for which you and a number of your colleagues on the bench seem to be the special pleaders) have a monopoly in their lines of trade, I submit that this is no good reason for their claim to have a monopoly on true patriotism or respect for the lawful institutions of the country. . . .

WHAT THE LABOR MOVEMENT IS FOR

Year by year man's liberties are trampled underfoot at the bidding of corporations and trusts, rights are invaded, and law perverted. In all ages, wherever a tyrant has shown himself, he has always found some willing judge to clothe that tyranny in the robes of legality, and modern capitalism has proven no exception to the rule.

You may not know that the labor movement as represented by the trades unions stands for right, for justice, for liberty. You may not imagine that the issuance of an injunction depriving men of a legal as well as a natural right to protect themselves, their wives, and little ones must fail of its purpose. Repression or oppression never yet succeeded in crushing the truth or redressing a wrong.

In conclusion let me assure you that labor will organize and more compactly than ever and upon practical lines; and despite relentless antagonism, achieve for humanity a nobler manhood, a more beautiful womanhood, and a happier childhood.

FOR FURTHER READING

John Avrich, *The Haymarket Tragedy*. Princeton, NJ: Princeton University Press, 1984.

Samuel Gompers, *Seventy Years of Life and Labor*. Ithaca, NY: ILR Press, 1984.

Harold C. Livesay, *Samuel Gompers and Organized Labor in America*. Boston: Little, Brown, 1978.

David Ray Papke, *The Pullman Case: The Clash of Labor and Capital in Industrial America*. Lawrence: University Press of Kansas, 1999.

Viewpoint 5A

A Populist Prescription for Social Reform (1892)

People's Party Platform of 1892

INTRODUCTION *The People's Party (or Populist Party) was organized in 1892; its presidential candidate,*

James Weaver, polled more than 1 million votes (out of 11 million cast) in the 1892 elections. Many of its participants and ideas can be traced back to the Farmers' Alliance and other agrarian movements of the 1870s and 1880s. Populist writers and speakers argued that farmers were being left behind in the industrial revolution and that the government should actively intervene in the economy to assure the welfare of farmers and workers. The following viewpoint consists of a preamble and policy platform adopted by the People's Party at its 1892 convention in Omaha, Nebraska, and provides a concise summary of what many Populists believed was wrong with America. Much of the preamble's writing has been attributed to Ignatius Donnelly, a radical newspaper editor and future congressman from Minnesota.

What were the main causes of social ills in America, according to Donnelly and the Populist Party? What do they assert about the established Republican and Democratic parties?

Assembled upon the one hundred and sixteenth anniversary of the Declaration of Independence, the People's Party of America in their first National Convention, invoking upon their action the blessing of Almighty God, puts forth, in the name and on behalf of the people of this country, the following preamble and declaration of principles:

PREAMBLE

The conditions which surround us best justify our co-operation. We meet in the midst of a nation brought to the verge of moral, political and material ruin. Corruption dominates the ballot box, the Legislatures, the Congress, and touches even the ermine of the Bench. The people are demoralized; most of the States have been compelled to isolate the voters at the polling places to prevent universal intimidation or bribery. The newspapers are largely subsidized or muzzled, public opinion silenced, business prostrated, our homes covered with mortgages, labor impoverished, and the land concentrating in the hands of the capitalists. The urban workmen are denied the right of organization for self-protection; imported pauperized labor beats down their wages; a hireling standing army, unrecognized by our laws, is established to shoot them down, and they are rapidly degenerating into European conditions. The fruits of the toil of millions are boldly stolen to build up colossal fortunes for a few, unprecedented in the history of mankind, and the possessors of these in turn despise the Republic and endanger liberty. From the same prolific womb of governmental injustice we breed the two great classes—tramps and millionaires.

The national power to create money is appropriated to enrich bond-holders; a vast public debt, payable in

From Edward McPherson, *A Handbook of Politics for 1892* (Washington, DC: Chapman, 1892).

legal tender currency, has been funded into gold-bearing bonds, thereby adding millions to the burdens of the people.

Silver, which has been accepted as coin since the dawn of history, has been demonetized to add to the purchasing power of gold by decreasing the value of all forms of property as well as human labor, and the supply of currency is purposely abridged to fatten usurers, bankrupt enterprise and enslave industry.

A vast conspiracy against mankind has been organized on two continents, and it is rapidly taking possession of the world. If not met and overthrown at once, it forebodes terrible social convulsions, the destruction of civilization, or the establishment of an absolute despotism.

A GREAT STRUGGLE

We have witnessed, for more than a quarter of a century, the struggles of the two great political parties for power and plunder, while grievous wrongs have been inflicted upon the suffering people. We charge that the controlling influences dominating both these parties have permitted the existing dreadful conditions to develop without serious effort to prevent or restrain them.

Neither do they now promise us any substantial reform. They have agreed together to ignore, in the coming campaign, every issue but one. They propose to drown the outcries of a plundered people with the uproar of a sham battle over the tariff, so that capitalists, corporations, national banks, rings, trusts, watered stock, the demonetization of silver and the oppressions of the usurers may all be lost sight of. They propose to sacrifice our homes, lives and children, on the altar of mammon; to destroy the multitude in order to secure corruption funds from the millionaires.

Assembled on the anniversary of the birthday of the nation, and filled with the spirit of the grand general and chieftain who established our independence, we seek to restore the Government of the Republic to the hands of the "plain people" with whose class it originated. We assert our purposes to be identical with the purposes of the National Constitution, to form a more perfect Union and establish justice, insure domestic tranquility, provide for the common defense, promote the general welfare and secure the blessings of liberty for ourselves and our posterity.

———————■———————

The powers of government . . . should be expanded . . . to the end that oppression, injustice and poverty, shall eventually cease in the land.

———————■———————

We declare that this Republic can only endure as a free government while built upon the love of the whole people for each other and for the nation; that it cannot be pinned together by bayonets; that the civil war is over and that every passion and resentment which grew out of it must die with it, and that we must be in fact, as we are in name, one united brotherhood of freedom.

Our country finds itself confronted by conditions for which there is no precedent in the history of the world; our annual agricultural productions amount to billions of dollars in value, which must within a few weeks or months be exchanged for billions of dollars' worth of commodities consumed in their production; the existing currency supply is wholly inadequate to make this exchange; the results are falling prices, the formation of combines and rings, the impoverishment of the producing class. We pledge ourselves that, if given power, we will labor to correct these evils by wise and reasonable legislation, in accordance with the terms of our platform.

PARTY PLATFORM

We believe that the powers of government—in other words, of the people—should be expanded (as in the case of the postal service) as rapidly and as far as the good sense of an intelligent people and the teachings of experience shall justify, to the end that oppression, injustice and poverty, shall eventually cease in the land.

While our sympathies as a party of reform are naturally upon the side of every proposition which will tend to make men intelligent, virtuous and temperate, we nevertheless regard these questions—important as they are—as secondary to the great issues now pressing for solution, and upon which not only our individual prosperity, but the very existence of free institutions depend; and we ask all men to first help us to determine whether we are to have a Republic to administer, before we differ as to the conditions upon which it is to be administered; believing that the forces of reform this day organized will never cease to move forward, until every wrong is righted, and equal rights and equal privileges securely established for all the men and women of this country. We declare, therefore,

First.—That the union of the labor forces of the United States this day consummated shall be permanent and perpetual; may its spirit enter into all hearts for the salvation of the Republic, and the uplifting of mankind.

Second.—Wealth belongs to him who creates it, and every dollar taken from industry without an equivalent is robbery. "If any will not work, neither shall he eat." The interests of rural and civic labor are the same; their enemies are identical.

Third.—We believe that the time has come when the railroad corporations will either own the people or the people must own the railroads; and should the Government enter upon the work of owning and managing all railroads, we should favor an amendment to the Constitution by which all persons engaged in the Government service shall be placed under a civil service regulation of the most rigid character, so as to prevent the increase of the power of the national administration by the use of such additional Government employes.

Finance.—We demand a national currency, safe, sound and flexible, issued by the General Government only [replacing notes issued by private banks], a full legal tender for all debts public and private....

1. We demand free and unlimited coinage of silver and gold at the present legal ratio of 16 to 1.
2. We demand that the amount of circulating medium [money] be speedily increased to not less than $50 per capita.
3. We demand a graduated income tax.
4. We believe that the money of the country should be kept as much as possible in the hands of the people, and hence we demand that all State and National revenues shall be limited to the necessary expenses of the Government, economically and honestly administered.
5. We demand that Postal Savings Banks be established by the Government for the safe deposit of the earnings of the people and to facilitate exchange.

Transportation.—Transportation being a means of exchange and a public necessity, the government should own and operate the railroads in the interest of the people.

The telegraph and telephone, like the post office system, being a necessity for the transmission of news, should be owned and operated by the Government in the interest of the people.

Land.—The land, including all the natural sources of wealth, is the heritage of the people and should not be monopolized for speculative purposes, and alien ownership of land should be prohibited. All land now held by railroads and other corporations in excess of their actual needs, and all lands now owned by aliens should be reclaimed by the Government and held for actual settlers only.

Viewpoint 5B

A Social Darwinist View of Social Reform (1914)

William Graham Sumner (1840–1910)

INTRODUCTION *Those who opposed the Populist Party and other movements calling for radical changes in American society during the Gilded Age often applied the ideas of British naturalist Charles Darwin. Darwin developed the theories of natural selection "survival of the fittest" to account for the development of biological species. "Social Darwinists" applied similar ideas to economic conditions in America and other nations to explain why social and economic inequality existed. One such theorist was William Graham Sumner, a professor of political and social science at Yale University from 1872 to 1909. Sumner's writings, in which he argued that attempts to reform society and help the disadvantaged were doomed because they flew in the face of nature itself, made him one of the leading defenders of the status quo during the Gilded Age. In the following viewpoint, excerpted from an essay first published in 1914 after Sumner's death, he argues that reforms helping the "unfit" would harm society.*

What is the burden nature places on humanity, according to Sumner? What does he argue are the causes of poverty? Which parts of the People's Party platform (see opposing viewpoint) might Sumner accept?

Socialism is no new thing. In one form or another it is to be found throughout all history. It arises from an observation of certain harsh facts in the lot of man on earth, the concrete expression of which is poverty and misery, These facts challenge us. It is folly to try to shut our eyes to them. We have first to notice what they are, and then to face them squarely.

---■---

Competition . . . is a law of nature.

---■---

A STRUGGLE AGAINST NATURE

Man is born under the necessity of sustaining the existence he has received by an onerous struggle against nature, both to win what is essential to his life and to ward off what is prejudicial to it. He is born under a burden and a necessity. Nature holds what is essential to him, but she offers nothing gratuitously. He may win for his use what she holds, if he can. Only the most meager and inadequate supply for human needs can be obtained directly from nature. There are trees which may be used for fuel and for dwellings, but labor is required to fit them for this use. There are ores in the ground, but labor is necessary to fit the products of nature for human use. In this struggle every individual is under the pressure of the necessities for food, clothing, shelter, fuel, and every individual brings with him more or less energy for the conflict necessary to supply his needs. . . .

The struggle for existence is aimed against nature. It is from her niggardly hand that we have to wrest the satisfactions for our needs, but our fellow-men are our

competitors for the meager supply. Competition, therefore, is a law of nature. Nature is entirely neutral; she submits to him who most energetically and resolutely assails her. She grants her rewards to the fittest, therefore, without regard to other considerations of any kind. If, then, there be liberty, men get from her just in proportion to their works, and their having and enjoying are just in proportion to their being and their doing. Such is the system of nature. If we do not like it, and if we try to amend it, there is only one way in which we can do it. We can take from the better and give to the worse. We can deflect the penalties of those who have done ill and throw them on those who have done better. We can take the rewards from those who have done better and give them to those who have done worse. We shall thus lessen the inequalities. We shall favor the survival of the unfittest, and we shall accomplish this by destroying liberty. Let it be understood that we cannot go outside of this alternative: Liberty, inequality, survival of the fittest; not liberty, equality, survival of the unfittest. The former carries society forward and favors all its best members; the latter carries society downwards and favors all its worst members. . . .

THE LAWS OF PROSPERITY

The sound student of sociology can hold out to mankind, as individuals or as a race, only one hope of better and happier living. That hope lies in an enhancement of the industrial virtues and of the moral forces which thence arise. Industry, self-denial, and temperance are the laws of prosperity for men and states; without them advance in the arts and in wealth means only corruption and decay through luxury and vice. With them progress in the arts and increasing wealth are the prime conditions of an advancing civilization which is sound enough to endure. The power of the human race to-day over the conditions of prosperous and happy living are sufficient to banish poverty and misery, if it were not for folly and vice. The earth does not begin to be populated up to its power to support population on the present stage of the arts; if the United States were as densely populated as the British Islands, we should have 1,000,000,000 people here. If, therefore, men were willing to set to work with energy and courage to subdue the outlying parts of the earth, all might live in plenty and prosperity. But if they insist on remaining in the slums of great cities or on the borders of an old society, and on a comparatively exhausted soil, there is no device of economists or statesmen which can prevent them from falling victims to poverty and misery or from succumbing in the competition of life to those who have greater command of capital.

William Graham Sumner, *The Challenge of Facts and Other Essays*, ed., Albert G. Keller (New Haven, CT: Yale University Press, 1914).

OPPOSING VIEWPOINTS IN AMERICAN HISTORY

Part 2
THE PROGRESSIVE ERA (1895–1920)

CHRONOLOGY

1895

July United States intervenes in boundary dispute between Great Britain and Venezuela.

February 24 Rebellion against Spanish rule breaks out in Cuba.

September 18 Booker T. Washington speaks at the Atlanta Exposition.

1896

January 4 Utah becomes the 45th state.

April 23 Demonstration of Thomas Edison's motion picture invention occurs.

May 18 Supreme Court in *Plessy v. Ferguson* legalizes segregation.

November 3 William McKinley elected president.

1897

January Gold rush starts in Klondike, Alaska.

1898

February 15 The U.S. battleship *Maine* sunk in Havana Harbor in Cuba after mysterious explosion.

April 21–December 10 Spanish-American War results in U.S. victory and acquisition of Guam, Puerto Rico, and the Philippines; Cuba gains independence from Spain.

July 28 Hawaii annexed by the United States.

1899

February 4 Filipino rebels under Emilio Aguinaldo attack American troops in Manila, starting rebellion that lasts three years.

September 6 United States proposes "Open Door" policy toward China.

1900

March 6 Social Democratic (later Socialist) Party founded by Eugene Debs.

September 18 First direct primary election in nation held in Hennepin County, Minnesota.

November 6 McKinley reelected president; Theodore Roosevelt elected vice president; noted Progressive Robert M. La Follette elected governor of Wisconsin.

1901

January 10 First great oil strike in Texas occurs.

February 25 U.S. Steel Corporation founded, which later grows into nation's first billion-dollar corporation.

March 2 Congress passes Platt Amendment making Cuba a quasi-protectorate of the United States.

September 14 McKinley dies eight days after assassination attempt; Roosevelt takes office.

November 9 Northern Securities Company, a railroad holding company controlled by J.P. Morgan, is incorporated.

1902

February *McClure's* magazine begins to publish articles by Lincoln Steffens, Ida M. Tarbell, and other "muckrackers."

March 10 Roosevelt sues Northern Securities Company in first "trust-busting" suit.

May 12 United Mine Workers strike idles 140,000 workers; President Roosevelt intervenes in October; strikers end walkout on October 21.

1903

June 16 Ford Motor Company formed.

February 1 *The Souls of Black Folk* by W.E.B. Du Bois published.

May 23 Wisconsin is first state to adopt direct primary for party elections.

October Baseball holds first World Series.

November United States secures rights to Panama Canal route after Panama, with assistance from the U.S. Navy, secedes from Colombia.

December 17 Wilbur and Orville Wright achieve world's first successful airplane flight.

1904

March 14 Supreme Court orders dissolution of Northern Securities Company for violating anti-trust laws.

December 6 Pronouncement of the "Roosevelt Corollary" to the Monroe Doctrine occurs.

1905

January 4 U.S. takes over customs and international debt of the Dominican Republic.

June Industrial Workers of the World (IWW) founded.

1906

February Upton Sinclair's *The Jungle* published.

April 18–19 Great San Francisco Earthquake devastates the city.

June 30 Pure Food and Drug Act and Meat Inspection Act passed by Congress.

April 17 In *Lochner v. New York* Supreme Court finds state law limiting maximum working hours unconstitutional.

September 29 U.S. troops occupy Cuba.

1907

January–December Peak year of immigration brings 1,285,349 immigrants to the United States.

October Panic of 1907 reveals pitfalls of U.S. monetary system.

November 16 Oklahoma enters the Union.

1908

February 24 Supreme Court in *Muller v. Oregon* upholds Oregon's law mandating ten-hour maximum workday for women.

October 1 Henry Ford's Model T automobile goes on the market.

November 3 William Howard Taft elected president.

1909

June 1 National Association for the Advancement of Colored People (NAACP) founded.

1910

March 26 United States forbids immigration of criminals, paupers, and anarchists.

August 31 Theodore Roosevelt gives his "New Nationalism" speech.

1911

March 25 Triangle Shirtwaist factory fire kills 141 trapped workers in New York City.

May 15 Supreme Court orders dissolution of Standard Oil Company.

1912

June 4 Massachusetts becomes first state to adopt minimum wage legislation for women and children.

January 6 New Mexico becomes the 47th state.

February 14 Arizona admitted as 48th state.

April 15 SS *Titanic* sinks on its maiden voyage.

August U.S. Marines land in Nicaragua.

August 24 Alaska receives territorial status.

November 5 Woodrow Wilson elected president.

1913

September 3 Congress passes Hetch Hetchy dam bill.

February 25 Sixteenth Amendment added to Constitution.

May 31 Seventeenth Amendment added to Constitution.

December 13 Federal Reserve System established.

1914

January 5 Henry Ford perfects assembly line; announces adoption of five-dollar minimum daily wage for his workers.

August World War I begins in Europe: President Wilson proclaims U.S. neutrality and offers to mediate the conflict.

August 15 Panama Canal opens.

September 26 Federal Trade Commission established.

1915

January 25 First transcontinental telephone call is made.

May 7 British passenger liner *Lusitania* sunk by a German submarine; 114 Americans drowned.

December 4 Ku Klux Klan revived in Georgia.

1916

March Clashes occur between U.S. troops and Mexican guerrilla leader "Pancho" Villa.

May 4 Germany pledges to restrict its submarine warfare and not to attack merchant ships without warning.

October 16 Margaret Sanger opens nation's first birth control clinic.

November 7 Woodrow Wilson reelected president.

1917

February 3 United States severs diplomatic relations with Germany after it resumes submarine attacks on U.S. ships.

March 2 Puerto Rico made a U.S. territory.

April 2 Wilson asks Congress for declaration of war against Germany; Jeannette Rankin of Montana, Congress's first woman, is one of the 50 representatives to vote no.

October First U.S. detachments arrive at military front lines in France.

November Bolshevist revolution in Russia occurs; United States refuses to recognize new regime.

1918

January 8 Wilson's "Fourteen Points" speech to Congress outlines U.S. war aims.

May 16 Sedition Act passed outlawing speech critical of the war effort.

November 11 World War I ends.

1919

January 29 Eighteenth Amendment added to Constitution; its prohibition of alcohol is to take effect January 16, 1920.

June 28 Treaty of Versailles signed and includes Wilson's proposal for a League of Nations.

1920

March 19 A final attempt to ratify the Treaty of Versailles fails in the Senate.

August 26 Nineteenth Amendment, guaranteeing women the right to vote, added to Constitution.

November 2 Warren G. Harding elected president.

PREFACE

Between 1895 and 1920 the United States witnessed significant developments in both domestic and foreign affairs. In the domestic sphere the country debated and enacted numerous social, economic, and political reforms that have become known collectively as progressivism. In foreign affairs the United States participated in two wars that signified the country's emergence as a world power. By 1920, however, the American people were reacting against both domestic reform and foreign entanglements.

THE PROGRESSIVE MOVEMENT

The progressive movement was a response to trends in the country's social and economic conditions since the Civil War—trends many Americans found disturbing. These changes included the rise of big business and the formation of monopolies; corruption in local, state, and federal governments; the widening of class divisions; and the growing numbers of poor people in the nation's cities. Progressives believed that all of these developments threatened American ideals of fairness and equal opportunity. To counter this threat they sponsored numerous reform efforts (although most progressives rejected radical changes such as those prescribed by socialism). While not all Americans agreed with progressives on the need for change, the reforms that were proposed, debated, and in many cases enacted during this time had a lasting impact on American society.

Progressivism had much in common with the agrarian-based Populist movement that peaked in the early and mid-1890s. Populists, like progressives, decried the unequal distribution of wealth and power in the nation. (At the turn of the century, 2 percent of the nation's population controlled 60 percent of its wealth.) Both movements condemned the power of large business corporations and trusts that controlled whole industries, and they called for greater government regulation of the economy. Both movements also advocated reformed and stronger governments to protect the public interest. Some former Populists played major roles in the progressive movement itself. Important differences between the two movements existed, however. Progressivism differed from Populism in that it had an urban rather than a rural base of support. Progressivism also had greater appeal among the educated middle class and therefore attracted the support of more writers, academics, and intellectuals than did the Populist movement. The progressives also opted to work within the two major political parties rather than try to repeat the Populist attempt to create a new third party.

Those who called themselves progressives varied widely in occupation and in their beliefs. They included politicians, preachers, social welfare workers, academics, business owners, journalists, and others. They often disagreed on particular issues or on which cause or reform was most important. Some progressives believed that the main problem to be addressed was the dominance of business monopolies; others believed it to be the unequal status of women. Some focused on the conservation of natural resources, while others focused on corruption in city government or the influx of immigrants. In many respects, progressivism can be considered an aggregate of causes rather than one cohesive movement.

PROGRESSIVE REFORMS AND REFORMERS

In its infancy, the progressive movement was most active at the state and local levels. Mayors such as Hazen Pingree of Detroit and Tom Johnson of Cleveland forcefully attacked urban poverty and municipal corruption. Governors such as Robert La Follette of Wisconsin and Hiram Johnson of California capitalized on reformist sentiment to break the control of business over their respective state governments. La Follette and other governors then helped create new laws regulating railroads and utilities, setting minimum wages and maximum hours for workers, abolishing child labor, and ensuring more democratic participation in the nomination and election of public officials.

Notable progressives worked outside of politics as well. Jane Addams founded Hull House in Chicago in 1889 and began a lifelong career of helping poor residents of urban slums. Journalist "muckrakers" such as Upton Sinclair, Ida Tarbell, and Lincoln Steffens exposed shady business practices and political scandals in widely read books and magazine articles. Scholars such as John Dewey and Charles A. Beard applied progressive ideas to the study of philosophy, history, and economics.

Three of the leading figures of the Progressive Era were U.S. presidents: Theodore Roosevelt, William H. Taft, and Woodrow Wilson. Roosevelt became president in 1901 following the assassination of William McKinley. The former New York governor immediately began to use his office (which he called his "bully pulpit") to give progressivism a place on the national agenda. Roosevelt was particularly concerned about environmental issues, but he also lent his support to strengthening antitrust laws and regulating business, including the railroad, meatpacking, and oil industries. Taft, president from 1909 to 1913, carried forward many of Roosevelt's policies (although by the end of his term many progressives were clamoring for a new president). Wilson, president from 1913 to 1921 and leader of the progressive wing of the Democratic Party, accomplished numerous government reforms, including the creation of the Federal Reserve System to manage the nation's currency and the Federal Trade Commission, a government agency with broad powers to regulate business practices.

The Progressive Era produced four constitutional amendments, each of which addressed a major progressive concern. The Sixteenth Amendment authorized a federal income tax, which was intended in part to ensure a greater measure of economic equality among American citizens. The Seventeenth Amendment established popular elections for U.S. senators (who had previously been selected by state legislators), advancing the progressive goal of increasing citizens' participation in the election of their representatives. Many progressives viewed alcohol consumption as a major social problem; the Eighteenth Amendment, which banned the "manufacture, sale, or transportation of intoxicating liquors," ushered in the era of Prohibition. Finally, the Nineteenth Amendment extended the right to vote to women, a victory for the women's suffrage movement, which was the leading feminist cause of the Progressive Era.

BLACKS AND OTHER MINORITIES

Blacks fared poorly during the Progressive Era. In the southern states, where most blacks lived, white-dominated state and local governments enforced the segregation of the races in schools, public buildings, and virtually all other areas of life. White politicians devised numerous mechanisms, such as literacy tests and poll taxes, designed to deny blacks the right to vote. Lynch mobs killed hundreds of blacks. Many southern blacks migrated to northern cities, hoping to find better jobs and more equal treatment. Those who moved north did find that jobs were plentiful (especially after the United States entered World War I), but gains in employment were offset by continued racial discrimination and poor living conditions in urban slums. The black community was divided over how best to respond to the continued denial of equal rights in American society.

Although a few progressives supported equal rights for blacks, many did not. President Woodrow Wilson, for example, formally segregated federal government employees. Other minorities were also adversely affected by some of the policies advocated by progressive reformers, many of whom believed that the quality of American life was threatened as much by unfamiliar immigrants as by corrupt politicians. Progressives in California supported the passage of laws restricting the ability of Japanese immigrants and other noncitizens to lease land. Many progressives advocated immigration restrictions to reduce America's intake of foreigners not of a northern European background. In his 1916 book *The Passing of the Great Race*, prominent progressive Madison Grant wrote in favor of immigration restrictions, racial segregation, and forced sterilization of "worthless race types" (which he defined to include blacks, Jews, and southern and eastern Europeans).

THE UNITED STATES BECOMES A WORLD POWER

Along with domestic reforms, significant developments in foreign affairs affected the United States during the Progressive Era. During the decades following the Civil War, most Americans paid relatively little attention to the world beyond America's shores. However, by the 1890s several trends came together to draw Americans' attention to international issues. One development was the growing importance of trade and investment in America's economy. Another was the increasing international competition for colonies. With Great Britain, France, Germany, and other European nations jockeying for colonies in Asia and Africa, some Americans worried that the United States was missing out on a potential source of wealth and international stature. They believed that in order to be recognized as a great nation, the United States needed an overseas empire. Other Americans sharply criticized such beliefs, arguing that a colonial empire was unworthy of America's heritage as a nation founded on an anticolonial statement, the Declaration of Independence.

America's first significant venture into colonialism followed the 1898 Spanish-American War. The war ended with the United States taking the Philippines, Guam, and Puerto Rico from the defeated Spanish. This decision to acquire colonies, especially the Philippines (the largest and most remote of the acquired territories), signaled a new American commitment to imperialism—a commitment that was further demonstrated by America's three-year war to put down a Filipino rebellion for independence. Under Presidents McKinley, Roosevelt, Taft, and Wilson, the United States undertook several ventures to expand and protect what were deemed to be America's strategic and economic interests abroad, especially in the Western Hemisphere. Between 1900 and 1914 American troops intervened repeatedly in Cuba, Panama, Nicaragua, the Dominican Republic, Haiti, and Mexico. Americans took over the customs houses and supervised elections of a number of these countries. One of the most celebrated—and criticized—foreign policy undertakings of the United States was its support of Panama's revolution from Colombia in 1903 in order to gain control of a site to build the Panama Canal, which was completed in 1914.

The progressive movement assumed no single position on foreign affairs or on American imperialism. Some progressives argued that imperialism betrayed American ideals of equality and self-government. Others held that America was in a good position to improve life in other countries by remaking their economies and governments in the image of the United States. "I will teach those Latin American countries to elect good men," said progressive president Woodrow Wilson near the start of his administration.

WORLD WAR I

Progressives were equally divided on the merits and drawbacks of entering World War I. When war began in Europe in 1914, few Americans, progressive or otherwise, favored taking sides in the conflict. However, in May 1915, when a German submarine sank the British passenger liner *Lusitania*, killing 128 Americans and hundreds of other people, ex-president Theodore Roosevelt and others argued that the United States should enter the war against Germany, or at least undergo a massive military "preparedness" program. But other notable progressives, including social reformer Jane Addams and Wisconsin leader Robert La Follette (by then a U.S. senator), argued that America should remain neutral in the war. They worried that domestic reforms would be sacrificed if the United States plunged into war. President Wilson himself struggled to maintain "peace with honor" for three years before finally asking Congress for a declaration of war against Germany on April 2, 1917, citing German submarine attacks on U.S. ships as the primary reason for his decision. America would subsequently send 2 million soldiers to fight in Europe, of which 112,000 would perish.

Both during and after the war, Wilson tried to preserve his progressive ideals by arguing that the United States, through its military and diplomatic interventions in Europe, sought to establish a world "safe for democracy" and to end the era of colonialism and power politics. The League of Nations, an international organization of member nations created by Woodrow Wilson during the 1919 peace talks in Europe, was to be the centerpiece of his vision of a progressive new world. However, the mood of the nation was changing. After long and acrimonious debate the Senate rejected U.S. membership in the League of Nations. Running for president in 1920, Republican Warren G. Harding promised a return to "normalcy," a word that to many Americans signified the rejection both of drastic domestic reforms and involvement in world affairs. Harding's 1920 election victory marked the end of the Progressive Era.

JIM CROW AND BLACK RESPONSE

Viewpoint 6A

Blacks Should Stop Agitating for Political Equality (1895)

Booker T. Washington (1856–1915)

INTRODUCTION *Born into slavery shortly before the Civil War, Booker T. Washington received his education at the Hampton Institute, an industrial school founded by a former Union general for the education of ex-slaves. After teaching at Hampton for a time, Washington founded the Tuskegee Institute in Alabama, a vocational institute for blacks. Under his leadership the school grew into one of the leading centers of black education in the United States. Washington's national prominence was assured by his speech at the 1895 Atlanta Exposition, reprinted here. For the next twenty years white America considered him the preeminent spokesperson for the nation's black population. Those years were marked by the growth of "Jim Crow" laws and other measures that disenfranchised blacks and increased racial segregation. Washington advocated a policy of accommodation on civil rights issues, arguing that blacks should concentrate on economic self-improvement rather than changes in the nation's laws.*

What reasons does Washington give for optimism on race relations? What elements of Washington's speech do you think account for his popularity with American political leaders such as President Grover Cleveland, who in a letter to Washington wrote that his 1895 speech "cannot fail to delight and encourage all who wish well for your race"?

Mr. President and Gentlemen of the Board of Directors and Citizens:

One-third of the population of the South is of the Negro race. No enterprise seeking the material, civil, or moral welfare of this section can disregard this element of our population and reach the highest success. I but convey to you, Mr. President and Directors, the sentiment of the masses of my race when I say that in no way have the value and manhood of the American Negro been more fittingly and generously recognized

From Booker T. Washington's speech at the Atlanta Exposition, September 18, 1895; reprinted in his book *Up From Slavery* (Doubleday, 1901).

than by the managers of this magnificent exposition at every stage of its progress. It is a recognition that will do more to cement the friendship of the two races than any occurrence since the dawn of our freedom.

Not only this, but the opportunity here afforded will awaken among us a new era of industrial progress. Ignorant and inexperienced, it is not strange that in the first years of our new life we began at the top instead of at the bottom; that a seat in Congress or the state legislature was more sought than real estate or industrial skill; that the political convention or stump speaking had more attractions than starting a dairy farm or truck garden.

CAST DOWN YOUR BUCKET

A ship lost at sea for many days suddenly sighted a friendly vessel. From the mast of the unfortunate vessel was seen a signal: "Water, water; we die of thirst!" The answer from the friendly vessel at once came back: "Cast down your bucket where you are." A second time the signal, "Water, water, send us water!" ran up from the distressed vessel, and was answered: "Cast down your bucket where you are." And a third and fourth signal for water was answered: "Cast down your bucket where you are." The captain of the distressed vessel, at last heeding the injunction, cast down his bucket, and it came up full of fresh, sparkling water from the mouth of the Amazon River.

To those of my race who depend on bettering their condition in a foreign land or who underestimate the importance of cultivating friendly relations with the Southern white man, who is their next-door neighbor, I would say: Cast down your bucket where you are; cast it down in making friends, in every manly way, of the people of all races by whom we are surrounded. Cast it down in agriculture, mechanics, in commerce, in domestic service, and in the professions. And in this connection it is well to bear in mind that whatever other sins the South may be called to bear, when it comes to business, pure and simple, it is in the South that the Negro is given a man's chance in the commercial world, and in nothing is this exposition more eloquent than in emphasizing this chance.

Our greatest danger is that, in the great leap from slavery to freedom, we may overlook the fact that the masses of us are to live by the productions of our hands and fail to keep in mind that we shall prosper in proportion as we learn to dignify and glorify common labor, and put brains and skill into the common occupations of life; shall prosper in proportion as we learn to draw the line between the superficial and the substantial, the ornamental gewgaws of life and the useful. No race can prosper till it learns that there is as much dignity in tilling a field as in writing a poem. It is at the bottom of life we must begin, and not at the top. Nor should we permit our grievances to overshadow our opportunities.

To those of the white race who look to the incoming of those of foreign birth and strange tongue and habits for the prosperity of the South, were I permitted I would repeat what I say to my own race, "Cast down your bucket where you are." Cast it down among the 8 million Negroes whose habits you know, whose fidelity and love you have tested in days when to have proved treacherous meant the ruin of your firesides. Cast down your bucket among these people who have, without strikes and labor wars, tilled your fields, cleared your forests, builded your railroads and cities, and brought forth treasures from the bowels of the earth and helped make possible this magnificent representation of the progress of the South. Casting down your bucket among my people, helping and encouraging them as you are doing on these grounds, and, with education of head, hand, and heart, you will find that they will buy your surplus land, make blossom the waste places in your fields, and run your factories.

The wisest among my race understand that the agitation of questions of social equality is the extremist folly.

While doing this, you can be sure in the future, as in the past, that you and your families will be surrounded by the most patient, faithful, law-abiding, and unresentful people that the world has seen. As we have proved our loyalty to you in the past, in nursing your children, watching by the sickbed of your mothers and fathers, and often following them with tear-dimmed eyes to their graves, so in the future, in our humble way, we shall stand by you with a devotion that no foreigner can approach, ready to lay down our lives, if need be, in defense of yours; interlacing our industrial, commercial, civil, and religious life with yours in a way that shall make the interests of both races one. In all things that are purely social we can be as separate as the fingers, yet one as the hand in all things essential to mutual progress.

There is no defense or security for any of us except in the highest intelligence and development of all. If anywhere there are efforts tending to curtail the fullest growth of the Negro, let these efforts be turned into stimulating, encouraging, and making him the most useful and intelligent citizen. Effort or means so invested will pay a thousand percent interest. These efforts will be twice blessed—"blessing him that gives and him that takes."...

AGAINST AGITATION

The wisest among my race understand that the agitation of questions of social equality is the extremest folly, and that progress in the enjoyment of all the privileges that will come to us must be the result of severe and constant struggle rather than of artificial forcing. No race that has anything to contribute to the markets of the world is long in any degree ostracized. It is important and right that all privileges of the law be ours, but it is vastly more important that we be prepared for the exercise of these privileges. The opportunity to earn a dollar in a factory just now is worth infinitely more than the opportunity to spend a dollar in an opera house.

In conclusion, may I repeat that nothing in thirty years has given us more hope and encouragement and drawn us so near to you of the white race as this opportunity offered by the exposition; and here bending, as it were, over the altar that represents the results of the struggles of your race and mine, both starting practically empty-handed three decades ago, I pledge that, in your effort to work out the great and intricate problem which God has laid at the doors of the South, you shall have at all times the patient, sympathetic help of my race; only let this be constantly in mind that, while from representations in these buildings of the product of field, of forest, of mine, of factory, letters, and art, much good will come—yet far above and beyond material benefits will be that higher good, that let us pray God will come, in a blotting out of sectional differences and racial animosities and suspicions, in a determination to administer absolute justice, in a willing obedience among all classes to the mandates of law. This, coupled with our material prosperity, will bring into our beloved South a new heaven and a new earth.

Viewpoint 6B
Blacks Should Strive for Political Equality (1903)
W.E.B. Du Bois (1868–1963)

INTRODUCTION *From 1895 until his death twenty years later, the most famous leader of black America was Booker T. Washington, a political moderate who argued that blacks should pursue economic self-improvement and political accommodation. An early critique of Washington's views comes from the following excerpts from* The Souls of Black Folk, *a noted 1903 study written by W.E.B. Du Bois. Du Bois, the first black to earn a doctorate from Harvard University in Massachusetts, later helped found the National Association for the Advancement of Colored People (NAACP) and was for many years America's leading black intellectual and civil rights activist. One of Du Bois's criticisms of Washington was that blacks should do more to pursue their civil and political rights.*

What connection does Du Bois see between Booker T. Washington's successes and potential problems for American blacks? Could Du Bois be considered more or less realistic about civil rights than Washington? Why or why not?

Easily the most striking thing in the history of the American Negro since 1876 is the ascendancy of Mr. Booker T. Washington. It began at the time when war memories and ideals were rapidly passing; a day of astonishing commercial development was dawning; a sense of doubt and hesitation overtook the freedmen's sons,— then it was that his leading began. Mr. Washington came, with a single definite programme, at the psychological moment when the nation was a little ashamed of having bestowed so much sentiment on Negroes, and was concentrating its energies on Dollars. His programme of industrial education, conciliation of the South, and submission and silence as to civil and political rights, was not wholly original; the Free Negroes from 1830 up to wartime had striven to build industrial schools, and the American Missionary Association had from the first taught various trades; and [Joseph C.] Price and others had sought a way of honorable alliance with the best of the Southerners. But Mr. Washington first indissolubly linked these things; he put enthusiasm, unlimited energy, and perfect faith into this programme, and changed it from a by-path into a veritable Way of Life....

Mr. Washington represents in Negro thought the old attitude of adjustment and submission; but adjustment at such a peculiar time as to make his programme unique. This is an age of unusual economic development, and Mr. Washington's programme naturally takes an economic cast, becoming a gospel of Work and Money to such an extent as apparently almost completely to overshadow the higher aims of life. Moreover, this is an age when the more advanced races are coming in closer contact with the less developed races, and the race-feeling is therefore intensified; and Mr. Washington's programme practically accepts the alleged inferiority of the Negro races. In our own land, the reaction from the sentiment of war time has given impetus to race-prejudice against Negroes, and Mr. Washington withdraws many of the high demands of Negroes as men and American citizens. In other periods of intensified prejudice all the Negro's tendency to self-assertion has been called forth; at this period a policy of submission is advocated. In the history of nearly all other races and peoples the doctrine preached at such crises has been that manly self-respect is worth more than lands and houses, and that a people who voluntarily

From W.E.B. Du Bois, *The Souls of Black Folk* (Chicago: A.C. McClurg, 1903).

surrender such respect, or cease striving for it, are not worth civilizing.

WASHINGTON'S PRESCRIPTION

In answer to this, it has been claimed that the Negro can survive only through submission. Mr. Washington distinctly asks that black people give up, at least for the present, three things,—

First, political power,

Second, insistence on civil rights,

Third, higher education of Negro youth,—and concentrate all their energies on industrial education, the accumulation of wealth, and the conciliation of the South. This policy has been courageously and insistently advocated for over fifteen years, and has been triumphant for perhaps ten years. As a result of this tender of the palm-branch, what has been the return? In these years there have occurred:

1. The disfranchisement of the Negro
2. The legal creation of a distinct status of civil inferiority for the Negro
3. The steady withdrawal of aid from institutions for the higher training of the Negro

These movements are not, to be sure, direct results of Mr. Washington's teachings; but his propaganda has, without a shadow of doubt, helped their speedier accomplishment. The question then comes: Is it possible, and probable, that nine millions of men can make effective progress in economic lines if they are deprived of political rights, made a servile caste, and allowed only the most meager chance for developing their exceptional men? If history and reason give any distinct answer to these questions, it is an emphatic *No*. And Mr. Washington thus faces the triple paradox of his career:

1. He is striving nobly to make Negro artisans business men and property-owners; but it is utterly impossible, under modern competitive methods, for workingmen and property-owners to defend their rights and exist without the right of suffrage.
2. He insists on thrift and self-respect, but at the same time counsels a silent submission to civic inferiority such as is bound to sap the manhood of any race in the long run.
3. He advocates common-school and industrial training, and depreciates institutions of higher learning; but neither the Negro common-schools, nor Tuskegee itself, could remain open a day were it not for teachers trained in Negro colleges, or trained by their graduates.

This triple paradox in Mr. Washington's position is the object of criticism by two classes of colored Americans. One class is spiritually descended from Toussaint the Savior [Haitian rebellion leader Toussaint L'Ouverture], through Gabriel, Vesey, and Turner [Gabriel Prosser, Denmark Vesey, Nat Turner], and they represent the attitude of revolt and revenge; they hate the white South blindly and distrust the white race generally, and so far as they agree on definite action, think that the Negro's only hope lies in emigration beyond the borders of the United States. And yet, by the irony of fate, nothing has more effectually made this programme seem hopeless than the recent course of the United States toward weaker and darker peoples in the West Indies, Hawaii, and the Philippines,—for where in the world may we go and be safe from lying and brute force?

The other class of Negroes who cannot agree with Mr. Washington has hitherto said little aloud. They deprecate the sight of scattered counsels, of internal disagreement; and especially they dislike making their just criticism of a useful and earnest man an excuse for a general discharge of venom from small-minded opponents. Nevertheless, the questions involved are so fundamental and serious that it is difficult to see how men like... Kelly Miller, J.W.E. Bowen, and other representatives of this group, can much longer be silent. Such men feel in conscience bound to ask of this nation three things:

1. The right to vote
2. Civic equality
3. The education of youth according to ability

They acknowledge Mr. Washington's invaluable service in counselling patience and courtesy in such demands; they do not ask that ignorant black men vote when ignorant whites are debarred, or that any reasonable restrictions in the suffrage should not be applied; they know that the low social level of the mass of the race is responsible for much discrimination against it, but they also know, and the nation knows, that relentless color-prejudice is more often a cause than a result of the Negro's degradation; they seek the abatement of this relic of barbarism, and not its systematic encouragement and pampering by all agencies of social power from the Associated Press to the Church of Christ. They advocate, with Mr. Washington, a broad system of Negro common schools supplemented by thorough industrial training; but they are surprised that a man of Mr. Washington's insight cannot see that no such educational system ever has rested or can rest on any other basis than that of the well-equipped college and university, and they insist that there is a demand for a few such institutions throughout the South to train the best of the Negro youth as teachers, professional men, and leaders.

This group of men honor Mr. Washington for his attitude of conciliation toward the white South; they accept the "Atlanta Compromise" in its broadest interpretation; they recognize, with him, many signs of promise, many

men of high purpose and fair judgment, in this section; they know that no easy task has been laid upon a region already tottering under heavy burdens. But, nevertheless, they insist that the way to truth and right lies in straightforward honesty, not in indiscriminate flattery; in praising those of the South who do well and criticising uncompromisingly those who do ill; in taking advantage of the opportunities at hand and urging their fellows to do the same, but at the same time in remembering that only a firm adherence to their higher ideals and aspirations will ever keep those ideals within the realm of possibility. They do not expect that the free right to vote, to enjoy civic rights, and to be educated, will come in a moment; they do not expect to see the bias and prejudices of years disappear at the blast of a trumpet; but they are absolutely certain that the way for a people to gain their reasonable rights is not by voluntarily throwing them away and insisting that they do not want them; that the way for a people to gain respect is not by continually belittling and ridiculing themselves; that, on the contrary, Negroes must insist continually, in season and out of season, that voting is necessary to modern manhood, that color discrimination is barbarism, and that black boys need education as well as white boys....

The growing spirit of kindliness and reconciliation between the North and South after the frightful difference of a generation ago ought to be a source of deep congratulation to all, and especially to those whose mistreatment caused the war; but if that reconciliation is to be marked by the industrial slavery and civic death of those same black men, with permanent legislation into a position of inferiority, then those black men, if they are really men, are called upon by every consideration of patriotism and loyalty to oppose such a course by all civilized methods, even though such opposition involves disagreement with Mr. Booker T. Washington. We have no right to sit silently by while the inevitable seeds are sown for a harvest of disaster to our children, black and white....

HALF-TRUTHS

It would be unjust to Mr. Washington not to acknowledge that in several instances he has opposed movements in the South which were unjust to the Negro; he sent memorials to the Louisiana and Alabama constitutional conventions, he has spoken against lynching, and in other ways has openly or silently set his influence against sinister schemes and unfortunate happenings. Notwithstanding this, it is equally true to assert that on the whole the distinct impression left by Mr. Washington's propaganda is, first, that the South is justified in its present attitude toward the Negro because of the Negro's degradation; secondly, that the prime cause of the Negro's failure to rise more quickly is his wrong education in the past; and, thirdly, that his future rise depends primarily on his own efforts. Each of these propositions is a dangerous half-truth. The supplementary truths must never be lost sight of: first, slavery and race-prejudice are potent if not sufficient causes of the Negro's position; second, industrial and common-school training were necessarily slow in planting because they had to await the black teachers trained by higher institutions,—it being extremely doubtful if any essentially different development was possible, and certainly a Tuskegee was unthinkable before 1880; and, third, while it is a great truth to say that the Negro must strive and strive mightily to help himself, it is equally true that unless his striving be not simply seconded, but rather aroused and encouraged, by the initiative of the richer and wiser environing group, he cannot hope for great success.

By every civilized and peaceful method we must strive for the rights which the world accords to men.

In his failure to realize and impress this last point, Mr. Washington is especially to be criticised. His doctrine has tended to make the whites, North and South, shift the burden of the Negro problem to the Negro's shoulders and stand aside as critical and rather pessimistic spectators; when in fact the burden belongs to the nation, and the hands of none of us are clean if we bend not our energies to righting these great wrongs.

The South ought to be led, by candid and honest criticism, to assert her better self and do her full duty to the race she has cruelly wronged and is still wronging. The North—her co-partner in guilt—cannot salve her conscience by plastering it with gold. We cannot settle this problem by diplomacy and suaveness, by "policy" alone. If worse comes to worst, can the moral fibre of this country survive the slow throttling and murder of nine millions of men?

The black men of America have a duty to perform, a duty stern and delicate,—a forward movement to oppose a part of the work of their greatest leader. So far as Mr. Washington preaches Thrift, Patience, and Industrial Training for the masses, we must hold up his hands and strive with him, rejoicing in his honors and glorying in the strength of this Joshua called of God and of man to lead the headless host. But so far as Mr. Washington apologizes for injustice, North or South, does not rightly value the privilege and duty of voting, belittles the emasculating effects of caste distinctions, and opposes the higher training and ambition of our brighter minds,—

so far as he, the South, or the Nation does this,—we must unceasingly and firmly oppose them. By every civilized and peaceful method we must strive for the rights which the world accords to men, clinging unwaveringly to those great words which the sons of the Fathers would fain forget: "We hold these truths to be self-evident: That all men are created equal; that they are endowed by their Creator with certain unalienable rights; that among these are life, liberty, and the pursuit of happiness."

FOR FURTHER READING

Rebecca Carroll, ed., *Uncle Tom or New Negro?: African Americans Reflect on Booker T. Washington and UP FROM SLAVERY 100 Years Later.* New York: Harlem Moon, 2006.

W.E.B. Du Bois et al., *The Souls of Black Folk: Authoritative Text, Contexts, Criticism.* New York: W.W. Norton, 1999.

Augustine Meier, *Negro Thought in America, 1880–1915.* Ann Arbor: University of Michigan Press, 1969.

Jacqueline M. Moore, *Booker T. Washington, W.E.B. Du Bois, and the Struggle for Racial Uplift.* Wilmington, DE: Scholarly Resources, 2003.

Viewpoint 7A
Racial Segregation Is Constitutional (1896)
Henry B. Brown (1836–1913)

INTRODUCTION *In 1890 the state of Louisiana passed a law requiring racial segregation on passenger trains (many states passed similar laws at this time). Homer A. Plessy, a person of mixed racial background, was forcibly ejected from a train, arrested, and tried and convicted for breaking the law after attempting to sit in a whites-only section. His appeal challenging the constitutionality of the segregation law made it to the U.S. Supreme Court, but the justices ruled 7–1 in 1896 to uphold his conviction under Louisiana's segregation statute. The following viewpoint is excerpted from the majority opinion, written by Henry B. Brown, an associate justice of the Supreme Court from 1890 to 1906. He argues that state-imposed racial segregation laws were constitutional as long as equal facilities were provided for whites and blacks. The case,* Plessy v. Ferguson, *established the "separate but equal" standard that remained the law of the land until the Supreme Court overturned it in 1954 in the case of* Brown v. Board of Education *(see viewpoint 28A).*

How does Brown distinguish between political and social equality, and what importance does this distinction have in his argument? What response does he make to the claim that segregation creates a "badge of inferiority" for blacks? Does the result of Plessy v. Ferguson *seem to vindicate either the arguments of*

Booker T. Washington or W.E.B. Du Bois found in viewpoints 6A and 6B?

This case turns upon the constitutionality of an act of the General Assembly of the State of Louisiana, passed in 1890, providing for separate railway carriages for the white and colored races....

The constitutionality of this act is attacked upon the ground that it conflicts both with the Thirteenth Amendment of the Constitution, abolishing slavery, and the Fourteenth Amendment, which prohibits certain restrictive legislation on the part of the States.

THE THIRTEENTH AMENDMENT

1. That it does not conflict with the Thirteenth Amendment, which abolished slavery and involuntary servitude, except as a punishment for crime, is too clear for argument. Slavery implies involuntary servitude—a state of bondage; the ownership of mankind as a chattel, or at least the control of the labor and services of one man for the benefit of another, and the absence of a legal right to the disposal of his own person, property and services....

In the *Civil Rights cases* [referring to an 1883 Supreme Court decision that collectively ruled on several challenges to the 1875 Civil Rights Act, including *United States v. Stanley*, and that declared sections of that national civil rights law unconstitutional],... it was said that the act of a mere individual, the owner of an inn, a public conveyance or place of amusement, refusing accommodations to colored people, cannot be justly regarded as imposing any badge of slavery or servitude upon the applicant, but only as involving an ordinary civil injury, properly cognizable by the laws of the State, and presumably subject to redress by those laws until the contrary appears. "It would be running the slavery argument into the ground," said Mr. Justice [Joseph P.] Bradley, "to make it apply to every act of discrimination which a person may see fit to make as to the guests he will entertain, or as to the people he will take into his coach or cab or car, or admit to his concert or theatre, or deal with in other matters of intercourse or business."

A statute which implies merely a legal distinction between the white and colored races—a distinction which is founded in the color of the two races, and which must always exist so long as white men are distinguished from the other race by color—has no tendency to destroy the legal equality of the two races, or reestablish a state of involuntary servitude. Indeed, we do not understand that the Thirteenth Amendment is strenuously relied upon by the plaintiff in error in this connection.

From the majority opinion in *Plessy v. Ferguson*, 163 U.S. 537 (1896).

THE FOURTEENTH AMENDMENT

2. By the Fourteenth Amendment, all persons born or naturalized in the United States, and subject to the jurisdiction thereof, are made citizens of the United States and of the State wherein they reside; and the States are forbidden from making or enforcing any law which shall abridge the privileges or immunities of citizens of the United States, or shall deprive any person of life, liberty or property without due process of law, or deny to any person within their jurisdiction the equal protection of the laws....

The object of the amendment was undoubtedly to enforce the absolute equality of the two races before the law, but in the nature of things it could not have been intended to abolish distinctions based upon color, or to enforce social, as distinguished from political equality, or a commingling of the two races upon terms unsatisfactory to either. Laws permitting, and even requiring, their separation in places where they are liable to be brought into contact do not necessarily imply the inferiority of either race to the other, and have been generally, if not universally, recognized as within the competency of the state legislatures in the exercise of their police power. The most common instance of this is connected with the establishment of separate schools for white and colored children, which has been held to be a valid exercise of the legislative power even by courts of States where the political rights of the colored race have been longest and most earnestly enforced.

One of the earliest of these cases is that of *Roberts v. City of Boston*,... in which the Supreme Judicial Court of Massachusetts held that the general school committee of Boston had power to make provision for the instruction of colored children in separate schools established exclusively for them, and to prohibit their attendance upon the other schools....

It was held that the powers of the committee extended to the establishment of separate schools for children of different ages, sexes and colors, and that they might also establish special schools for poor and neglected children, who have become too old to attend the primary school, and yet have not acquired the rudiments of learning, to enable them to enter the ordinary schools. Similar laws have been enacted by Congress under its general power of legislation over the District of Columbia,... as well as by the legislatures of many of the States, and have been generally, if not uniformly, sustained by the courts....

Laws forbidding the intermarriage of the two races may be said in a technical sense to interfere with the freedom of contract, and yet have been universally recognized as within the police power of the State....

CIVIL RIGHTS AND STATE LAWS

In the [1883 Supreme Court] *Civil Rights case,* . . . it was held that an act of Congress, entitling all persons within the jurisdiction of the United States to the full and equal enjoyment of the accommodations, advantages, facilities and privileges of inns, public conveyances, on land or water, theatres and other places of public amusement, and made applicable to citizens of every race and color, regardless of any previous condition of servitude, was unconstitutional and void, upon the ground that the Fourteenth Amendment was prohibitory upon the States only. . . . Positive rights and privileges are undoubtedly secured by the Fourteenth Amendment; but they are secured by way of prohibition against state laws and state proceedings affecting those rights and privileges, and by power given to Congress to legislate for the purpose of carrying such prohibition into effect; and such legislation must necessarily be predicated upon such supposed state laws or state proceedings, and be directed to the correction of their operation and effect. . . .

———————◼———————

If one race be inferior to the other socially, the Constitution of the United States cannot put them upon the same plane.

———————◼———————

So far, then, as a conflict with the Fourteenth Amendment is concerned, the case reduces itself to the question whether the statute of Louisiana is a reasonable regulation, and with respect to this there must necessarily be a large discretion on the part of the legislature. In determining the question of reasonableness it is at liberty to act with reference to the established usages, customs and traditions of the people, and with a view to the promotion of their comfort, and the preservation of the public peace and good order. Gauged by this standard, we cannot say that a law which authorizes or even requires the separation of the two races in public conveyances is unreasonable, or more obnoxious to the Fourteenth Amendment than the acts of Congress requiring separate schools for colored children in the District of Columbia, the constitutionality of which does not seem to have been questioned, or the corresponding acts of state legislatures.

RACIAL PREJUDICE AND THE LAW

We consider the underlying fallacy of the plaintiff's argument to consist in the assumption that the enforced separation of the two races stamps the colored race with a badge of inferiority. If this be so, it is not by reason of anything found in the act, but solely because the colored race chooses to put that construction upon it. The argument necessarily assumes that if, as has been more than once the case, and is not unlikely to be so again, the colored race should become the dominant power in the state legislature, and should enact a law in precisely similar terms, it would thereby relegate the white race to an inferior position. We imagine that the white race, at least, would not acquiesce in this assumption. The argument also assumes that social prejudices may be overcome by legislation, and that equal rights cannot be secured to the negro except by an enforced commingling of the two races. We cannot accept this proposition. If the two races are to meet upon terms of social equality, it must be the result of natural affinities, a mutual appreciation of each other's merits and a voluntary consent of individuals. As was said by the Court of Appeals of New York in *People v. Gallagher,* . . . "this end can neither be accomplished nor promoted by laws which conflict with the general sentiment of the community upon whom they are designed to operate. When the government, therefore, has secured to each of its citizens equal rights before the law and equal opportunities for improvement and progress, it has accomplished the end for which it was organized and performed all of the functions respecting social advantages with which it is endowed." Legislation is powerless to eradicate racial instincts or to abolish distinctions based upon physical differences, and the attempt to do so can only result in accentuating the difficulties of the present situation. If the civil and political rights of both races be equal one cannot be inferior to the other civilly or politically. If one race be inferior to the other socially, the Constitution of the United States cannot put them upon the same plane.

Racial Segregation Is Unconstitutional (1896)

John Marshall Harlan (1833–1911)

INTRODUCTION *In the 1896 case of* Plessy v. Ferguson, *the U.S. Supreme Court upheld a Louisiana state law requiring the racial segregation of train passengers. The sole dissenter was John Marshall Harlan, who served as an associate justice of the Supreme Court from 1877 to 1911. Portions of his dissenting opinion appear below. A Kentuckian and former slaveholder, Harlan is best remembered today for his dissents in this and other cases in which the Supreme Court upheld racial segregation and limited black civil rights.*

What personal liberties are being abridged by the Louisiana law, according to Harlan? How does he respond to the argument that the Louisiana law applies to both races equally?

From John Marshall Harlan's dissenting opinion in *Plessy v. Ferguson* 163 U.S. 537 (1896).

By the Louisiana statute, the validity of which is here involved, all railway companies (other than street railroad companies) carrying passengers in that State are required to have separate but equal accommodations for white and colored persons, "by providing two or more passenger coaches for each passenger train, *or* by dividing the passenger coaches by a *partition* so as to secure separate accommodations." Under this statute, no colored person is permitted to occupy a seat in a coach assigned to white persons; nor any white person, to occupy a seat in a coach assigned to colored persons. . . .

So . . . we have before us a state enactment that compels, under penalties, the separation of the two races in railroad passenger coaches, and makes it a crime for a citizen of either race to enter a coach that has been assigned to citizens of the other race.

Thus the State regulates the use of a public highway by citizens of the United States solely upon the basis of race.

However apparent the injustice of such legislation may be, we have only to consider whether it is consistent with the Constitution of the United States. . . .

CIVIL RIGHTS AND THE CONSTITUTION

In respect of civil rights, common to all citizens, the Constitution of the United States does not, I think, permit any public authority to know the race of those entitled to be protected in the enjoyment of such rights. Every true man has pride of race, and under appropriate circumstances when the rights of others, his equals before the law, are not to be affected, it is his privilege to express such pride and to take such action based upon it as to him seems proper. But I deny that any legislative body or judicial tribunal may have regard to the race of citizens when the civil rights of those citizens are involved. Indeed, such legislation, as that here in question, is inconsistent not only with that equality of rights which pertains to citizenship, National and State, but with the personal liberty enjoyed by every one within the United States.

The Thirteenth Amendment does not permit the withholding or the deprivation of any right necessarily inhering in freedom. It not only struck down the institution of slavery as previously existing in the United States, but it prevents the imposition of any burdens or disabilities that constitute badges of slavery or servitude. It decreed universal civil freedom in this country. This court has so adjudged. But that amendment having been found inadequate to the protection of the rights of those who had been in slavery, it was followed by the Fourteenth Amendment, which added greatly to the dignity and glory of American citizenship, and to the security

of personal liberty, by declaring that "all persons born or naturalized in the United States, and subject to the jurisdiction thereof, are citizens of the United States and of the State wherein they reside," and that "no State shall make or enforce any law which shall abridge the privileges or immunities of citizens of the United States; nor shall any State deprive any person of life, liberty or property without due process of law, nor deny to any person within its jurisdiction the equal protection of the laws." These two amendments, if enforced according to their true intent and meaning, will protect all the civil rights that pertain to freedom and citizenship. Finally, and to the end that no citizen should be denied, on account of his race, the privilege of participating in the political control of his country, it was declared by the Fifteenth Amendment that "the right of citizens of the United States to vote shall not be denied or abridged by the United States or by any State on account of race, color or previous condition of servitude."

These notable additions to the fundamental law were welcomed by the friends of liberty throughout the world. They removed the race line from our governmental systems. They had, as this court has said, a common purpose, namely, to secure "to a race recently emancipated, a race that through many generations have been held in slavery, all the civil rights that the superior race enjoy." . . .

Our Constitution is color-blind, and neither knows nor tolerates classes among citizens.

THE LOUISIANA LAW

It was said in argument that the statute of Louisiana does not discriminate against either race, but prescribes a rule applicable alike to white and colored citizens. But this argument does not meet the difficulty. Every one knows that the statute in question had its origin in the purpose, not so much to exclude white persons from railroad cars occupied by blacks, as to exclude colored people from coaches occupied by or assigned to white persons. Railroad corporations of Louisiana did not make discrimination among whites in the matter of accommodation for travellers. The thing to accomplish was, under the guise of giving equal accommodation for whites and blacks, to compel the latter to keep to themselves while travelling in railroad passenger coaches. No one would be so wanting in candor as to assert the contrary. The fundamental objection, therefore, to the statute is that it interferes with the personal freedom of citizens. If a white man and a black man choose to occupy the same public conveyance on a public highway, it is their right to do so, and no government, proceeding alone on grounds of race, can prevent it without infringing the personal liberty of each. . . .

THE COLOR-BLIND CONSTITUTION

The white race deems itself to be the dominant race in this country. And so it is, in prestige, in achievements, in education, in wealth and in power. So, I doubt not, it will continue to be for all time, if it remains true to its great heritage and holds fast to the principles of constitutional liberty. But in view of the Constitution, in the eye of the law, there is in this country no superior, dominant, ruling class of citizens. There is no caste here. Our Constitution is color-blind, and neither knows nor tolerates classes among citizens. In respect of civil rights, all citizens are equal before the law. The humblest is the peer of the most powerful. The law regards man as man, and takes no account of his surroundings or of his color when his civil rights as guaranteed by the supreme law of the land are involved. It is, therefore, to be regretted that this high tribunal, the final expositor of the fundamental law of the land, has reached the conclusion that it is competent for a State to regulate the enjoyment by citizens of their civil rights solely upon the basis of race.

In my opinion, the judgment this day rendered will, in time, prove to be quite as pernicious as the decision made by this tribunal in the [1857] *Dred Scott case.* It was adjudged in that case that the descendants of Africans who were imported into this country and sold as slaves were not included nor intended to be included under the word "citizens" in the Constitution, and could not claim any of the rights and privileges which that instrument provided for and secured to citizens of the United States; that at the time of the adoption of the Constitution they were "considered as a subordinate and inferior class of beings, who had been subjugated by the dominant race, and, whether emancipated or not, yet remained subject to their authority, and had no rights or privileges but such as those who held the power and the government might choose to grant them." . . . The recent amendments of the Constitution, it was supposed, had eradicated these principles from our institutions. But it seems that we have yet, in some of the States, a dominant race—superior class of citizens, which assumes to regulate the enjoyment of civil rights, common to all citizens, upon the basis of race. The present decision, it may well be apprehended, will not only stimulate aggressions, more or less brutal and irritating, upon the admitted rights of colored citizens, but will encourage the belief that it is possible, by means of state enactments, to defeat the beneficent purposes which the people of the United States had in

view when they adopted the recent amendments of the Constitution, by one of which the blacks of this country were made citizens of the United States and of the States in which they respectively reside, and whose privileges and immunities, as citizens, the States are forbidden to abridge. Sixty millions of whites are in no danger from the presence here of eight millions of blacks. The destinies of the two races, in this country, are indissolubly linked together, and the interests of both require that the common government of all shall not permit the seeds of race hate to be planted under the sanction of law. What can more certainly arouse race hate, what more certainly create and perpetuate a feeling of distrust between these races, than state enactments, which, in fact, proceed on the ground that colored citizens are so inferior and degraded that they cannot be allowed to sit in public coaches occupied by white citizens? That, as all will admit, is the real meaning of such legislation as was enacted in Louisiana. . . .

A BADGE OF SERVITUDE

The arbitrary separation of citizens, on the basis of race, while they are on a public highway, is a badge of servitude wholly inconsistent with the civil freedom and the equality before the law established by the Constitution. It cannot be justified upon any legal grounds.

If evils will result from the commingling of the two races upon public highways established for the benefit of all, they will be infinitely less than those that will surely come from state legislation regulating the enjoyment of civil rights upon the basis of race. We boast of the freedom enjoyed by our people above all other peoples. But it is difficult to reconcile that boast with a state of the law which, practically, puts the brand of servitude and degradation upon a large class of our fellow-citizens, our equals before the law. The thin disguise of "equal" accommodations for passengers in railroad coaches will not mislead any one, nor atone for the wrong this day done. . . .

I am of opinion that the statute of Louisiana is inconsistent with the personal liberty of citizens, white and black, in that State, and hostile to both the spirit and letter of the Constitution of the United States. If laws of like character should be enacted in the several States of the Union, the effect would be in the highest degree mischievous. Slavery, as an institution tolerated by law would, it is true, have disappeared from our country, but there would remain a power in the States, by sinister legislation, to interfere with the full enjoyment of the blessings of freedom; to regulate civil rights, common to all citizens, upon the basis of race; and to place in a condition of legal inferiority a large body of American citizens, now constituting a part of the political community called the People of the United States, for whom, and by whom through representatives, our government is administered. Such a system is inconsistent with the guarantee given by the Constitution to each State of a republican form of government, and may be stricken down by Congressional action, or by the courts in the discharge of their solemn duty to maintain the supreme law of the land, anything in the constitution or laws of any State to the contrary notwithstanding.

For the reasons stated, I am constrained to withhold my assent from the opinion and judgment of the majority.

FOR FURTHER READING

Loren P. Beth, *John Marshall Harlan: The Last Whig Justice.* Lexington: University of Kentucky Press, 1992.

Harvey Fireside, *Separate and Unequal: Homer Plessy and the Supreme Court Decision that Legalized Racism.* New York: Carroll & Graf, 2004.

Keith Weldon Medley, *We as Freemen: Plessy v. Ferguson,* Gretna, LA: Pelican Publishing Company, 2003.

Brook Thomas, *Plessy v. Ferguson: A Brief History with Documents.* Boston: Bedford Books, 1997.

Richard Wormser, *The Rise and Fall of Jim Crow.* New York: St. Martin's Press, 2003.

AMERICAN EMPIRE

Viewpoint 8A

America Should Retain the Philippines (1900)

Albert J. Beveridge (1862–1937)

INTRODUCTION *America's victory in the Spanish-American War in 1898 left the United States in possession of former Spanish colonies Puerto Rico, Guam, and the Philippine Islands. The peace treaty with Spain was ratified by the Senate in February 1899 by only a one-vote margin, in part because some Americans were disturbed by the idea of the United States holding foreign colonies. Concern over the Philippines intensified in 1899 when Filipino nationalists, led by Emilio Aguinaldo, waged guerilla warfare against U.S. soldiers in the Philippines. Members of what became known as the anti-imperialist movement called for U.S. withdrawal from the Philippines and other foreign possessions.*

One of the leading opponents of the anti-imperialist movement was Albert J. Beveridge, author of the following viewpoint. Elected to the U.S. Senate in 1899 at the age of 36, Beveridge toured the Philippines just prior to taking office. On January 9, 1900, he addressed the Senate in support of the following proposition: "Resolved . . . that the Philippine Islands are territory belonging to the United States; that it is the intention of the United States to retain them as such

and to establish and maintain such governmental control throughout the archipelago as the situation may demand." The following excerpts from that speech provide his economic and moral reasons why the United States should retain control over the Philippines, even in the face of violent resistance.

Are the reasons for retaining the Philippines primarily economic, moral, or both, according to Beveridge? Is racial prejudice important to his arguments? Beverdige is considered one of the most progressive senators of his era. What does this say about American progressivism?

I address the Senate at this time because Senators and Members of the House on both sides have asked that I give to Congress and the country my observations in the Philippines and the Far East, and the conclusions which those observations compel; and because of hurtful resolutions introduced and utterances made in the Senate, every word of which will cost and is costing the lives of American soldiers.

The times call for candor. The Philippines are ours forever, "territory belonging to the United States," as the Constitution calls them. And just beyond the Philippines are China's illimitable markets. We will not retreat from either. We will not repudiate our duty in the archipelago. We will not abandon our opportunity in the Orient. We will not renounce our part in the mission of our race, trustee, under God, of the civilization of the world. And we will move forward to our work, not howling out regrets like slaves whipped to their burdens, but with gratitude for a task worthy of our strength, and thanksgiving to Almighty God that He has marked us as His chosen people, henceforth to lead in the regeneration of the world.

This island empire is the last land left in all the oceans. If it should prove a mistake to abandon it, the blunder once made would be irretrievable. If it proves a mistake to hold it, the error can be corrected when we will. Every other progressive nation stands ready to relieve us.

But to hold it will be no mistake. Our largest trade henceforth must be with Asia. The Pacific is our ocean. More and more Europe will manufacture the most it needs, secure from its colonies the most it consumes. Where shall we turn for consumers of our surplus? Geography answers the question. China is our natural customer. She is nearer to us than to England, Germany, or Russia, the commercial powers of the present and the future. They have moved nearer to China by securing permanent bases on her borders. The Philippines give us a base at the door of all the East.

From Albert J. Beveridge, *Congressional Record,* 56th Cong., 1st sess., 1900, pp. 704–712.

Lines of navigation from our ports to the Orient and Australia; from the [proposed Central American] Isthmian Canal to Asia; from all Oriental ports to Australia, converge at and separate from the Philippines. They are a self-supporting, dividend-paying fleet, permanently anchored at a spot selected by the strategy of Providence, commanding the Pacific. And the Pacific is the ocean of the commerce of the future. Most future wars will be conflicts for commerce. The power that rules the Pacific, therefore, is the power that rules the world. And, with the Philippines, that power is and will forever be the American Republic....

The Philippines command the commercial situation of the entire East. Can America best trade with China from San Francisco or New York? From San Francisco, of course. But if San Francisco were closer to China than New York is to Pittsburgh, what then? And Manila is nearer Hongkong than Habana [Havana] is to Washington. And yet American statesmen plan to surrender this commercial throne of the Orient where Providence and our soldiers' lives have placed us. When history comes to write the story of that suggested treason to American supremacy and therefore to the spread of American civilization, let her in mercy write that those who so proposed were merely blind and nothing more.

RESOURCES OF THE ISLANDS

But if they did not command China, India, the Orient, the whole Pacific for purposes of offense, defense, and trade, the Philippines are so valuable in themselves that we should hold them. I have cruised more than 2,000 miles through the archipelago, every moment a surprise at its loveliness and wealth. I have ridden hundreds of miles on the islands, every foot of the way a revelation of vegetable and mineral riches....

Luzon is larger and richer than New York, Pennsylvania, Illinois, or Ohio. Mindanao is larger and richer than all New England, exclusive of Maine. Manila, as a port of call and exchange, will, in the time of men now living, far surpass Liverpool. Behold the exhaustless markets they command. It is as if a half dozen of our States were set down between Oceania [islands of the South Pacific] and the Orient, and those States themselves undeveloped and unspoiled of their primitive wealth and resources....

THE CHARACTER OF THE PEOPLE

It will be hard for Americans who have not studied them to understand the people. They are a barbarous race, modified by three centuries of contact with a decadent race. The Filipino is the South Sea Malay, put through a process of three hundred years of superstition in religion, dishonesty in dealing, disorder in habits of industry, and cruelty, caprice, and corruption in government. It is barely possible that 1,000 men in all the archipelago are capable of self-government in the Anglo-Saxon sense.

My own belief is that there are not 100 men among them who comprehend what Anglo-Saxon self-government even means, and there are over 5,000,000 people to be governed.... [Emilio] Aguinaldo is a clever, popular leader, able, brave, resourceful, cunning, ambitious, unscrupulous, and masterful. He is full of decision, initiative, and authority, and had the confidence of the masses. He is a natural dictator. His ideas of government are absolute orders, implicit obedience, or immediate death. He understands the character of his country men. He is...not a Filipino Washington....

ABANDONMENT IMPOSSIBLE

Here, then, Senators, is the situation. Two years ago there was no land in all the world which we could occupy for any purpose. Our commerce was daily turning toward the Orient, and geography and trade developments made necessary our commercial empire over the Pacific. And in that ocean we had no commercial, naval, or military base. To-day we have one of the three great ocean possessions of the globe, located at the most commanding commercial, naval, and military points in the eastern seas, within hail of India, shoulder to shoulder with China, richer in its own resources than any equal body of land on the entire globe, and peopled by a race which civilization demands shall be improved. Shall we abandon it? That man little knows the common people of the Republic, little understands the instincts of our race, who thinks we will not hold it fast and hold it forever, administering just government by simplest methods. We may trick up devices to shift our burden and lessen our opportunity; they will avail us nothing but delay. We may tangle conditions by applying academic arrangements of self-government to a crude situation; their failure will drive us to our duty in the end.

The military situation, past, present, and prospective, is no reason for abandonment. Our campaign has been as perfect as possible with the force at hand. We have been delayed, first, by a failure to comprehend the immensity of our acquisition; and, second, by insufficient force; and, third, by our efforts for peace....

This war is like all other wars. It needs to be finished before it is stopped. I am prepared to vote either to make our work thorough or even now to abandon it. A lasting peace can be secured only by overwhelming forces in ceaseless action until universal and absolutely final defeat is inflicted on the enemy. To halt before every armed force, every guerrilla band, opposing us is dispersed or exterminated will prolong hostilities and leave alive the seeds of perpetual insurrection.

Even then we should not treat [negotiate]. To treat at all is to admit that we are wrong. And any quiet so secured will be delusive and fleeting. And a false peace will betray us; a sham truce will curse us. It is not to serve the purposes of the hour, it is not to salve a present situation, that peace should be established. It is for the tranquillity of the archipelago forever. It is for an orderly government for the Filipinos for all the future. It is to give this problem to posterity solved and settled; not vexed and involved. It is to establish the supremacy of the American Republic over the Pacific and throughout the East till the end of time.

It has been charged that our conduct of the war has been cruel. Senators, it has been the reverse. I have been in our hospitals and seen the Filipino wounded as carefully, tenderly cared for as our own. Within our lines they may plow and sow and reap and go about the affairs of peace with absolute liberty. And yet all this kindness was misunderstood, or rather not understood. Senators must remember that we are not dealing with Americans or Europeans. We are dealing with Orientals. We are dealing with Orientals who are Malays. We are dealing with Malays instructed in Spanish methods. They mistake kindness for weakness, forbearance for fear. It could not be otherwise unless you could erase hundreds of years of savagery, other hundreds of years of orientalism, and still other hundreds of years of Spanish character and custom.

Our mistake has not been cruelty; it has been kindness....

The news that 60,000 American soldiers have crossed the Pacific; that, if necessary, the American Congress will make it 100,000 or 200,000 men; that, at any cost, we will establish peace and govern the islands, will do more to end the war than the soldiers themselves. But the report that we even discuss the withdrawal of a single soldier at the present time and that we even debate the possibility of not administering government throughout the archipelago ourselves will be misunderstood and misrepresented and will blow into a flame once more the fires our soldiers' blood has almost quenched.

WAR OPPONENTS BETRAY SOLDIERS

Reluctantly and only from a sense of duty am I forced to say that American opposition to the war has been the chief factor in prolonging it. Had Aguinaldo not understood that in America, even in the American Congress, even here in the Senate, he and his cause were supported; had he not known that it was proclaimed on the stump and in the press of a faction in the United States that every shot his misguided followers fired into the breasts of American soldiers was like the volleys fired by

Washington's men against the soldiers of King George his insurrection would have dissolved before it entirely crystallized.

The utterances of American opponents of the war are read to the ignorant soldiers of Aguinaldo and repeated in exaggerated form among the common people. Attempts have been made by wretches claiming American citizenship to ship arms and ammunition from Asiatic ports to the Filipinos, and these acts of infamy were coupled by the Malays with American assaults on our Government at home. The Filipinos do not understand free speech, and therefore our tolerance of American assaults on the American President and the American Government means to them that our President is in the minority or he would not permit what appears to them such treasonable criticism. It is believed and stated in Luzon, Panay, and Cebu that the Filipinos have only to fight, harass, retreat, break up into small parties, if necessary, as they are doing now, but by any means hold out until the next Presidential election, and our forces will be withdrawn.

All this has aided the enemy more than climate, arms, and battle. Senators, I have heard these reports myself; I have talked with the people; I have seen our mangled boys in the hospital and field; I have stood on the firing line and beheld our dead soldiers, their faces turned to the pitiless southern sky, and in sorrow rather than anger I say to those whose voices in America have cheered those misguided natives on to shoot our soldiers down, that the blood of those dead and wounded boys of ours is on their hands, and the flood of all the years can never wash that stain away. In sorrow rather than anger I say these words, for I earnestly believe that our brothers knew not what they did.

FILIPINOS AND SELF-GOVERNMENT

But, Senators, it would be better to abandon this combined garden and Gibraltar of the Pacific, and count our blood and treasure already spent a profitable loss, than to apply any academic arrangement of self-government to these children. They are not capable of self-government. How could they be? They are not of a self-governing race. They are Orientals, Malays, instructed by Spaniards in the latter's worst estate.

They know nothing of practical government except as they have witnessed the weak, corrupt, cruel, and capricious rule of Spain. What magic will anyone employ to dissolve in their minds and characters those impressions of governors and governed which three centuries of misrule has created? What alchemy will change the oriental quality of their blood and set the self-governing currents of the American pouring through their Malay veins? How shall they, in the twinkling of an eye, be exalted to the heights of self-governing peoples which required a thousand years for us to reach, Anglo-Saxon though we are?

Let men beware how they employ the term "self-government." It is a sacred term. It is the watchword at the door of the inner temple of liberty, for liberty does not always mean self-government. Self-government is a method of liberty—the highest, simplest, best—and it is acquired only after centuries of study and struggle and experiment and instruction and all the elements of the progress of man. Self-government is no base and common thing, to be bestowed on the merely audacious. It is the degree which crowns the graduate of liberty, not the name of liberty's infant class, who have not yet mastered the alphabet of freedom. Savage blood, oriental blood, Malay blood, Spanish example—are these the elements of self-government?

We must act on the situation as it exists, not as we would wish it. . . .

AN ELEMENTAL QUESTION

This question is deeper than any question of party politics; deeper than any question of the isolated policy of our country even; deeper even than any question of constitutional power. It is elemental. It is racial. God has not been preparing the English-speaking and Teutonic peoples for a thousand years for nothing but vain and idle self-contemplation and self-admiration. No! He has made us the master organizers of the world to establish system where chaos reigns. He has given us the spirit of progress to overwhelm the forces of reaction throughout the earth. He has made us adept in government that we may administer government among savage and senile peoples. Were it not for such a force as this the world would relapse into barbarism and night. And of all our race He has marked the American people as His chosen nation to finally lead in the regeneration of the world. This is the divine mission of America, and it holds for us all the profit, all the glory, all the happiness possible to man. We are trustees of the world's progress, guardians of its righteous peace. The judgment of the Master is upon us: "Ye have been faithful over a few things; I will make you ruler over many things."

What shall history say of us? Shall it say that we renounced that holy trust, left the savage to his base condition, the wilderness to the reign of waste, deserted duty, abandoned glory, forgot our sordid profit even, because we feared our strength and read the charter of our powers with the doubter's eye and the quibbler's mind? Shall it say that, called by events to captain and command the proudest, ablest, purest race of history in history's noblest work, we declined that great commission? Our fathers would not have had it so. No! They founded no paralytic government, incapable of the simplest acts of administration.

They planted no sluggard people, passive while the world's work calls them. They established no reactionary nation. They unfurled no retreating flag.

GOD'S HAND IN ALL

That flag has never paused in its onward march. Who dares halt it now—now, when history's largest events are carrying it forward; now, when we are at last one people, strong enough for any task, great enough for any glory destiny can bestow? How comes it that our first century closes with the process of consolidating the American people into a unit just accomplished, and quick upon the stroke of that great hour presses upon us our world opportunity, world duty, and world glory, which none but a people welded into an indivisible nation can achieve or perform?

Blind indeed is he who sees not the hand of God in events so vast, so harmonious, so benign. Reactionary indeed is the mind that perceives not that this vital people is the strongest of the saving forces of the world; that our place, therefore, is at the head of the constructing and redeeming nations of the earth; and that to stand aside while events march on is a surrender of our interests, a betrayal of our duty as blind as it is base. Craven indeed is the heart that fears to perform a work so golden and so noble; that dares not win a glory so immortal.

Viewpoint 8B

America Should Not Rule the Philippines (1900)
Joseph Henry Crooker (1850–1931)

INTRODUCTION *The American Anti-Imperialist League was founded in 1898 to protest the U.S. acquisition of Spanish colonies following the Spanish-American War. The following viewpoint is taken from a 1900 pamphlet by league member Joseph Henry Crooker, a clergyman and author of several books on religious issues. A central area of concern of Crooker and other anti-imperialists was the Philippines, a group of islands ten thousand miles from California with a population of 7 million. In 1899 the newly annexed American colony became the site of a prolonged military struggle between American soldiers stationed there and nationalist rebels; the military conflict intensified the domestic controversy over America's role in the Philippines.*

What does Crooker see as most alarming about American acquisition of the Philippines? How does he differentiate between continental and overseas expansion?

A political doctrine is now preached in our midst that is the most alarming evidence of moral decay that ever appeared in American history. Its baleful signifi-

From Joseph Henry Crooker, *The Menace to America* (Chicago: American Anti-Imperialist League, 1900).

cance consists, not simply in its moral hatefulness, but in the fact that its advocates are so numerous and so prominent.

It is this: A powerful nation, representative of civilization, has the right, for the general good of humanity, to buy, conquer, subjugate, control, and govern feeble and backward races and peoples, without reference to their wishes or opinions.

This is preached from pulpits as the gospel of Christ. It is proclaimed in executive documents as American statesmanship. It is defended in legislative halls as the beginning of a more glorious chapter in human history. It is boastfully declaimed from the platform as the first great act in the regeneration of mankind. It is published in innumerable editorials, red with cries for blood and hot with lust for gold, as the call of God to the American people....

If this be Duty, let us recite no more the Master's [Jesus] creed of love. If this be Destiny, let us proclaim no more the rights of men. If this be Patriotism, let us sing no more "America." We must rewrite the "Star Spangled Banner," and make its theme the praise of conquest and colonization. We must erase the motto, "E Pluribus Unum," and inscribe instead: "One nation in authority over many people." We must tear up the Declaration of Independence and put in its place "A Summary of the Duties of Colonists to Their Master."...

OUR NATIONAL SHAME

We cannot worship this golden calf and go unscourged. We cannot violate the principles of our government and enjoy the blessings of those principles. We cannot deny freedom across the ocean and maintain it at home. This Nation cannot endure with part of its people citizens and part colonists. The flag will lose all its glory if it floats at once over freemen and subjects. We cannot long rule other men and keep our own liberty. In the high and holy name of humanity, we are trampling upon the rights of men. But Nemesis will wake. The mask will fall; our joy will turn to bitterness; we shall find ourselves in chains.

Most of all, we lament the stain that has come to our flag, not from the soldier carrying it, but from the policy that has compelled him to carry it in an unjust cause. On executive hands falls, not only the blood of the hunted islander, but the blood of the American murdered by the ambition that sent him to invade distant lands. What we most deplore is the surrender that we as a nation have made of our leadership in the world's great work of human emancipation. What we most bitterly mourn is that we, by our selfish dreams of mere commercialism, have piled obstacles mountain high in the way of progress.

What is most surprising and most alarming is the fact that large numbers of our people still call this national ambition for conquest and dominion a form of exalted patriotism. But we are surely under the spell of a malign influence. A false Americanism has captivated our reason and corrupted our conscience. May this hypnotic lethargy, induced by the glittering but deceptive bauble of imperialism, speedily pass away; and may these fellow citizens become again true Americans, free to labor for the liberty of all men and intent on helping the lowly of all lands to independence.

It is time that all American citizens should look more carefully into the conditions and tendencies which constitute what may well be called, "The Menace to America." Let me discuss briefly certain phases of what rises ominously before us as the Philippine problem....

SLAUGHTER AND DESTRUCTION

The following is one phase of the popular argument in justification of our oriental aggressions: The obligations of humanity demanded that we take possession of the Philippine Islands in order to prevent the anarchy which would certainly have followed had we taken any other course than that which we did.

But would a little native-grown anarchy have been as bad as the slaughter and destruction which we have intruded? Let us remember that we ourselves have already killed and wounded thousands of the inhabitants. We have arrayed tribe against tribe; we have desolated homes and burned villages; agriculture and commerce have been prostrated; and finally, we have created hatred of ourselves in the breasts of millions of people to remain for years to plague us and them. It is not likely that if left to themselves anything half so serious would have occurred. It is perfectly clear that some other attitude towards those Islands besides that of domination, which this Nation most unfortunately took, would have prevented these results.

And we are not yet at the end. Recurring outbreaks against us as intruders, by people desirous of independence, will undoubtedly produce more distress and disorder in the next ten years (if our present policy is maintained) than would have resulted from native incapacity. Moreover, there are no facts in evidence that warrant the assertion that anarchy would have followed had we left them more to themselves. This is wholly an unfounded assumption. It would certainly have been well to have waited and given them a chance before interfering. That we did not wait, that we did not give them a chance, is proof positive that our national policy was not shaped by considerations of humanity or a reasonable desire to benefit them, but by a spirit of selfish aggrandizement....

WHOSE FINANCIAL GAIN?

It is pitiful that our people, and especially the common people, should be so carried away by wild and baseless dreams of the commercial advantage of these Islands. It is bad enough to sacrifice patriotism upon the altar of Mammon; but it is clear that in this case the sacrifice will be made without securing any benefit, even from Mammon.

The annual expense our Nation will incur by the military and naval establishment in the Philippines will be at least $100,000,000. This the taxpayer of America must pay. On the other hand the trade profits from these Islands—from the very nature of the case—will go directly into the pockets of millionaire monopolists, the few speculators who will get possession of the business interests there, in the line of hemp, sugar, tobacco and lumber.

The proposition is a plain one. These Islands will cost us, the common people, a hundred million dollars a year. The profits from them, possibly an equal sum, will go directly to a few very rich men. This is a very sleek speculative scheme for transferring vast sums of money from the people at large to the bank accounts of a few monopolists. Can any one see anything very helpful to the common taxpayer in such a policy? This is a serious problem for consideration, in addition to the competition of American labor with cheap Asiatic workmen—in itself sufficiently serious.

The question I press is this: Can such a policy work anything but financial harm to the average American citizen? For one, I do not care to pay this tribute money every time I draw a check or buy a bottle of medicine, tribute money that means oppression to those distant islanders, unnecessary burdens to our own people, and a still larger store for speculators to be used in corrupting American politics!

WHAT IS "EXPANSION"?

A passionate demand for expansion has taken possession of the American imagination. It is contended, We must come out of our little corner and take our place on the worldstage of the nations.

The expansion of military rule and sordid commercialism is not the expansion of our real strength or true glory.

But what has been the real expansion of our Nation for over a century? It has been two-fold. (1) The extension of our free institutions westward across the continent to the Pacific coast; (2) the powerful influence of our republican principles throughout the world. Our political ideals have modified the sentiments of great nations; our people have flowed over contiguous territories and planted there the same civic, social, religious and educational institutions that they possessed in their Eastern home. All this has been a normal and natural growth of true Americanism.

The policy that now popularly bears the name "expansion" is something radically different; and it is in no sense the expansion of America. Our people have been sadly deceived by something far worse than an optical illusion—a deceptive phrase has lured them into danger and toward despotism. To buy 10,000,000 distant islanders is the expansion of Jefferson Davis, not the expansion of Abraham Lincoln. To tax far-off colonists without their consent is the expansion of the policy of [British king] George III, not the expansion of the patriotism of George Washington. To rule without representation subject peoples is not the expansion of Americanism, but the triumph of imperialism.

The policy advocated is the suppression of American principles, the surrender of our sublime ideals, and the end of our beneficent ministry of liberty among the nations. Just because I want to see America expand I condemn the policy as unpatriotic. Let us not deceive ourselves; the expansion of military rule and sordid commercialism is not the expansion of our real strength or true glory. Let us not mistake the renunciation of American ideals for the expansion of American institutions.

FLAG AND CONSTITUTION

Wherever the flag goes, there the constitution must go. Wherever the flag waves, there the whole of the flag must be present. Wherever the constitution is extended, there the entire constitution must rule. If any one does not wish to accept these consequences, then let the flag be brought back to the spot where it can represent true Americanism, and Americanism in its entirety. What shall our banner be to the Filipino? A symbol of his own liberty or the hated emblem of a foreign oppressor? Shall it float over him in Manila as a mere subject and say to him when he lands in San Francisco that he is an alien? Then that flag will become the object of the world's derision!

If it does not symbolize American institutions in their fullness wherever it floats, then our starry banner becomes false to America and oppressive to those who may fear its authority, but do not share its freedom. Disgrace and harm will not come from taking the flag down, but rather from keeping it where it loses all that our statesmen, prophets and soldiers have put into it. The only way to keep "Old Glory" from becoming a falsehood is to give all under it the liberty that it represents. Nowhere must it remain simply to represent a power to be dreaded, but everywhere it must symbolize rights and privileges shared by all.

FOR FURTHER READING

John Braeman, *Albert J. Beveridge: American Nationalist.* Chicago: University of Chicago Press, 1971.

A.B. Feuer, ed., *America at War: The Philippines, 1898–1913.* Westport, CT: Praeger Press, 2002.

Thomas G. Paterson, ed., *American Imperialism and Anti-Imperialism.* New York: Crowell, 1973.

James C. Thomas Jr. et al., *Sentimental Imperialists.* New York: Harper & Row, 1981.

Richard E. Welch, *Response to Imperialism: The United States and the Philippine-American War, 1899–1902.* Chapel Hill: University of North Carolina Press, 1979.

PROGRESSIVE ERA REFORMS AND ISSUES

Viewpoint 9A

Child Labor Should Be Abolished (1906)

Edwin Markham (1852–1940)

INTRODUCTION *One of the reforms supported by many Progressive Era reformers was the abolition of child labor. Children in America had traditionally worked on farms or as apprentices learning a craft, but many reformers argued that the industrial revolution had changed the nature of child labor. They contended that many children worked in horrible conditions in mines, factories, and sweatshops, and were deprived of an education. The following viewpoint is excerpted from a September 1906 article by journalist and poet Edwin Markham. A former schoolteacher, Markham was one of the "muckrakers" of the era who penned exposés on political corruption and other social and economic ills of American society. This essay, focusing on children working in textile mills in the South, was one of several articles Markham wrote for* Cosmopolitan *magazine.*

What kinds of harms to children does Markham describe? What significance does he attach to the race of the children? Cosmopolitan *was (and is) a magazine directed at women readers; what parts of Markham's article do you find revealing about social views on women in the early twentieth century?*

Once, so the story goes, an old Indian chieftain was shown the ways and wonders of New York. He saw the cathedrals, the skyscrapers, the bleak tenements, the blaring mansions, the crowded circus, the airy span of the

From Edwin Markham, "The Hoe Man in the Making," *Cosmopolitan,* September 1906.

Brooklyn Bridge. "What is the most surprising thing you have seen?" asked several comfortable Christian gentlemen of this benighted pagan whose worship was a "bowing down to sticks and stones." The savage shifted his red blanket and answered in three slow words, "Little children working."

It has remained, then, for civilization to give the world an abominable custom which shocks the social ethics of even an unregenerate savage. For the Indian father does not ask his children to work, but leaves them free till the age of maturity, when they are ushered with solemn rites into the obligations of their elders. Some of us are wondering why our savage friends do not send their medicine men as missionaries, to shed upon our Christian darkness the light of barbarism. Child labor is a new thing in human affairs. Ancient history records no such infamy. "Children," says the Talmud, "must not be taken from the schools even to rebuild the temple." In Greece and Rome the children of both slave and master fared alike in a common nursery. The trainers worked to build up strong and beautiful bodies, careless of the accident of lineage or fortune. But how different is our "Christian civilization"! Seventeen hundred thousand children at work! Does the enumeration bring any significance to our minds when we say that an army of one million seven hundred thousand children are at work in our "land of the free"? This was the figure in 1900; now there are hundreds of thousands more. And many of them working their long ten or fourteen hours by day or by night, with only a miserable dime for a wage! Can the heart take in the enormity? . . .

COTTON MILLS

More children are crowded into this limbo of the loom than into any other cavern of our industrial abyss. In the southern cotton mills, where the doors shut out the odor of the magnolia and shut in the reeking damps and clouds of lint, and where the mocking bird outside keeps obbligato to the whirring wheels within, we find a gaunt goblin army of children keeping their forced march on the factory floors—an army that outwatches the sun by day and the stars by night. Eighty thousand children, mostly girls, are at work in the textile mills of the United States. The South, the center of the cotton industry, happens to have the eminence of being the leader in this social infamy. At the beginning of 1903 there were in the South twenty thousand children at the spindles. *The Tradesman,* of Chattanooga, estimates that with the springing up of new mills there must now be fifty thousand children at the southern looms. This is 30 per cent of all the cotton workers of the South—a spectral army of pygmy people sucked in from the hills to dance beside the crazing wheels.

Let us again reckon up this Devil's toll. In the North (where, God knows, conditions are bad enough), for every one thousand workers over sixteen years of age there are eighty-three workers under sixteen (that young old-age of the working-child); while in the South, for every one thousand workers in the mills over sixteen years of age there are three hundred and fifty-three under sixteen. Some of these are eight and nine years old, and some are only five and six. For a day or a night at a stretch these little children do some one monotonous thing—abusing their eyes in watching the rushing threads; dwarfing their muscles in an eternity of petty movements; befouling their lungs by breathing flecks of flying cotton; bestowing ceaseless, anxious attention for hours, where science says that "a twenty-minute strain is long enough for a growing mind." And these are not the children of recent immigrants, hardened by the effete conditions of foreign servitude. Nor are they Negro children who have shifted their shackles from field to mill. They are white children of old and pure colonial stock. Think of it! Here is a people that has outlived the bondage of England, that has seen the rise and fall of slavery—a people that must now fling their children into the clutches of capital, into the maw of the blind machine; must see their latest-born drag on in a face of servility that reminds us of the Saxon churl under the frown of the Norman lord. For Mammon is merciless.

Fifty thousand children, mostly girls, are in the textile mills of the South. Six times as many children are working now as were working twenty years ago. Unless the conscience of the nation can be awakened, it will not be long before one hundred thousand children will be hobbling in hopeless lock-step to these Bastilles of labor. It will not be long till these little spinners shall be "far on the way to be spiders and needles."

We boast that we are leading the commercialism of the world and we grind in our mills the bones of the little ones to make good our boast.

DEADLY DRUDGERY

Think of the deadly drudgery in these cotton mills. Children rise at half-past four, commanded by the ogre scream of the factory whistle; they hurry, ill fed, unkempt, unwashed, half dressed, to the walls which shut out the day and which confine them amid the din and dust and merciless maze of the machines. Here, penned in little narrow lanes, they look and leap and reach and tie among acres and acres of looms. Always the snow of lint in their faces, always the thunder of the machines

in their ears. A scant half hour at noon breaks the twelve-hour vigil, for it is nightfall when the long hours end and the children may return to the barracks they call "home," often too tired to wait for the cheerless meal which the mother, also working in the factory, must cook, after her factory day is over. Frequently at noon and at night they fall asleep with the food unswallowed in the mouth. Frequently they snatch only a bite and curl up undressed on the bed, to gather strength for the same dull round tomorrow, and tomorrow, and tomorrow. . . .

And why do these children know no rest, no play, no learning, nothing but the grim grind of existence? Is it because we are all naked and shivering? Is it because there is sudden destitution in the land? Is it because pestilence walks at noonday? Is it because war's red hand is pillaging our storehouses and burning our cities? No, forsooth! Never before were the storehouses so crammed to bursting with bolts and bales of every warp and woof. No, forsooth! The children, while yet in the gristle, are ground down that a few more useless millions may be heaped up. We boast that we are leading the commercialism of the world, and we grind in our mills the bones of the little ones to make good our boast.

Rev. Edgar Murphy of Montgomery, Alabama, has photographed many groups of these pathetic little toilers, all under twelve. Jane Addams saw in a night-factory a little girl of five, her teeth blacked with snuff, like all the little girls about her—a little girl who was busily and clumsily tying threads in coarse muslin. The average child lives only four years after it enters the mills. Pneumonia stalks in the damp, lint-filled rooms, and leads hundreds of the little ones out to rest. Hundreds more are maimed by the machinery, two or three for each of their elders. One old mill hand carries sixty-four scars, the cruel record of the shuttles.

The labor commissioner of North Carolina reports that there are two hundred and sixty-one cotton mills in that state, in which nearly forty thousand people are employed, including nearly eight thousand children. The average daily wage of the men is fifty-seven cents, of the women thirty-nine cents, of the children twenty-two cents. The commissioner goes on to say: "I have talked with a little boy of seven years who worked for forty nights in Alabama, and with another child who, at six years of age, had been on the night shift eleven months. Little boys turned out at two o'clock in the morning, afraid to go home, would beg a clerk in the mill for permission to lie down on the office floor. In one city mill in the South, a doctor said he had amputated the fingers of more than one hundred children, mangled in the mill machinery, and that a horrible form of dropsy occurs frequently among the overworked children." . . .

These little white children often begin work in the mill with no fragment of education. And often after a year of this brain-blasting labor they lose the power to learn even the simple art of reading. There is sometimes a night school for the little workers, but they often topple over with sleep at the desks, after the long grind of the day. Indeed they must not spend too many wakeful hours in the night school, shortening their sleep-time; for the ogre of the mill must have all their strength at full head in the morning. . . .

But worse than all is the breakdown of the soul in these God-forgetting mills. Here boys and girls are pushed into the company of coarse men who are glib with oaths and reeking jests. Torrents of foul profanity from angry overseers wash over the souls of the children, till they, too, grow hardened in crusts of coarseness. Piled on all these are the fearful risks that the young girls run from the attentions of men "higher up," especially if the girls happen to be cursed with a little beauty. . . .

The poor remnant of these young toilers, they who do not crumble down in an early death, or drift to the gutter or the brothel are left alas! to become fathers and mothers. Fathers and mothers, forsooth! What sort of fatherhood and motherhood can we hope for from these children robbed of childhood, from these children with the marrow sucked out of their bones and the beauty run out of their faces? Tragical is it beyond words to think that any of these poor human effigies should ever escape to engender their kind and to send on a still more pitiable progeny. What child worthy of the name can spring from the loins of these withered effigies of men? What babe worthy of the name can be mothered in the side of this wasted and weakened woman who has given her virgin vitality to the Moloch of the mill? And what wonder that, if expelled from the factory as no longer competent to be a cog or a pulley in the vast machine, they have no ambition but to sit idly in the sun? What wonder that the commonwealth, having fostered these dull degenerates, should be forced to care for them in her almshouses, her jails, her asylums? . . .

DRIVEN BY PROFIT

The factory, we are told, must make a certain profit, or the owners (absentee proprietors generally, living in larded luxury) will complain. Therefore the president is goaded on by the directors. He in turn whips up the overseer; the overseer takes it out on the workers. So the long end of the lash cuts red the backs of the little children. Need we wonder, then, that cotton-factory stock gives back portly profits—25, 35, yes, even 50 per cent? It pays, my masters, to grind little children into dividends! And the silks and muslins do not show the stain of blood, although they are splashed with scarlet on God's side. . . .

"Rob us of child labor and we will take our mills from your state." This is the frequent threat of the mill owners in the chambers and lobbies of legislation. And, alas! we are in a civilization where such a threat avails. Still, in spite of the apathy of the church, in spite of the assault of the capital, the friends of mercy have in all but four states forced some sort of a protective law: no child under twelve years of age shall work for longer than eight hours, nor any without a common-school education. This reads fairly well; but a law on the statute book is not always a law on the factory-floor. The inspectors are often vigilant and quick with conscience. Some mills desire to keep the law. But others are crooked: they have their forged and perjured certificates, their double payrolls—one for the inspector, another for the counting-house. They have, also, the device of bringing children in as "mothers' helps," giving the mothers a few more pennies for the baby fingers.

Hard masters of mills, shiftless or hapless parents, even misguided children themselves, all conspire to hold the little slaves to the wheel. Yes, even the children are taught to lie about their age, and their tongues are ever ready with the glib rehearsal. Some mills keep a lookout for the inspector, and at the danger signal the children scurry like rats to hide in attics, to crouch in cellars, behind bales of cotton, under heaps of old machinery. But God's battle has begun. Still there must be a wider unification of the bands of justice and mercy, a fusing and forcing of public opinion. Let the women of America arise, unite, and resolve in a great passion of righteousness to save the children of the nation. Nothing can stand against the fire of an awakened and banded womanhood.

Viewpoint 9B

Child Labor May Be Beneficial (1883, 1906)

Thomas L. Livermore and a North Carolina mill worker
(dates unknown)

INTRODUCTION *In 1870 the Census Bureau established a separate category of workers who were between the ages of ten and fifteen; the bureau estimated that one of eight American children in this age group was in the labor force. By 1900 that number had risen to one in six, and the practice of child labor had come under increasing attack from politicians and social reformers. The following two-part viewpoint presents opinions of two people intimately involved in factory child labor. The first part is excerpted from testimony by Thomas L. Livermore, a manager of a textile factory in New Hampshire, before an 1883 congressional committee investigating labor conditions. Responding to questions from New Hampshire senator Henry W. Blair, Livermore concedes that children need some classroom education, but asserts that factory employment is a worthwhile source of "practical" learning for many children. The second part of the viewpoint is taken from a handbill that was circulated in cotton mills in North Carolina around 1906. In it, the anonymous author states that he and his family, including his two boys and three girls, are much better off employed together in a cotton mill than they had been previously on a two-hundred-acre farm.*

What benefits of child labor do the authors describe? What is revealed about their views on schooling and education? Do you believe that their respective positions as a factory manager and a parent enable them to speak for the children's interest?

I

Senator Henry W. Blair: Won't you please tell us your experience with the question of child labor; how it is and to what extent it exists here; why it exists, and whether, as it is actually existing here, it is a hardship on a child or on a parent; or whether there is any evil in that direction that should be remedied?

Livermore: There is a certain class of labor in the mills which, to put it in very common phrase, consists mainly in running about the floor—where there is not as much muscular exercise required as a child would put forth in play, and a child can do it about as well as a grown person can do it—not quite as much of it, but somewhere near it—and with proper supervision of older people, the child serves the purpose. That has led to the employment of children in the mills, I think. . . .

Now, a good many heads of families, without any question in my mind, were not sufficiently considerate of the mental and physical welfare of their children, and they put them to work in the mills, perhaps too early, and certainly kept them there too much of the time in former years, and the legislature had to step in and protect the children against the parents by requiring that they should go to school a certain number of months or weeks in a year, or else they should not be allowed to work in the mills; and at the present time there is a very severe law in this state applicable to children—I think some under twelve and some under sixteen. I do not remember the terms of it, but the child has to have a certificate of the authorities in control of the schools that he has been to school the time required by the statute before the mill manager is able to employ him. I think the mill manager is subject to a very considerable penalty for non-compliance with that law.

In this city in our mills, and as far as I know in the rest of the mills, we have been very particular to observe the statute. I do not know how it is outside of the city. I suppose that it may depend a good deal upon public sentiment. If public sentiment supports the law, it will be enforced; if it does not, it will not be. I think public sentiment does support it here to an extent, although I think it extends a little too far in preventing children up to sixteen working in mills more than a given time. . . . The city authorities here have an officer who makes it his business to go through the mills to see whether the law is complied with or not.

WORK AND EDUCATION

Now, I think that when it is provided that a child shall go to school as long as it is profitable for a workman's child (who has got to be a workingman himself) to go to school, the limit has been reached at which labor in the mills should be forbidden. There is such a thing as too much education for working people sometimes. I do not mean to say by that that I discourage education to any person on earth, or that I think that with good sense any amount of education can hurt anyone, but I have seen cases where young people were spoiled for labor by being educated to a little too much refinement.

You have known something of farm life and the necessity that a boy is put under of learning to farm while he is still a boy?

Yes.

Now, with reference to the acquirement of the necessary skill to earn a living, without which an education would amount to little—a man having enough knowledge to starve upon has not much advantage—do you think that the child should be withheld from the educating idea in the industrial line to so large an extent as the law now requires?

I do not.

Is there danger of too much abstention from that sort of practical education which enables a child when grown to earn his living?

I think so. I will state that in our machine shops we take apprentices to learn the trade of a machinist, which is one of the best trades that any man in this country can have. We agree that if they will agree to serve three years for pay which enables them to live, we will teach them the trade of a machinist; and it is a curious illustration of the effect of very advanced common schools that our foremen prefer apprentice boys from the country, who have worked on farms and been to a district school a little while, to boys that have been educated in the city. They say that the city boys do not stick to their work as the others do. They are a little above the employment.

Part I: From testimony of Thomas L. Livermore, *Report of the Committee of the Senate Upon the Relations Between Labor and Capital* (Washington, DC: GPO, 1885). Part II: From August Kohn, *The Cotton Mills of South Carolina* (Columbia, SC: 1907).

Is this employment that you speak about in the mills in which children are engaged of a character to tax their muscular or physical frame more than it ought to during their growing period?

No, sir; I don't know of any such employment in the mills being put upon children.

———————— ■ ————————

At the mills, children over 12 years old, after they learn their job, can make more than men can make on farms.

———————— ■ ————————

II

Three years ago I owned a little mountain farm of two hundred acres. I had two good horses, two good cows, plenty of hogs, sheep and several calves. I had three girls and two boys; ages run from 11 to 21. On my little farm I raised about four hundred bushels of corn, thirty to forty bushels of wheat, two hundred to three hundred dozen oats, and cut from four to eight stacks of hay during the summer. After I clothed my family, fed all my stock during the winter, I had only enough provisions and feed to carry me through making another crop, and no profit left. I sold my farm and stock, paid up all my debts and moved my family to a cotton mill. At that time green hands had to work for nothing til they learned their job, about one month, but now my youngest daughter, only 14 years old, is making $6 per week, my other two are making $7.50 each per week and my two boys are making $8 per week and I am making $4.50 per week; a total of $166 per month. My provisions average $30, house rent $2, coal and wood $4, total $36; leaving a balance of $130, to buy clothes and deposit in the bank.

FACTORY WORK VS. FARM TOILING

My experience is that, while you are on the farm toiling in rain and snow, feeding away what you have made during the summer and making wood to keep fires to keep your family from freezing, you could at the same time be in a cotton mill and in a good, comfortable room, making more than you can make in the summer time on the farm, and there is no stock to eat up what you make. At the mills, children over 12 years old, after they learn their job, can make more than men can make on farms. It is not every family that can do as well as the above family, but it only shows what a family can do that will try and work. Most any family can do half as well—so divide the above number of workers' wages by two and see if you would not still be doing well.

Give this matter your careful thought.

FOR FURTHER READING

Russell Freedman, *Kids at Work: Lewis Hine and the Crusade Against Child Labor*. New York: Clarion Books, 1998.

Hugh D. Hindman, *Child Labor: An American History*. Armonk, NY: M.E. Sharpe, 2002.

Arthur and Lila Weinburg, eds., *The Muckrakers: The Era in Journalism that Moved America to Reform*. New York: Simon & Schuster, 1961.

Viewpoint 10A
American Women Should Have the Right to Vote (1909)
Julia Ward Howe (1819–1910)

INTRODUCTION *Julia Ward Howe, a noted writer, lecturer, and social reformer, is perhaps best known as the author of "The Battle Hymn of the Republic," written during the Civil War. In 1869 she helped found the American Woman Suffrage Association, an organization that worked to gain the vote for women in individual states. In the following viewpoint, excerpted from a 1909 article, she describes the positive results of women's suffrage in Colorado and other places, and argues for the right to vote for all American women.*

Does Howe exhibit racial prejudice in her comments on black suffrage? Does Howe argue that women's suffrage would cause radical changes in American society?

When the stripling David, having rashly undertaken to encounter the Philistine giant [Goliath], found himself obliged to choose a weapon for the unequal fight, he dismissed the costly armament offered him by the king, and went back to the simple stone and sling with which he was familiar. Even in like manner will I, pledged just now to make a plain statement of the claims of woman to suffrage, trust myself to state the case as it appeared to me when, after a delay of some years, I finally gave it my adhesion [assent].

Having a quick and rather preponderating sense of the ridiculous, I had easily apprehended the humorous associations which would at first attach themselves to any change in the political status of women. It had once appeared to me answer enough to the new demand to ask the mothers what they proposed to do with their babies, with their husbands, that they should find time for the exercise of these very superfluous functions.

BLACK MEN GAIN SUFFRAGE

While I still so spake and so thought, behold, a race of men became enfranchised by the appeal to arms. The conquest of their rights demanded the power to defend those rights, and this power the logic of history had placed in the ballot, whose object it is to secure to

From Julia Ward Howe, "The Case for Woman Suffrage," *Outlook*, April 3, 1909.

every person of sane and sound mind the availing expression of his political faith and individual will.

———— ■ ————

Experience has shattered... all the old predictions that [women's suffrage] would... have a ruinous influence both on womanly delicacy and on public affairs.

———— ■ ————

I had by this time cast in my lot with those to whom the right of the negro to every human function and privilege appeared a point to be maintained at all hazards. It had been determined that the slave should become a free man, and, further than this, that, in order to maintain his freedom, he must perform the offices of a free citizen.

Two new thoughts now came to me in the shape of questions: Why was the vote so vital a condition of the freedom of an American citizen? And, if it was held to be so vital, why should every man possess it, and no woman? I did and do believe in equal civic rights for all human beings, without regard to race, subject only to such tests as may be applied impartially to all alike. But there seemed a special incongruity in putting this great mass of ignorant men into a position of political superiority to all women. The newly enfranchised men were generally illiterate and of rather low morality. Should they, simply on account of sex, be invested with a power and dignity withheld from women, who at that time were unquestionably better fitted to intervene in matters of government than men could be who for many generations past had been bought and sold like cattle, men who would have the whole gamut of civilization to learn by heart before they could have any availing knowledge of what a vote should really mean? Here were ignorance and low life commissioned to lord it over the august company of the mothers. Here were the natural guardians of childhood debarred from the highest office in its defense. I felt that this could not be right; and when the foremost friends of the negro showed themselves as the foremost champions of the political enfranchisement of women, I had no longer any hesitation in saying, This must be the keystone of the arch, whose absence leaves so sad and strange a gap in the construction of our political morality.

Since then the question of suffrage for women has passed out of the academic stage, and has become a matter of practical observation and experience in an ever-growing number of States and countries. Experience has shattered, like a house of cards, all the old predictions that it would destroy the home, subvert the foundations

of society, and have a ruinous influence both on womanly delicacy and on public affairs....

The fundamental argument for woman suffrage, of course, is its justice, and this would be enough were there no other. But a powerful argument can also be made for it from the standpoint of expediency. It has now been proved to demonstration, not only that woman suffrage has no bad results, but that it has certain definite good results.

1. It gives women a position of increased dignity and influence. On this point I will quote from... people whose word has weight in our own land and abroad.

Miss Margaret Long, daughter of the ex-Secretary of the Navy, who has resided for years in Denver, has written: "It seems impossible to me that any one can live in Colorado long enough to get into touch with the life here, and not realize that women count for more in all the affairs of this State than they do where they have not the power that the suffrage gives. More attention is paid to their wishes, and much greater weight given to their opinions and judgment."

Mrs. K.A. Sheppard, President of the New Zealand Council of Women, says: "Since women have become electors, their views have become important and command respect. Men listen to and are influenced by the opinions of women to a far greater degree than was the case formerly. There is no longer heard the contemptuous 'What do women know of such matters?' And so out of the greater civil liberty enjoyed by women has come a perceptible rise in the moral and humanitarian tone of the community. A young New Zealander in his teens no longer regards his mother as belonging to a sex that must be kept within a prescribed sphere. That the lads and young men of a democracy should have their whole conception of the rights of humanity broadened and measured by truer standards is in itself an incalculable benefit."...

IMPROVING THE LAWS

2. It leads to improvements in the laws. No one can speak more fitly of this than Judge Lindsey, of the Denver Juvenile Court. He writes: "We have in Colorado the most advanced laws of any State in the Union for the care and protection of the home and the children, the very foundation of the Republic. We owe this more to woman suffrage than to any one cause. It does not take any mother from her home duties to spend ten minutes in going to the polls, casting her vote, and returning to the bosom of her home; but during those ten minutes she wields a power which is doing more to protect that home, and all other homes, than any other power or influence in Colorado."

Mrs. Helen L. Grenfell, of Denver, served three terms as State Superintendent of Public Instruction for

Colorado, and is highly esteemed by educators throughout the State. She introduced in Colorado the system of leasing instead of selling the lands set apart by the Government for the support of the public schools, thereby almost doubling the annual revenue available for education. Mrs. Grenfell was appointed by the Governor to represent Colorado at the Congress of the International Woman Suffrage Alliance at Amsterdam last summer. In her report to that Congress she enumerated a long list of improved laws obtained in Colorado since women were granted the ballot, and added: "Delegates of the Interparliamentary Union who visited different parts of the United States for the purpose of studying American institutions declared concerning our group of laws relating to child life in its various aspects of education, home, and labor, that 'they are the sanest, most humane, most progressive, most scientific laws relating to the child to be found on any statute-books in the world.'" . . .

Since women attained the ballot, all the four equal suffrage States have raised the age of protection for girls to eighteen. In Idaho and Wyoming the repeal of the laws that formerly licensed gambling is universally ascribed to the women. The Colorado statutes against cruelty to animals and against obscene literature are said to be models of their kind. . . .

WOMEN'S INFLUENCE

3. Women can bring their influence to bear on legislation more quickly and with less labor by the direct method than by the indirect. In Massachusetts the suffragists worked for fifty-five years before they succeeded in getting a law making mothers equal guardians of their minor children with the fathers. After half a century of effort by indirect influence, only twelve out of our forty-six States have taken similar action. In Colorado, when the women were enfranchised, the very next Legislature passed such a bill.

4. Equal suffrage often leads to the defeat of bad candidates. This is conceded even by Mr. A. Lawrence Lewis, whose article in *The Outlook* against woman suffrage in Colorado has been reprinted by the anti-suffragists as a tract. He says:

"Since the extension of the franchise to women, political parties have learned the inadvisability of nominating for public offices drunkards, notorious libertines, gamblers, retail liquor dealers, and men who engage in similar discredited occupations, because the women almost always vote them down." . . .

And quoting once more from Judge Lindsey, of Denver: "One of the greatest advantages from woman suffrage is the fear on the part of the machine politicians to nominate men of immoral character. While many bad men have been elected in spite of woman suffrage, they have not been elected because of woman suffrage. If the women alone had a vote, it would result in a class of men in public office whose character for morality, honesty, and courage would be of a much higher order."

5. Equal suffrage broadens women's minds, and leads them to take a more intelligent interest in public affairs. President Slocum, of Colorado College, Enos A. Mills, the forestry expert, Mrs. Decker, and many others, bear witness to this. The Hon. W.E. Mullen, Attorney-General of Wyoming, who went there opposed to woman suffrage and has been converted, writes: "It stimulates interest and study, on the part of women, in public affairs. Questions of public interest are discussed in the home. As the mother, sister, or teacher of young boys, the influence of woman is very great. The more she knows about the obligations of citizenship, the more she is able to teach the boys." A leading bookseller of Denver says he sold more books on political economy in the first eight months after women were given the ballot than he had sold in fifteen years before.

6. It makes elections and political meetings more orderly. The Hon. John W. Kingman, of the Wyoming Supreme Court, says: "In caucus discussions the presence of a few ladies is worth a whole squad of police."

7. It makes it easier to secure liberal appropriations for educational and humanitarian purposes. In Colorado the schools are not scrimped for money, as they are in the older and richer States. So say Mrs. Grenfell, General Irving Hale, and others.

8. It opens to women important positions now closed to them because they are not electors. Throughout England, Scotland, Ireland, and a considerable part of Europe, a host of women are rendering admirable service to the community in offices from which women in America are still debarred.

9. It increases the number of women chosen to such offices as are already open to them. Thus, in Colorado women were eligible as county superintendents of schools before their enfranchisement; but when they obtained the ballot the number of women elected to those positions showed an immediate and large increase.

10. It raises the average of political honesty among the voters. Judge Lindsey says: "Ninety-nine per cent of our election frauds are committed by men."

11. It tends to modify a too exclusively commercial view of public affairs. G.W. Russell, Chairman of the Board of Governors of Canterbury College, New Zealand, writes: "Prior to women's franchise the distinctive feature of our politics was finance. Legislative proposals were regarded almost entirely from the point of view of (1) What would they cost? and (2) What would be their effect from a commercial standpoint? The woman's

view is not pounds nor pence, but her home, her family. In order to win her vote, the politicians had to look at public matters from her point of view. Her ideal was not merely money, but happy homes and a fair chance in life for her husband, her intended husband, and her present or prospective family."

SUFFRAGE AND THE FAMILY

12. Last, but not least, it binds the family more closely together. I say this with emphasis, though it is in direct opposition to an argument much brought forward by the opponents of woman suffrage. Let us give ear to words that are written, like the last, from a region where equal suffrage has been tried and proved.

The Hon. Hugh Lusk, ex-member of the New Zealand Parliament, says: "We find that equal suffrage is the greatest family bond and tie, the greatest strengthener of family life. It seemed odd at first to find half the benches at a political meeting occupied by ladies; but when men have got accustomed to it they do not like the other thing. When they found that they could take their wives and daughters to these meetings, and afterwards go home with them and talk it over, it was often the beginning of a new life for the family—a life of ideas and interests in common, and of a unison of thought."

It is related that the Japanese Government many years ago sent a commission to the United States to study the practical working of Christianity, with a view to introducing it into Japan as the State religion if the report of the commission proved favorable. The commission saw many evils rampant in America, and went home reporting that Christianity was a failure. The opponents of woman suffrage argue in the same way. They find evils in the enfranchised States, and straightway draw the conclusion that woman suffrage is a failure. But it may be said with truth of woman suffrage, as of Christianity, that these evils exist not because of it but in spite of it; and that it has effected a number of distinct improvements, and is on the way to effect yet more.

I have sat in the little chapel at Bethlehem in which tradition places the birth of the Saviour. It seemed fitting that it should he adorned with offerings of beautiful things. But while I mused there a voice seemed to say to me: "Look abroad! This divine child is a child no more. He has grown to be a man and a deliverer. Go out into the world! Find his footsteps and follow them. Work, as he did, for the redemption of mankind. Suffer as he did, if need be, derision and obloquy. Make your protest against tyranny, meanness, and injustice!"

The weapon of Christian warfare is the ballot, which represents the peaceable assertion of conviction and will. Society everywhere is becoming converted to its use.

Adopt it, O you women, with clean hands and a pure heart! Verify the best word written by the apostle—"In Christ Jesus there is neither bond nor free, neither male nor female, but a new creature," the harbinger of a new creation!

Viewpoint 10B
American Women Should Not Have the Right to Vote (1909)
Emily P. Bissell (1861–1948)

INTRODUCTION *Emily P. Bissell was an organizer of the Delaware chapter of the American Red Cross and the first president of the Consumers' League of Delaware, where she helped secure passage of state laws regulating child and women labor. She was also an active opponent of the movement to secure a woman's right to vote who testified before Congress, gave lectures, and wrote pamphlets on the issue. Bissell did not find any inconsistencies in her political positions, arguing that women had greater influence in promoting beneficial legislation precisely because of their position as nonvoters, removed from the political process. The following viewpoint is taken from a 1909 pamphlet distributed by the New York State Association Opposed to Women Suffrage.*

Why is suffrage different from reforms opening up higher education and work opportunities for women who desire them, according to Bissell? What opinions does she express about voting rights and restrictions in America compared with other countries? What distinctions does she make between "good" and "bad" women, and how important are these distinctions in her argument?

There are three points of view from which woman today ought to consider herself—as an individual, as a member of a family, as a member of the state. Every, woman stands in those three relations to American life. Every woman's duties and rights cluster along those three lines; and any change in woman's status that involves all of them needs to be very carefully considered by every thoughtful woman.

———————◼———————

The suffragists cannot get the vote without forcing it on all the rest of womankind in America.

———————◼———————

The proposal that women should vote affects each one of these three relations deeply. It is then a proposal

From Emily P. Bissell, "A Talk to Women on the Suffrage Question," in *Selected Articles on Woman Suffrage*, 3rd rev. ed. (New York: H.W. Wilson, 1916).

that the American woman has been considering for sixty years, without accepting it. Other questions, which have been only individual, as the higher education for such individual women as desire it, or the opening of various trades and professions to such individual women as desire to enter them have not required any such thought or hesitation. They are individual, and individuals have decided on them and accepted them. But this great suffrage question, involving not only the individual, but the family and the state, has hung fire. There are grave objections to woman suffrage on all these three counts. Sixty years of argument and of effort on the part of the suffragists have not in the least changed these arguments, because they rest on the great fundamental facts of human nature and of human government. The suffrage is "a reform against nature" and such reforms are worse than valueless.

A MISTAKE FOR INDIVIDUALS?

Let us take these three points of view singly. Why, in the first place, is the vote a mistake for women as individuals? I will begin discussing that by another question. "How many of you have leisure to spare now, without the vote?" The claims upon a woman's time, in this twentieth century, are greater than ever before. Woman, in her progress, has taken up many important things to deal with, and has already overloaded herself beyond her strength. If she is a working-woman, her day is full—fuller than that of a workingman, since she has to attend, in many cases, to home duties or to sewing and mending for herself when her day's toil is over. If she is a wife and mother, she has her hands full with the house and the children. If she is a woman of affairs and charities, she has to keep a secretary or call in a stenographer to get through her letters and accounts. Most of the self-supporting women of my acquaintance do not want the ballot. They have no time to think about it. Most of the wives and mothers I know do not want to vote. They are too busy with other burdens. Most of the women of affairs I know do not want to vote. They are doing public work without it better than they could with it, and consider it a burden, not a benefit. The ballot is a duty, a responsibility; and most intelligent, active women to-day believe that it is man's duty and responsibility, and that they are not called to take it up in addition to their own share. The suffragists want the ballot individually. They have a perfect right to want it. They ask no leisure. And if it were only an individual question, then I should say heartily "Let them have it, as individuals, and let us refuse to take it, as individuals, and then the whole matter can be individually settled." But that is impossible, for there are two other aspects. The suffragists cannot get the vote without forcing it on all the rest of womankind in America; for America means unrestricted manhood suffrage, and an equal suffrage law would mean unrestricted womanhood suffrage, from the college girl to the immigrant woman who cannot read and the negro woman in the cotton-field, and from the leader of society down to the drunken woman in the police court. The individual aspect is only one of the three, and after all, the least important.

DUTY TO THE FAMILY

For no good woman lives to herself. She has always been part of a family as wife or sister or daughter from the time of Eve.... The American home is the foundation of American strength and progress. And in the American home woman has her own place and her own duty to the family.

It is an axiom in physics that two things cannot be in the same place at the same time. Woman, as an individual, apart from all home ties, can easily enough get into a man's place. There are thousands of women in New York to-day—business women, professional women, working girls, who are almost like men in their daily activity. But nearly all these women marry and leave the man's place for the woman's, after a few years of business life. It is this fact which makes their wages lower than men's, and keeps them from being a highly skilled class. They go back into the home, and take up a woman's duties in the family. If they are wise women, they give up their work; they do not try to be in a man's place and a woman's too. But when they do make this foolish resolve to keep on working the home suffers. There are no children; or the children go untrained; housekeeping is given up for boarding; there is no family atmosphere. The woman's place is vacant—and in a family, that is the most important place of all. The woman, who might be a woman, is half a man instead.

The family demands from a woman her very best. Her highest interests, and her unceasing care, must be in home life, if her home is to be what it ought to be. Here is where the vote for woman comes in as a disturbing factor. The vote is part of man's work. Ballot-box, cartridge box, jury box, sentry box, all go together in his part of life. Woman cannot step in and take the responsibilities and duties of voting without assuming his place very largely. The vote is a symbol of government, and leads at once into the atmosphere of politics; to make herself an intelligent voter (and no other kind is wanted) a woman must study up the subjects on which she is to vote and cast her ballot with a personal knowledge of current politics in every detail. She must take it all from her husband, which means that he is thus given two votes instead of one, not equal suffrage, but a double suffrage for the man....

The vote, which means public life, does not fit into the ideal of family life. The woman who is busy training a family is doing her public service right in the home. She cannot be expected to be in two places at the same time doing the work of the state as the man does....

THE WOMEN'S VOTE

This brings us to the third point, which is, the effect on the state of a vote for women. Let us keep in mind, always, that in America we cannot argue about municipal suffrage, or taxpaying suffrage, or limited suffrage of any kind—"to one end they must all come," that of unrestricted woman suffrage, white and colored, illiterate and collegebred alike having the ballot. America recognizes no other way. Do not get the mistaken idea—which the suffragists cleverly present all the while—that the English system of municipal or restricted suffrage, or the Danish system, or any other system, is like ours. It is *not*. Other countries have restricted forms of suffrage by which individual women can be sorted out, so to speak. But America has equal manhood suffrage ingrained in her very state, in her very law. Once begin to give the suffrage to women, and there is but one end in this country. The question is always with us, "What effect will unrestricted female suffrage have on the state?" We must answer that question or beg the subject.

One thing is sure—the women's vote would be an indifferent one. The majority of women do not want to vote—even the suffragists acknowledge that. Therefore, if given the vote, they would not be eager voters. There would be a number of highly enthusiastic suffrage voters—for a while. But when the coveted privilege became a commonplace, or even an irksome duty, the stay-at-home vote would grow larger and larger. The greatest trouble in politics to-day is the indifferent vote among men. Equal suffrage would add a larger indifferent vote among women.

Then there is the corrupt vote to-day. Among men it is bad enough. But among women it would be much worse. What, for example, would the Tenderloin [red-light district] woman's vote be in New York? for good measures and better city politics? In Denver, it has been found to work just as might be supposed, and in Denver the female ward politician appeared full-fledged in the Shafroth case, in the full swing of bribery, and fraud. Unrestricted suffrage must reckon with all kinds of women, you see—and the unscrupulous woman will use her vote for what it is worth and for corrupt ends.

Today, without the vote, the women who are intelligent and interested in public affairs use their ability and influence for good measures. And the indifferent woman does not matter. The unscrupulous woman has no vote. We get the best, and bar out the rest. The state gets all the benefit of its best women, and none of the danger from its worst women. The situation is too

beneficial to need any change in the name of progress. We have now two against one, a fine majority, the good men and the good women against the unscrupulous men. Equal suffrage would make it two to two—the good men and the good women against the unscrupulous men and the unscrupulous women—a tie vote between good and evil instead of a safe majority for good.

Then, beside the indifferent vote and the corrupt vote, there would be, in equal suffrage, a well-meaning, unorganized vote. But government is not run in America by unorganized votes—it is run by organized parties. To get results, one vote is absurd. An effectual vote means organization; and organization means primaries and conventions, and caucuses and office-holding, and work, and work, and more work. A ballot dropped in a box is not government, or power. This is what men are fighting out in politics, and we women ought to understand their problem. One reason that I, personally, do not want the ballot is that I have been brought up, in the middle of politics in a state that is full of them, and I know the labor they entail on public-spirited men. Politics, to me, does not mean unearned power, or the registering of one's opinion on public affairs—it means hard work, incessant organization and combination, continual perseverance against disappointment and betrayal, steadfast effort for small and hard-fought advance. I have seen too many friends and relatives in that battle to want to push any woman into it. And unless one goes into the battle the ballot is of no force. The suffragists do not expect to. They expect and urge that all that will be necessary will be for each woman to "register her opinion" and cast her ballot and go home.

Where would the state be then—with an indifferent vote, a corrupt vote, and a helpless, unorganized vote, loaded on to its present political difficulties? Where would the state be with a doubled negro vote in the Black Belt? Where would New York and Chicago be with a doubled immigrant vote? I have two friends, sisters, one of them living in Utah, the other in Colorado—both suffrage states. The one in Colorado belongs to the indifferent vote. She is too busy to vote, and doesn't believe in it anyhow. The one in Utah goes to the polls regularly, not because she wants to vote, but because as she says "The Mormons vote all their women solidly, and we Gentiles have to vote as a duty—and how we wish we were back again under manhood suffrage." Is the state benefited by an unwilling electorate such as that?

FOR FURTHER READING

Jane Jerome Camhi, *Women Against Women: American Anti-Suffragism, 1880–1920.* Brooklyn, NY: Carlson Publishing, 1994.

Eleanor Cliff, *Founding Sisters and the Nineteenth Amendment.* Hoboken, NJ: John Wiley & Sons, 2003.

Mary H. Grant, *Private Woman, Public Person: An Account of the Life of Julia Ward Howe.* Brooklyn, NY: Carlson Publishing, 1994.

Jeff Hill, *Women's Suffrage.* Detroit, MI: Omnigraphics, 2006.

Thomas J. Jablonsky, *The Home, Heaven, and Mother Party: Female Anti-Suffragists in the United States, 1868–1920.* Brooklyn, NY: Carlson Publishing, 1994.

Rosalyn Terbog-Penn, *African American Women in the Struggle for the Vote, 1850–1920.* Bloomington: Indiana University Press, 1998.

Viewpoint 11A

Hetch Hetchy Valley Should Be Preserved (1912)

John Muir (1838–1914)

INTRODUCTION *John Muir, an explorer and naturalist, played a leading role in starting the conservation movement in the United States. A founder of the Sierra Club, Muir's writings and public campaigning led to the establishment in 1890 of Yosemite National Park (an area in California he had explored years earlier). The following viewpoint is taken from a chapter in Muir's 1912 book* The Yosemite, *describing the Hetch Hetchy Valley. The valley was the subject of an intense national debate when San Francisco city officials proposed to dam it to create a water supply for the city. Muir was the leading advocate for the "preservationist" view that Hetch Hetchy Valley and other wilderness areas should remain in their natural states.*

How does Muir characterize proponents of the dam? How are his views different from the conservation beliefs of Gifford Pinchot, author of the opposing viewpoint? What does the national controversy over the project reveal about changing American attitudes about natural resources?

Yosemite [Valley] is so wonderful that we are apt to regard it as an exceptional creation, the only valley of its kind in the world; but Nature is not so poor as to have only one of anything. Several other yosemites have been discovered in the Sierra that occupy the same relative positions on the [Sierra Nevada] Range and were formed by the same forces in the same kind of granite. One of these, the Hetch Hetchy Valley, is in the Yosemite National Park about twenty miles from Yosemite and is easily accessible to all sorts of travelers by a road and trail that leaves the Big Oak Flat road at Bronson Meadows a few miles below Crane Flat, and to mountaineers by way of Yosemite Creek basin and the head of the middle fork of the Tuolumne [River]. . . .

The floor of the Valley is about three and a half miles long, and from a fourth to half a mile wide. The lower portion is mostly a level meadow about a mile long, with the trees restricted to the sides and the river banks, and partially separated from the main, upper, forested portion by a low bar of glacier-polished granite across which the river breaks in rapids.

The principal trees are the yellow and sugar pines, digger pine, incense cedar, Douglas spruce, silver fir, the California and golden-cup oaks, balsam cottonwood, Nuttall's flowering dogwood, alder, maple, laurel, tumion, etc. The most abundant and influential are the great yellow or silver pines like those of Yosemite, the tallest over two hundred feet in height, and the oaks assembled in magnificent groves with massive rugged trunks four to six feet in diameter, and broad, shady, wide-spreading heads. The shrubs forming conspicuous flowery clumps and tangles are manzanita, azalea, spiraea, brier-rose, several species of ceanothus, calycanthus, philadelphus, wild cherry, etc.; with abundance of showy and fragrant herbaceous plants growing about them or out in the open in beds by themselves—lilies, Mariposa tulips, brodiaeas, orchids, iris, spraguea, draperia, collomia, collinsia, castilleja, nemophila, larkspur, columbine, goldenrods, sunflowers, mints of many species, honeysuckle, etc. Many fine ferns dwell here also, especially the beautiful and interesting rockferns—pellaea and cheilanthes of several species—fringing and rosetting dry rock-piles and ledges; woodwardia and asplenium on damp spots with fronds six or seven feet high; the delicate maidenhair in mossy nooks by the falls, and the sturdy, broad-shouldered pteris covering nearly all the dry ground beneath the oaks and pines.

It appears, therefore, that Hetch Hetchy Valley, far from being a plain, common, rock-bound meadow, as many who have not seen it seem to suppose, is a grand landscape garden, one of Nature's rarest and most precious mountain temples. As in Yosemite, the sublime rocks of its walls seem to glow with life, whether leaning back in repose or standing erect in thoughtful attitudes, giving welcome to storms and calms alike, their brows in the sky, their feet set in the groves and gay flowery meadows, while birds, bees, and butterflies help the river and waterfalls to stir all the air into music—things frail and fleeting and types of permanence meeting here and blending, just as they do in Yosemite, to draw her lovers into close and confiding communion with her.

THE VALLEY IN DANGER

Sad to say, this most precious and sublime feature of the Yosemite National Park, one of the greatest of all our natural resources for the uplifting joy and peace and health of the people, is in danger of being dammed and made

From John Muir, *The Yosemite* (New York: Century, 1912).

OPPOSING VIEWPOINTS IN AMERICAN HISTORY

into a reservoir to help supply San Francisco with water and light, thus flooding it from wall to wall and burying its gardens and groves one or two hundred feet deep. This grossly destructive commercial scheme has long been planned and urged (though water as pure and abundant can be got from sources outside of the people's park, in a dozen different places), because of the comparative cheapness of the dam and of the territory which it is sought to divert from the great uses to which it was dedicated in the Act of 1890 establishing the Yosemite National Park.

The making of gardens and parks goes on with civilization all over the world, and they increase both in size and number as their value is recognized. Everybody needs beauty as well as bread, places to play in and pray in, where Nature may heal and cheer and give strength to body and soul alike. This natural beauty-hunger is made manifest in the little windowsill gardens of the poor, though perhaps only a geranium slip in a broken cup, as well as in the carefully tended rose and lily gardens of the rich, the thousands of spacious city parks and botanical gardens, and in our magnificent National parks—the Yellowstone, Yosemite, Sequoia, etc.—Nature's sublime wonderlands, the admiration and joy of the world. Nevertheless, like anything else worth while, from the very beginning, however well guarded, they have always been subject to attack by despoiling gain-seekers and mischief-makers of every degree from Satan to Senators, eagerly trying to make everything immediately and selfishly commercial, with schemes disguised in smug-smiling philanthropy, industriously, sham-piously crying, "Conservation, conservation, panutilization," that man and beast may be fed and the dear Nation made great. . . .

MISLEADING ARGUMENTS

That any one would try to destroy such a place seems incredible; but sad experience shows that there are people good enough and bad enough for anything. The proponents of the dam scheme bring forward a lot of bad arguments to prove that the only righteous thing to do with the people's parks is to destroy them bit by bit as they are able. Their arguments are curiously like those of the devil, devised for the destruction of the first garden—so much of the very best Eden fruit going to waste; so much of the best Tuolumne water and Tuolumne scenery going to waste. Few of their statements are even partly true, and all are misleading.

Thus, Hetch Hetchy, they say, is a "low-lying meadow." On the contrary, it is a high-lying natural landscape garden. . . .

"It is a common minor feature, like thousands of others." On the contrary it is a very uncommon feature;

after Yosemite, the rarest and in many ways the most important in the National Park.

> *These . . . devotees of ravaging commercialism, seem to have a perfect contempt for Nature.*

"Damming and submerging it 175 feet deep would enhance its beauty by forming a crystal-clear lake." Landscape gardens, places of recreation and worship, are never made beautiful by destroying and burying them. The beautiful sham lake, forsooth, would be only an eyesore, a dismal blot on the landscape, like many others to be seen in the Sierra. For, instead of keeping it at the same level all the year, allowing Nature centuries of time to make new shores, it would, of course, be full only a month or two in the spring, when the snow is melting fast; then it would be gradually drained, exposing the slimy sides of the basin and shallower parts of the bottom, with the gathered drift and waste, death and decay of the upper basins, caught here instead of being swept on to decent natural burial along the banks of the river or in the sea. Thus the Hetch Hetchy dam-lake would be only a rough imitation of a natural lake for a few of the spring months, an open sepulcher for the others.

"Hetch Hetchy water is the purest of all to be found in the Sierra, unpolluted, and forever unpollutable." On the contrary, excepting that of the Merced below Yosemite, it is less pure than that of most of the other Sierra streams, because of the sewerage of camp grounds draining into it, especially of the Big Tuolumne Meadows camp ground, occupied by hundreds of tourists and mountaineers, with their animals, for months every summer, soon to be followed by thousands from all the world.

These temple destroyers, devotees of ravaging commercialism, seem to have a perfect contempt for Nature, and, instead of lifting their eyes to the God of the mountains, lift them to the Almighty Dollar.

Dam Hetch Hetchy! As well dam for water-tanks the people's cathedrals and churches, for no holier temple has ever been consecrated by the heart of man.

Viewpoint 11B
Hetch Hetchy Valley Should Be Dammed (1913)
Gifford Pinchot (1865–1946)

INTRODUCTION *Gifford Pinchot was director of the U.S. Department of Agriculture's Division of Forestry from 1898 to 1910 (the division was reorganized and renamed the U.S. Forest Service in 1905). His position and his friendship with Theodore Roosevelt, president of the United States from 1901 to 1909, made Pinchot one of America's leading conservationists. Pinchot advocated a multi-use approach to using federal lands and other natural resources—a position that sometimes placed him at odds with "preservationists" such as Sierra Club founder John Muir who called for the setting aside of lands for the sole purpose of wilderness protection.*

Pinchot's differences with preservationists were evident in the national debate over whether to dam the remote Hetch Hetchy Valley in Yosemite National Park. The project—intended to provide water for San Francisco—was bitterly opposed by Muir and other environmentalists. In the following viewpoint, taken from testimony given before Congress in 1913, Pinchot defends his support of the proposed dam as part of his general philosophy favoring the utilization of America's natural resources for the greatest good of the people. Pinchot's testimony helped persuade Congress to pass a bill authorizing the Hetch Hetchy dam.

What does Pinchot consider to be the fundamental goal of conservation? Judging from arguments presented in viewpoint 11A, how might John Muir respond to Pinchot's fundamental principle? How does Pinchot describe his differences with Muir?

We come now face to face with the perfectly clean question of what is the best use to which this water that flows out of the Sierras can be put. As we all know, there is no use of water that is higher than the domestic use. Then, if there is, as the engineers tell us, no other source of supply that is anything like so reasonably available as this one; if this is the best, and within reasonable limits of cost, the only means of supplying San Francisco with water, we come straight to the question of whether the advantage of leaving this valley in a state of nature is greater than the advantage of using it for the benefit of the city of San Francisco.

Now, the fundamental principle of the whole conservation policy is that of use, to take every part of the land and its resources and put it to that use in which it will best serve the most people, and I think there can be no question at all but that in this case we have an instance in which all weighty considerations demand the passage of the bill. There are, of course, a very large number of incidental changes that will arise after the passage of the bill. The construction of roads, trails, and telephone systems which will follow the passage of this bill will be a very important help in the park and forest reserves. The national forest telephone system and the roads and trails to which this bill will lead will form an important additional help in fighting fire in the forest reserves. . . . The

From Gifford Pinchot, testimony on the Hetch Hetchy dam site, *Congressional Record*, 63rd Cong., 1st sess., June 25, 1913.

presence of these additional means of communication will mean that the national forest and the national park will be visited by very large numbers of people who cannot visit them now. I think that the men who assert that it is better to leave a piece of natural scenery in its natural condition have rather the better of the argument, and I believe if we had nothing else to consider than the delight of the few men and women who would yearly go into the Hetch Hetchy Valley, then it should be left in its natural condition. But the considerations on the other side of the question to my mind are simply overwhelming, and so much so that I have never been able to see that there was any reasonable argument against the use of this water supply by the city of San Francisco. . . .

THE GREATEST GOOD

Mr. [John E.] Raker [U.S. Congressman from California]. Taking the scenic beauty of the park as it now stands, and the fact that the valley is sometimes swamped along in June and July, is it not a fact that if a beautiful dam is put there, as is contemplated, and as the picture is given by the engineers, with the roads contemplated around the reservoir and with other trails, it will be more beautiful than it is now, and give more opportunity for the use of the park?

Mr. Pinchot. Whether it will be more beautiful, I doubt, but the use of the park will be enormously increased. I think there is no doubt about that.

Mr. Raker. In other words, to put it a different way, there will be more beauty accessible than there is now?

Mr. Pinchot. Much more beauty will be accessible than now.

Mr. Raker. And by putting in roads and trails the Government, as well as the citizens of the Government, will get more pleasure out of it than at the present time?

Mr Pinchot. You might say from the standpoint of enjoyment of beauty and the greatest good to the greatest number, they will be conserved by the passage of this bill, and there will be a great deal more use of the beauty of the park than there is now.

Mr. Raker. Have you seen Mr. John Muir's criticism of the bill? You know him?

Mr. Pinchot. Yes, sir; I know him very well. He is an old and very good friend of mine. I have never been able to agree with him in his attitude toward the Sierras for the reason that my point of view has never appealed to him at all. When I became Forester and denied the right to exclude sheep and cows from the Sierras, Mr. Muir thought I had made a great mistake, because I allowed the use by an acquired right of a large number of people to interfere with what would have been the utmost beauty of the forest. In this case I think he has unduly given away to beauty as against use.

FOR FURTHER READING

William Dudley, ed., *The Environment (History of Issues)*. Farmington Hills, MI: Greenhaven, 2006.

Stephen R. Fox, *The American Conservation Movement: John Muir and His Legacy*. Madison: University of Wisconsin Press, 1985.

Samuel P. Hays, *Conservation and the Gospel of Efficiency: The Progressive Conservation Movement, 1890–1920*. New York: Atheneum, 1969.

Char Miller, *Gifford Pinchot and the Making of Modern Environmentalism*. Washington, DC: Island Press/Shearwater Books, 2001.

Robert W. Righter, *The Battle over Hetch Hetchy: America's Most Controversial Dam and the Birth of Modern Environmentalism*. New York: Oxford University Press, 2005.

Viewpoint 12A

The Federal Government Should Regulate Trusts: Roosevelt's New Nationalism (1910)

Theodore Roosevelt (1858–1919)

INTRODUCTION *Theodore Roosevelt served as president of the United States for seven-and-a-half years following the assassination of William McKinley in 1901. Under the slogan of giving Americans the "square deal," he instituted several Progressive reforms, including federal regulation of the railroad, food, and drug industries, federal "trust busting" lawsuits against large and monopolistic corporations, and expansion of the national parks system. Roosevelt remained active in politics after leaving office in 1909. Disappointed in the relatively conservative policies of his handpicked successor as president, William Howard Taft, Roosevelt became a leading advocate for greater federal government intervention in the economic and social development of the United States.*

In a famous speech to Civil War veterans at Osawatomie, Kansas, on August 31, 1910, Roosevelt spelled out his political philosophy, which he called the "New Nationalism." Roosevelt called for the establishment of government commissions to control (rather than break up) the large corporations and business trusts (monopolies) that were playing a growing role in American life. The speech, excerpted here, became the springboard for Roosevelt's political comeback, which ultimately split the Republican Party. Taft and Roosevelt both ran for president in 1912 (Roosevelt as candidate of the Progressive or "Bull Moose" Party), only to finish behind the Democratic candidate, Woodrow Wilson.

What does Roosevelt argue to be the proper function of government? What parts of the speech do you believe would be considered most objectionable to conservatives? Which elements differ most from the views of Woodrow Wilson as expressed in the opposing

viewpoint? How would you concisely define the New Nationalism?

In every wise struggle for human betterment one of the main objects, and often the only object, has been to achieve in large measure equality of opportunity. In the struggle for this great end, nations rise from barbarism to civilization, and through it people press forward from one stage of enlightenment to the next. One of the chief factors in progress is the destruction of special privilege. The essence of any struggle for healthy liberty has always been, and must always be, to take from some one man or class of men the right to enjoy power, or wealth, or position, or immunity, which has not been earned by service to his or their fellows. That is what you fought for in the Civil War, and that is what we strive for now....

Practical equality of opportunity for all citizens, when we achieve it, will have two great results. First, every man will have a fair chance to make of himself all that in him lies; to reach the highest point to which his capacities, unassisted by special privilege of his own and unhampered by the special privilege of others, can carry him, and to get for himself and his family substantially what he has earned. Second, equality of opportunity means that the commonwealth will get from every citizen the highest service of which he is capable. No man who carries the burden of the special privileges of another can give to the commonwealth that service to which it is fairly entitled.

THE SQUARE DEAL

I stand for the square deal. But when I say that I am for the square deal, I mean not merely that I stand for fair play under the present rules of the game, but that I stand for having those rules change so as to work for a more substantial equality of opportunity and of reward for equally good service....

Now, this means that our government, National and State, must be freed from the sinister influence or control of special interests. Exactly as the special interests of cotton and slavery threatened our political integrity before the Civil War, so now the great special business interests too often control and corrupt the men and methods of government for their own profit. We must drive the special interests out of politics. That is one of our tasks today. Every special interest is entitled to justice—full, fair, and complete—and, now, mind you, if there were any attempt by mob-violence to plunder and work harm to the special interest, whatever it may be, that I most dislike, and the wealthy man, whomsoever he may be, for whom I have the greatest contempt, I would

Excerpted from Theodore Roosevelt's campaign speech at Osawatomie, Kansas, August 31, 1910.

fight for him, and you would if you were worth your salt. He should have justice. For every special interest is entitled to justice, but not one is entitled to a vote in Congress, to a voice on the bench, or to representation in any public office. The Constitution guarantees protection to property, and we must make that promise good. But it does not give the right of suffrage to any corporation.

The true friend of property, the true conservative, is he who insists that property shall be the servant and not the master of the commonwealth; who insists that the creature of man's making shall be the servant and not the master of the man who made it. The citizens of the United States must effectively control the mighty commercial forces which they have themselves called into being. There can be no effective control of corporations while their political activity remains. To put an end to it will be neither a short nor an easy task, but it can be done.

We must have complete and effective publicity of corporate affairs, so that the people may know beyond peradventure whether the corporations obey the law and whether their management entitles them to the confidence of the public. It is necessary that laws should be passed to prohibit the use of corporate funds directly or indirectly for political purposes; it is still more necessary that such laws should be thoroughly enforced. Corporate expenditures for political purposes, and especially such expenditures by public service corporations, have supplied one of the principal sources of corruption in our political affairs.

GOVERNMENT SUPERVISION OF TRUSTS

It has become entirely clear that we must have government supervision of the capitalization, not only of public-service corporations, including, particularly, railways, but of all corporations doing an interstate business. I do not wish to see the nation forced into the ownership of the railways if it can possibly be avoided, and the only alternative is thoroughgoing and effective regulation, which shall be based on a full knowledge of all the facts, including a physical valuation of property. This physical valuation is not needed, or, at least, is very rarely needed, for fixing rates; but it is needed as the basis of honest capitalization.

---■---

The effort at prohibiting all combination has substantially failed.

---■---

We have come to recognize that franchises should never be granted except for a limited time, and never without proper provision for compensation to the public.

It is my personal belief that the same kind and degree of control and supervision which should be exercised over public-service corporations should be extended also to combinations which control necessaries of life, such as meat, oil, and coal, or which deal in them on an important scale. I have no doubt that the ordinary man who has control of them is much like ourselves. I have no doubt he would like to do well, but I want to have enough supervision to help him realize that desire to do well.

I believe that the officers, and, especially, the directors, of corporations should be held personally responsible when any corporation breaks the law.

Combinations in industry are the result of an imperative economic law which cannot be repealed by political legislation. The effort at prohibiting all combination has substantially failed. The way out lies, not in attempting to prevent such combinations, but in completely controlling them in the interest of the public welfare. For that purpose the Federal Bureau of Corporations is an agency of first importance. Its powers, and, therefore, its efficiency, as well as that of the Interstate Commerce Commission, should be largely increased. We have a right to expect from the Bureau of Corporations and from the Interstate Commerce Commission a very high grade of public service. We should be as sure of the proper conduct of the interstate railways and the proper management of interstate business as we are now sure of the conduct and management of the national banks, and we should have as effective supervision in one case as in the other. . . .

NATIONAL REGULATION OF WEALTH

Nothing is more true than that excess of every kind is followed by reaction; a fact which should be pondered by reformer and reactionary alike. We are face to face with new conceptions of the relations of property to human welfare, chiefly because certain advocates of the rights of property as against the rights of men have been pushing their claims too far. The man who wrongly holds that every human right is secondary to his profit must now give way to the advocate of human welfare, who rightly maintains that every man holds his property subject to the general right of the community to regulate its use to whatever degree the public welfare may require it.

But I think we may go still further. The right to regulate the use of wealth in the public interest is universally admitted. Let us admit also the right to regulate the terms and conditions of labor, which is the chief element of wealth, directly in the interest of the common good. The fundamental thing to do for every man is to give him a chance to reach a place in which he will make the greatest possible contribution to the public welfare.

Understand what I say there. Give him a chance, not push him up if he will not be pushed. Help any man who stumbles; if he lies down, it is a poor job to try to carry him; but if he is a worthy man, try your best to see that he gets a chance to show the worth that is in him. No man can be a good citizen unless he has a wage more than sufficient to cover the bare cost of living, and hours of labor short enough so that after his day's work is done he will have time and energy to bear his share in the management of the community, to help in carrying the general load. We keep countless men from being good citizens by the conditions of life with which we surround them. We need comprehensive workmen's compensation acts, both State and national laws to regulate child labor and work for women, and, especially we need in our common schools not merely education in book-learning, but also practical training for daily life and work. We need to enforce better sanitary conditions for our workers and to extend the use of safety appliances for our workers in industry and commerce, both within and between the States. Also, friends, in the interest of the working man himself we need to set our faces like flint against mob-violence just as against corporate greed; against violence and injustice and lawlessness by wage-workers just as much as against lawless cunning and greed and selfish arrogance of employers....

NATIONAL EFFICIENCY

National efficiency has many factors. It is a necessary result of the principle of conservation widely applied. In the end it will determine our failure or success as a nation. National efficiency has to do, not only with natural resources and with men, but it is equally concerned with institutions. The State must be made efficient for the work which concerns only the people of the State; and the nation for that which concerns all the people. There must remain no neutral ground to serve as a refuge for lawbreakers, and especially for lawbreakers of great wealth, who can hire the vulpine legal cunning which will teach them how to avoid both jurisdictions. It is a misfortune when the national legislature fails to do its duty in providing a national remedy, so that the only national activity is the purely negative activity of the judiciary in forbidding the State to exercise power in the premises.

I do not ask for overcentralization; but I do ask that we work in a spirit of broad and far-reaching nationalism when we work for what concerns our people as a whole. We are all Americans. Our common interests are as broad as the continent. I speak to you here in Kansas exactly as I would speak in New York or Georgia, for the most vital problems are those which affect us all alike. The National Government belongs to the whole American people, and

where the whole American people are interested, that interest can be guarded effectively only by the National Government. The betterment which we seek must be accomplished, I believe, mainly through the National Government.

The American people are right in demanding that New Nationalism, without which we cannot hope to deal with new problems. The New Nationalism puts the national need before sectional or personal advantage. It is impatient of the utter confusion that results from local legislatures attempting to treat national issues as local issues. It is still more impatient of the impotence which springs from overdivision of governmental powers, the impotence which makes it possible for local selfishness or for legal cunning, hired by wealthy special interests, to bring national activities to a deadlock. This New Nationalism regards the executive power as the steward of the public welfare. It demands of the judiciary that it shall be interested primarily in human welfare rather than in property, just as it demands that the representative body shall represent all the people rather than any one class or section of the people.

I believe in shaping the ends of government to protect property as well as human welfare. Normally, and in the long run, the ends are the same; but whenever the alternative must be faced, I am for men and not for property, as you were in the Civil War. I am far from underestimating the importance of dividends; but I rank dividends below human character. Again, I do not have any sympathy with the reformer who says he does not care for dividends. Of course, economic welfare is necessary, for a man must pull his own weight and be able to support his family. I know well that the reformers must not bring upon the people economic ruin, or the reforms themselves will go down in the ruin. But we must be ready to face temporary disaster, whether or not brought on by those who will war against us to the knife. Those who oppose all reform will do well to remember that ruin in its worst form is inevitable if our national life brings us nothing better than swollen fortunes for the few and the triumph in both politics and business of a sordid and selfish materialism.

The Federal Government Should Oppose Trusts: Wilson's New Freedom (1913)
Woodrow Wilson (1856–1924)

INTRODUCTION *Woodrow Wilson was elected president of the United States in 1912 and served two terms. The former academic, college president, and New Jersey governor benefited from a split in the Republican Party between supporters of incumbent president William Howard Taft and former president Theodore Roosevelt.*

In his campaign speeches, Wilson, a Democrat, differentiated himself from his opponents by emphasizing his opposition to business trusts and monopolies. He argued that the national government should take action to prevent large business concerns from squelching free market competition and amassing too much political and economic power. Wilson's proposals became known as the "New Freedom" in contrast to Roosevelt's "New Nationalism," which emphasized government regulations, not dismantling, of large corporations and trusts. Wilson's speeches were collected and edited into book form by William B. Hale and published in 1913 under the title The New Freedom. *The following viewpoint consists of excerpts from that volume.*

How does Wilson differentiate between big businesses and trusts? What are the main areas of disagreement between Wilson and Theodore Roosevelt, author of the opposing viewpoint? Are these differences fundamental, in your view?

Since I entered politics, I have chiefly had men's views confided to me privately. Some of the biggest men in the United States, in the field of commerce and manufacture, are afraid of somebody, are afraid of something. They know that there is a power somewhere so organized, so subtle, so watchful, so interlocked, so complete, so pervasive, that they had better not speak above their breath when they speak in condemnation of it.

They know that America is not a place of which it can he said, as it used to be, that a man may choose his own calling and pursue it just as far as his abilities enable him to pursue it; because to-day, if he enters certain fields, there are organizations which will use means against him that will prevent his building up a business which they do not want to have built up; organizations that will see to it that the ground is cut from under him and the markets shut against him. For if he begins to sell to certain retail dealers, to any retail dealers, the monopoly will refuse to sell to those dealers, and those dealers, afraid, will not buy the new man's wares.

NO LONGER A LAND
OF OPPORTUNITY

And this is the country which has lifted to the admiration of the world its ideals of absolutely free opportunity, where no man is supposed to be under any limitation except the limitations of his character and of his mind; where there is supposed to be no distinction of class, no distinction of blood, no distinction of social status, but where men win or lose on their merits.

I lay it very close to my own conscience as a public man whether we can any longer stand at our doors and

Excerpted from Woodrow Wilson, *The New Freedom* (New York: Doubleday, Page, and Co., 1913).

welcome all newcomers upon those terms. American industry is not free, as once it was free; American enterprise is not free; the man with only a little capital is finding it harder to get into the field, more and more impossible to compete with the big fellow. Why? Because the laws of this country do not prevent the strong from crushing the weak. That is the reason, and because the strong have crushed the weak the strong dominate the industry and the economic life of this country. No man can deny that the lines of endeavor have more and more narrowed and stiffened; no man who knows anything about the development of industry in this country can have failed to observe that the larger kinds of credit are more and more difficult to obtain, unless you obtain them upon the terms of uniting your efforts with those who already control the industries of the country; and nobody can fail to observe that any man who tries to set himself up in competition with any process of manufacture which has been taken under the control of large combinations of capital will presently find himself either squeezed out or obliged to sell and allow himself to be absorbed....

ARE TRUSTS INEVITABLE?

Gentlemen say, they have been saying for a long time, and, therefore, I assume that they believe, that trusts are inevitable. They don't say that big business is inevitable. They don't say merely that the elaboration of business upon a great co-operative scale is characteristic of our time and has come about by the natural operation of modern civilization. We would admit that. But they say that the particular kind of combinations that are now controlling our economic development came into existence naturally and were inevitable; and that, therefore, we have to accept them as unavoidable and administer our development through them. They take the analogy of the railways. The railways were clearly inevitable if we were to have transportation, but railways after they are once built stay put. You can't transfer a railroad at convenience; and you can't shut up one part of it and work another part. It is in the nature of what economists, those tedious persons, call natural monopolies; simply because the whole circumstances of their use are so stiff that you can't alter them. Such are the analogies which these gentlemen choose when they discuss the modern trust.

I admit the popularity of the theory that the trusts have come about through the natural development of business conditions in the United States, and that it is a mistake to try to oppose the processes by which they have been built up, because those processes belong to the very nature of business in our time, and that therefore the only thing we can do, and the only thing we ought to attempt to do, is to accept them as inevitable arrangements and make the best out of it that we can by regulation.

I answer, nevertheless, that this attitude rests upon a confusion of thought. Big business is no doubt to a large extent necessary and natural. The development of business upon a great scale, upon a great scale of cooperation, is inevitable, and, let me add, is probably desirable. But that is a very different matter from the development of trusts, because the trusts have not grown. They have been artificially created; they have been put together, not by natural processes, but by the will, the deliberate planning will, of men who were more powerful than their neighbors in the business world, and who wished to make their power secure against competition.

The trusts do not belong to the period of infant industries. They are not the products of the time, that old laborious time, when the great continent we live on was undeveloped, the young nation struggling to find itself and get upon its feet amidst older and more experienced competitors. They belong to a very recent and very sophisticated age, when men knew what they wanted and knew how to get it by the favor of the government.

Did you ever look into the way a trust was made? It is very natural, in one sense, in the same sense in which human greed is natural. If I haven't efficiency enough to beat my rivals, then the thing I am inclined to do is to get together with my rivals and say: "Don't let's cut each other's throats; let's combine and determine prices for ourselves; determine the output, and thereby determine the prices: and dominate and control the market." That is very natural. That has been done ever since freebooting was established. That has been done ever since power was used to establish control. . . .

I take my stand . . . on the proposition that private monopoly is indefensible and intolerable.

A trust is formed in this way: a few gentlemen "promote" it—that is to say, they get it up, being given enormous fees for their kindness, which fees are loaded on to the undertaking in the form of securities of one kind or another. The argument of the promoters is, not that every one who comes into the combination can carry on his business more efficiently than he did before; the argument is: we will assign to you as your share in the pool twice, three times, four times, or five times what you could have sold your business for to an individual competitor who would have to run it on an economic and competitive basis. We can afford to buy it at such a figure because we are shutting out competition. We can afford to make the stock of the combination half a dozen times what it naturally would be and pay dividends

on it, because there will be nobody to dispute the prices we shall fix.

Talk of that as sound business? Talk of that as inevitable? It is based upon nothing except power. It is not based upon efficiency. It is no wonder that the big trusts are not prospering in proportion to such competitors as they still have in such parts of their business as competitors have access to; they are prospering freely only in those fields to which competition has no access. . . .

UNFAIR COMPETITION

I take my stand absolutely, where every progressive ought to take his stand, on the proposition that private monopoly is indefensible and intolerable. And there I will fight my battle. And I know how to fight it. Everybody who has even read the newspapers knows the means by which these men built up their power and created these monopolies. Any decently equipped lawyer can suggest to you statutes by which the whole business can be stopped. What these gentlemen do not want is this: they do not want to be compelled to meet all comers on equal terms. I am perfectly willing that they should beat any competitor by fair means; but I know the foul means they have adopted, and I know that they can be stopped by law. If they think that coming into the market upon the basis of mere efficiency, upon the mere basis of knowing how to manufacture goods better than anybody else and to sell them cheaper than anybody else, they can carry the immense amount of water that they have put into their enterprises in order to buy up rivals, then they are perfectly welcome to try it. But there must be no squeezing out of the beginner, no crippling his credit; no discrimination against retailers who buy from a rival; no threats against concerns who sell supplies to a rival; no holding back of raw material from him; no secret arrangements against him. All the fair competition you choose, but no unfair competition of any kind. And then when unfair competition is eliminated, let us see these gentlemen carry their tanks of water on their backs. All that I ask and all I shall fight for is that they shall come into the field against merit and brains everywhere. If they can beat other American brains, then they have got the best brains. . . .

MONOPOLIES AND ROOSEVELT

The doctrine that monopoly is inevitable and that the only course open to the people of the United States is to submit to and regulate it found a champion during the campaign of 1912 in the new [Progressive] party, or branch of the Republican party, founded under the leadership of Mr. [Theodore] Roosevelt. . . .

You know that Mr. Roosevelt long ago classified trusts for us as good and bad, and he said that he was afraid only of the bad ones. Now he does not desire that there should be any more bad ones, but proposes that they should all be made good by discipline, directly applied by a commission of executive appointment. All he explicitly complains of is lack of publicity and lack of fairness; not the exercise of power, for throughout that plank [of the new party platform] the power of the great corporations is accepted as the inevitable consequence of the modern organization of industry. All that it is proposed to do is to take them under control and regulation. The national administration having for sixteen years been virtually under the regulation of the trusts, it would be merely a family matter were the parts reversed and were the other members of the family to exercise the regulation. And the trusts, apparently, which might, in such circumstances, comfortably continue to administer our affairs under the mollifying influences of the federal government, would then, if you please, be the instrumentalities by which all the humanistic, benevolent program of the rest of that interesting platform would be carried out!

The third [Roosevelt's] party says that the present system of our industry and trade has come to stay. Mind you, these artificially built up things, these things that can't maintain themselves in the market without monopoly, have come to stay, and the only thing that the government can do, the only thing that the third party proposes should be done, is to set up a commission to regulate them. It accepts them. It says: "We will not undertake, it were futile to undertake, to prevent monopoly, but we will go into an arrangement by which we will make these monopolies kind to you. We will guarantee that they shall be pitiful. We will guarantee that they shall pay the right wages. We will guarantee that they shall do everything kind and public-spirited, which they have never heretofore shown the least inclination to do."

Don't you realize that that is a blind alley? You can't find your way to liberty that way. You can't find your way to social reform through the forces that have made social reform necessary. . . .

When you have thought the whole thing out, therefore, you will find that the program of the new party legalizes monopolies and systematically subordinates workingmen to them and to plans made by the government both with regard to employment and with regard to wages. Take the thing as a whole, and it looks strangely like economic mastery over the very lives and fortunes of those who do the daily work of the nation; and all this under the overwhelming power and sovereignty of the national government. What most of us are fighting for is to break up this very partnership between big business and the government. We call upon all intelligent men to bear witness that if this plan were consummated, the great employers and capitalists of the country would be under a more overpowering temptation than ever to take control

of the government and keep it subservient to their purpose. . . .

MONOPOLIES CANNOT CHANGE

I do not trust any promises of a change of temper on the part of monopoly. Monopoly never was conceived in the temper of tolerance. Monopoly never was conceived with the purpose of general development. It was conceived with the purpose of special advantage. Has monopoly been very benevolent to its employees? Have the trusts had a soft heart for the working people of America? Have you found trusts that cared whether women were sapped of their vitality or not? Have you found trusts who are very scrupulous about using children in their tender years? Have you found trusts that were keen to protect the lungs and the health and the freedom of their employees? Have you found trusts that thought as much of their men as they did of their machinery? Then who is going to convert these men into the chief instruments of justice benevolence? . . .

The reason that America was set up was that she might be different from all the nations of the world in this: that the strong could not put the weak to the wall, that the strong could not prevent the weak from entering the race. America stands for opportunity. America stands for a free field and no favor. America stands for a government responsive to the interests of all. And until America recovers those ideals in practice, she will not have the right to hold her head high again amidst the nations as she used to hold it.

FOR FURTHER READING

James Chace, *1912: Wilson, Roosevelt, Taft & Debs—The Election that Changed the Country*. New York: Simon & Schuster, 2004.

John Milton Cooper, *The Warrior and the Priest: Woodrow Wilson and Theodore Roosevelt*. Cambridge, MA: Belknap Press, 1983.

John A. Gable, *The Bull Moose Years: Theodore Roosevelt and the Progressive Party*. Port Washington, NY: Kennikat Press, 1978.

Edwin Charles Rozwenc, *Roosevelt, Wilson and the Trusts*. Boston: D.C. Heath, 1953.

WORLD WAR I AND THE LEAGUE OF NATIONS

Viewpoint 13A

America Should Enter World War I (1917)

Woodrow Wilson (1856–1917)

INTRODUCTION *When the countries of Europe plunged into war in 1914, Woodrow Wilson asked all Americans to "act and speak in the true spirit of neutrality." Wilson managed to maintain U.S. neutrality for the next thirty months, and made the slogan "He kept us out of war" part of his successful reelection campaign in 1916. On April 2, 1917, however, he appeared before a joint session of Congress to ask for a declaration of war against Germany.*

Wilson's address, excerpted here, tried to answer two major questions: (1) Why had America changed its stance from neutrality to hostility toward Germany? and (2) What did America hope to achieve by entering the war? Wilson emphasized the problems caused by German submarine warfare in answering the first question. Through diplomatic pressure, Wilson had managed to get Germany to restrict its use of submarines against American ships and those of other neutral nations. In January 1917, however, Germany resumed a policy of unrestricted submarine warfare, and American ships were being sunk without warning. In answering the second question Wilson established some idealistic goals beyond the mere defeat of Germany: America was fighting to "end all wars" and make the world "safe for democracy."

How has Germany effectively declared war on the United States, according to Wilson? What does he consider to be America's wartime objectives? What does he say are not *America's objectives?*

I have called the Congress into extraordinary session because there are serious, very serious, choices of policy to be made, and made immediately, which it was neither right nor constitutionally permissible that I should assume the responsibility of making.

On the 3rd of February last, I officially laid before you the extraordinary announcement of the Imperial German government that on and after the 1st day of February it was its purpose to put aside all restraints of law or of humanity and use its submarines to sink every vessel that sought to approach either the ports of Great Britain and Ireland or the western coasts of Europe or any of the ports controlled by the enemies of Germany within the Mediterranean.

That had seemed to be the object of the German submarine warfare earlier in the war, but since April of last year (1916) the Imperial government had somewhat restrained the commanders of its undersea craft in conformity with its promise then given to us that passenger boats should not be sunk and that due warning would be given to all other vessels which its submarines might seek to destroy, when no resistance was offered or escape attempted, and care taken that their crews were given at least a fair chance to save their lives in their open boats. The precautions taken were meager and haphazard enough, as was proved in distressing instance after instance in the progress of the cruel and

Excerpted from Woodrow Wilson's April 2, 1917, address to Congress, 65th Cong., 1st sess., Sen. Doc. 5.

unmanly business, but a certain degree of restraint was observed.

The new policy has swept every restriction aside. Vessels of every, kind, whatever their flag, their character, their cargo, their destination, their errand, have been ruthlessly sent to the bottom without warning and without thought of help or mercy for those on board, the vessels of friendly neutrals along with those of belligerents. Even hospital ships and ships carrying relief to the sorely bereaved and stricken people of Belgium, though the latter were provided with safe conduct through the proscribed areas by the German government itself and were distinguished by unmistakable marks of identity, have been sunk with the same reckless lack of compassion or of principle. . . .

We will not choose the path of submission and suffer the most sacred rights of . . . our people to be ignored or violated.

NOT JUST AMERICA'S WAR

The present German submarine warfare against commerce is a warfare against mankind. It is a war against all nations. American ships have been sunk, American lives taken in ways which it has stirred us very deeply to learn of; but the ships and people of other neutral and friendly nations have been sunk and overwhelmed in the waters in the same way. There has been no discrimination. The challenge is to all mankind.

Each nation must decide for itself how it will meet it. The choice we make for ourselves must be made with a moderation of counsel and a temperateness of judgment befitting our character and our motives as a nation. We must put excited feeling away. Our motive will not be revenge or the victorious assertion of the physical might of the nation, but only the vindication of right, of human right, of which we are only a single champion.

When I addressed the Congress on the 26th of February last, I thought that it would suffice to assert our neutral rights with arms, our right to use the seas against unlawful interference, our right to keep our people safe against unlawful violence. But armed neutrality, it now appears, is impracticable. Because submarines are in effect outlaws when used as the German submarines have been used against merchant shipping, it is impossible to defend ships against their attacks as the law of nations has assumed that merchantmen would defend themselves against privateers or cruisers, visible craft giving chase upon the open sea. . . .

There is one choice we cannot make, we are incapable of making: we will not choose the path of submission and suffer the most sacred rights of our nation and our people to be ignored or violated. The wrongs against which we now array ourselves are no common wrongs; they cut to the very roots of human life.

With a profound sense of the solemn and even tragical character of the step I am taking and of the grave responsibilities which it involves, but in unhesitating obedience to what I deem my constitutional duty, I advise that the Congress declare the recent course of the Imperial German government to be in fact nothing less than war against the government and people of the United States; that it formally accept the status of belligerent which has thus been thrust upon it; and that it take immediate steps, not only to put the country in a more thorough state of defense but also to exert all its power and employ all its resources to bring the government of the German Empire to terms and end the war. . . .

AMERICA'S OBJECT

Our object now, as then, is to vindicate the principles of peace and justice in the life of the world as against selfish and autocratic power and to set up among the really free and self-governed peoples of the world such a concert of purpose and of action as will henceforth ensure the observance of those principles. Neutrality is no longer feasible or desirable where the peace of the world is involved and the freedom of its peoples, and the menace to that peace and freedom lies in the existence of autocratic governments backed by organized force which is controlled wholly by their will, not by the will of their people. We have seen the last of neutrality in such circumstances. We are at the beginning of an age in which it will be insisted that the same standards of conduct and of responsibility for wrong done shall be observed among nations and their governments that are observed among the individual citizens of civilized states.

We have no quarrel with the German people. We have no feeling toward them but one of sympathy and friendship. It was not upon their impulse that their government acted in entering this war. It was not with their previous knowledge or approval. It was a war determined upon as wars used to be determined upon in the old, unhappy days when peoples were nowhere consulted by their rulers and wars were provoked and waged in the interest of dynasties or of little groups of ambitious men who were accustomed to use their fellowmen as pawns and tools.

Self-governed nations do not fill their neighbor states with spies or set the course of intrigue to bring about some critical posture of affairs which will give them an opportunity to strike and make conquest. Such designs can be successfully worked out only under cover and where no one has the right to ask questions. Cunningly contrived plans of deception or aggression, carried, it may be, from generation to generation, can be worked out and kept from the light only within the privacy of courts or behind the carefully guarded confidences of a narrow and privileged class. They are happily impossible where public opinion commands and insists upon full information concerning all the nation's affairs. . . .

The world must be made safe for democracy. Its peace must be planted upon the tested foundations of political liberty. We have no selfish ends to serve. We desire no conquest, no dominion. We seek no indemnities for ourselves, no material compensation for the sacrifices we shall freely make. We are but one of the champions of the rights of mankind. We shall be satisfied when those rights have been made as secure as the faith and the freedom of nations can make them. . . .

We have borne with their present government through all these bitter months because of that friendship—exercising a patience and forbearance which would otherwise have been impossible. We shall, happily, still have an opportunity to prove that friendship in our daily attitude and actions toward the millions of men and women of German birth and native sympathy who live among us and share our life, and we shall be proud to prove it toward all who are in fact loyal to their neighbors and to the government in the hour of test. They are, most of them, as true and loyal Americans as if they had never known any other fealty or allegiance. They will be prompt to stand with us in rebuking and restraining the few who may be of a different mind and purpose. If there should be disloyalty, it will be dealt with with a firm hand of stern repression; but, if it lifts its head at all, it will lift it only here and there and without countenance except from a lawless and malignant few.

FIGHT FOR DEMOCRACY

It is a distressing and oppressive duty, gentlemen of the Congress, which I have performed in thus addressing you. There are, it may be, many months of fiery trial and sacrifice ahead of us. It is a fearful thing to lead this great peaceful people into war, into the most terrible and disastrous of all wars, civilization itself seeming to be in the balance. But the right is more precious than peace, and we shall fight for the things which we have always carried nearest our hearts—for democracy, for the right of those who submit to authority to have a voice in their own governments, for the rights and liberties of small nations, for a universal dominion of right by such a concert of free peoples as shall bring peace and safety to all nations and make the world itself at last free.

To such a task we can dedicate our lives and our fortunes, everything that we are and everything that we have, with the pride of those who know that the day has come when America is privileged to spend her blood and her might for the principles that gave her birth and happiness and the peace which she has treasured. God helping her, she can do no other.

America Should Not Enter World War I (1917)

George W. Norris (1861–1944)

INTRODUCTION *President Woodrow Wilson's call in 1917 for a declaration of war against Germany was opposed in Congress by fifty representatives and six senators, one of whom was George W. Norris of Nebraska. Norris, a Progressive Republican, had served for thirteen years in Congress. The following viewpoint is excerpted from his speech before Congress given on April 4, 1917, opposing war. Norris questions America's prior commitment to neutrality (arguing that U.S. policy had actually favored Germany's enemy Great Britain), and contends that the main supporters and beneficiaries of war would be Wall Street financiers (who had loaned money to Great Britain), industrialists, and wealthy Americans in general.*

Why is Great Britain as much to blame as Germany for violating American neutrality rights, according to Norris? What are America's objectives in entering the war, according to Norris? How do they differ from those offered by Woodrow Wilson in the opposing viewpoint?

The resolution now before the Senate is a declaration of war. Before taking this momentous step, and while standing on the brink of this terrible vortex, we ought to pause and calmly and judiciously consider the terrible consequences of the step we are about to take. We ought to consider likewise the route we have recently traveled and ascertain whether we have reached our present position in a way that is compatible with the neutral position which we claimed to occupy at the beginning and through the various stages of this unholy and unrighteous war.

No close student of recent history will deny that both Great Britain and Germany have, on numerous occasions since the beginning of the war, flagrantly violated in the most serious manner the rights of neutral vessels and neutral nations under existing international law as recognized up to the beginning of this war by the civilized world.

The reason given by the President in asking Congress to declare war against Germany is that the German Government has declared certain war zones, within which, by the use of submarines, she sinks, without notice, American ships and destroys American lives.

From George W. Norris, *Congressional Record*, 65th Cong., 1st sess. (April 4, 1917), pp. 212–214.

WAR ZONES

Let us trace briefly the origin and history of these so-called war zones. The first war zone was declared by Great Britain. She gave us and the world notice of it on the 4th day of November, 1914. The zone became effective November 5, 1914, the next day after the notice was given. This zone so declared by Great Britain covered the whole of the North Sea....

The first German war zone was declared on the 4th day of February, 1915, just three months after the British war zone was declared. Germany gave 15 days' notice of the establishment of her zone, which became effective on the 18th day of February, 1915. The German war zone covered the English Channel and the high sea waters around the British Isles....

It will thus be seen that the British Government declared the north of Scotland route into the Baltic Sea as dangerous and the English Channel route into the Baltic Sea as safe.

The German Government in its order did exactly the reverse. It declared the north of Scotland route into the Baltic Sea as safe and the English Channel route into the Baltic Sea as dangerous....

Thus we have the two declarations of the two Governments, each declaring a military zone and warning neutral shipping from going into the prohibited area. England sought to make her order effective by the use of submerged mines. Germany sought to make her order effective by the use of submarines. Both of these orders were illegal and contrary to all international law as well as the principles of humanity. Under international law no belligerent Government has the right to place submerged mines in the high seas. Neither has it any right to take human life without notice by the use of submarines. If there is any difference on the ground of humanity between these two instrumentalities, it is certainly in favor of the submarines. The submarine can exercise some degree of discretion and judgment. The submerged mine always destroys without notice, friend and foe alike, guilty and innocent the same. In carrying out these two policies, both Great Britain and Germany have sunk American ships and destroyed American lives without provocation and without notice. There have been more ships sunk and more American lives lost from the action of submarines than from English mines in the North Sea: for the simple reason that we finally acquiesced in the British war zone and kept our ships out of it, while in the German war zone we have refused to recognize its legality and have not kept either our ships or our citizens out of its area. If American ships had gone into the British war zone in defiance of Great Britain's order, as they have gone into the German war zone in defiance of the German Government's order, there would have been many more American lives lost and many more American ships sunk by the instrumentality of the mines than the instrumentality of the submarines....

What was our duty as a Government and what were our rights when we were confronted with these extraordinary orders declaring these military zones? First, we could have defied both of them and could have gone to war against both of these nations for this violation of international law and interference with our neutral rights. Second, we had the technical right to defy one and to acquiesce in the other. Third, we could, while denouncing them both as illegal, have acquiesced in them both and thus remained neutral with both sides, although not agreeing with either as to the righteousness of their respective orders.

There are a great many American citizens who feel that we owe it as a duty to humanity to take part in this war. Many instances of cruelty and inhumanity can be found on both sides. Men are often biased in their judgment on account of their sympathy and their interests. To my mind, what we ought to have maintained from the beginning was the strictest neutrality. If we had done this I do not believe we would have been on the verge of war at the present time. We had a right as a nation, if we desired, to cease at any time to be neutral. We had a technical right to respect the English war zone and to disregard the German war zone, but we could not do that and be neutral. I have no quarrel to find with the man who does not desire our country to remain neutral. While many such people are moved by selfish motives and hopes of gain, I have no doubt but that in a great many instances, through what I believe to be a misunderstanding of the real condition, there are many honest, patriotic citizens who think we ought to engage in this war and who are behind the President in his demand that we should declare war against Germany. I think such people err in judgment and to a great extent have been misled as to the real history and the true facts by the almost unanimous demand of the great combination of wealth that has a direct financial interest in our participation in the war. We have loaned many hundreds of millions of dollars to the allies in this controversy. While such action was legal and countenanced by international law, there is no doubt in my mind but the enormous amount of money loaned to the allies in this country has been instrumental in bringing about a public sentiment in favor of our country taking a course that would make every bond worth a hundred cents on the dollar and making the payment of every debt certain and sure. Through this instrumentality and also through the instrumentality of others who have not only made millions out of the war in the manufacture of munitions, etc., and who would expect to make millions more if our country can be drawn into the catastrophe, a large

number of the great newspapers and news agencies of the country have been controlled and enlisted in the greatest propaganda that the world has ever known, to manufacture sentiment in favor of war. It is now demanded that the American citizens shall be used as insurance policies to guarantee the safe delivery of munitions of war to belligerent nations. The enormous profits of munition manufacturers, stockbrokers, and bond dealers must be still further increased by our entrance into the war. This has brought us to the present moment, when Congress, urged by the President and backed by the artificial sentiment, is about to declare war and engulf our country in the greatest holocaust that the world has ever known....

WAR BRINGS PROSPERITY TO SOME

To whom does war bring prosperity? Not to the soldier who for the munificent compensation of $16 per month shoulders his musket and goes into the trench, there to shed his blood and to die if necessary; not to the brokenhearted widow who waits for the return of the mangled body of her husband; not to the mother who weeps at the death of her brave boy; not to the little children who shiver with cold; not to the babe who suffers from hunger; nor to the millions of mothers and daughters who carry broken hearts to their graves. War brings no prosperity to the great mass of common and patriotic citizens. It increases the cost of living of those who toil and those who already must strain every effort to keep soul and body together. War brings prosperity to the stock gambler on Wall Street—to those who are already in possession of more wealth than can be realized or enjoyed....

Their object in having war and in preparing for war is to make money. Human suffering and the sacrifice of human life are necessary, but Wall Street considers only the dollars and the cents. The men who do the fighting, the people who make the sacrifices, are the ones who will not be counted in the measure of this great prosperity.... The stock brokers would not, of course, go to war, because the very object they have in bringing on the war is profit, and therefore they must remain in their Wall Street offices in order to share in that great prosperity which they say war will bring. The volunteer officer, even the drafting officer, will not find them. They will be concealed in their palatial offices on Wall Street, sitting behind mahogany desks, covered up with clipped coupons—coupons soiled with the sweat of honest toil, coupons stained with mothers' tears, coupons dyed in the lifeblood of their fellow men.

———————◼———————

The troubles of Europe ought to be settled by Europe.

———————◼———————

We are taking a step to-day that is fraught with untold danger. We are going into war upon the command of gold. We are going to run the risk of sacrificing millions of our countrymen's lives in order that other countrymen may coin their lifeblood into money. And even if we do not cross the Atlantic and go into the trenches, we are going to pile up a debt that the toiling masses that shall come many generations after us will have to pay. Unborn millions will bend their backs in toil in order to pay for the terrible step we are now about to take. We are about to do the bidding of wealth's terrible mandate. By our act we will make millions of our countrymen suffer, and the consequences of it may well be that millions of our brethren must shed their lifeblood, millions of broken-hearted women must weep, millions of children must suffer with cold, and millions of babes must die from hunger, and all because we want to preserve the commercial right of American citizens to deliver munitions of war to belligerent nations....

A DOLLAR SIGN ON THE FLAG

I know that I am powerless to stop it. I know that this war madness has taken possession of the financial and political powers of our country. I know that nothing I can say will stay the blow that is soon to fall. I feel that we are committing a sin against humanity and against our countrymen. I would like to say to this war god, You shall not coin into gold the lifeblood of my brethren. I would like to prevent this terrible catastrophe from falling upon my people. I would be willing to surrender my own life if I could cause this awful cup to pass. I charge no man here with a wrong motive, but it seems to me that this war craze has robbed us of our judgment. I wish we might delay our action until reason could again be enthroned in the brain of man. I feel that we are about to put the dollar sign upon the American flag.

I have no sympathy with the military spirit that dominates the Kaiser and his advisers. I do not believe that they represent the heart of the great German people. I have no more sympathy with the submarine policy of Germany than I have with the mine-laying policy of England. I have heard with rejoicing of the overthrow of the Czar of Russia and the movement in that great country toward the establishment of a government where the common people will have their rights, liberty, and freedom respected. I hope and pray that a similar revolution may take place in Germany that the Kaiser may be overthrown, and that on the ruins of his military despotism may be established a German republic, where the great German people may work out their world destiny. The working out of that problem is not an American burden. We ought to remember the advice of the Father of our Country [George Washington] and keep out of entangling alliances. Let Europe solve her problems as we have solved ours. Let Europe bear her burdens as we have borne ours. In the greatest war of our history and at the time it occurred, the greatest war in the world's history, we were engaged in solving an American problem. We settled the question of human slavery and washed our flag clean by the sacrifice of human blood. It was a great problem and a great burden, but we solved it ourselves. Never once did we think of asking Europe to take part in its solution. Never once did any European nation undertake to settle the great question. We solved it, and history has rendered a unanimous verdict that we solved it right. The troubles of Europe ought to be settled by Europe, and wherever our sympathies may lie, disagreeing as we do, we ought to remain absolutely neutral and permit them to settle their questions without our interference. We are now the greatest neutral nation. Upon the passage of this resolution we will have joined Europe in the great catastrophe and taken America into entanglements that will not end with this war, but will live and bring their evil influences upon many generations yet unborn.

FOR FURTHER READING

Martin Marix Evans, ed., *American Voices of World War I*, Chicago: Fitzroy Dearborn, 2001.

Robert H. Ferrell, *Woodrow Wilson and World War I*. New York: Harper & Row, 1985.

Seward W. Livermore, *Politics Is Adjourned: Woodrow Wilson and the War Congress, 1916–1918*. Middletown, CT: Wesleyan University Press, 1966.

Earnest R. May, *The World War and American Isolation, 1914–1917*. Cambridge, MA: Harvard University Press, 1959.

H.C. Peterson and Gilbert C. Fite, *Opponents of War, 1917–1918*. Seattle: University of Washington Press, 1968.

Viewpoint 14A

War Dissenters' Freedoms of Speech and Assembly Must Be Preserved (1917)

Robert La Follette (1855–1925)

INTRODUCTION *Robert La Follette, a senator representing Wisconsin from 1906 to 1925, was one of six members of the U.S. Senate who voted against President Woodrow Wilson's call for a declaration of war against Germany in 1917. His opposition made the senator and former Wisconsin governor, previously best known for his oratory and success in bringing progressive reforms to fruition, an object of national vilification. Former president Theodore Roosevelt and others called for his expulsion from the Senate. A judge in Texas suggested in one instance that La Follette and his dissenting colleagues should be shot as traitors.*

The following viewpoint is excerpted from an October 1917 speech La Follette made in the Senate in response to criticism he and other war critics were receiving. La Follette argues that many Americans who opposed sending soldiers to fight in Europe had been unlawfully jailed or had their constitutional rights of free speech and assembly violated by overzealous supporters of the war. He contends that the nation's civil liberties should not be dropped in time of war.

What examples of violations of civil liberties does La Follette describe? How does war affect the citizen's relationship with the government, according to La Follette?

Six Members of the Senate and 50 Members of the House voted against the declaration of war. Immediately there was let loose upon those Senators and Representatives a flood of invective and abuse from newspapers and individuals who had been clamoring for war, unequaled, I believe, in the history of civilized society.

Prior to the declaration of war every man who had ventured to oppose our entrance into it had been condemned as a coward or worse, and even the President had by no means been immune from these attacks.

Since the declaration of war the triumphant war press has pursued those Senators and Representatives who voted against war with malicious falsehood and recklessly libelous attacks, going to the extreme limit of charging them with treason against their country.

This campaign of libel and character assassination directed against the Members of Congress who opposed our entrance into the war has been continued down to the present hour, and I have upon my desk newspaper clippings, some of them libels upon me alone, some directed as well against other Senators who voted in opposition to the declaration of war....

If I alone had been made the victim of these attacks, I should not take one moment of the Senate's time for their consideration, and I believe that other Senators who have been unjustly and unfairly assailed, as I have been, hold the same attitude upon this that I do. *Neither the clamor of the mob nor the voice of power will ever turn me by the breadth of a hair from the course I mark out for myself, guided by such knowledge as I can obtain and controlled and directed by a solemn connection of right and duty....*

But, sir, it is not alone Members of Congress that the war party in this country has sought to intimidate. The mandate seems to have gone forth to the sovereign people of this country that they must be silent while those things are being done by their Government which most vitally concern their well-being, their happiness, and their lives.

Robert La Follette, address to the U.S. Senate, *Congressional Record*, October 6, 1917, 65th Cong., 1st sess., pp. 7878–79.

PEOPLE BEING TERRORIZED

Today—for weeks past—honest and law-abiding citizens of this country are being terrorized and outraged in their rights by those sworn to uphold the laws and protect the rights of the people. I have in my possession numerous affidavits establishing the fact that people are being unlawfully arrested, thrown into jail, held incommunicado for days, only to be eventually discharged without ever having been taken into court, because they have committed no crime. Private residences are being invaded, loyal citizens of undoubted integrity and probity arrested, cross-examined, and the most sacred constitutional rights guaranteed to every American citizen are being violated.

It appears to be the purpose of those conducting this campaign to throw the country into a state of terror, to coerce public opinion, to stifle criticism, and suppress discussion of the great issues involved in this war.

I think all men recognize that in time of war the citizen must surrender some rights for the common good which he is entitled to enjoy in time of peace. *But, sir, the right to control their own Government, according to constitutional forms, is not one of the rights that the citizens of this country are called upon to surrender in time of war.*

Rather, in time of war, the citizen must be more alert to the preservation of his right to control his Government. He must be most watchful of the encroachment of the military upon the civil power. He must beware of those precedents in support of arbitrary action by administrative officials which, excused on the plea of necessity in wartime, become the fixed rule when the necessity has passed and normal conditions have been restored.

Our government . . . is founded on the right of the people to freely discuss all matters pertaining to their Government, in war not less than in peace.

PROTECTING FREE SPEECH

More than all, the citizen and his representative in Congress in time of war must maintain his right of free speech. More than in times of peace, it is necessary that the channels for free public discussion of governmental policies shall be open and unclogged.

I believe, Mr. President, that I am now touching upon the most important question in this country today—and that is the right of the citizens of this country and their representatives in Congress to discuss in an orderly way, frankly and publicly and without fear, from the platform and through the press, every important phase of this war; its causes, the manner in which it should be conduced, and the terms upon which peace should be made. . . .

I am contending for this right, because the exercise of it is necessary to the welfare, to the existence, of this Government, to the successful conduct of this war, and to a peace which shall be enduring and for the best interest of this country. . . .

Mr. President, our Government, above all others, is founded on the right of the people freely to discuss all matters pertaining to their Government, in war not less than in peace. . . . How can that popular will express itself between elections except by meetings, by speeches, by publications, by petitions, and by addresses to the representatives of the people?

Any man who seeks to set a limit upon those rights, whether in war or peace, aims a blow at the most vital part of our Government. And then as the time for election approaches, and the official is called to account for his stewardship—not a day, not a week, not a month, before the election, but a year or more before it, if the people choose—they must have the right to the freest possible discussion of every question upon which their representative has acted, of the merits of every measure he has supported or opposed, of every vote he has cast and every speech that he has made. And before this great fundamental right every other must, if necessary, give way, for in no other manner can representative government be preserved.

Viewpoint 14B

War Dissenters' Freedoms of Speech and Assembly Must Be Limited (1917)

Outlook

INTRODUCTION *Opponents and critics of America's decision to enter World War I often faced significant obstacles in acting on their beliefs. For example, when the People's Council for Democracy and Peace, an antiwar organization, tried to hold a national convention, they found themselves unable to find a meeting place as cities and states issued edicts banning all meetings of groups opposing the war. The following viewpoint in support of such measures is excerpted from an editorial in the magazine* Outlook. *Referring briefly to the controversy over the People's Council's troubles, the editors argue that speech and public meetings that give "aid and comfort to the enemy" are not protected under the Constitution, and that state and local governments have the right to prevent such meetings from taking place.*

What responsibilities do local authorities have in protecting the right of free assembly, according to Outlook? *What constitutes treason, according to the editors?*

There are no rights which do not imply corresponding duties and obligations. Of no rights is this truer than of the right of free speech and public assembly.

Apparently the great majority of those who are agitating against the Draft Law [the 1917 Selective Service Act] and who are pleading for an early peace—a peace which of necessity would be a German peace—have failed to understand this fundamental principle which underlies the right of free speech and free public assembly. A concrete instance of this misunderstanding has recently occupied a larger space than it deserved in the public prints. We refer to the agitation over the pacifist convention which has been denied the right of assembly in more than one State of the Union.

A FUNDAMENTAL RIGHT

No one denies, on the one hand, that the right of free assembly in a republic is one of the fundamental rights of the citizen. Democracy is imperiled without it. The people must be free to meet and to discuss public questions. And the mere fact that there is such a state of public feeling that an assembly may be broken into by a mob does not justify the prohibition of such an assembly. The right of free assembly must, however, be maintained by the authorities even in the face of threatened riots. This right to assemble is based on the purpose of the assembly. It is not limited by the danger or lack of danger of public disorder.

For example, the citizens of East St. Louis have a lawful right to meet and protest against the recent lynching of Negroes in that city. Any fear of riots caused by the rougher elements of East St. Louis would not justify the authorities from prohibiting such an assembly. If the Mayor did not have the power to protect such an assembly, he might temporarily postpone it, but only in order to enable him to call on the Governor, and, if necessary, on the President, for forces sufficient to keep order and to protect the right of free assembly. It must always be remembered that this right to free assembly even under the circumstances which we have described does not justify any body of citizens in claiming a right to use the public streets or the public parks for the purpose of such an assembly. They have no more right to take public property for such a purpose than they have to take private property without the consent of its owner.

There is, on the other hand, nothing in the right of free assembly which entitles any body of citizens to hold a meeting for an unlawful purpose on either public or private property, no matter how freely permission to hold such a meeting may be granted by the owners or owner. Burglars or train robbers have no right to meet for the purpose of planning a robbery. Before the Civil

Reprinted from "The Right of Public Assembly," *Outlook*, September 17, 1917.

War the border ruffians of Missouri had no right to meet for the purpose of planning a raid upon Kansas, and to-day the liquor-sellers and bootleggers of Kansas have no right to meet in order to plan a scheme of organized resistance to the Prohibition Law of that State.

Such offenses against the public peace can be readily recognized by even the most pro-German of our pacifists. But they fail to recognize what the overwhelming majority of our citizens do recognize—that treason in time of war is an attack on public security enormously greater than any of the peace-time offenses which we have above described.

———————■———————

The executive departments of the State . . . are under a very solemn obligation to do whatever is necessary to prevent action . . . which will interfere with the prosecution of the war.

———————■———————

WAR AND TREASON

In time of war any overt act which gives aid and comfort to the enemy is treason. The intent of an act is determined by its evident effect. It is entirely possible that the effect of the mere call for such an assembly as certain pacifists have recently attempted to hold was to give aid and comfort to the enemies of the United States, the effect of such a call is rightly judged, not only from the announced purpose of the assembly, but also from the private utterances of the leaders of the movement. Certainly, in any case, the people of the country have a right to assume that the decisions of the governors and mayors who prohibit such an assembly within their several jurisdictions were based on just and reasonable grounds. If these executive officers were convinced that the intent or effect of such a meeting would have been to give aid and comfort to our enemies, no one, no matter how passionate his championship of the right of free assembly, need complain of its prohibition.

Preventive law is as legitimate as preventive medicine. The law continually steps in to prevent a wrong from being perpetrated. It does not wait until it is perpetrated before it attempts to prohibit or punish. If a policeman sees a thug holding a blackjack over the head of an unarmed citizen, he does not wait until the blackjack falls before he attempts to arrest the offender.

In war time the duty of prompt preventive action is especially laid upon the executive. We do not have to wait until injury is done, until the blackjack falls, or conscription is halted or the collection of taxes made difficult, or

until that public confidence necessary to the vigorous prosecution of a war is undermined, before our executives can act. The executive departments of the State and Nation are under a very solemn obligation to do whatever is necessary to prevent action by irresponsible or malicious parties which will interfere with the prosecution of the war, and so bring aid and comfort to our enemies.

FOR FURTHER READING

Frederick C. Griffin, *Six Who Protested: Radical Opposition to the First World War.* Port Washington, NY: Kenikat Press, 1977.

David M. Kennedy, *Over Here: The First World War and American Society.* New York: Oxford University Press, 1980.

Paul L. Murphy, *World War I and the Origins of Civil Liberties in the United States.* New York: Norton, 1979.

Richard Polenberg, *Fighting Faiths: The Abrams Case, the Supreme Court, and Free Speech.* New York: Viking, 1987.

Viewpoint 15A

The United States Should Join the League of Nations (1919)

James D. Phelan (1861–1930)

INTRODUCTION *A crucial decision facing America following World War I was whether to join the League of Nations. The league was largely the creation of President Woodrow Wilson. As early as January 8, 1918, Wilson was calling for "a general association of nations" to protect the territorial integrity of countries and to prevent future war. In 1919 he strove to make his vision a reality as head of the U.S. peace delegation in Versailles, France, by insisting that the Treaty of Versailles being negotiated include the creation of such an international organization. The League of Nations that was drawn up after World War I consisted of an Assembly to represent all member nations, a Council controlled by leading powers including the United States, and a Permanent Court of International Justice to arbitrate disputes between nations.*

Wilson's vision faced a serious obstacle in the U.S. Senate, where the Treaty of Versailles, like all U.S. treaties, had to be ratified by a two-thirds majority. Many opponents cited what they viewed as America's historic tradition, dating back to George Washington, of avoiding "foreign entanglements." These arguments and others are addressed in the following viewpoint, taken from a speech by one of the League's supporters, Democratic senator James D. Phelan of California. The February 20, 1919, address excerpted here was originally given before a group of internationalist Republicans led by former president William Howard Taft.

How does Phelan respond to isolationist arguments based on George Washington's 1796 Farewell Address?

What analogy does he make between the League of Nations and civil society?

Now, I should think that all men of good will would support the principle of the league of nations. We may differ as to the details of the power which might be granted to the league. But as to the essential principle, to organize to avert the horrors of war, if possible, in this world, there can be no question. . . .

There is no partisanship involved in this. As President Taft said the other day, "In matters international, Woodrow Wilson and myself stand together." [Applause.] And the gentlemen who are so fond these days of quoting George Washington must have forgotten that in the Farewell Address there is a condemnation of partisan spirit. It was one of the things against which he warned his countrymen. And now they are suffering the partisan spirit to influence their sober judgment.

Woodrow Wilson declared long ago that the object of this war . . . was to establish "a reign of law with the consent of the governed and sustained by the organized opinion of mankind." [Applause.] The organized opinion of mankind means nothing less than a league of nations, because it is only through the nations, unless you are ready to destroy all international barriers, that the opinion of mankind can be organized. And he has been busy ever since in making good his word.

But those Senators—and you see I am not in accord with their utterances, and they represent, I am glad to assure the league, a very small minority, I believe, of that body [applause]—are fond of quoting Washington, who warned us also against international entanglements. That sounds very good. But Washington also said in a letter to one of his contemporaries that we can not participate in European affairs for at least 20 years, because we have not the power to treat with them on terms of equality, and we might endanger our hard-won independence. But 120 years have passed, and the United States is the most powerful Nation in the world. [Applause.] So what Washington said at that time, modified by his own words in private correspondence, certainly does not apply to the United States today. And, as the object of this war was to give democracy to the small nations, and to the large ones as well, and to destroy autocracy and tyranny, George Washington, undoubtedly, if consulted, would say, "Those are the very purposes to which I have dedicated my word and my sword," and he would speed us on that road.

If we were acting contrary to the principles of Washington and the Fathers, it might be well to call a halt and say that we are traveling upon forbidden ground. But we have gone to Europe, and our boys have given the

James D. Phelan, *Congressional Record*, 66th Cong., 1st sess. (March 3, 1919), pp. 4870–71.

decisive blow to autocracy [applause], and this is merely a question in the organization of a league, of something to sustain them in their work. And I feel that there should be as much enthusiasm in this cause as there was in that other cause when we believed that our national rights at home and abroad, aye, our national existence, perhaps was involved in the issue of the conflict; because we can not sit down now and serenely regard Europe. On the contrary, the situation is full of misgivings. I will not enlarge upon the argument, which has been so elaborately set forth by our worthy President. But he has told you again and again that a large number of small countries have been set up and given democracy, and if they be abandoned to their fate we will have, within a very short time, the most horrible war in history in its ferocity, outclassing and distancing the conflict through which we have just passed. Because racial animosities would be aroused, and the old order, often sleeping but never dying, in clashes like this will reassert itself, and the little countries will make a futile resistance and be again amalgamated in the great nations over which tyrants will rule.

A PLEA FOR THE LEAGUE

So, unless this league is established, there is absolutely no hope for democratic Europe; there will be no hope for the men, women, and children; there will be no hope for the workers, because their protection is in the establishment and in the maintenance of democracy, in which their voices are so tremendously potent. They are rudely expressing themselves in some of the countries today. But looking back upon history, we must not be alarmed, because it is only through revolution that order comes. That is the world's history. That must not discourage us. But when they return to reason and know that in this world there must be responsible government, without which there will be neither labor nor wages, then and in that event they will, I am convinced, yield to the arguments which have been advanced in their interests.

It has been said that a league of nations is impossible. When the American Engineers went to Europe, and when we shipped over two millions of men, with all the accessories of war, and built railroads and built great warehouses and provided the food not only for our own men but for the men of other lands, it was an achievement of great magnitude. And somebody said, and I believe it has clung as a sentiment to the American Engineers, "It can not be done, but here it is!" A league can not be formed, but here it is. [Applause.] The President is on the ocean bearing the first draft, adopted unanimously, under pressure which I believe he exerted, as the one thing that he desired of all others to bring back to his countrymen as the reward of the war—not captives, not lands and territory, but peace for all the world. What greater ideal could there be? What greater achievement could he have won?...

We are disloyal to our ideals if we refuse to let our country enlist in this cause.

INDIVIDUALS AND NATIONS

One word more, Mr. President. I suppose the argument has often been made; but it seems to me that in its simplest form a league of nations bears a close analogy to civil society. Democracy is a league of men, banded together for mutual protection. And they yield certain of their natural rights for the purpose of establishing this democracy as ordered government. In a league of nations the nations must necessarily yield some of the exclusive rights which they now hold for the same purpose—their mutual protection. Is there anything wrong with that? Is the right of the individual more sacred than the right of the nation? But grant for the moment that it is. It is yielded willingly in the interest of organized government, organized democracies, where all have a voice and where all thrive; it is their self-determination, freely given, and all abide by the result of the expression of that voice, and the minorities are given protection. They are not destroyed, as in the old days of the Crusaders. And you may recall in this connection the story of the Crusader, who was told on his deathbed that he had to repent and forgive his enemies, and he naively responded, "Why, I have no enemies; I have killed them all." But a democracy respects the minority which does not quite agree with the majority government, and that is a little sacrifice they must make in order to preserve the peace of society.

Now, the United States, going into a compact of this kind will, let us concede to the objecting Senators, yield apart of what they regard as their exclusive rights about which they are very tender. But is not the prize worth the game? Is not the peace of the world worth the sacrifice? [Applause.] Is there anything more terrible than unleashed human beings destroying each other under circumstances of greatest cruelty? War, we are told, burdens a people with debt to go down from one generation to another, like the curse of original sin. It wipes the people from the earth as though Heaven had repented the making of man. Its evils can not be written, even in human blood. And our campaign is against war. And in that campaign every man is enlisted as a patriot, just as much as every man was enlisted in our recent campaign, where his loyalty was never questioned, to carry the Stars and Stripes, standing for equal rights and justice throughout the benighted countries of Europe and bringing hope

and succor to those who for centuries have been the victims of oppression.

But we are disloyal to our ideals if we refuse to let our country enlist in this cause. We are all, by sacrifice and concession, working for a perfect State at home. The league is working for a more perfect world. And, my friends, just as the organization of society has abolished violence in the settlement of disputes and set up legislatures and courts, so this league of nations, if it carries its purpose through to the finish by creating international tribunals, will abolish war, which is only violence on a broader scale. Let us not dismiss this question by saying it belongs only to the sentimental. Sentiment is the best thing in the world, and the difficulty is in living up to it. Human nature is the meanest thing about us, and we are always trying to keep it down. That is the function of society; it is as well the function of the league.

The United States Should Not Join the League of Nations (1919)

Lawrence Sherman (1858–1939)

INTRODUCTION *The League of Nations was the center-piece of President Woodrow Wilson's vision for reshaping the world order and America's place in it. Wilson succeeded in incorporating the league's creation within the Treaty of Versailles, negotiated in 1919 by the nations that had fought World War I. But the president faced significant opposition in the U.S. Senate, which had to ratify the treaty. Opponents contended that the League represented a major break from America's traditional isolationist foreign policy of self-protective neutrality and avoidance of foreign entanglements. A faction of senators, dubbed the "irreconcilables," was steadfastly and philosophically opposed to American participation in the League of Nations. One of these senators was Lawrence Sherman, a Republican from Illinois who served in the Senate from 1913 to 1921. In the following viewpoint, excerpted from remarks on the Senate floor on March 13, 1919, Sherman stakes out a position of classic American isolationism and emphasizes the danger of burdening the new nation of America with the conflicts of the old nations of Europe.*

What contrasts does Sherman draw between the United States and Europe? What attitudes about racial and ethnic groups does he reveal? What distinction does he make between the decision to enter World War I and the decision to enter the League of Nations?

Nearly four months ago the belligerent nations signed the armistice that saved Germany from a

From Lawrence Sherman, *Congressional Record*, 66th Cong., 1st sess. (March 3, 1919), pp. 4865–57.

destructive atonement for her crimes. In that time the responsible agents of the United States of America have not occupied themselves in ending the war and writing terms of peace upon which Germany shall pay the penalty of acknowledged defeat in her attempts against civilized mankind. They have busied themselves with an effort to create a superstate above the governments and peoples of nations to exercise supersovereignty over both nations and their individual citizens and subjects.

Advantage is taken of a wish for universal and permanent peace to present this device as a certain instrumentality to that desired end. . . .

[But] the constitution of the league of nations must be submitted to that scrutiny which will assay its service as a charter prescribing a rule of conduct among nations and whether obedience can be secured. It must be tested by the peoples grouped under sovereign governments to ascertain how it will affect them and what burdens are likely to be assumed; what measure of relief is practicable. Does this document give it, or if not, what can be written reasonably calculated to accomplish that measure of relief? These are inquiries which merit the highest effort of which this Senate and the American Nation are capable. Such a momentous issue seldom challenges free people for decision. . . .

All nations with organic government sufficient to be dealt with as responsible powers can be assembled by their voluntary act under a code of international law. Twenty-six nations so obligated themselves in 1899 in the first Hague convention. Forty-four nations were signatory in 1907 to the second Hague convention. When the armistice was signed November 11, 1918, all the warring nations were contracting parties agreeing in 1907 to arbitrate differences as a substitute for war. Every outrage perpetrated by Germany she had bound herself not to commit. Her deliberate policy of frightfulness she had solemnly covenanted should never be pursued. The indispensable end to be sought, therefore, is not to multiply international agreements, but to discover means of compelling or persuading nations to keep them when made. . . .

CONFLICTS IN EUROPE

Europe contains many independent sovereign nations. Some submerged nationalities, overwhelmed by wars reaching back some centuries, will undoubtedly rise to reassumed sovereignty. With the latter we may be concerned. They might be converted into warlike forces against us if subject to a dominant government, our enemy. Much European bloodshed has had its origin in commercial rivalry resulting in territorial aggression. It may be repeated. Most wars of modern times have begun in Europe. Kings have fought to gain thrones for their kin and subordinates. Ancient feuds of reigning families have sent armies into many a disastrous field. Ambitious men have risen to shake continents with their struggles for power.

That is all to end, however, because we now hear that kings are no more and the people will administer all future governments. We fervently pray it may be so. Yet some of the people we are asked by this league to invest with sovereign power over us may well engage our concern.

Russia is the fountainhead of bloody chaos and the attempted dissolution of every civil and domestic tie dear to the Anglo-Saxon race. Germany may be passing from despotic rule to class government founded on Marxian socialism.

The constitution of the league of nations is a Pandora's box of evil to empty up on the American people the aggregated calamities of the world.

The restless elements of Europe, inured to violence and disliking the monotony of private industry, are always explosive material. Erecting them into states does not insure tranquillity. To all such people, if they have not wisdom and virtue, self-restraint and justice to the minority, liberty is the greatest of all possible evils, not only to them but to the world.

If we ratify this league in its present form, we invest such people with equal power over us. Their vices and misfortunes react upon us. Their follies and crimes become in turn a menace, because we have given them an equal vote in the league with our own country. It may become not a means of removing a menace but of creating one beyond our power either to abate or to remove.

The constitution of the league of nations is a Pandora's box of evil to empty upon the American people the aggregated calamities of the world, and only time is the infallible test even of our own institutions.

WORLD WAR I

When the United States by joint resolution of Congress entered the war April 6, 1917, we signed no pact with the Governments arrayed against the central powers. The American felt in his heart Germany was a menace to the free governments of the world. There was an instinctive horror at Germany's methods of making war and her avowed policy of frightfulness. It was known she aimed at world dominion. Those in authority at this Capitol knew we must fight the danger alone or jointly with the allies.

We chose to make common cause against a common danger. To do so we abdicated no sovereign power. We bound ourselves in no perpetual alliance to draw the sword whenever and so long as a majority of European governments voted it upon us. Our practical expression in this crisis was to reserve for ourselves the power to decide when and how long a controversy between two or more nations in some quarter of the globe was of such magnitude as to warrant our interference even to the extremity of war.

A working status was in fact established between our Government and the allies. Under it the war was fought successfully to the armistice of November 11, 1918. No nation surrendered its sovereignty. They voluntarily combined their strength against the common peril. It was a union of equals, and each was in an equally common self-defense bound to give all it had if the struggle demanded it. This is the key to any league of nations that will survive the ephemeral theories and impossible yearnings of the alleged friends of humanity who are more fertile in phrase making than successful in the practical affairs of men. . . .

The actual working alliance between our Government and Germany's European enemies . . . implies no loss of sovereignty and no violence to national sentiment. It is a cooperative expression of the law of self-defense, an American doctrine on which every patriot can join his fellow man. It impairs no constitutional power of Congress. It invades no executive domain, and it leaves our Government the responsible instrumentality to direct the will of our people. We escape the perils of surrendering our country to the mandates of a majority of the Governments of the Old World by this course.

The same public opinion in a free government that would unite our people under the proposed league would lead to concerted action under a treaty whose obligation rests in good faith. If public opinion does not support the league, it can not send armies into the field. America will not sacrifice her lives and her treasure unless her heart is in the war. No mere language written on parchment can in practice make any compact between sovereign nations more binding than a treaty unless some supersovereign force be contemplated as a coercive agent upon the American Government and its people. Force converts such a league into a tyranny and international oppressor. Such a compact becomes the source of universal war, not the means of permanent peace. . . .

ARTICLE 10

In article 10 [of the Covenant (constitution) of the league of nations] the members of the league bind themselves to preserve each other, and the executive council is required to advise upon the means by which all the league members shall be protected against external aggression which will impair their territorial integrity and political independence. If this article avails anything it binds our Government, its Army, its Navy, its people, and its Treasury to defend Great Britain's colonial dependencies any place in the world. A like obligation attends us for France, Italy, and every other league member. England's territorial possessions are in every part of the globe. Russia is a vast area with 180,000,000 people, and Germany with 70,000,000. The United Kingdom of Great Britain has in Europe fewer than 50,000,000 population. More than 300,000,000 souls acknowledge the supremacy of England's flag in Asia. Great Britain feels, as seldom before, the need of help to maintain her territorial integrity. . . .

I decline to vote to bind the American people to maintain the boundary lines and political independence of every nation that may be a league member. It ought to be done only when the question menaces our peace and safety. It must be a treaty uniting our associated nations in the mutual and common bonds of self-defense. It becomes, then a league of sovereigns acting with the common purpose of self-preservation. The law of nations is like the law of individuals. Self-defense is the first law and is justified before every tribunal known to civilized man. . . .

This league, Mr. President, sends the angel of death to every American home. In every voice to ratify it we can hear the beating of his wing. There will be none to help; no decrees from omniscience will direct us to sprinkle with blood the lintel of every American home. If this supersovereignty be created, conscription will take from all, and we will bear the white man's burden in every quarter of the world.

FOR FURTHER READING

Robert E. Hennings, *James D. Phelan and the Wilson Progressives of California.* New York: Garland, 1985.

Herbert F. Margulies, *The Mild Reservationists and the League of Nations Controversy in the Senate.* Columbia: University of Missouri Press, 1989.

Ralph A. Stone, *The Irreconcilables.* Lexington: University of Kentucky Press, 1970.

Ralph A. Stone, ed., *Wilson and the League of Nations.* New York: Holt, Rinehart and Winston, 1967.

Part 3
PROSPERITY, DEPRESSION, AND WAR (1920–1945)

CHRONOLOGY

1920

January 1 Government agents in several cities arrest thousands of suspected communist and anarchist immigrants in "Palmer raids."

January 16 Eighteenth Amendment (alcohol prohibition) goes into effect.

March 19 U.S. Senate rejects Treaty of Versailles and the League of Nations.

May 5 Anarchists Nicola Sacco and Bartolomeo Vanzetti arrested for murder.

May 31 U.S. government ends price guarantees on wheat, triggering a downward spiral for all crop prices.

August 26 Nineteenth Amendment, granting women the right to vote, is ratified.

November 2 Warren G. Harding elected president.

1921

May 9 Emergency Quota Act restricts the number of immigrants allowed into the country.

November 2 Margaret Sanger founds American Birth Control League (later called Planned Parenthood).

1923

March 3 Henry Luce publishes the first issue of *Time* magazine.

August 2 President Harding dies; Vice President Calvin Coolidge succeeds to the presidency.

December Equal Rights Amendment to Constitution introduced in Congress.

1924

June 2 Act of Congress makes American Indians full U.S. citizens.

November 4 Calvin Coolidge elected president; two women elected as state governors: Nellie Tayloe Ross in Wyoming and Miriam ("Ma") Ferguson in Texas.

1925

July 10–21 The Scopes evolution trial is held in Dayton, Tennessee.

August 8 40,000 Ku Klux Klan members march in Washington D.C.

1926

March Robert Goddard test-flies world's first liquid-fueled rocket.

1927

February 23 Congress creates the Federal Radio Commission to regulate radio broadcasters.

April 7 First successful demonstration of television occurs.

May 20–21 Charles Lindbergh flies his solo flight across the Atlantic Ocean.

August 23 Sacco and Vanzetti are executed.

October Premiere of *The Jazz Singer* ushers in era of sound movies.

1928

August 27 The Kellogg-Briand Pact outlawing war is signed by the U.S. and other nations.

November 6 Herbert Hoover elected president.

79

December 17 Clark Memorandum repudiates 1904 Roosevelt Corollary to Monroe Doctrine and pledges that U.S. will stop intervening in Latin America.

1929

October The stock market crashes, triggering the Great Depression.

1930

June 17 Smoot-Hawley Tariff Act drastically raises duties on numerous industrial and agricultural products.

1932

January The Stimson Doctrine states that the U.S. refuses to recognize the 1931 Japanese conquest of Manchuria.

January 22 Reconstruction Finance Corporation established by President Hoover.

November 8 Franklin D. Roosevelt elected president.

1933

February 6 Twentieth Amendment to Constitution ratified, moving future presidential inauguration dates from March 4 to January 20.

March 4 Frances Perkins, appointed secretary of labor, becomes first woman to hold cabinet-level post.

March 5 Roosevelt declares a national bank holiday.

March 9–June 16 In the "First Hundred Days" of New Deal, special session of Congress results in creation of Federal Deposit Insurance Corporation, National Recovery Administration, the Federal Emergency Relief Administration, and other programs.

April 19 U.S. abandons gold standard.

November 16 Roosevelt extends formal diplomatic recognition to the Soviet Union.

December 5 Prohibition ends when Eighteenth Amendment is repealed.

1934

May Dust storm destroys topsoil in Texas, Oklahoma, and other states.

May 29 1901 Platt Amendment superseded by new U.S.-Cuba treaty that ends Cuba's status as U.S. protectorate.

June 18 Congress enacts the Indian Reorganization Act to help preserve Indian tribal culture; reverses Dawes Act of 1887.

1935

May 27 The Supreme Court strikes down several New Deal measures as unconstitutional.

July 5 President Roosevelt signs the National Labor Relations Act.

August Congress passes the first in a series of neutrality acts designed to prevent American entry into another European war.

August 14 The Social Security Act is signed by Roosevelt.

1936

November 3 Roosevelt reelected president.

December United Automobile Workers stage a successful sit-down strike against General Motors in Detroit.

1937

February 5 President Roosevelt proposes his plan (rejected by Congress) to expand size of Supreme Court.

April 12 The Supreme Court upholds the constitutionality of the National Labor Relations Act.

May 6 *Hindenburg* airship disaster occurs.

1939

February 27 Supreme Court outlaws sit-down strikes.

August 22 Germany and Soviet Union sign nonaggression pact.

September 3 France and Great Britain declare war on Germany following German invasion of Poland.

1940

June Germany conquers France; controls most of Europe.

September America First Committee is organized to oppose U.S. involvement in war in Europe.

September 3 U.S. exchanges 50 destroyers to Great Britain for leases on naval and air bases.

September 16 Congress passes first peacetime draft in American history.

September 27 Germany, Italy, and Japan sign military alliance.

November 5 President Roosevelt wins an unprecedented third term.

1941

March Lend-lease aid to Great Britain and other nations authorized by Congress.

June 22 Nazi Germany invades the Soviet Union.

June 25 Roosevelt establishes Fair Employment Practices Board and bans racial discrimination by defense contractors.

August 1 U.S. bans exports of aviation oil to Japan.

August 9 Roosevelt and Churchill meet off Newfoundland and formulate the Atlantic Charter.

September 11 Roosevelt orders navy to shoot German submarines "on sight."

December 7–11 Japanese attack on Pearl Harbor; Congress declares war against Japan; Germany and Italy declare war on the U.S.

1942

February 20 Roosevelt authorizes the military internment and relocation of Japanese Americans.

June 3–6 Battle of Midway is the turning point in U.S. war against Japan.

1943

June 4 White soldiers invade Mexican-American communities in "zoot-suit" riots of Los Angeles.

June 20–22 Race riot in Detroit occurs.

November 28–December 1 Roosevelt, British prime minister Winston Churchill, and Soviet leader Joseph Stalin meet together for first time at the Teheran Conference.

1944

June 6 Allied forces cross English Channel and land in Normandy, France, on D-Day.

November 7 Roosevelt reelected to a fourth term.

1945

February Yalta Conference occurs between Roosevelt, Churchill, and Stalin.

April 12 President Roosevelt dies; Vice President Harry S. Truman succeeds to the presidency.

May 8 Victory in Europe Day occurs.

June 26 United Nations Charter signed by U.S. and 50 other nations in San Francisco.

July 16 United States successfully explodes first atomic bomb in New Mexico.

July 17–August 2 Truman meets Stalin and Churchill at Potsdam Conference in suburb of Berlin.

August 6 Atomic bomb dropped on Hiroshima.

August 8 The Soviet Union declares war on Japan.

August 9 Atomic bomb dropped on Nagasaki.

August 14 The Japanese government announces its intention to surrender.

September 2 Victory over Japan Day signals the end of World War II.

PREFACE

The quarter century following World War I was one of the most eventful periods of American history. These years featured new heights in economic prosperity and technological development, the most severe financial crash in all of American history and a corresponding economic depression, revolutionary developments in the role of the national government in American life, and another cataclysmic world conflict. Americans often profoundly disagreed on how to meet the challenges created by these events.

UNEVEN ECONOMIC PROSPERITY

Following World War I, and especially from 1923 to 1929, America enjoyed significant economic growth. Experts believed that a "permanent plateau" of prosperity had been reached. Innovative methods of manufacturing, such as the use of the assembly line and the replacement of steam power with electricity, greatly improved productivity. These and other technologies led to the development of new consumer goods—including the radio, the vacuum cleaner, and the refrigerator—and the creation of entire industries, including that of the automobile.

The automobile was perhaps the single key factor behind America's economic growth in the 1920s. Due to the manufacturing innovations of Henry Ford, the automobile was transformed from an expensive plaything for an elite few into an affordable necessity for the middle class. Passenger-car registrations rose from 8 million in 1920 to 23 million in 1930. The automobile industry employed thousands of workers and spurred the development of many secondary industries, including rubber and oil.

The development of the auto industry helped fuel a growing economy and rising standard of living for many Americans. During the 1920s, per capita income rose 20 percent, unemployment averaged 3.7 percent, and inflation was virtually nonexistent at less than 1 percent. Low inflation and steady economic growth meant higher standards of living; by the mid-1920s the typical middle-class family owned a car, a radio, a phonograph, a telephone, and other consumer goods. These goods were often purchased on installment plans from national chain stores—two other important economic developments of the 1920s.

Not all Americans shared in the economic good times. Older industries, such as the railroads and coal mines, struggled in the face of new competition. Due in part to a reduction of union membership, workers received a declining share of business profits. Farmers were hit hard by falling crop prices; net farm income dropped from $9.5 billion in 1920 to $5.3 billion in 1928.

However, despite the economic hardships of some, the majority of Americans continued to have confidence in the economy and in the pro-business Republican leadership in Washington, as evidenced by the Republican presidential election victories of 1920, 1924, and 1928 (despite significant political scandals during the Warren G. Harding administration in the early 1920s). In many respects, the Democrats followed the Republicans' lead and offered few alternative economic proposals. Although in the country at large there were debates over taxes, the Federal Reserve System, and the stock market, these issues were not of fundamental concern to most Americans.

CULTURE CLASH

The most burning controversies of the 1920s were not economic or political, but rather cultural. The decade was marked by numerous national disagreements on various social and cultural issues, ranging from the teaching of Darwinian evolution in public schools to the impact of immigrants on American society. To some degree the cultural debates of the 1920s reveal a clash between the traditional values of small-town America and the new values emerging in the modernizing American cities.

One of the defining controversies of the era was the national debate over the prohibition of alcohol, instituted by the Eighteenth Amendment to the Constitution in 1919 and eventually repealed by the Twenty-First Amendment in 1933. Prohibition was enthusiastically supported by many white Protestant residents of America's rural areas and small towns, especially in the South and the Midwest. It was generally opposed by several distinct groups of Americans—urban Catholic immigrants, the wealthy and cosmopolitan elite, intellectuals, and social liberals—whom many of Prohibition's supporters viewed with profound suspicion. In many respects, the debate for and against Prohibition reflected the underlying cultural divide in America at this time.

The most extreme reactionary movement of the 1920s was the revival of the Ku Klux Klan. Its members preached American racial, ethnic, and moral purity against the presumed threats posed by blacks, immigrants, Catholics, and others. At its height, membership in the Ku Klux Klan reached 5 million and attained significant political power in several states far beyond the boundaries of the Old South, the territory of the original Klan of the post–Civil War period. But financial and sexual scandals caused the membership and power of the new Klan to greatly decline after 1925.

THE GREAT DEPRESSION
AND THE NEW DEAL

Debate on cultural issues was overshadowed by concern about the state of the economy following the stock market crash of October 1929 and the onset of the worst and longest economic collapse in America's history. The human suffering of the Great Depression can be only dimly perceived by looking at economic statistics, but a few numbers can provide a glimpse. Between 1929 and 1932, unemployment rose from 3 percent to nearly 25 percent. America's gross national product (GNP) plunged from $104 billion in 1929 to $59 billion in 1932. More than five thousand banks closed, wiping out the savings of millions of Americans. Farm and home foreclosures skyrocketed. All these economic calamities came at a time when there was little or no safety net of government relief, welfare programs, or unemployment compensation. Care of the unemployed was primarily a responsibility of private charities, which often found themselves stretched beyond their capabilities during the depression.

The initial response of government at all levels to this economic disaster was limited. At the federal level President Herbert Hoover strongly believed that government intrusion into the private sphere would undermine American individualism and contribute to the creation of an oppressive bureaucracy at best or full-blown socialism at worst. Elected president in 1928 with the promise of continued prosperity, Hoover saw his role as that of an "influential adviser and well-placed cheerleader." As such he exhorted business leaders to maintain high levels of employment while cutting back on production (since he believed that the country's economic dilemma resulted from an excess of goods in circulation). He also urged banking leaders to cooperate among themselves to prevent weak banks from failing. And he encouraged American workers and consumers to spend with the confidence that recovery was just around the corner. Hoover's approach proved unsuccessful at alleviating the Great Depression. He was defeated for reelection in 1932 by a wide margin.

Hoover's vanquisher was Franklin D. Roosevelt, a New York governor and Democratic politician who would go on to win an unprecedented four consecutive presidential elections and dominate American political life until his death in 1945. Roosevelt led the country both in its fight against the Great Depression and in its fight against Germany and Japan in World War II.

Pledging a "New Deal" to the American people, in his first term Roosevelt launched a flurry of federal programs aimed at bringing relief to beleaguered people and recovery and reform to the economy. These programs included public works projects to create jobs, government regulation and reform of the nation's financial institutions, a social security system for the elderly and retired, natural resource preservation, and collective bargaining guarantees for the American worker. Conservatives on the right argued that the New Deal was drifting dangerously into socialism; radicals on the left argued that the New Deal was too concerned with preserving an obsolete and disgraced capitalism. But such criticisms did not prevent Roosevelt's reelection by large margins to three subsequent terms in 1936, 1940, and 1944. Historians and economists still argue over the benefits of Roosevelt's New Deal and how much it helped America end its Great Depression (most conclude that the nation's involvement in World War II had a greater role). However, the New Deal did, for better or worse, greatly expand the size, reach, and responsibilities of the federal government in managing America's economy and providing for the people's welfare.

THE END OF ISOLATIONISM

Even as Franklin D. Roosevelt and his political opponents were arguing over various aspects of the New Deal, events in Europe and Asia were beginning to turn the country's attention to world affairs. Within a few years America would have to make the crucial decision over whether or not to intervene in yet another world war.

Following the rejection of American membership in the League of Nations, the new international organization championed by President Woodrow Wilson after World War I, most Americans shared an isolationist outlook. The Senate repeatedly rebuffed presidential efforts to sanction American membership on the World Court (an arm of the League of Nations). Congress passed immigration laws in the early 1920s that sharply limited the number of immigrants allowed into the country—another reflection of the isolationist spirit of the times.

In addition, many historians, writers, and some congressional committees severely criticized America's 1917 decision to intervene in World War I, blaming that choice on the conspirings of British diplomats, international bankers, and arms manufacturers. So persuasive were their arguments that isolationism returned in full force after World War I, reaching a peak in the mid-1930s when Congress passed a series of neutrality laws designed to prohibit Americans from lending money and selling arms to warring nations. These laws were an attempt to prevent repetition of what were viewed as the mistakes of 1917.

Meanwhile, international tensions were building around the world. The League of Nations, bereft of American support, was unable to prevent wars or protect nations from attack. Japan invaded the northern Chinese province of Manchuria in 1931. In Europe the countries of Italy and Germany had adopted fascist regimes and had become increasingly aggressive toward their neighbors. In 1937 Roosevelt suggested that such aggressor nations be "quarantined" by the collective action of peace-loving nations. But he quickly backed away from concrete action to carry out such a quarantine in the face of strong isolationist sentiment from members of Congress and the media.

Thus, when war broke out in Europe in 1939, Roosevelt had almost no choice but to proclaim American neutrality (although he did not follow Woodrow Wilson's 1914 lead by asking Americans to be neutral in their "hearts and minds" as well). For the next two years Roosevelt prodded Congress to modify the neutrality laws to permit American trade and aid to Great Britain, France (conquered by Germany in June 1940), and the Soviet Union (invaded by Germany in June 1941). He also presided over an American military buildup, pressed for the country's first peacetime draft, negotiated a controversial agreement to trade American destroyers for rights to British naval bases, and deployed the U.S. Navy to patrol the Atlantic Ocean against German submarines. All of these actions were opposed by a vociferous isolationist movement that abated only after Japan's surprise attack on Pearl Harbor on December 7, 1941.

WORLD WAR II

The United States was far more heavily involved in World War II than it had been in World War I. Fifteen million men and 338,000 women served in America's armed forces. The United States suffered 1 million casualties during the war, including 292,000 battlefield deaths. The war affected most Americans at home as well. Income taxes increased significantly. The government rationed food and goods, including beef and gasoline, and housing shortages were a critical problem in many areas. However, by 1943 unemployment had almost vanished as millions of men and women went to

work in defense plants manufacturing war materials. Most historians have credited the war and its massive military spending (the United States spent an estimated $350 billion during the war) for finally bringing the country out of the Great Depression.

World War II brought new challenges and opportunities for women and minorities. Between 1941 and 1945, 6 million women entered the labor force. Many worked in manufacturing jobs previously dominated by men. The war also opened up new roles and opportunities for blacks. Some fought in World War II in segregated units; others found employment in American factories. In response to pressure from A. Philip Randolph and other black leaders, President Roosevelt in June 1941 issued an executive order banning discriminatory employment practices in federal agencies and companies doing defense-related work. However, fearing sabotage and disloyalty, the U.S. government interned 112,000 members of another minority—Japanese Americans—in detention camps during the war. Many of those detained lost their homes, businesses, and farms as a result of their internment.

The war in Europe ended in the spring of 1945 with the surrender of Germany. The war in Asia ended in August 1945 following the dropping of atomic bombs on the Japanese cities of Hiroshima and Nagasaki in early August 1945. The decision to use this new weapon, developed by a massive research effort during World War II, contributed to Japan's surrender, but it also engendered great controversy around the world.

With the war's end America faced the challenge of attempting to return its economy to peacetime conditions and reintegrate its soldiers into civilian life. There also came an American resolve not to repeat the retreat to isolationism that followed World War I. In 1945 America's political leadership was willing to assume a significant role in world politics. Not all Americans shared this determination, however. The years after World War II brought renewed debate on both the government's role in American life and America's role in the world.

SOCIAL AND CULTURAL ISSUES OF THE 1920s

The Department of Justice Is Defending America from Communist Subversion (1920)

A. Mitchell Palmer (1872–1936)

INTRODUCTION *A. Mitchell Palmer was appointed attorney general of the United States by President Woodrow Wilson in 1919 and served until 1921. A person who harbored presidential ambitions of his own, he was one of the leading figures of America's first "Red Scare." The successful Bolshevik revolution in Russia in 1917 seemed poised to spread to other nations following World War I. The fear (and, for some, the hope) of communist revolution in America grew in 1919 with the formation of two communist parties in the United States and the establishment of the Comintern (Communist International) in Russia to promote world revolution. The year 1919 was also one of social unrest in America as the nation struggled with high rates of inflation and unemployment. Americans also endured thousands of strikes and a wave of violent bomb scares and explosions—actions many blamed on communist radicals (one bomb damaged Palmer's house).*

In 1919 the Palmer-led Department of Justice launched a nationwide crackdown against "suspicious" foreigners. In a series of well-publicized actions, offices of labor unions and radical organizations were raided and suspected radicals and anarchism apprehended. Some were charged with breaking laws originally passed to limit opposition to World War I. Many of the foreign immigrants captured were ultimately deported. These actions, which became known as "Palmer raids," were criticized by some for disregarding civil liberties. In the following viewpoint, taken from a February 1920 article, Palmer justifies his actions as necessary to defend America from subversion from within.

On what grounds does Palmer refuse to make "nice distinctions" between criminal violations and radical ideas? How does he respond to charges that his deportations of suspicious immigrants were unjust? Why might he include extended quotations of the Communist Manifesto in his article?

Excerpted from A. Mitchell Palmer, "The Case Against the 'Reds,'" *Forum*, February 1920.

Like a prairie-fire, the blaze of revolution was sweeping over every American institution of law and order a year ago. It was eating its way into the homes of the American workman, its sharp tongues of revolutionary heat were licking the altars of the churches, leaping into the belfry of the school bell, crawling into the sacred corners of American homes, seeking to replace marriage vows with libertine laws, burning up the foundations of society.

Robbery, not war, is the ideal of communism. This has been demonstrated in Russia, Germany, and in America. As a foe, the anarchist is fearless of his own life, for his creed is a fanaticism that admits no respect of any other creed. Obviously it is the creed of any criminal mind, which reasons always from motives impossible to clean thought. Crime is the degenerate factor in society.

Upon these two basic certainties, first that the "Reds" were criminal aliens, and secondly that the American Government must prevent crime, it was decided that there could be no nice distinctions drawn between the theoretical ideals of the radicals and their actual violations of our national laws. An assassin may have brilliant intellectuality, he may be able to excuse his murder or robbery with fine oratory, but any theory which excuses crime is not wanted in America. This is no place for the criminal to flourish, nor will he do so, so long as the rights of common citizenship can be exerted to prevent him.

OUR GOVERNMENT IN JEOPARDY

It has always been plain to me that when American citizens unite upon any national issue, they are generally right, but it is sometimes difficult to make the issue clear to them. If the Department of Justice could succeed in attracting the attention of our optimistic citizens to the issue of internal revolution in this country, we felt sure there would be no revolution. The Government was in jeopardy. My private information of what was being done by the organization known as the Communist Party of America, with headquarters in Chicago, of what was being done by the Communist Internationale under their manifesto planned at Moscow last March [1919] by Trotzky [Leon Trotsky], Lenine [Vladimir Lenin] and others, addressed "To the Proletariats of All Countries," of what strides the Communist Labor Party was making, removed all doubt. In this conclusion we did not ignore the definite standards of personal liberty, of free speech, which is the very temperament and heart of the people. The evidence was examined with the utmost care, with a personal leaning toward freedom of thought and word on all questions.

The whole mass of evidence, accumulated from all parts of the country, was scrupulously scanned, not merely for the written or spoken differences of viewpoint as to the Government of the United States, but, in spite of these things, to see if the hostile declarations might not be sincere in their announced motive to improve our social order. There was no hope of such a thing....

My information showed that communism in this country was an organization of thousands of aliens, who were direct allies of Trotzky. Aliens of the same misshapen caste of mind and indecencies of character, and it showed that they were making the same glittering promises of lawlessness, of criminal autocracy to Americans, that they had made to the Russian peasants. How the Department of Justice discovered upwards of 60,000 of these organized agitators of the Trotzky doctrine in the United States, is the confidential information upon which the Government is now sweeping the nation clean of such alien filth....

WILL DEPORTATIONS CHECK BOLSHEVISM?

Behind, and underneath, my own determination to drive from our midst the agents of Bolshevism with increasing vigor and with greater speed, until there are no more of them left among us, so long as I have the responsible duty of that task, I have discovered the hysterical methods of these revolutionary humans with increasing amazement and suspicion. In the confused information that sometimes reaches the people, they are compelled to ask questions which involve the reasons for my acts against the "Reds." I have been asked, for instance, to what extent deportation will check radicalism in this country. Why not ask what will become of the United States Government if these alien radicals are permitted to carry out the principles of the Communist Party as embodied in its so-called laws, aims and regulations?

There wouldn't be any such thing left. In place of the United States Government we should have the horror and terrorism of bolsheviki tyranny such as is destroying Russia now. Every scrap of radical literature demands the overthrow of our existing government. All of it demands obedience to the instincts of criminal minds, that is, to the lower appetites, material and moral. The whole purpose of communism appears to be a mass formation of the criminals of the world to overthrow the decencies of private life, to usurp property that they have not earned, to disrupt the present order of life regardless of health, sex or religious rights. By a literature that promises the wildest dreams of such low aspirations, that can occur to only the criminal minds, communism distorts our social law.

The chief appeal communism makes is to "The Worker." If they can lure the wage-earner to join their own gang of thieves, if they can show him that he will be rich if he steals, so far they have succeeded in betraying him to their own criminal course.

Read this manifesto issued in Chicago:

THE COMMUNIST PARTY MANIFESTO

The world is on the verge of a new era. Europe is in revolt. The masses of Asia are stirring uneasily.

Capitalism is in collapse. The workers of the world are seeing a new light and securing new courage. Out of the night of war is coming a new day.

The spectre of communism haunts the world of capitalism. Communism, the hope of the workers to end misery and oppression.

The workers of Russia smashed the front of international Capitalism and Imperialism. They broke the chains of the terrible war; and in the midst of agony, starvation and the attacks of the Capitalists of the world, they are creating a new social order.

The class war rages fiercely in all nations. Everywhere the workers are in a desperate struggle against their capitalist masters. The call to action has come. The workers must answer the call!

The Communist Party of America is the party of the working class. The Communist Party proposes to end Capitalism and organize a workers' industrial republic. The workers must control industry and dispose of the product of industry. The Communist Party is a party realizing the limitation of all existing workers' organizations and proposes to develop the revolutionary movement necessary to free the workers from the oppression of Capitalism. The Communist Party insists that the problems of the American worker are identical with the problems of the workers of the world.

These are the revolutionary tenets of Trotzky and the Communist Internationale. Their manifesto further embraces the various organizations in this country of men and women obsessed with discontent, having disorganized relations to American society. These include the I.W.W.'s [International Workers of the World], the most radical socialists, the misguided anarchists, the agitators who oppose the limitations of unionism, the moral perverts and the hysterical neurasthenic women who abound in communism. The phraseology of their manifesto is practically the same wording as was used by the Bolsheviks for their International Communist Congress....

There is no legislation at present which can reach an American citizen who is discontented with our system of American Government, nor is it necessary. The dangerous fact to us is that the Communist Party of America is actually affiliated and adheres to the teaching program and tactics of the 3d Internationale. Consider what this means. The first congress of the Communist Nationale held March 6, 1919, in Moscow, subscribed to by Trotzky and Lenine, adopted the following:

———————————■———————————

No alien, advocating the overthrow of existing law and order in his country shall escape arrest and prompt deportation.

———————————■———————————

This makes necessary the disarming of the bourgeoisie at the proper time, the arming of the laborer, and the formation of a communist army as the protectors of the rules of the proletariat and the inviolability of the social structure.

When we realize that each member of the Communist Party of America pledges himself to the principles above set forth, deportation of men and women bound to such a theory is a very mild reformatory sentence....

It has been inferred by the "Reds" that the United States Government, by arresting and deporting them, is returning to the autocracy of Czardom, adopting the system that created the severity of Siberian banishment. My reply to such charges is, that in our determination to maintain our government we are treating our alien enemies with extreme consideration. To deny them the privilege of remaining in a country which they have openly deplored as an unenlightened community, unfit for those who prefer the privileges of Bolshevism, should be no hardship. It strikes me as an odd form of reasoning that these Russian Bolsheviks who extol the Bolshevik rule, should be so unwilling to return to Russia. The nationality of most of the alien "Reds" is Russian and German. There is almost no other nationality represented among them.

It has been impossible in so short a space to review the entire menace of the internal revolution in this country as I know it, but this may serve to arouse the American citizen to its reality, its danger, and the great need of united effort to stamp it out, under our feet, if needs be. It is being done. The Department of Justice will pursue the attack of these "Reds" upon the Government of the United States with vigilance, and no alien, advocating the overthrow of existing law and order in this country, shall escape arrest and prompt deportation.

It is my belief that while they have stirred discontent in our midst, while they have caused irritating strikes, and while they have infected our social ideas with the disease of their own minds and their unclean morals, we can get rid of them! and not until we have done so shall we have removed the menace of Bolshevism for good.

Viewpoint 16B

The Department of Justice Is Violating Constitutional Freedoms (1920)

National Popular Government League

INTRODUCTION *From 1919 to 1921 the federal government engaged in a series of controversial actions against suspected radicals and anarchists. One large burst of such activity occurred in January 1920 when the U.S. Department of Justice, under the leadership of Attorney General A. Mitchell Palmer and his assistant J. Edgar Hoover, launched surprise raids on meetings of suspected*

communist and anarchist agitators. The law enforcement actions were generally performed without arrest warrants. The main targets were foreign immigrants, many of whom were detained for months and/or subsequently deported by federal immigration officials.

Many Americans questioned the tactics of these "Palmer raids." Among them were members of the National Popular Government League (NPGL), a group of prominent liberal lawyers and others including Felix Frankfurter (a future Supreme Court justice), Zechariah Chafee Jr. (Harvard law professor and author), and Roscoe Pound (dean of Harvard Law School). The league investigated raids and in May 1920 released a stinging report, excerpted here, accusing the U.S. government of wholesale violations of civil liberties.

Do the members of the National Popular Government League take a stand here on radicalism? What do they find most disturbing about the government's actions? What parts of the Constitution do they argue are being violated?

TO THE AMERICAN PEOPLE:

For more than six months we, the undersigned lawyers, whose sworn duty it is to uphold the Constitution and Laws of the United States, have seen with growing apprehension the continued violation of that Constitution and breaking of those Laws by the Department of Justice of the United States government.

Under the guise of a campaign for the suppression of radical activities, the office of the Attorney General, acting by its local agents throughout the country, and giving express instructions from Washington, has committed continual illegal acts. Wholesale arrests both of aliens and citizens have been made without warrant or any process of law; men and women have been jailed and held *incommunicado* without access of friends or counsel; homes have been entered without search-warrant and property seized and removed; other property has been wantonly destroyed; workingmen and workingwomen suspected of radical views have been shamefully abused and maltreated. Agents of the Department of Justice have been introduced into radical organizations for the purpose of informing upon their members or inciting them to activities; these agents have even been instructed from Washington to arrange meetings upon certain dates for the express object of facilitating wholesale raids and arrests. In support of these illegal acts, and to create sentiment in its favor, the Department of Justice has also constituted itself a propaganda bureau, and has sent to newspapers and magazines of this country quantities of material designed to excite public opinion against radicals,

From the National Popular Government League, *Report Upon the Illegal Practices of the United States Department of Justice.* Washington, DC: National Popular Government League, 1920.

all at the expense of the government and outside the scope of the Attorney General's duties.

ILLEGAL ACTS

We make no argument in favor of any radical doctrine as such, whether Socialist, Communist or Anarchist. No one of us belongs to any of these schools of thought. Nor do we now raise any question as to the Constitutional protection of free speech and a free press. We are concerned solely with bringing to the attention of the American people the utterly illegal acts which have been committed by those charged with the highest duty of enforcing the laws—acts which have caused widespread suffering and unrest, have struck at the foundation of American free institutions, and have brought the name of our country into disrepute.

These acts may be grouped under the following heads:

(1) Cruel and Unusual Punishments:

The Eighth Amendment to the United States Constitution provides:

Excessive bail shall not be required nor excessive fines imposed, nor cruel and unusual punishments inflicted.

Punishments of the utmost cruelty, and heretofore unthinkable in America, have become usual. Great numbers of persons arrested, both aliens and citizens, have been threatened, beaten with blackjacks, struck with fists, jailed under abominable conditions, or actually tortured. . . .

(2) Arrests without Warrant:

The Fourth Amendment to the Constitution provides:

The right of the people to be secure in their persons, houses, papers, and effects, against unreasonable searches and seizures, shall not be violated, and no Warrants shall issue, but upon probable cause, supported by Oath or affirmation, and particularly describing the place to be searched, and the persons or things to be seized.

Many hundreds of citizens and aliens alike have been arrested in wholesale raids, without warrants or pretense of warrants. They have then either been released, or have been detained in police stations or jails for indefinite lengths of time while warrants were being applied for. This practice of making mass raids and mass arrests without warrant has resulted directly from the instructions, both written and oral, issued by the Department of Justice at Washington. . . .

(3) Unreasonable Searches and Seizures:

The Fourth Amendment has been quoted above.

In countless cases agents of the Department of Justice have entered the homes, offices, or gathering places of persons suspected of radical affiliations, and, without pretense of any search warrant, have seized and removed property belonging to them for use by the Department of Justice. In many of these raids property which could not be removed or was not useful to the Department, was intentionally smashed and destroyed. . . .

(4) Provocative Agents:

We do not question the right of the Department of Justice to use its agents in the Bureau of Investigation to ascertain when the law is being violated. But the American people has never tolerated the use of undercover provocative agents or "agents provocateurs," such as have been familiar in old Russia or Spain. Such agents have been introduced by the Department of Justice into the radical movements, have reached positions of influence therein, have occupied themselves with informing upon or instigating acts which might be declared criminal, and at the express direction of Washington have brought about meetings of radicals in order to make possible wholesale arrests at such meetings. . . .

(5) Compelling Persons to be Witnesses against Themselves:

The Fifth Amendment provides as follows:

No person . . . shall be compelled in any criminal case to be a witness against himself, nor be deprived of life, liberty, or property, without due process of law.

It has been the practice of the Department of Justice and its agents, after making illegal arrests without warrant, to question the accused person and to force admissions from him by terrorism, which admissions were subsequently to be used against him in deportation proceedings. . . .

(6) Propaganda by the Department of Justice:

The legal functions of the Attorney General are: to advise the Government on questions of law, and to prosecute persons who have violated federal statutes. For the Attorney General to go into the field of propaganda against radicals is a deliberate misuse of his office and a deliberate squandering of funds entrusted to him by Congress. . . .

Since these illegal acts have been committed by the highest legal powers in the United States, there is no final appeal from them except to the conscience and condemnation of the American people. American institutions have not in fact been protected by the Attorney General's ruthless suppression. On the contrary those institutions have been seriously undermined, and revolutionary unrest has been vastly intensified. No organizations of radicals acting through propaganda over the last six months could have created as much revolutionary sentiment in America as has been created by the acts of the Department of Justice itself.

Even were one to admit that there existed any serious "Red menace" before the Attorney General started his "unflinching war" against it, his campaign has been singularly fruitless. Out of the many thousands suspected by the Attorney General (he had already listed 60,000 by name and history on Nov. 14, 1919, aliens and citizens), what do the figures show of net results? Prior to January 1, 1920, there were actually deported 263 persons. Since January 1 there have been actually deported 18 persons. Since January 1 there have been ordered deported an additional 529 persons, and warrants for 1,547 have been cancelled (after full hearings and consideration of the evidence) by Assistant Secretary of Labor Louis F. Post, to whose courageous reestablishment of American Constitutional Law in deportation proceedings are due the attacks that have been made upon him. The Attorney General has consequently got rid of 810 alien suspects, which, on his own showing, leaves him at least 59,160 persons (aliens and citizens) still to cope with.

A GOVERNMENT OF LAWS

It has always been the proud boast of America that this is a government of laws and not of men. Our Constitution and laws have been based on the simple elements of human nature. Free men cannot be driven and repressed; they must be led. Free men respect justice and follow truth, but arbitrary power they will oppose until the end of time. There is no danger of revolution so great as that created by suppression, by ruthlessness, and by deliberate violation of the simple rules of American law and American decency.

It is a fallacy to suppose that, any more than in the past, any servant of the people can safely arrogate to himself unlimited authority. To proceed upon such a supposition is to deny the fundamental American theory of the consent of the governed. Here is no question of a vague and threatened menace, but a present assault upon the most sacred principles of our Constitutional liberty.

FOR FURTHER READING

Stanley Coben, *A. Mitchell Palmer, Politican.* New York: Columbia University Press, 1963.

David Cole, *Enemy Aliens: Double Standards and Constitutional Freedoms in the War on Terrorism.* New York: New Press, 2003.

Edwin P. Hoyt, *The Palmer Raids, 1919–1920.* New York: Seabury Press, 1969.

Kim E. Nielsen, *Un-American Womanhood: Antiradicalism, Antifeminism, and the First Red Scare.* Columbus: Ohio State University Press, 2001.

Viewpoint 17A

H.L. Mencken Critiques America (1922)

H.L. Mencken (1880–1956)

INTRODUCTION *H.L. Mencken was a noted journalist, writer, and satirist. He was a columnist for the* Baltimore Sun *from 1906 to 1948 and the founder and editor of the magazine* American Mercury. *Mencken became celebrated during the 1920s for his caustic commentaries on the "traditional" American values of rural and small-town America, in which he criticized in colorful prose the American "booboisie" for their narrow-mindedness. His social and literary criticism greatly influenced a generation of intellectuals, some of whom became part of the "Lost Generation" that moved to Europe in the 1920s while decrying the limits of American culture. The following example of Mencken's writing is taken from* Prejudices: Third Series, *a collection of newspaper and magazine essays published in book form in 1922.*

On what points does Mencken agree with the intellectuals leaving America? Which portions of this viewpoint would you rate most controversial? Why?

Apparently there are those who begin to find it disagreeable—nay, impossible. Their anguish fills the Liberal weeklies and every ship that puts out from New York carries a groaning cargo of them, bound for Paris, London, Munich, Rome and way points—anywhere to escape the great curses and atrocities that make life intolerable for them at home. Let me say at once that I find little to cavil at in their basic complaints. In more than one direction, indeed, I probably go a great deal further than even the Young Intellectuals. It is, for example, one of my firmest and most sacred beliefs, reached after an inquiry extending over a score of years and supported by incessant prayer and meditation, that the government of the United States, in both its legislative arm and its executive arm, is ignorant, incompetent, corrupt, and disgusting—and from this judgment I except no more than twenty living lawmakers and no more than twenty executioners of their laws. It is a belief no less piously cherished that the administration of justice in the Republic is stupid, dishonest, and against all reason and equity—and from this judgment I except no more than thirty judges, including two upon the bench of the Supreme Court of the United States. It is another that the foreign policy of the United States—its habitual manner of dealing with other nations, whether friend or foe—is hypocritical, disingenuous, knavish, and dishonorable—and from this judgment I consent to no exceptions whatever, either recent or long past. And it is my fourth (and, to avoid too depressing a bill, final) conviction that the American people, taking one with another, constitute the most timorous, sniveling, poltroonish, ignominious mob of serfs and goose-steppers ever gathered under one flag in Christendom since the end of the Middle Ages, and that they grow more timorous, more sniveling, more poltroonish, more ignominious every day....

Excerpted from "On Being an American" by H.L. Mencken, in *Prejudices: Third Series* (New York: Knopf, 1922).

WHY I STAY

Well, then, why am I still here? Why am I so complacent (perhaps even to the point of offensiveness), so free from bile, so little fretting and indignant, so curiously happy?... To be happy (reducing the thing to its elementals) I must be:

a. Well-fed, unbounded by sordid cares, at ease in Zion.

b. Full of a comfortable feeling of superiority to the masses of my fellow-men.

c. Delicately and unceasingly amused according to my taste.

It is my contention that, if this definition be accepted, there is no country on the face of the earth wherein a man roughly constituted as I am—a man of my general weaknesses, vanities, appetites, prejudices, and aversions—can be so happy, or even one-half so happy, as he can be in these free and independent states.... Here the business of getting a living, particularly since the war brought the loot of all Europe to the national strong-box, is enormously easier than it is in any other Christian land—so easy, in fact, that an educated and forehanded man who fails at it must actually make deliberate efforts to that end. Here the general average of intelligence, of knowledge, of competence, of integrity, of self-respect, of honor is so low that any man who knows his trade, does not fear ghosts, has read fifty good books, and practices the common decencies stands out as brilliantly as a wart on a bald head, and is thrown willy-nilly into a meager and exclusive aristocracy. And here, more than anywhere else that I know of or have heard of, the daily panorama of human existence, of private and communal folly—the unending procession of governmental extortions and chicaneries, of commercial brigandages and throat-slittings, of theological buffooneries, of aesthetic ribaldries, of legal swindles and harlotries, of miscellaneous rogueries, villainies, imbecilities, grotesqueries, and extravagances—is so inordinately gross and preposterous, so perfectly brought up to the highest conceivable amperage, so steadily enriched with an almost fabulous daring and originality, that only the man who was born with a petrified diaphragm can fail to laugh himself to sleep every night, and to awake every morning with all the eager, unflagging expectation of a Sunday-school superintendent touring the Paris peep-shows....

A THIRD-RATE COUNTRY

The United States is essentially a commonwealth of third-rate men—that distinction is easy here because the general level of culture, of information, of taste and judgment, of ordinary competence is so low. No sane man, employing an American plumber to repair a leaky drain, would expect him to do it at the first trial, and in precisely the same way no sane man, observing an American Secretary of State in negotiation with Englishmen and Japs, would expect him to come off better than second best. Third-rate men, of course, exist in all countries, but it is only here that they are in full control of the state, and with it of all the national standards. The land was peopled, not by the hardy adventurers of legend, but simply by incompetents who could not get on at home, and the lavishness of nature that they found here, the vast ease with which they could get livings, confirmed and augmented their native incompetence....

The United States, to my eye, is incomparably the greatest show on earth. It is a show which avoids diligently all the kinds of clowning which tire me most quickly—for example royal ceremonials, the tedious hocus-pocus of *haute politique*, the taking of politics seriously—and lays chief stress upon the kinds which delight me unceasingly—for example, the ribald combats of demagogues, the exquisitely ingenious operations of master rogues, the pursuit of witches and heretics, the desperate struggles of inferior men to claw their way into Heaven. We have clowns in constant practice among us who are as far above the clowns of any great state as a Jack Dempsey is above a paralytic—and not a few dozen or score of them, but whole droves and herds. Human enterprises which, in all other Christian countries, are resigned despairingly to an incurable dullness—things that seem devoid of exhilarating amusement by their very nature—are here lifted to such vast heights of buffoonery that contemplating them strains the midriff almost to breaking. I cite an example: the worship of God. Everywhere else on earth it is carried on in a solemn and dispiriting manner; in England, of course, the bishops are obscene, but the average man seldom gets a fair chance to laugh at them and enjoy them. Now come home. Here we not only have bishops who are enormously more obscene than even the most gifted of the English bishops; we have also a huge force of lesser specialists in ecclesiastical mountebankery—tin-horn Loyolas, Savonarolas and Xaviers of a hundred fantastic rites, each performing untiringly and each full of a grotesque and illimitable whimsicality. Every American town, however small, has one of its own: a holy clerk with so fine a talent for introducing the arts of jazz into the salvation of the damned that his performance takes on all the gaudiness of a four-ring circus, and the bald announcement that he will raid Hell on such and such a night is enough to empty all the town blind-pigs and bordellos and pack his sanctuary to the doors. And to aid him and inspire him there are traveling experts to whom he stands in the relation of a wart to the Matterhorn—stupendous masters of theological imbecility, contrivers of doctrines utterly preposterous, heirs to the Joseph Smith, Mother Eddy and John Alexander Dowie tradition—[William J.]

Bryan, [Billy] Sunday, and their like. These are the eminences of the American Sacred College. I delight in them. Their proceedings make me a happier American.

Turn, now, to politics. Consider, for example, a campaign for the Presidency. Would it be possible to imagine anything more uproariously idiotic—a deafening, nerve-wracking battle to the death between Tweedledum and Tweedledee, Harlequin and Sganarelle, Gobbo and Dr. Cook—the unspeakable, with fearful snorts, gradually swallowing the inconceivable? I defy any one to match it elsewhere on this earth. In other lands, at worst, there are at least intelligible issues, coherent ideas, salient personalities. Somebody says something, and somebody replies. But what did [Warren G.] Harding say in 1920, and what did [James] Cox reply? Who was Harding, anyhow, and who was Cox? Here, having perfected democracy, we lift the whole combat to symbolism, to transcendentalism, to metaphysics. Here we load a pair of palpably tin cannon with blank cartridges charged with talcum powder, and so let fly. Here one may howl over the show without any uneasy reminder that it is serious, and that some one may be hurt. I hold that this elevation of politics to the plane of undiluted comedy is peculiarly American, that nowhere else on this disreputable ball has the art of the sham-battle been developed to such fineness. . . .

Mirth is necessary to wisdom, to comfort, above all, to happiness. Well, here is the land of mirth, as Germany is the land of metaphysics and France is the land of fornication. Here the buffoonery never stops. What could be more delightful than the endless struggle of the Puritan to make the joy of the minority unlawful and impossible? The effort is itself a greater joy to one standing on the sidelines than any or all of the carnal joys that it combats. . . . One man prefers the Republic because it pays better wages than Bulgaria. Another because it has laws to keep him sober and his daughter chaste. Another because the Woolworth Building is higher than the cathedral at Chartres. Another because, living here, he can read the New York *Evening Journal*. Another because there is a warrant out for him somewhere else. Me, I like it because it amuses me to my taste. I never get tired of the show. It is worth every cent it costs.

Viewpoint 17B
A Critique of H.L. Mencken (1928)
Catherine Beach Ely (1873–1936)

INTRODUCTION *Catherine Beach Ely was a teacher and a writer on art criticism and social issues. In the following viewpoint, taken from a 1928 article published in the* North American Review, *she takes aim at H.L. Mencken, perhaps America's most prominent cultural critic of the 1920s. Her criticism of Mencken is also a defense of the American society Mencken made a point*

of satirizing, with its optimism, religious faith, and patriotism.

How does Ely describe Mencken? Does her description of Mencken and his writing accurately describe the tone of the opposing viewpoint? Do you think she presents an adequate response to Mencken's arguments? Why or why not?

The exile of Henry Mencken among us ignorant, naïve Americans is a tragedy of modern letters. Self-condemned to this unhappy existence by his own decision, and not by our insistence, he continues to afford us the unparalleled spectacle of his supreme condescension. He endures our stupidities and crudenesses with pained disgust. With what one would call a missionary's zeal, were not the concept missionary so foreign to his taste, he labors to convert us to the sophisticate's viewpoint. He abandons the civilizations of other lands, presumably more in harmony with his fastidious predilections, in order that we Americans may feel the contrast between his lofty intelligence and our inane futilities.

What desperate isolation, that of this apostle of pessimism stranded on the shores of cheerful, constructive America! Constructive—the very word makes the indignant Mencken shudder at the rawness of a nation bent on erecting its own destiny and well being, though undoubtedly this egregiously prosperous country of ours offers a convenient financial environment to the mental alien. . . .

AMERICA'S EXASPERATING QUALITIES

Our idiotic cheerfulness aggravates Mencken. Destitute of the acrimony which marks the superiority of the alien *literati*, we pursue our inferior bourgeois objectives with hopeful vigor, with candid and unseemly optimism. The world has been revolving on its axis since 1492, and America has not yet learned the proper attitude of cynical acquiescence to fate and of jesting unconcern for human responsibility. She insists on being useful and altruistic in spite of the oral and written precepts of our conspicuous intellectual, Mencken the Mentor. Full many a time he pushes us Yankees beneath the dark waters of pessimism, but unfailingly we bob up again on the life-preserver of our buoyant instinct for overcoming difficulties and dangers. In America apparently we cannot realize that conquering obstacles is obsolete.

Mencken deplores our antiquated regard for the sacredness of home, church, and history. We are so slow to learn that there is no such word as tradition in the lexicon of modern thought. Tradition implies affection for the past, whereas the Mencken school would

Catherine Beach Ely, ("The Sorrows of Mencken,") *North American Review*, vol. 225, no. 1 (January 1928).

have us understand that we have no past and no future worth cherishing, only the present for donning harlequin's attire and proclaiming the farcical futility of human endeavor.

Hero worship exasperates the cynics as the most foolish phase of tradition. To make a hero of an American is to imply that there is something fine in human nature and, worst of all, in American human nature. Acknowledging gratitude for a salient personality in public life runs counter to the sophisticate's assumption that gratitude is a weakness and that there is no greatness of character. Yet, in spite of Mencken's tutoring, incorrigibly stupid America continues to cherish her sacred memories and hopes. She persists in erecting monuments to her heroes, and in teaching her school-children to believe in Country and Flag—foolish America! disgruntled Mencken!

Patriotism heads Mencken's list of bourgeois offences. To be a patriot is to stir the risibles of advanced thinkers. How arrogant of America to value her experiences as a Nation, how tasteless her self-reminders of her evolution as a Republic! Columbus might better have remained comfortably in Italy; as for the Puritans, if they had foundered in the deep sea, we should have been spared the record of their austere follies. England was well rid of us, yet we are none the better for our independence. This dollar-chasing America presumes to prate of patriotism, to sing the glories of her birth, and to seek divine guidance. Mencken sorrows over all these childish tendencies, sorrows because our Nation will not cast aside her preoccupation with reminiscent emotions. Patriotism implies teamwork, the submersion of the Ego, the upward look, the strong right arm, the romance of history, whereas Menckenism puts the individual in a vacuum and tells him to exist without the atmosphere of enthusiasm expressed in national service and devotion.

America is incurably religious, although Mencken points inexorably to the signposts of modern intellectualism. She persists in putting faith and will power above barren mental cerebration. Underneath her crust of materialism she cherishes spiritual ideals. America's spiritual energy angers Mencken, because he makes himself believe that the religion of America is synonymous with hypocrisy, superstition and wrong-headedness. What right have we Americans to the consolations and inspirations of piety—we least of all peoples!

For the Mencken school faith is demoded, aspiration a weak delusion. Yet America refuses to repudiate religion. She makes it the foundation of her institutions, the motive-power of her charities, the keynote of her progress. Mencken sorrows over America's narrow conformities, so contrary to the self-sufficiency of intellectualism.

The American bourgeois blunders onward and upward instead of reclining at full length in the dry lands of Rationalism.

MENCKEN'S IMITATORS

As an alleviation for the crass stupidities of the American "booboisie", Mencken has founded a school of congenial spirits. A select inner circle of Americans choose him as their guide and pattern. Our Menckenites form an esoteric band of superior minds, whose special function it is to deride all things American. They reflect his prejudices and imitate his cawings and croakings at our absurdities. Chief among them in stereotyped implicit obedience is Sinclair Lewis. Self-acknowledged star pupil of Menckenism, Lewis incorporates his master's theories into novels which put the dunce cap on America and condemn her to the dark corner as the world's most imbecile race.

Mencken's band of imitators—the bad boys of literature—console him for his grievance at sentimental America. He has imparted to them his swagger, his bravado. They jeer at the plain person, who in the grapple with life turns to sentiments which brighten the bleakness of an unkind environment by revealing a goal worth a struggle. Like street arabs pelting strangers in comely garments, they throw derisive epithets at the kindly virtues and gracious deeds which brighten sombre places.

They have the brawler's delight in destruction—the instinct to break the bright wings of idealism, to silence the song of hope, the flutter of expectation. They love to tease, to worry, to injure the purposeful citizen pursuing the round of homely existence. "What's the use!" they sneer; "your work is futile, your faith nonsensical, your courage childish—you poor dupe, you preposterous bourgeois!" Thumbing the nose, they scoff at the harmless effusions of life. Parades, both literal and figurative, with the old fellows in uniform, the young ones beating the drum and playing the fife, the applause and enthusiasms of the crowd as an outlet for human ardor, offend the superiority complex of the Mencken coterie.

Mencken, critic *in perpetuum*, assuages his vexation at our perverse Americanisms with the cup of malice which he prepares for himself. His caustic middle age will pass into tart old age spent in the America he disdains but refuses to desert. For, were he absent from foolish America, his occupation would cease. With no America to berate, his career would vanish, his mentality atrophy. Having stored up for himself no gentle thoughts, no mellow traditions, no mild benignant pleasures of the mind, how could he live in a land he did not despise? How could he endure a congenial environment after the bracing air of antagonism to all things American? On his peak of scorn he noisily bewails America; but he enjoys his sorrows.

FOR FURTHER READING

Lorin Baritz, ed., *The Culture of the Twenties*. Indianapolis: Bobbs-Merrill, 1970.

Stanley Coben, *Rebellion Against Victorianism*. New York: Oxford University Press, 1991.

Edward A. Martin, *H.L. Mencken and the Debunkers*. Athens: University of Georgia Press, 1984.

Marion Elizbeth Rodgers, *Mencken: The American Iconoclast*. New York: Oxford University Press, 2005.

Viewpoint 18A

Prohibition Is a Success (1924)

John Gordon Cooper (1872–1955)

INTRODUCTION *Prohibition was a significant issue during the 1920s. The Eighteenth Amendment to the Constitution, which was ratified in 1919 and took effect in 1920, prohibited the manufacture, transportation, and sale of "intoxicating liquors" in the United States. Congress passed the Volstead Act in 1919 to enforce the amendment, and consumption of alcoholic beverages at first declined. However, federal and state enforcement efforts failed to stop the making, smuggling, and selling of alcohol. Much of the illicit activity was controlled by organized crime syndicates. Within a few years there was discussion of modifying the Volstead Act to allow the sale of wine and beer or to turn over its enforcement to the states. Some people began calling for the repeal of the Eighteenth Amendment altogether. The following viewpoint, a defense of Prohibition, is taken from a 1924 magazine article by John Gordon Cooper, a former railroad worker who served as a Republican congressman from Ohio from 1915 to 1937.*

What importance does Cooper attach to the fact that Prohibition is not just a federal law, but part of the Constitution? What benefits of the ban on alcohol does he list? What arguments does he make about opponents of Prohibition?

That prohibition should be strictly enforced as long as it is a part of the Constitution of the United States, and that as part of the Constitution it is deserving of the respect and support of the citizens of the United States, is not a debatable question. Our whole system of government, our greatness as a nation, and the unequaled benefits, opportunities, and privileges which we enjoy as individual Americans are all based on the Constitution. A blow at the Constitution is a blow at all that is near and dear to us. The Eighteenth Amendment prohibiting the traffic in intoxicating liquor as a beverage is an integral part of the Constitution and as such is as much entitled to respect and obedience as any other part of the fundamental law of the land. Disregard of the Eighteenth

John Gordon Cooper, "The Benefits of Prohibition," *Forum*, June 1924.

Amendment is just as serious as disregard of the guarantee that life, liberty, and property may not be taken from a citizen without due process of law. Disobedience of one law inevitably breeds disobedience of other laws and leads to anarchy. We may change the Constitution but we can not nullify it.

Even the most active enemies of prohibition do not openly advocate disobedience to the Constitution. They propose instead that the sale of beer and wine be legalized on the claim that such beverages are not intoxicating. It is not within the scope of this article to go at length into this phase of the subject, but experience has amply proved that the liquor traffic cannot be regulated, that when it is granted an inch it will take a mile, that the only way to meet the evil is to place it outside the law and then enforce the law. To legalize the sale and traffic in wine and beer would enormously increase illicit traffic in "hard" liquor.

THE EFFECTIVENESS OF PROHIBITION

The extent to which prohibition is effective today depends on the point of view. To contend that it is entirely effective in parts of some of our great cities where the entire population is of foreign extraction and where the law officers wink at violations is, of course, useless. But it is just as far from the fact to argue, as do some liquor advocates, that prohibition has increased drinking and intemperance throughout the country. Relatively, prohibition is effective and it will advance toward complete effectiveness just as rapidly as citizens come to a full realization that it is a vital part of the fundamental law of the land, and to the degree that enforcement officers are selected because of fitness and determination to do their duty instead of because of political influence and "pull". Of course it will become more effective as a new generation which never knew the open saloon takes the place of those who cannot forget their appetites for strong drink.

The effectiveness of prohibition has been a varying quantity. When war-time prohibition went into effect July 1, 1919, it was obeyed even by the hardened bootleggers and moonshiners to a remarkable degree because the people were still living under the influence of the discipline and unselfish zeal of war days. Our police statistics mirror this condition. Then came the reaction from the strain of the war, such reaction as has always followed war. There was a moral let down. Violations of the prohibition law were the result, not the cause, of this moral reaction and a turn toward the pursuit of selfish pleasures and desires.

The liquor interests soon saw what they believed to be a chance to resurrect their outlawed business. They began their smuggling operations and encouraged moonshining in order to secure supplies of intoxicating beverages for the thoughtless and the indifferent. They revived their slimy tactics of graft and bribery so that they might secure permits to withdraw bonded liquor and secure the protection of officers sworn to enforce the law. They formed alliances with corrupt politicians, and the whole country has been subjected to an unceasing propaganda aimed at law and order and a sober and decent America. . . .

Despite all obstacles and handicaps the social, economic, and industrial reforms accomplished by prohibition are so numerous that it is impossible even to catalogue them within the limited scope of this statement. No longer are there 177,790 open, legalized saloons inviting patronage and serving as centers of evil, vice, corruption, and death. The country has never been so rich and the people so sober. But for prohibition, readjustment from the war could not have gone forward so rapidly and successfully.

BENEFITS OF PROHIBITION

The death rate in the United States has fallen amazingly. In the first four years under prohibition the decrease was equivalent to saving 873,000 lives. Crime has lessened. More people may be arrested,—but for traffic law violations, breaches of some automobile, food, or sanitary regulation and not for drunkenness. The federal census shows a decrease of 5.8 per 100,000 in our criminal population from 1917 to 1922. Hundreds of penal institutions have been closed since prohibition. Judge William M. Gemmill, of Chicago, a foremost criminal authority, says that the drop in the number of arrests for drunkenness is equivalent to 500,000 a year. The licensed liquor traffic was the most fertile source of crime, and much of the existing criminality is traceable to the now outlawed liquor traffic which is encouraged by the advocates of nullification of the Constitution.

America's prosperity is the wonder of the whole world. We have five-sixths of the world's motor vehicles. Mr. R.T. Hodgkins, Vice-President of the Rollin Motors Company, asserts that at least seven million motor cars have been bought with money that formerly went to the saloon. [Business statistician] Roger Babson says that prohibition turned what would normally have been a downward trend into an upward one and thus accounts for much of our recent and present prosperity. Two or three billion dollars yearly were turned from the destructive channels of drink to the constructive channels of legitimate business.

———————— ■ ————————

The average man is the greatest gainer from prohibition.

———————— ■ ————————

Last year alone the savings deposits of the country increased a billion dollars. Insurance holdings gained eleven billion dollars and vast sums were expended for the radio, moving pictures, and other entertainments. Stock in the nation's great enterprises has been acquired by a much larger number of people. The growth of the Labor Banks is another indication that the workers are saving their money more than ever before.

That drunkenness has dropped to a minimum under prohibition is proved by the fact that in most cities a drunkard is a rare sight on the streets, and the homes for alcoholics have decreased from 238 in the time of the licensed saloon to 38 last year. There are few communities in America where it is not almost as easy to enter the lodge of a secret society without a password as it is for any one to buy a drink of intoxicating liquor without being sponsored by an acquaintance of the dealer.

The average man is the greatest gainer from prohibition. In the past ten years the per capita wealth of America has increased from $968 to $2,918, most of the gain coming after the adoption of prohibition. It is not the men and women who work for a living and are busily engaged in producing the wealth and prosperity of the nation who are agitating against prohibition. Such agitation finds far more willing supporters among the wealthy idle who want liquor to stimulate their jaded appetites in their pursuit of pleasure. It is among these people far more than among those who work with their hands that the advocates of beer and wine find aid and comfort and sympathy.

Viewpoint 18B
Prohibition Is a Failure (1926)
William H. Stayton (1861–1942)

INTRODUCTION *Throughout the 1920s a political divide grew between "wets" who wanted the federal prohibition of the sale of alcohol relaxed or repealed, and "drys" who supported the Eighteenth Amendment to the Constitution creating Prohibition. This political fault line in some respects reflected a deeper social division between America's urban and rural areas.*

In 1926 the U.S. Senate held hearings on the effectiveness of Prohibition. Among those testifying was William H. Stayton, the founder and leader of the Association Against the Prohibition Amendment. The AAPA, begun in 1922, consisted of wealthy industrialists who supported "wet" candidates for political office. Stayton in his testimony, excerpted here, summarizes what he considered to be the harmful effects of Prohibition on American society.

What has been the effect of Prohibition on the nation's drinking habits, according to Stayton? How has Prohibition changed the role of the federal government, in his opinion? How does Stayton respond to arguments that Prohibition has contributed to American economic prosperity?

The evidence presented in the hearings before the subcommittee of the Senate Judiciary Committee, uncontroverted and unchallenged, shows:

That authenticated statistics compiled and reported by the police departments of practically all of the larger cities of the United States, and many smaller ones, reveal a progressive and continuous increase in arrests for drunkenness from 1920, the first year of constitutional prohibition, to 1925, inclusive, thereby proving that prohibition is not now effectively enforced anywhere in the United States.

That arrests for drunkenness began to decline in practically all cities of the United States in 1917 and continued to drop rapidly during 1918 and 1919, and that during the period of this decline in arrests for public intoxication, milder beverages, such as beer and wine, were the principal drinks readily available for public consumption.

That by 1924 the arrests for drunkenness in the principal cities of the United States were practically as great in number as in 1916 and 1917 when they reached the high peak, and that available reports show that in 1925 they had gone higher than the pre-prohibition peak, thus proving that prohibition as a remedy for intemperance is a total failure.

FAILURE OF ENFORCEMENT

That attempted prohibition enforcement, for the first time in the history of the Republic, has introduced into important departments of the Federal Government, corruption on a colossal scale, and scandals of such magnitude as to bring discredit upon the agencies of the Government and shake the faith of the people in the integrity of the government they set up for their protection.

The testimony of Assistant Secretary of the Treasury, General Andrews, revealed that 875 prohibition agents have been dismissed for corruption. These figures represent only the discovered corruption, and there are none so sanguine as to believe that they represent more than a small proportion of the actual corruption that has existed in the prohibition unit from the day it was originated.

That after six years of national prohibition, and the expenditure of vast sums of money to enforce the law, the manufacture of alcoholic beverages by illicit distillation and diversion and conversion of denatured industrial alcohol, has become a great and growing industry. The money value of the output of these products was estimated by accredited agents of the Federal Government, charged with the duty of enforcing the prohibition law, as several times as great as the combined expenditures

William H. Stayton, *Congressional Digest*, vol. 5, no. 6 (June 1926).

for whisky, wine, beer, and other alcoholic beverages before the ratification of the Eighteenth Amendment.

Federal District Attorney Buckner of New York estimated the money value of alcoholic liquor fabricated from redistilled denatured alcohol in the States of New York and Pennsylvania alone, to be more than $3,600,000,000 a year, and Federal Prohibition Administrator Frederick C. Baird of the Pittsburgh district, estimated the value of the moonshine products of the stills he had captured in his district, in an eight-months period, to be in excess of $2,000,000,000 a year.

These facts show the value of the unlawful output of alcoholic liquor in a very small territory of the United States, not including any smuggled liquors, to be approximately $5,600,000,000 a year—about four times the value of all alcoholic liquors consumed in the United States before prohibition. In these calculations no account is taken of moonshining, unlawful distilling, diversion and conversion of industrial alcohol, outside of the States of New York and Pennsylvania, nor has consideration been given to the facts that moonshining is a much more general practice at points removed from the seaboard, and in so-called dry territory, than in the Eastern part of the United States where there has been an almost uninterrupted supply of smuggled liquors.

Furthermore, these estimates do not touch the value of the quantity of liquors—whisky, gin, wine, cider, beer, applejack, and other alcoholic concoctions now generally made in the homes throughout the length and breadth of the country—in the cities, in the suburbs, and on the farms.

That the manufacture of moonshine whisky is an almost universal practice, as illustrated by the fact that 172,000 stills or parts of stills were captured in 1925, and that the number captured year after year, has increased rather than diminished, and that the Federal Administrator of Prohibition admitted that not one still in ten in actual operation is captured by the agents of the Government.

That the stills and parts of stills were captured in vastly greater numbers in so-called dry States than in wet States, proving conclusively that where it is more difficult to obtain smuggled or diverted whisky, the demand is supplied by local manufacture.

Prohibition has created a vast army of rum-runners, moonshiners, bootleggers, and corrupt public officials.

That the enforcement of the prohibition law in centers where the sentiment of the people is strongly arrayed against it—which condition prevails in most of the populous centers of the United States and in many of the smaller cities—has become such a difficult, corrupting and crime breeding problem, that the time and effort of public officials is so largely occupied in attempted suppression of its evils that they are compelled to neglect other vastly more important public duties.

INCREASED DRINKING

That prohibition has led to increased drinking of intoxicating liquor on the part of women and children; that it has popularized the hip pocket flask; that it has made the serving of liquors in the homes a social custom; that it has contributed directly to a condition of immorality graphically and tragically illustrated in an alarming increase in social diseases, especially among the youth of the land.

That prohibition has created a vast army of rum-runners, moonshiners, bootleggers, and corrupt public officials, thereby directly breeding a condition of lawlessness unequaled in the history of the Republic, and that this era of lawlessness has been disastrous to the moral standards of government and individual citizenship, and that its evil outcroppings have been evidenced by the preponderance of desperate and violent crime now being perpetrated by the very young.

That the cost of even moderately effective control of the commercialized traffic would mount to prohibitive sums, it being estimated by United States District Attorney Buckner of New York that it would require an appropriation of at least $75,000,000 a year to restrain the commercialized industry in the State of New York.

That in addition to its complete failure as a temperance measure, as shown by the fact that public drunkenness is now as great as in any period before prohibition, it has visited upon the country a train of evils of far reaching and deadening effect upon the public morals and public conscience; that it has been a prolific breeder of crime; that it has demoralized the youth of the land, and that altogether it has been the greatest curse that ever came upon the country disguised as a blessing....

PROHIBITION AND BUSINESS

It has been the boast of the drys that prohibition is good for business. We beg to remind you that prohibition was put forward as being good for public morals, and that it has been shown that it has been disastrous to public morals. The only defense that can now be made of it is that it is a good economic measure. Prohibitionists have quoted glibly many captains of industry as being favorable to prohibition, but they did not bring any industrial leaders here to so testify. They fall back upon the testimony of Professor [Irving] Fisher of Yale University that it has saved the country $6,000,000,000 a year.

The defect in Professor Fisher's testimony is that he did not take into consideration the desperate financial plight of American farmers, who, according to Senator Capper of Kansas, have sustained a loss of $20,000,000,000 in farm values during the past five years [due to a decrease in demand for crops previously used in alcoholic beverages]; and who are now pressing before this Congress numerous bills designed to relieve them from an almost bankrupt condition.

Neither did Professor Fisher take into account the fact that men who are actually engaged in banking and business admit freely that much of present day prosperity is due to unparalleled buying on installments, with 75 to 85 per cent of all automobiles, furniture, jewelry and numerous other commodities being bought on time payments. The estimates of bankers who have studied the problem, and who have actual knowledge of the question through handling the installment paper, is that in 1925 this installment buying aggregated more than five billion dollars. It is admitted by bankers and real economists actually engaged in business that the present flourishing volume of business in the automobile industry—of which we have heard so much—is due entirely to the installment buying of motor cars. It is not, in any sense, due to prohibition, because the evidence in this case shows that a vastly greater amount of money is now being spent for some kind of alcoholic liquors than before prohibition.

FOR FURTHER READING

Norman H. Clark, *Deliver Us from Evil: An Interpretation of American Prohibition.* New York: Norton, 1976.

Thomas M. Coffey, *The Long Thirst: Prohibition in America, 1920–1933.* New York: Norton, 1975.

Thomas R. Pegram, *Battling Demon Rum: The Struggle for a Dry America, 1880–1933.* Chicago: Ivan R. Dee, 1998.

Kenneth D. Rose, *American Women and the Repeal of Prohibition.* New York: New York University Press, 1996.

THE GREAT DEPRESSION
AND THE NEW DEAL
Viewpoint 19A
Self-Help Is the Best Response to Unemployment (1932)
Henry Ford (1863–1947)

INTRODUCTION *Henry Ford, pioneering automaker and founder of the Ford Motor Company, was perhaps the most famous American businessman of his time. A self-made man with little formal schooling, he occasionally wrote newspaper and magazine articles expounding his views on American social problems. The following viewpoint is taken from two such editorials inserted by*

Ford Motor Company into the magazine Literary Digest *in 1932, during the Great Depression. To cope with America's economic difficulties, Ford advocates encouraging the unemployed to help themselves rather than depend on charity or government relief. He also idealizes rural life, encouraging people to live off the land. In June 1932, when these articles first appeared, approximately 13 million workers—about one-quarter of America's labor force—were unemployed.*

What objections does Ford have to "routine" charity? What steps has his company taken to reduce unemployment and to help the poor, according to Ford?

I have always had to work, whether any one hired me or not. For the first forty years of my life, I was an employee. When not employed by others, I employed myself. I found very early that being out of hire was not necessarily being out of work. The first means that your employer has not found something for you to do; the second means that you are waiting until he does.

We nowadays think of work as something that others find for us to do, call us to do, and pay us to do. No doubt our industrial growth is largely responsible for that. We have accustomed men to think of work that way.

In my own case, I was able to find work for others as well as myself. Outside my family life, nothing has given me more satisfaction than to see jobs increase in number and in profit to the men who handle them. And beyond question, the jobs of the world today are more numerous and profitable in wages than they were even eighteen years ago.

THE PROBLEM OF UNEMPLOYMENT

But something entirely outside the workshops of the nation has affected this hired employment very seriously. The word "unemployment" has become one of the most dreadful words in the language. The condition itself has become the concern of every person in the country.

When this condition arrived, there were just three things to be done. The first, of course, was to maintain employment at the maximum by every means known to management. Employment—hire—was what the people were accustomed to; they preferred it; it was the immediate solution of the difficulty. In our plants we used every expedient to spread as much employment over as many employes as was possible. I don't believe in "make work"—the public pays for all unnecessary work—but there are times when the plight of others compels us to do the human thing even though it be but a makeshift; and I am obliged to admit that, like most manufacturers, we avoided layoffs by continuing work that good business judgment would have halted. All of our non-profit work was continued in full force and much of the shop work.

Henry Ford, "On Unemployment," *Literary Digest*, June 11 & 18, 1932.

There were always tens of thousands employed—the lowest point at Dearborn [Michigan] was 40,000—but there were always thousands unemployed or so meagerly employed, that the situation was far from desirable.

When all possible devices for providing employment have been used and fall short, there remains no alternative but self-help or charity.

I do not believe in routine charity. I think it a shameful thing that any man should have to stoop to take it, or give it. I do not include human helpfulness under the name of charity. My quarrel with charity is that it is neither helpful nor human. The charity of our cities is the most barbarous thing in our system, with the possible exception of our prisons. What we call charity is a modern substitute for being personally kind, personally concerned and personally involved in the work of helping others in difficulty. True charity is a much more costly effort than money-giving. Our donations too often purchase exemption from giving the only form of help that will drive the need for charity out of the land.

Our own theory of helping people has been in operation for some years. We used to discuss it years ago—when no one could be persuaded to listen. Those who asked for public attention to these matters were ridiculed by the very people who now call most loudly for some one to do something.

Our own work involves the usual emergency relief, hospitalization, adjustment of debt, with this addition—we help people to alter their affairs in common-sense accordance with changed conditions, and we have an understanding that all help received should be repaid in reasonable amounts in better times. Many families were not so badly off as they thought; they needed guidance in the management of their resources and opportunities. Human nature, of course, presented the usual problems. Relying on human sympathy many develop a spirit of professional indigence. But where co-operation is given, honest and self-respecting persons and families can usually be assisted to a condition which is much less distressing than they feared. . . .

Great numbers of people have made the stimulating discovery that they need not depend on employers to find work for them—they can find work for themselves.

SELF-HELP

But there is still another way, a third way, so much better than the very best charitable endeavor that it simply forbids us to be satisfied with anything less. That is the way of Self-Help....

If it is right and proper to help people to become wise managers of their own affairs in good times, it cannot be wrong to pursue the same object in dull times. Independence through self-dependence is a method which must commend itself when understood.

Methods of self-help are numerous and great numbers of people have made the stimulating discovery that they need not depend on employers to find work for them—they can find work for themselves. I have more definitely in mind those who have not yet made that discovery, and I should like to express certain convictions I have tested.

The land! That is where our roots are. There is the basis of our physical life. The farther we get away from the land, the greater our insecurity. From the land comes everything that supports life, everything we use for the service of physical life. The land has not collapsed or shrunk in either extent or productivity. It is there waiting to honor all the labor we are willing to invest in it, and able to tide us across any dislocation of economic conditions.

No unemployment insurance can be compared to an alliance between a man and a plot of land. With one foot in industry and another foot in the land, human society is firmly balanced against most economic uncertainties. With a job to supply him with cash, and a plot of land to guarantee him support, the individual is doubly secure. Stocks may fail, but seedtime and harvest do not fail.

I am not speaking of stop-gaps or temporary expedients. Let every man and every family at this season of the year cultivate a plot of land and raise a sufficient supply for themselves or others. Every city and village has vacant space whose use would be permitted. Groups of men could rent farms for small sums and operate them on the co-operative plan. Employed men, in groups often, twenty or fifty, could rent farms and operate them with several unemployed families. Or, they could engage a farmer with his farm to be their farmer this year, either as employee or on shares. There are farmers who would be glad to give a decent indigent family a corner of a field on which to live and provide against next winter. Industrial concerns everywhere would gladly make it possible for their men, employed and unemployed, to find and work the land. Public-spirited citizens and institutions would most willingly assist in these efforts at self-help.

I do not urge this solely or primarily on the ground of need. It is a definite step to the restoration of normal business activity. Families who adopt self-help have that amount of free money to use in the channels of trade. That in turn means a flow of goods, an increase in employment, a general benefit.

NO ONE IS HURT

When I suggested this last year and enabled our own people to make the experiment, the critics said that it would mean competition with the farmer. If that were true it would constitute a serious defect in the plan. My interest in the success and prosperity of the farmer is attested by my whole business career. The farmer is carrying in the form of heavy taxes the burden of families who cannot afford to buy his produce. Enabling them to raise their own food would not be taking a customer away from the farmer, but would be actually lifting a family off the tax-payer's back. It is argued that farm products are so cheap that it is better to buy than to grow them. This would be impressive if every one had money to spend. Farm products are cheap because purchasing power is low. And the farmer paying taxes helps to pay the difference. The course I suggest is not competition with the farmer; it deprives him of no customer; it does not affect the big market crops. Gardens never hurt the farmer. Partnerships between groups of city men and individual farmers certainly help the farmer. When a family lifts itself off the welfare lists or increases its free cash by raising its food, it actually helps the farmer as it does every one else, including itself. In fact, it is fundamental that *no one is hurt by self-help.* In the relief of tax burdens and the revival of industry the farmer would share the benefit.

Viewpoint 19B
Self-Help Is Not Enough (1932)
Charles R. Walker (1893–1974)

INTRODUCTION *Unemployment during the Great Depression was high, eventually peaking at about 25 percent of America's labor force. In the following viewpoint, Charles R. Walker examines the fate of one laborer who was laid off from the Ford Motor Company. In his depiction of John Boris and workers in similar situations, Walker exposes the limits of self-help as advocated by Henry Ford (see viewpoint 19A). Walker, a former steelworker, was a writer whose works examined the effects of industrial technology on the American laborer.*

How does John Boris, the Ford worker Walker profiles, respond to losing his job? Why is Boris relatively lucky, in Walker's view? Does Boris's situation provide an example of the efficacy as well as the limits of self-help? Why or why not?

In 1914 an extraordinary thing occurred in America. An automobile manufacturer in Detroit announced that he was raising wages for common labor to five dollars a day. Newspaper headlines in Detroit went a little crazy;

Excerpted from Charles Walker, "Down and Out in Detroit," in *America Faces the Future*, edited by Charles A. Beard (Boston: Houghton Mifflin, 1932).

the streets of the city and of the [nearby] little town of Dearborn were packed with workmen fighting for a chance to work at the new wage. And automobile manufacturers of Detroit and elsewhere raged and gave out desperate interviews prophesying doom. Detectives came to Detroit to investigate Henry Ford. But above all, workmen from all over the United States bought railroad tickets and boarded trains for Detroit. Among the latter was John (once Anton) Boris, American citizen of Slav descent, father of a family, who had ambitions to be a 'millerwright' and needed cash for an expanding family. He had been a logger in a Michigan lumber camp, then a worker in an Ohio steel mill where he earned from two to three dollars a day. With thousands of others, he now came to Detroit.

WORKING AT FORD

'In dose days work was hard all right at Ford's, but dey treat us like mens.' . . .

John Boris's wages at Ford's rose steadily as the years passed, till he was making eight dollars a day: His young wife, whom he had found it a delight to cherish as he had promised the priest, had borne him eight children, five of whom were living and going to Michigan schools. One day a letter arrived from a friend in a Texas oil field, saying to come out there for a good job. 'I think I go all right,' he told me, 'can get twenty dollar a day.' But his wife expressed other ideas. 'You stay wid Ford; here steady job—better dan big money for you; las' all de years what you live.' Boris stayed at Ford's.

'The American way,' said the automobile manufacturer in 1927, 'is to pay wages sufficient to guarantee the workingman not only subsistence, but the comforts and some of the luxuries of life. Let him buy a car, a radio, and an American home!' The children wanted a radio, so John got one; but he resisted his foreman's appeal to buy a car, even though American salesmanship did what it could against his Slavic conservatism. Public advice to 'buy a home,' however, appealed to an instinct. The real estate agent made out his contract. There was a five hundred dollars down payment and fifty dollars a month. He started payments and moved in. The house seemed in a sense to be rounding out his millwright's career for him; and better, he thought, than a car—even though the neighbors boasted of both.

It was in this house, under the shaded light of the 'parlor lamp,' that Boris the other day gave me in his own words the final chapter of this history. The house was subject to foreclosure in default of payment, but the furniture was still intact. The radio stood at the left of the chair where Boris sat; a double door led into a pleasant dining-room.

'Fourteen year,' said Boris, leaning forward, 'I work for Henry Ford. All kin' jobs . . . millerwright, danger jobs; I put in all my young days Henry Ford. Las' July, what you know, he lay me off. When I go out of factory that day I don' believe; I don' believe he do such ting to me. I tink trouble wid man in de office who don' un'erstan'.' His voice ceased and he took a deep breath which was expended in the earnest emphasis of his next words: 'I tink,' he said, 'I go Henry Ford *pers'nally!* But what you know!' He looked like a boy whom a drunken father had whipped into physical submission. His voice was angry, but with a deep hurt at the core of it. 'I can' get close to him,' he cried, 'I can' get clos' even employment man. De guard say, "We got your name in dere all right, we let you know when we wan' you." Nine mont',' he concluded, 'I go no work.'

COPING WITH UNEMPLOYMENT

Figures show that 14.2 per cent of Detroit's normally employed are out of jobs. Other cities follow close, with Cleveland at 13.8 per cent and Chicago at 13.3. The distinction of Detroit, however, is not that she has been hardest hit in the depression, but that she has done something to buck it. Municipal and community leadership—not the manufacturers—are doing what they can.

During the first of his workless periods, Boris was able to support his family and to continue regular payments on his home. Against public pressure he had exercised thrift, and had in reserve a few hundred dollars. But misfortunes did not attack him singly. His wife fell ill and an operation for a tumor was demanded. Boris met the emergency and hired the best doctor he could find. A kidney operation on the woman followed the first, running up medical charges for hospital and doctor to eight hundred dollars. Somewhere during this epoch the son of John Boris, who had gone to an American school and could put matters clearly in written English, composed a letter to the welfare department of the Ford Motor Company.

An 'investigator' arrived promptly, and took the chair, Boris informed me, in which I was sitting. 'Investigator say, "Boris, employment have no right do that to you. You get job back right away. Seven o'clock tomorrow morning you go employment; he put you back on job; tak' this slip." '

Going back the next morning through the high mill gate, with the slip tightly held in his fingers, Boris found delightedly that he was admitted to the office. 'We cannot give you your old job,' they told him, 'at eight dollars a day, but we will give you a new one at six dollars for three days a week.' 'Yes, all right,' said Boris. Lay-off and rehire with a dock of a dollar or two a day is common in the automobile industry. It enables the manufacturer to give the appearance of 'maintaining wages' while effecting the needed economies in his payroll. The same work is performed on 'the new job.' Boris was glad. 'Hard times for everybody,' he explained, 'sure, I take.' The employment manager continued courteously: 'After you work sixty days, you will receive seven dollars a day.' ...

On the sixty-first day, Boris received the promised seven dollars. On the sixty-third his foreman fired him. 'You're finished, Boris,' he said. To Boris it seemed clear that he had been dropped because he was 'making too much money.' And because there were thousands waiting to take his job at minimum pay. But he repressed this resentment and went to the office. 'Anything wrong wid my work for comp'ny?' he asked earnestly. No, the employment man assured him; his work was satisfactory. 'Wid my records for comp'ny?' he persisted, knowing that in hard times a man's record is his friend. 'No,' said the employment man, 'you have a good record with the company. But there is no longer any work for you.' The office then stated that this was not a lay-off, but, as Boris had expressed it, 'finish.' Boris then exploded. In reminiscence of what he had said, his voice came somewhere from the middle of his chest; it was compacted of fourteen years of exploded loyalty.

'I haf' no money now,' he cried, 'lose my home quick, what I do chil'ren, what I do doctor? Fourteen years!' he returned to his original cry, 'I work Henry Ford!'

The employment man looked at him. 'That is a long time; you should have saved money, Boris, to take care of you in your old age.'

Boris trembled. 'You say dat to me!' he cried, struggling for possession of himself. 'I give up my strength to you; I put in all my young days work good for Henry Ford—you can' do dis to me now!'

'Why did you spend all your money? asked the employment man.

'For why? I tell you. I spen' money for house,' replied John Boris, 'to raise fam'ly, to sen' my chil'ren school, to buy foods, *dat's how I spen' money*—'

'Your children are your own business,' said the other, 'not Henry Ford's.'

BETRAYED LOYALTY

Even in recollection of this episode which terminated his career and hastened the break-up of his family, I was struck by the special character of Boris's resentment. It seemed clear that he was torn as terribly by the blasting of his workman's loyalty as by the enormity of his personal loss.

'I go out from mill,' he continued. 'I try tink what I do help mysel'. Who I go to? I use tink,' he cried, 'if

something come like dis, go to Henry Ford yoursel'. But I tell you no workman beeg enough see Henry Ford! Well, I go lawyer—I happen to know him once—who knows ting like dis more what I do. I say: "What can I do now?" He say: "Nutting, John, ain' nutting you can do!"'

His particular case, in which job, savings, and home were wiped out, was one of the lucky ones.

John Boris refused to accept the dictum of the lawyer that there was nothing he could do. In accordance with the formula that 'there is plenty of work in the world if a man be willing to take it,' he buried the pride of a skilled maturity, and found a few hours' work in a cushion factory, accepting a wage twenty-seven and one half cents an hour less than Ford's minimum rate in 1914. But long before he managed this, his daughters had taken jobs in the same factory to which he came ultimately. They carried and are still carrying the bulk of the family load.

These latter items make the story of John Boris a relatively lucky one. The family enjoys a small income from wages; John Boris is not, and except only for a few weeks between the time of 'finish' at Ford's and the cushion factory job, has not been rated as one of the unemployed. And he is lucky enough to have escaped charity. ...

ONE OF THE LUCKY ONES

With some effort I looked into the work of the Ford employment office and of the welfare department of the Ford Motor Company. A comprehensive stagger system I found had been organized to spread work among the largest possible number. Further than this, a sincere effort was being made everywhere to give jobs to the neediest. Boris was dismissed, I am ready to believe, not through carelessness—but because relatively worse cases needed his job more. In fact the wealth of data put before me by the mayor's unemployment committee of the city of Detroit confirms me in the belief that his particular case, in which job, savings, and home were wiped out, was one of the lucky ones.

In addition to Mr. Boris's case, there are 227,000 men totally unemployed. Let us consider some of these. Out of the number, fifteen thousand are reported homeless. Boris as yet is not of this class and will probably escape it by living with relatives. These men are now housed in the 'emergency lodges,' better known as 'flop houses,' which are maintained at the city's expense. What are they like? Take the 'Fisher East Side Lodge.' It is a huge unused factory building lent to the city by Fisher Brothers and housing, when I visited it, sixteen hundred men. Here I found bank tellers with twenty to thirty years' experience, traveling salesmen, expert toolmakers, a vice-president or two, and workmen of every variety.

FOR FURTHER READING

Edward Keller, *Mister Ford—What Have You Done?: Henry Ford's Views on Economics.* Qubin, MO: Keaton Keller, 1993.

Milton Meltzer, *Brother, Can You Spare a Dime? The Great Depression, 1929–1933.* New York: New American Library, 1977.

Studs Terkel, *Hard Times: An Oral History of the Great Depression.* New York: Pantheon Books, 1986.

T.H. Watkins, *The Hungry Years: A Narrative History of the Great Depression in America.* New York: Henry Holt, 1999.

Viewpoint 20A
America Needs a New Deal (1932)
Franklin D. Roosevelt (1882–1945)

INTRODUCTION *In July 1932, with the nation in the depths of the Great Depression, the Democratic Party nominated Franklin D. Roosevelt to run for president. Roosevelt was then governor of New York, where he had presided over the expansion of state government programs to deal with unemployment and other economic problems. In accepting the presidential nomination, Roosevelt broke with tradition by personally addressing the Democratic National Convention. In his speech, excerpted here, Roosevelt describes what he holds as fundamental differences between the nation's two main political parties concerning government, and proposes new actions by the federal government to help farmers, the unemployed, and others hurt by the Great Depression. It was in this speech that he introduced the term "New Deal" to the American public.*

How does Roosevelt describe the differences between America's political parties? What "simple moral principle" does he state as the basis for his program?

There are two ways of viewing the Government's duty in matters affecting economic and social life. The first sees to it that a favored few are helped and hopes that some of their prosperity will leak through, sift through, to labor, to the farmer, to the small business man. That theory belongs to the party of Toryism, and I had hoped that most of the Tories left this country in 1776.

But it is not and never will be the theory of the Democratic Party. This is no time for fear, for reaction or for

Franklin D. Roosevelt, from his address to the Democratic National Convention, July 2, 1932. Reprinted in *Nothing to Fear: The Selected Addresses of Franklin Delano Roosevelt*, edited by B.C. Zevin (Boston: Houghton Mifflin, 1946).

timidity. Here and now I invite those nominal Republicans who find that their conscience cannot be squared with the groping and the failure of their party leaders to join hands with us; here and now, in equal measure, I warn those nominal Democrats who squint at the future with their faces turned toward the past, and who feel no responsibility to the demands of the new time, that they are out of step with their Party.

Yes, the people of this country want a genuine choice this year, not a choice between two names for the same reactionary doctrine. Ours must be a party of liberal thought, of planned action, of enlightened international outlook, and of the greatest good to the greatest number of our citizens.

Now it is inevitable—and the choice is that of the times—it is inevitable that the main issue of this campaign should revolve about the clear fact of our economic condition, a depression so deep that it is without precedent in modern history. It will not do merely to state, as do Republican leaders to explain their broken promises of continued inaction, that the depression is worldwide. That was not their explanation of the apparent prosperity of 1928. The people will not forget the claim made by them then that prosperity was only a domestic product manufactured by a Republican President and a Republican Congress. If they claim paternity for the one they cannot deny paternity for the other.

RECENT HISTORY

I cannot take up all the problems today. I want to touch on a few that are vital. Let us look a little at the recent history and the simple economics, the kind of economics that you and I and the average man and woman talk.

In the years before 1929 we know that this country had completed a vast cycle of building and inflation; for ten years we expanded on the theory of repairing the wastes of the War, but actually expanding far beyond that, and also beyond our natural and normal growth. Now it is worth remembering, and the cold figures of finance prove it, that during that time there was little or no drop in the prices that the consumer had to pay, although those same figures proved that the cost of production fell very greatly; corporate profit resulting from this period was enormous; at the same time little of that profit was devoted to the reduction of prices. The consumer was forgotten. Very little of it went into increased wages; the worker was forgotten, and by no means an adequate proportion was even paid out in dividends—the stockholder was forgotten.

And, incidentally, very little of it was taken by taxation to the beneficent Government of those years.

What was the result? Enormous corporate surpluses piled up—the most stupendous in history. Where, under the spell of delirious speculation, did those surpluses go? Let us talk economies that the figures prove and that we can understand. Why, they went chiefly in two directions: first, into new and unnecessary plants which now stand stark and idle; and second, into the call-money market [options to buy stock based on the belief the price will rise] of Wall Street, either directly by the corporations, or indirectly through the banks. Those are the facts. Why blink at them?

THE STOCK MARKET CRASH

Then came the crash. You know the story. Surpluses invested in unnecessary plants became idle. Men lost their jobs; purchasing power dried up; banks became frightened and started calling loans. Those who had money were afraid to part with it. Credit contracted. Industry stopped. Commerce declined, and unemployment mounted.

And there we are today.

Translate that into human terms. See how the events of the past three years have come home to specific groups of people: first, the group dependent on industry; second, the group dependent on agriculture; third, and made up in large part of members of the first two groups, the people who are called "small investors and depositors." In fact, the strongest possible tie between the first two groups, agriculture and industry, is the fact that the savings and to a degree the security of both are tied together in that third group—the credit structure of the Nation.

Never in history have the interests of all the people been so united in a single economic problem. Picture to yourself, for instance, the great groups of property owned by millions of our citizens, represented by credits issued in the form of bonds and mortgages—Government bonds of all kinds, Federal, State, county, municipal; bonds of industrial companies, of utility companies; mortgages on real estate in farms and cities, and finally the vast investments of the Nation in the railroads. What is the measure of the security of each of those groups? We know well that in our complicated, interrelated credit structure if any one of these credit groups collapses they may all collapse. Danger to one is danger to all.

How, I ask, has the present Administration in Washington treated the interrelationship of these credit groups? The answer is clear: It has not recognized that interrelationship existed at all. Why, the Nation asks, has Washington failed to understand that all of these groups, each and every one, the top of the pyramid and the bottom of the pyramid, must be considered together, that each and every one of them is dependent on every other; each and every one of them affecting the whole financial fabric?

Statesmanship and vision, my friends, require relief to all at the same time.

TAXES AND SPENDING

Just one word or two on taxes, the taxes that all of us pay toward the cost of Government of all kinds.

I know something of taxes. For three long years I have been going up and down this country preaching that Government—Federal and State and local—costs too much. I shall not stop that preaching. As an immediate program of action we must abolish useless offices. We must eliminate unnecessary functions of Government—functions, in fact, that are not definitely essential to the continuance of Government. We must merge, we must consolidate subdivisions of Government, and, like the private citizen, give up luxuries which we can no longer afford.

By our example at Washington itself, we shall have the opportunity of pointing the way of economy to local government, for let us remember well that out of every tax dollar in the average State in this Nation, forty cents enter the treasury in Washington, D.C., ten or twelve cents only go to the State capitals, and forty-eight cents are consumed by the costs of local government in counties and cities and towns.

I propose to you, my friends, and through you, that Government of all kinds, big and little, be made solvent and that the example be set by the President of the United States and his Cabinet....

UNEMPLOYMENT

And now one word about unemployment, and incidentally about agriculture. I have favored the use of certain types of public works as a further emergency means of stimulating employment and the issuance of bonds to pay for such public works, but I have pointed out that no economic end is served if we merely build without building for a necessary purpose. Such works, of course, should insofar as possible be self-sustaining if they are to be financed by the issuing of bonds. So as to spread the points of all kinds as widely as possible, we must take definite steps to shorten the working day and the working week.

Let us use common sense and business sense. Just as one example, we know that a very hopeful and immediate means of relief, both for the unemployed and for agriculture, will come from a wide plan of the converting of many millions of acres of marginal and unused land into timberland through reforestation. There are tens of millions of acres east of the Mississippi River alone in abandoned farms, in cut-over land, now growing up in worthless brush. Why, every European Nation has a definite land policy, and has had one for generations. We have none. Having none, we face a future of soil erosion and timber famine. It is clear that economic foresight and immediate employment march hand in hand in the call for the reforestation of these vast areas. In so doing, employment can be given to a million men. That is the kind of public work that is self-sustaining, and therefore capable of being financed by the issuance of bonds which are made secure by the fact that the growth of tremendous crops will provide adequate security for the investment.

Yes, I have a very definite program for providing employment by that means. I have done it, and I am doing it today in the State of New York. I know that the Democratic Party can do it successfully in the Nation. That will put men to work, and that is an example of the action that we are going to have.

AID TO AGRICULTURE

Now as a further aid to agriculture, we know perfectly well—but have we come out and said so clearly and distinctly?—we should repeal immediately those provisions of law that compel the Federal Government to go into the market to purchase, to sell, to speculate in farm products in a futile attempt to reduce farm surpluses. And they are the people who are talking of keeping Government out of business. The practical way to help the farmer is by an arrangement that will, in addition to lightening some of the impoverishing burdens from his back, do something toward the reduction of the surpluses of staple commodities that hang on the market. It should be our aim to add to the world prices of staple products the amount of a reasonable tariff protection, to give agriculture the same protection that industry has today.

And in exchange for this immediately increased return I am sure that the farmers of this Nation would agree ultimately to such planning of their production as would reduce the surpluses and make it unnecessary in later years to depend on dumping those surpluses abroad in order to support domestic prices. That result has been accomplished in other Nations; why not in America, too? . . .

WORK AND SECURITY

My program, of which I can only touch on these points, is based upon this simple moral principle: the welfare and the soundness of a nation depend first upon what the great mass of the people wish and need; and second, whether or not they are getting it.

What do the people of America want more than anything else? To my mind, they want two things: work, with all the moral and spiritual values that go with it; and with work, a reasonable measure of security—security for themselves and for their wives and children. Work and security—these are more than words. They are more than

facts. They are the spiritual values, the true goal toward which our efforts of reconstruction should lead. These are the values that this program is intended to gain; these are the values we have failed to achieve by the leadership we now have.

Our Republican leaders tell us economic laws—sacred, inviolable, unchangeable—cause panics which no one could prevent. But while they prate of economic laws, men and women are starving. We must lay hold of the fact that economic laws are not made by nature. They are made by human beings.

Never before in modern history have the essential differences between the two major American parties stood out in such striking contrast as they do today.

Yes, when—not if—when we get the chance, the Federal Government will assume bold leadership in distress relief. For years Washington has alternated between putting its head in the sand and saying there is no large number of destitute people in our midst who need food and clothing, and then saying the State should take care of them, if there are. Instead of planning two and a half years ago to do what they are now trying to do, they kept putting it off from day to day, week to week, and month to month, until the conscience of America demanded action.

I say that while primary responsibility for relief rests with localities now, as ever, yet the Federal Government has always had and still has a continuing responsibility for the broader public welfare. It will soon fulfill that responsibility. . . .

A NEW DEAL

Never before in modern history have the essential differences between the two major American parties stood out in such striking contrast as they do today. Republican leaders not only have failed in material things, they have failed in national vision, because in disaster they have held out no hope, they have pointed out no path for the people below to climb back to places of security and of safety in our American life.

Throughout the Nation men and women, forgotten in the political philosophy of the Government of the last years, look to us here for guidance and for more equitable opportunity to share in the distribution of national wealth.

On the farms, in the large metropolitan areas, in the smaller cities and in the villages, millions of our citizens cherish the hope that their old standards of living and of thought have not gone forever. Those millions cannot and shall not hope in vain.

I pledge you, I pledge myself, to a new deal for the American people. Let us all here assembled constitute ourselves prophets of a new order of competence and of courage. This is more than a political campaign; it is a call to arms. Give me your help, not to win votes alone, but to win in this crusade to restore America to its own people.

Viewpoint 20B

Roosevelt's New Deal Would Destroy America (1932)

Herbert Hoover (1874–1964)

INTRODUCTION *Elected in 1928, Herbert Hoover was president of the United States during the first years of the Great Depression. His popularity suffered as economic conditions worsened in the early 1930s. Nonetheless, the Republican Party chose him to run for reelection as president in 1932. During the campaign he both defended his presidency and attacked his Democratic opponent, Franklin D. Roosevelt. In the following viewpoint, excerpted from a campaign address given at New York City's Madison Square Garden on October 31, 1932, Hoover defends his record and what he calls the "American system" of individual freedom and limited government.*

What does Hoover see as the proper role for the federal government in managing America's economy? What aspects of the "American system" are most threatened by a Roosevelt presidency, according to Hoover? What hope does Hoover offer the nation about its future?

This campaign is more than a contest between two men. It is more than a contest between two parties. It is a contest between two philosophies of government.

We are told by the opposition that we must have a change, that we must have a new deal. It is not the change that comes from normal development of national life to which I object, but the proposal to alter the whole foundations of our national life which have been builded through generations of testing and struggle, and of the principles upon which we have builded the Nation. The expressions our opponents use must refer to important changes in our economic and social system and our system of Government, otherwise they are nothing but vacuous words. And I realize that in this time of distress many of our people are asking whether our social and economic system is incapable of that great primary

Herbert Hoover, from a campaign speech delivered at Madison Square Garden, New York City, October 31, 1932. Reprinted in *The State Papers and other Public Writings of Herbert Hoover*, vol. 2, edited by William Starr Myers (New York: Doubleday, Dorian & Co., 1934).

function of providing security and comfort of life to all of the firesides of our 25,000,000 homes in America, whether our social system provides for the fundamental development and progress of our people, whether our form of government is capable of originating and sustaining that security and progress.

This question is the basis upon which our opponents are appealing to the people in their fears and distress. They are proposing changes and so-called new deals which would destroy the very foundations of our American system. . . .

THE AMERICAN SYSTEM

Let us pause for a moment and examine the American system of government, of social and economic life, which it is now proposed that we should alter. Our system is the product of our race and of our experience in building a nation to heights unparalleled in the whole history of the world. It is a system peculiar to the American people. It differs essentially from all others in the world. It is an American system.

It is founded on the conception that only through ordered liberty, through freedom to the individual, and equal opportunity to the individual will his initiative and enterprise be summoned to spur the march of progress.

It is by the maintenance of equality of opportunity and therefore of a society absolutely fluid in freedom of the movement of its human particles that our individualism departs from the individualism of Europe. We resent class distinction because there can be no rise for the individual through the frozen strata of classes, and no stratification of classes can take place in a mass livened by the free rise of its particles. Thus in our ideals the able and ambitious are able to rise constantly from the bottom to leadership in the community.

This freedom of the individual creates of itself the necessity and the cheerful willingness of men to act cooperatively in a thousand ways and for every purpose as occasion arises; and it permits such voluntary cooperations to be dissolved as soon as they have served their purpose, to be replaced by new voluntary associations for new purposes.

There has thus grown within us, to gigantic importance, a new conception. That is, this voluntary cooperation within the community. Cooperation to perfect the social organization; cooperation for the care of those in distress; cooperation for the advancement of knowledge, of scientific research, of education; for cooperative action in the advancement of many phases of economic life. This is self-government by the people outside of Government; it is the most powerful development of individual freedom and equal opportunity that has taken place in the century and a half since our fundamental institutions were founded.

It is in the further development of this cooperation and a sense of its responsibility that we should find solutions for many of our complex problems, and not by the extension of government into our economic and social life. The greatest function of government is to build up that cooperation, and its most resolute action should be to deny the extension of bureaucracy. We have developed great agencies of cooperation by the assistance of the Government which promote and protect the interests of individuals and the smaller units of business. The Federal Reserve System, in its strengthening and support of the smaller banks; the Farm Board, in its strengthening and support of the farm cooperatives; the Home Loan Banks, in the mobilizing of building and loan associations and savings banks; the Federal Land Banks, in giving independence and strength to land mortgage associations; the great mobilization of relief to distress, the mobilization of business and industry in measures of recovery, and a score of other activities are not socialism—they are the essence of protection to the development of free men.

The primary conception of this whole American system is not the regimentation of men but the cooperation of free men. It is founded upon the conception of responsibility of the individual to the community, of the responsibility of local government to the state, of the state to the National Government.

It is founded on a peculiar conception of self-government designed to maintain this equal opportunity to the individual, and through decentralization it brings about and maintains these responsibilities. The centralization of government will undermine responsibilities and will destroy the system. . . .

DEMOCRATIC PROPOSALS

A proposal of our opponents which would break down the American system is the expansion of Government expenditure by yielding to sectional and group raids on the Public Treasury. The extension of Government expenditures beyond the minimum limit necessary to conduct the proper functions of the Government enslaves men to work for the Government. If we combine the whole governmental expenditures—National, state, and municipal—we will find that before the World War each citizen worked, theoretically, 25 days out of each year for the Government. In 1924 he worked 46 days a year for the Government. Today he works for the support of all forms of government 61 days out of the year.

No nation can conscript its citizens for this proportion of men's time without national impoverishment and destruction of their liberties. Our Nation cannot do it without destruction to our whole conception of the American system. The Federal Government has been forced in this emergency to unusual expenditures but in partial alleviation of these extraordinary and unusual expenditures, the Republican Administration has made a successful effort to reduce the ordinary running expenses of the Government. Our opponents have persistently interfered with such policies. I only need recall to you that the Democratic House of Representatives passed bills in the last session that would have increased our expenditures by $3,500,000,000, or 87 per cent. Expressed in day's labor, this would have meant the conscription of 16 days' additional work from every citizen for the Government. This I stopped. . . . But the major point I wish to make—the disheartening part of these proposals of our opponents—is that they represent successful pressures of minorities. They would appeal to sectional and group political support, and thereby impose terrific burdens upon every home in the country. These things can and must be resisted. But they can only be resisted if there shall be live and virile public support to the Administration, in opposition to political log-rolling and the sectional and group raids on the Treasury for distribution of public money, which is cardinal in the congeries of elements which make up the Democratic party.

These expenditures proposed by the Democratic House of Representatives for the benefit of special groups and special sections of our country directly undermine the American system. Those who pay are, in the last analysis, the man who works at the bench, the desk, and on the farm. They take away his comfort, stifle his leisure, and destroy his equal opportunity. . . .

ENDING POVERTY

I am not setting up the contention that our American system is perfect. No human ideal has ever been perfectly attained, since humanity itself is not perfect. But the wisdom of our forefathers and the wisdom of the 30 men who have preceded me in this office hold to the conception that progress can only be attained as the sum of accomplishments of free individuals, and they have held unalterably to these principles.

In the ebb and flow of economic life our people in times of prosperity and ease naturally tend to neglect the vigilance over their rights. Moreover, wrongdoing is obscured by apparent success in enterprise. Then insidious diseases and wrongdoings grow apace. But we have in the past seen in times of distress and difficulty that wrongdoing and weakness come to the surface and our people, in their endeavors to correct these wrongs, are tempted to extremes which may destroy rather than build.

It is men who do wrong, not our institutions. It is men who violate the laws and public rights. It is men, not institutions, which must be punished.

In my acceptance speech four years ago at Palo Alto I stated that—

One of the oldest aspirations of the human race was the abolition of poverty. By poverty I mean the grinding by under-nourishment, cold, ignorance, fear of old age to those who have the will to work.

I stated that—

In America today we are nearer a final triumph over poverty than in any land. The poorhouse has vanished from amongst us; we have not reached that goal, but given a chance to go forward, we shall, with the help of God, be in sight of the day when poverty will be banished from this Nation.

Our Democratic friends have quoted this passage many times in this campaign. I do not withdraw a word of it. When I look about the world even in these times of trouble and distress I find it more true in this land than anywhere else under the traveling sun. I am not ashamed of it, because I am not ashamed of holding ideals and purposes for the progress of the American people. Are my Democratic opponents prepared to state that they do not stand for this ideal or this hope? For my part, I propose to continue to strive for it, and I hope to live to see it accomplished. . . .

AMERICA'S CHOICE

My countrymen, the proposals of our opponents represent a profound change in American life—less in concrete proposal, bad as that may be, than by implication and by evasion. Dominantly in their spirit they represent a radical departure from the foundations of 150 years which have made this the greatest nation in the world. This election is not a mere shift from the ins to the outs. It means deciding the direction our Nation will take over a century to come.

FOR FURTHER READING

Frank Freidel, *FDR: Rendezvous with Destiny.* Boston: Little, Brown, 1990.

Louise W. Liebovich, *Bylines in Despair: Herbert Hoover, the Great Depression, and the U.S. News Media.* Westport, CT: Praeger, 1994.

Steve Neal, *Happy Days Are Here Again: The 1932 Democratic Convention, the Emergence of FDR—And How America Was Changed Forever.* New York: William Morrow, 2004.

Elliot A. Rosen, *Hoover, Roosevelt, and the Brains Trust: From Depression to New Deal.* New York: Columbia University Press, 1977.

Joan Hoff Wilson, *Herbert Hoover, Forgotten Progressive.* Boston: Little, Brown, 1975.

Redistributing America's Wealth Would Solve the Depression (1934)

Huey P. Long (1893–1935)

INTRODUCTION *During President Franklin D. Roosevelt's first term, he was beset both by conservative detractors of his New Deal and from liberal critics who argued that Roosevelt's reforms had not gone far enough. In the 1930s Huey P. Long, a powerful Democratic senator and governor of Louisiana, emerged as a potential Roosevelt opponent from the left, arguing that the federal government should do more to help poor Americans. In his Senate speeches and elsewhere Long touted a plan to tax the wealthy and redistribute the money to everyone else. The following viewpoint is a brief excerpt from one of his speeches explaining his plan and encouraging the formation of "Share-Our-Wealth" clubs nationwide.*

What limits on the wealth of individuals does Long propose? What conveniences does he say all Americans should have?

People of America: In every community get together at once and organize a share-our-wealth society—Motto: Every man a king

Principles and platform:

1. To limit poverty by providing that every deserving family shall share in the wealth of America for not less than one third of the average wealth, thereby to possess not less than $5,000 free of debt.
2. To limit fortunes to such a few million dollars as will allow the balance of the American people to share in the wealth and profits of the land.
3. Old-age pensions of $30 per month to persons over 60 years of age who do not earn as much as $1,000 per year or who possess less than $10,000 in cash or property, thereby to remove from the field of labor in times of unemployment those who have contributed their share to the public service.
4. To limit the hours of work to such an extent as to prevent overproduction and to give the workers of America some share in the recreations, conveniences, and luxuries of life.
5. To balance agricultural production with what can be sold and consumed according to the laws of God, which have never failed.
6. To care for the veterans of our wars.
7. Taxation to run the Government to be supported, first, by reducing big fortunes from the top, thereby to improve the country and provide employment in public works whenever agricultural surplus is such as to render unnecessary, in whole or in part, any particular crop.

Huey P. Long, address to Congress, *Congressional Record,* February 5, 1934.

SIMPLE AND CONCRETE—NOT AN EXPERIMENT

To share our wealth by providing for every deserving family to have one third of the average wealth would mean that, at the worst, such a family could have a fairly comfortable home, an automobile, and a radio, with other reasonable home conveniences, and a place to educate their children. Through sharing the work, that is, by limiting the hours of toil so that all would share in what is made and produced in the land, every family would have enough coming in every year to feed, clothe, and provide a fair share of the luxuries of life to its members. Such is the result to a family, at the worst.

From the worst to the best there would be no limit to opportunity. One might become a millionaire or more. There would be a chance for talent to make a man big, because enough would be floating in the land to give brains its chance to be used. As it is, no matter how smart a man may be, everything is tied up in so few hands that no amount of energy or talent has a chance to gain any of it.

There should be every man a king in this land flowing with milk and honey instead of lords of finance at the top and slaves and peasants at the bottom.

Would it break up big concerns? No. It would simply mean that, instead of one man getting all the one concern made, that there might be 1,000 or 10,000 persons sharing in such excess fortune, any one of whom, or all of whom, might be millionaires and over.

I ask somebody in every city, town, village, and farm community of America to take this as my personal request to call a meeting of as many neighbors and friends as will come to it to start a share-our-wealth society. Elect a president and a secretary and charge no dues. The meeting can be held at a courthouse, in some town hall or public building, or in the home of someone.

It does not matter how many will come to the first meeting. Get a society organized, if it has only two members. Then let us get to work quick, quick, quick to put an end by law to people starving and going naked in this land of too much to eat and too much to wear.

There is nothing wrong with the United States. We have more food than we can eat. We have more clothes and things out of which to make clothes than we can wear. We have more houses and lands than the whole 120 million can use if they all had good homes. So what is the trouble? Nothing except that a handful of men have everything and the balance of the people have nothing if their debts were paid. There should be every man a king in this land flowing with milk and honey instead of the lords of finance at the top and slaves and peasants at the bottom.

Viewpoint 21B
Long's "Share-Our-Wealth" Plan Is Impractical (1935)
Hamilton Basso (1904–1964)

INTRODUCTION *Huey P. Long was a powerful and skilled politician who championed the poor during the Great Depression. In the 1930s he built up a national following of supporters of his "Share-Our-Wealth" plan, in which Long promised American families an income of $2,500 paid for by taxing the wealthy. Hamilton Basso profiled Long in the May 1935 issue of* Harper's Magazine, *portions of which are excerpted here. Basso was a native of Long's home state of Louisiana and a writer and associate editor of the* New Yorker *magazine. Basso contends that Long's plans are economically impractical and that Long himself had dictatorial ambitions. Long's aspirations to become president were cut short in 1935 when he was shot and killed by political enemies in Louisiana.*

How much money is involved in Long's plan, according to Basso? What fundamental economic problem is never addressed by Long and his supporters, according to Basso?

The [Share-Our-Wealth] plan proposes, first of all, to liquidate all fortunes of more than "three or four million" dollars. The possessors of such fortunes will be required, not to sell their holdings, but to transfer ownership to the United States Treasury. Long declares that this will return to the government some $170,000,000,000.

A VAGUE PLAN

It next proposes (with considerable vagueness as to how it is to be done) to give every family in the United States a home, an automobile, and a radio; representing an approximate value of $5,000. To do this, according to Mr. Long, it is necessary to spend about $100,000,000,000.

It is highly doubtful... even if the great American fortunes were dissolved, that we should all be able to have... a minimum wage of $2,500 a year.

From Hamilton Basso, "Huey Long and His Background," *Harper's Magazine*, May 1935, pp. 664, 672–673.

The plan further proposes a minimum wage intended to give each family a cash income of not less than $2,500 a year. As an attack on unemployment, it is suggested that the working week be lengthened or reduced each year in order to maintain a balance between production and consumption. When reduced, the industrial and agricultural workers thus freed would be employed, upon governmental projects.

With the $70,000,000,000 left over from the liquidation of the great fortunes, the plan proposes to give every child in the country (provided he can show he deserves it by passing an intelligence test) a college education; the government, if necessary, supporting the student through college. Old-age pensions will also be provided for every United States citizen, beginning at the age of sixty-five, and the soldiers' bonus will be paid in full.

UNFEASIBLE

Mr. Long is an economic ignoramus, still thinking of the nation's wealth as so many poker chips which are to be piled on the table and redistributed among the players. He takes no cognizance of the instruments of production—mines, railroads, factories—by which wealth is produced. It is highly doubtful, furthermore, even if the great American fortunes were dissolved, that we should all be able to have $5,000 and a minimum wage of $2,500 a year. . . . The problem is not one of merely redistributing the poker chips which symbolize dollars and cents but of producing income. This, it seems, has never occurred to Mr. Long. . . . It is too much to ask his millions of supporters to stop and consider whether or not his plan is feasible. Its very naiveté makes it sound plausible, and plausibility goes farther in politics than economics.

Once Mr. Long reaches the White House we shall, of course, be living under a dictatorship. . . . If this sounds like an alarmist statement, I ask only that you remember the way democratic processes have been flouted in Louisiana; the attempt to gag and muzzle the press; the fiasco of the legislature which passed forty-four laws in just about as many minutes; the use of the courts and civil authorities to break the longshoremen's strike; the way in which any citizen known to be opposed to Long may be deprived of the right to vote. Mr. Long, in his own little sphere, has power equal to that of Hitler's. It is a power, I assure you, he is not reluctant to employ.

FOR FURTHER READING

Alan Brinkley, *Voices of Protest: Huey Long, Father Coughlin, and the Great Depression.* New York: Random House, 1983.

William E. Leuchtenburg, *The New Deal: A Documentary History.* New York: Harper & Row, 1968.

Robert S. McElvaine, *The Great Depression, America, 1929–1941.* New York: Random House, 1985.

Richard H. Pells, *Radical Visions and American Dreams: Culture and Social Thought During the Depression Years.* Chicago: University of Illinois Press, 1998.

Richard D. White Jr., *Kingfish: The Reign of Huey P. Long.* New York: Random House, 2006.

WORLD WAR II

Viewpoint 22A

The United States Should Give Lend-Lease Aid to Great Britain (1940)

Franklin D. Roosevelt (1882–1945)

INTRODUCTION *The outbreak of war in Europe in 1939, much like the outbreak of war in 1914, forced the United States to make a series of choices on how to respond. Some Americans, believing that the United States should not repeat its 1917 decision to send troops to Europe, urged that America remain strictly neutral. This stance was consistent with a series of Neutrality Acts passed by Congress in the 1930s that prohibited U.S. companies from providing arms or monetary loans to warring nations or in other ways becoming embroiled in foreign wars. President Franklin D. Roosevelt, in the early months of World War II, successfully pressed Congress to relax the arms embargo and to sell arms to the Allies (Great Britain and France) on a limited "cash and carry" basis (the Allies needed to pay upfront and provide their own shipping). Controversy remained as to whether such limited aid would be enough for the Allies, and if not, whether America should do more.*

The following viewpoint is taken from one of Roosevelt's "fireside chats"—his radio speeches in which he discussed issues and decisions of his presidency. Roosevelt made this particular speech on December 29, 1940, at the close of an eventful year that saw the fall of France, Denmark, Norway, Belgium, and Holland to Nazi Germany; the passage of the first peacetime military draft in U.S. history; and Roosevelt's own reelection to an unprecedented third term as president. The government of Great Britain informed the United States that it was running out of cash to pay for needed arms, planes, and other supplies. Roosevelt responded by proposing what became known as the Lend-Lease Act, under which the United States would provide military supplies to Great Britain with repayment decisions deferred to the end of the war. His plan needed Congressional approval, and his speech was part of the president's campaign to garner public support for the idea—and to defend such aid against charges that it would inevitably lead America into war. Roosevelt in his speech emphasizes the dangers posed to the United States by Germany, Italy, and Japan—nations that in September 1939 had signed a mutual defense pact aimed at the United States.

What would happen to the United States if Great Britain fell to Germany, according to Roosevelt? How does he characterize those who oppose aiding the Allies? What does Roosevelt assert concerning the possibility of lend-lease aid leading to sending U.S. soldiers to war?

My friends, this is not a fireside chat on war. It is a talk on national security, because the nub of the whole purpose of your president is to keep you now, and your children later, and your grandchildren much later, out of a last-ditch war for the preservation of American independence and all of the things that American independence means to you and to me and to ours....

Never before since Jamestown and Plymouth Rock has our American civilization been in such danger as now.

THE AXIS THREAT

For, on September 27th, 1940, this year, by an agreement signed in Berlin, three powerful nations, two in Europe and one in Asia, joined themselves together in the threat that if the United States of America interfered with or blocked the expansion program of these three nations—a program aimed at world control—they would unite in ultimate action against the United States.

The Nazi masters of Germany have made it clear that they intend not only to dominate all life and thought in their own country, but also to enslave the whole of Europe, and then to use the resources of Europe to dominate the rest of the world....

In view of the nature of this undeniable threat, it can be asserted, properly and categorically, that the United States has no right or reason to encourage talk of peace, until the day shall come when there is a clear intention on the part of the aggressor nations to abandon all thought of dominating or conquering the world.

At this moment, the forces of the states that are leagued against all peoples who live in freedom are being held away from our shores. The Germans and the Italians are being blocked on the other side of the Atlantic by the British, and by the Greeks, and by thousands of soldiers and sailors who were able to escape from subjugated countries. In Asia the Japanese are being engaged by the Chinese nation in another great defense.

In the Pacific Ocean is our fleet.

Some of our people like to believe that wars in Europe and in Asia are of no concern to us. But it is a matter of most vital concern to us that European and Asiatic war-makers should not gain control of the oceans which lead to this hemisphere.

One hundred and seventeen years ago the Monroe Doctrine [which stated that the United States opposed further European colonization of or intervention in the Western Hemisphere] was conceived by our government as a measure of defense in the face of a threat against this hemisphere by an alliance in Continental Europe. Thereafter, we stood guard in the Atlantic, with the British as neighbors. There was no treaty. There was no "unwritten agreement."

And yet, there was the feeling, proven correct by history, that we as neighbors could settle any disputes in peaceful fashion. And the fact is that during the whole of this time the Western Hemisphere has remained free from aggression from Europe or from Asia.

Does anyone seriously believe that we need to fear attack anywhere in the Americas while a free Britain remains our most powerful naval neighbor in the Atlantic? And does anyone seriously believe, on the other hand, that we could rest easy if the Axis powers were our neighbors there?

If Great Britain goes down, the Axis powers will control the continents of Europe, Asia, Africa, Australasia, and the high seas—and they will be in a position to bring enormous military and naval resources against this hemisphere. It is no exaggeration to say that all of us, in all the Americas, would be living at the point of a gun—a gun loaded with explosive bullets, economic as well as military.

We should enter upon a new and terrible era in which the whole world, our hemisphere included, would be run by threats of brute force. And to survive in such a world, we would have to convert ourselves permanently into a militaristic power on the basis of war economy.

THE OCEANS ARE NO PROTECTION

Some of us like to believe that even if Britain falls, we are still safe, because of the broad expanse of the Atlantic and of the Pacific.

But the width of those oceans is not what it was in the days of clipper ships. At one point between Africa and Brazil the distance is less from Washington to Denver, Colorado—five hours for the latest type of bomber. And at the North end of the Pacific Ocean America and Asia almost touch each other.

Why even today we have planes that could fly from the British Isles to New England and back again without refueling. And remember that the range of the modern bomber is ever being increased.

During the past week many people in all parts of the nation have told me what they wanted me to say tonight. Almost all of them expressed a courageous desire to hear the plain truth about the gravity of the situation. One telegram, however, expressed the attitude of the small minority who want to see no evil and hear no evil, even

Excerpted from Franklin D. Roosevelt's "fireside chat" radio broadcast of December 29, 1940.

though they know in their hearts that evil exists. That telegram begged me not to tell again of the ease with which our American cities could be bombed by any hostile power which had gained bases in this Western Hemisphere. The gist of that telegram was: "Please, Mr. President, don't frighten us by telling us the facts."

Frankly and definitely there is danger ahead—danger against which we must prepare. But we well know that we cannot escape danger, or the fear of danger, by crawling into bed and pulling the covers over our heads.

Some nations of Europe were bound by solemn non-intervention pacts with Germany. Other nations were assured by Germany that they need *never* fear invasion. Non-intervention pact or not, the fact remains that they *were* attacked, overrun, thrown into modern slavery at an hour's notice, or even without any notice at all. As an exiled leader of one of these nations said to me the other day, "The notice was a minus quantity. It was given to my Government two hours after German troops had poured into my country in a hundred places."

The fate of these nations tells us what it means to live at the point of a Nazi gun.

THE NAZI THREAT

The Nazis have justified such actions by various pious frauds. One of these frauds is the claim that they are occupying a nation for the purpose of "restoring order." Another is that they are occupying or controlling a nation on the excuse that they are "protecting it" against the aggression of somebody else.

For example, Germany has said that she was occupying Belgium to save the Belgians from the British. Would she then hesitate to say to any South American country, "We are occupying you to protect you from aggression by the United States?"

Belgium today is being used as an invasion base against Britain, now fighting for its life. And any South American country, in Nazi hands, would always constitute a jumping-off place for German attack on any one of the other republics of this hemisphere. . . .

There are those who say that the Axis powers would never have any desire to attack the Western Hemisphere. That is the same dangerous form of wishful thinking which has destroyed the powers of resistance of so many conquered peoples. The plain facts are that the Nazis have proclaimed, time and again, that all other races are their inferiors and therefore subject to their orders. And most important of all, the vast resources and wealth of this American Hemisphere constitute the most tempting loot in all of the round world.

Let us no longer blind ourselves to the undeniable fact that the evil forces which have crushed and undermined and corrupted so many others are already within

our own gates. Your Government knows much about them and every day is ferreting them out.

Their secret emissaries are active in our own and in neighboring countries. They seek to stir up suspicion and dissension to cause internal strife. They try to turn capital against labor, and vice versa. They try to reawaken long-slumbering racial and religious enmities which should have no place in this country. They are active in every group that promotes intolerance. They exploit for their own ends our own natural abhorrence of war. These trouble-breeders have but one purpose. It is to divide our people, to divide them into hostile groups and to destroy our unity and shatter our will to defend ourselves.

AMERICAN APPEASERS

There are also American citizens, many of them in high places, who, unwittingly in most cases, are aiding and abetting the work of these agents. I do not charge these American citizens with being foreign agents. But I do charge them with doing exactly the kind of work that the dictators want done in the United States.

These people not only believe that we can save our own skins by shutting our eyes to the fate of other nations. Some of them go much further than that. They say that we can and should become the friends and even the partners of the Axis powers. Some of them even suggest that we should imitate the methods of the dictatorships. But Americans never can and never will do that.

The experience of the past two years has proven beyond doubt that no nation can appease the Nazis. No man can tame a tiger into a kitten by stroking it. There can be no appeasement with ruthlessness. There can be no reasoning with an incendiary bomb. We know now that a nation can have peace with the Nazis only at the price of total surrender.

Even the people of Italy have been forced to become accomplices of the Nazis, but at this moment they do not know how soon they will be embraced to death by their allies.

The American appeasers ignore the warning to be found in the fate of Austria, Czechoslovakia, Poland, Norway, Belgium, the Netherlands, Denmark and France. They tell you that the Axis powers are going to win anyway; that all of this bloodshed in the world could be saved, that the United States might just as well throw its influence into the scale of a dictated peace, and get the best out of it that we can.

They call it a "negotiated peace." Nonsense! Is it a negotiated peace if a gang of outlaws surrounds your community and on threat of extermination makes you pay tribute to save your own skins?

For such a dictated peace would be no peace at all. It would be only another armistice, leading to the most gigantic armament race and the most devastating trade wars in all history. And in these contests the Americas would offer the only real resistance to the Axis powers....

KEEPING AMERICA OUT OF WAR

The British people and their allies today are conducting an active war against this unholy alliance. Our own future security is greatly dependent on the outcome of that fight. Our ability to "keep out of war" is going to be affected by that outcome.

Thinking in terms of today and tomorrow, I make the direct statement to the American people that there is far less chance of the United States getting into war if we do all we can now to support the nations defending themselves against attack by the Axis than if we acquiesce in their defeat, submit tamely to an Axis victory, and wait our turn to be the object of attack in another war later on.

If we are to be completely honest with ourselves, we must admit that there is risk in any course we may take. But I deeply believe that the great majority of our people agree that the course that I advocate involves the least risk now and the greatest hope for world peace in the future.

The people of Europe who are defending themselves do not ask us to do their fighting. They ask us for the implements of war, the planes, the tanks, the guns, the freighters which will enable them to fight for their liberty and for our security. Emphatically we must get these weapons to them, get them to them in sufficient volume and quickly enough, so that we and our children will be saved the agony and suffering of war which others have had to endure.

Let not the defeatists tell us that it is too late. It will never be earlier. Tomorrow will be later than today.

Certain facts are self-evident.

In a military sense Great Britain and the British Empire are today the spearhead of resistance to world conquest. And they are putting up a fight which will live forever in the story of human gallantry.

---■---

We must be the great arsenal of democracy.

---■---

There is no demand for sending an American Expeditionary Force outside our own borders. There is no intention by any member of your Government to send such a force. You can, therefore, nail, nail any talk about sending armies to Europe as deliberate untruth.

Our national policy is not directed toward war. Its sole purpose is to keep war away from our country and away from our people.

Democracy's fight against world conquest is being greatly aided, and must be more greatly aided, by the rearmament of the United States and by sending every ounce and every ton of munitions and supplies that we can possibly spare to help the defenders who are in the front lines. And it is no more unneutral for us to do that than it is for Sweden, Russia and other nations near Germany to send steel and ore and oil and other war materials into Germany every day in the week....

THE ARSENAL OF DEMOCRACY

We must be the great arsenal of democracy. For us this is an emergency as serious as war itself. We must apply ourselves to our task with the same resolution, the same sense of urgency, the same spirit of patriotism and sacrifice as we would show were we at war.

We have furnished the British great material support and we will furnish far more in the future.

There will be no "bottlenecks" in our determination to aid Great Britain. No dictator, no combination of dictators, will weaken that determination by threats of how they will construe that determination.

The British have received invaluable military support from the heroic Greek army and from the forces of all the governments in exile. Their strength is growing. It is the strength of men and women who value their freedom more highly than they value their lives.

I believe that the Axis powers are not going to win this war. I base that belief on the latest and best of information.

We have no excuse for defeatism. We have every good reason for hope—hope for peace, yes, and hope for the defense of our civilization and for the building of a better civilization in the future.

I have the profound conviction that the American people are now determined to put forth a mightier effort than they have ever yet made to increase our production of all the implements of defense, to meet the threat to our democratic faith.

As President of the United States I call for that national effort. I call for it in the name of this nation which we love and honor and which we are privileged and proud to serve. I call upon our people with absolute confidence that our common cause will greatly succeed.

Viewpoint 22B

Lend-Lease Aid Will Drag the United States into War (1941)

James F. O'Connor (1878–1945)

INTRODUCTION *In January 1941 Congress began debate on H.R. 1776, later known as the Lend-Lease Act. Prompted by British pleas to President Franklin*

D. Roosevelt for help against Germany, the bill gave sweeping new powers to the president to provide assistance to any nation he designated as vital for America's defense. The proposed measure created vigorous debate in Congress, where it was strenuously opposed by members who feared American involvement in yet another European war. One of the opponents of lend-lease was James F. O'Connor, a Democratic representative from Montana, whose remarks on January 21, 1941, on the floor of Congress are excerpted here. O'Connor, a former rancher, banker, and judge, served in Congress from 1937 to 1945. In his speech he argues against the passage of H.R. 1776, claiming that it would eventually cause the United States to "plunge headlong into war." He states that while he shares with others a desire for British victory over Germany, such a goal is not worth risking American lives.

Despite the efforts of O'Connor and others, the Lend-Lease Act was passed by Congress in March 1941. Eventually the United States sent $50 billion in such aid to Great Britain and other countries during World War II.

What does the "average American" want, according to O'Connor? Is Franklin D. Roosevelt's proposal (see viewpoint 22A) consistent with this, in your view? Why or why not? What arguments does O'Connor make about the proper duties and responsibilities of Congress and the president? How important to his position is the opinion about the likelihood of Germany invading the United States?

On its face, H.R. 1776 is a bill "to promote the defense of the United States."

If the 435 Members of this House believed that this really is a bill "to promote the defense of the United States" then this bill would be passed in a few minutes' time without a single vote being cast against it, because every one of us here believes in defending the United States.

I speak to you today, my colleagues, as one of many who feels that this legislation would not do what it proposes to accomplish, namely: "To promote the defense of the United States."

The decision this Congress makes in passing on this bill will affect the lives of millions of people throughout the world. I want that decision to be in favor of the American people.

The American people do not want this country to plunge headlong into war.

James F. O'Connor, *Congressional Record*, 77th Cong, 1st sess., January 21, 1941, pp. 211–213.

I do not propose, myself, and I do not think that you intend, to support this, or any other measure that is not in the best interests of the American people.

There is not a question in my mind as to where the sympathies of our people lie in regard to the wars raging across the oceans. By thought, word, deed, and prayer Americans have indicated plainly they prefer that the victors of these wars shall be the democracies of Great Britain, China, and Greece.

The average American, in my opinion, is thinking something like this: "Let us give them anything we have in the way of materials that will help them win the war so long as it does not jeopardize the safety and security of the United States."

But the American people do not want this country to plunge headlong into war.

Help Britain? Help China? Help Greece? Emphatically "Yes."

But to the extent of sending troops their answer, a thousand times more emphatic, is "No."

This Nation has been committed to a policy, so far as the democracies are concerned, of "all aid short of war."

The people, at least up to now, have taken those words at their literal meaning.

Perhaps, now, they finally have come to realize that "short of war" is vague and may be misleading.

This bill, H.R. 1776, is an act to carry out the "short of war" policy.

LEND-LEASE WILL LEAD TO WAR

Under this bill, in its present form, it would be possible, without any doubt whatsoever, for circumstances to arise which most certainly would involve the United States in war.

Let me illustrate just one such circumstance.

Suppose we were to send our warships into danger zones or use them to convoy supply ships to Great Britain or Ireland. Is there any doubt whatever that Britain's foes would attempt to sink our vessels? Is there any doubt that such an attack on our ships would not plunge the United States into war?

And this is but one of similar situations that could arise.

And let me ask you this question, colleagues:

Would any of us whom the American people honored by election to public office last November be here today if, prior to election day, we had stood before the American voters and openly proclaimed:

"I am in favor of the United States entering war."

Or if we had proclaimed:

"I will support legislation that may involve the United States in war."

Of course we would not be here if we had made any such campaign statement. No Member here, I am confident, will dispute me on this point.

If, then, I gave my pledge to Montana voters to do my best to "promote the defense of the United States," and keep us out of war, how can I be expected to support a bill that my conscience tells me exposes the United States to the gravest danger of being forced into war?

As it now reads, this bill, in my opinion, would do just that. . . .

What condition exists now that did not exist last fall when I gave my pledge to Montana voters—except the emotional hysteria that has been manufactured by the press, the radio, and the motion-picture theaters? . . .

GIVING THE PRESIDENT TOO MUCH POWER

In the first place, passage of this bill would amount to a complete abdication of the legislative branch of the Government. Congress already has surrendered so much of its authority as to be virtually incapable of discharging its duty as the law-making representatives of the electorate.

By the unprecedented powers this bill gives to the Office of the Chief Executive, powers that easily could lead to involvement of the Nation in war, Congress would give up the authority vested in it, exclusively, under the Constitution, to decide when the United States shall go to war.

Let us, my friends, keep faith with our people. Let us take no affirmative action that seems to me, without a doubt, will cause our naval and military forces to go into this war in Europe. . . .

Already, out of the Constitution and the interpretations by our Supreme Court, the President has plenary power in our external affairs. He is the sole agency and representative of our policy with foreign nations. Pass this bill, as it stands, and it would give him the same total power over our domestic defense powers.

While I am 100 percent for the purpose of the bill—to promote the defense of the United States—I cannot support this bill in its present form.

Please understand that I do not contend that any course, in these days, is bulletproof against involvement of this Nation in war. The only thing Congress can do is keep its pledge to the people to try to keep them out of war. We cannot keep that pledge by supporting bills that permit aggressive and unneutral acts that are sure to get us into war.

Perhaps the course I suggest is wrong. I do not know. Only the future holds the answer. No human being has it. . . .

What is going to happen when "Hitlerism" is crushed? How much further will Britain want to go? Has Britain said she wants to restore the status quo in Europe as it existed as of August 31, 1939? Has she said that France, Poland, Austria, Belgium, Holland, Poland, Rumania, and the other countries are to be restored? Would Britain need troops to accomplish this? Would we be asked to supply them?

A DARK FUTURE

If so, the future looks dark for the flower of American manhood.

If we are to attempt to right the wrongs of Europe, 3,000 miles away, God help America.

Let us think a little further.

Suppose Germany is licked. That will not mean she is conquered. Great nations never are conquered, unless they are exterminated, which is impossible.

France is prostrated today, but not conquered. The spirit of France will rise. On the ruins perhaps a greater nation than ever before will be born. France may profit by her mistakes.

If Germany should defeat Great Britain, would the English people be conquered? Oh, no; they are not made of faulty fiber. The fight would have just begun.

The seed for disorder in the world is planted by selfish, greedy, war-minded men who find themselves adrift from Christianity.

Europe is dark today because most of Europe has forsaken Christian principles.

As I see it, the duty of this Congress is not to take any step that might involve this Nation in war, but rather to assume a statesmanlike leadership toward the goal of peace.

Involving this Nation, the most powerful on earth, in war certainly is not a step toward peace. You cannot quench a fire by adding a huge amount of new fuel to it.

Peace is an active and positive thing. Peace is not merely a cessation of war through some peace treaty. History is filled with the fragments of broken pledges for peace. . . .

THE FIRST WORLD WAR

Do you wonder, my friends, that I shudder at the prospects of America becoming embroiled in Europe's wars? At the prospect of having to pledge not only the lives of American young men but the homes of the people who have worked and saved a lifetime to own—in fact, their all—to prosecute a war in Europe?

The first World War, you will recall, was fought to "save democracy."

Today the same nations are taking part in another great conflict, eyed in the same purpose, only with added fury, cruelty, barbarity, hatred, and viciousness.

What is it about? The same things that caused the first World War.

The picture is reprinted, of course, by adding a touch here and there—but the face of the war monster is still vivid. The mask does not hide the horrid expression of greed, desire for power, trade, gold, land, hatred of fellow man, and the hideous gaunt jaws and empty eye sockets.

The President, in recent eloquent speeches, visualized a world of religious freedom, freedom of speech, freedom from want, freedom from fear.

What a great and happy world that would be. Christ visualized such a world. As I heard the President's words, I pondered the picture he painted.

But we are not living today in that God-like world. This is a world of chaos created by man's greed.

Can we wipe out want in Europe when we have not wiped out want here?

I can take you into any town, city, village, or county in this country and show you want.

A MILITARY BLOOD BANK

Dare we set America up and commit her as the financial and military blood bank of the rest of the world when the proportion of want in this country is still so great that by doing this our country would become a victim of financial and military pernicious anemia? . . .

Should we not appreciate the fact that we cannot right every wrong in this man-made world? We cannot police this world. To do so would require many millions of soldiers and billions more dollars of armaments.

The forgotten man, to my way of thinking, was the American soldier of World War No. 1. When he came home he found his job gone. He had to abandon gradually the ideals he thought he had fought for. He saw his hope of material prosperity dwindle. He took any job he could get.

If he were so unfortunate as to be injured in body or in mind, he found himself, perhaps, in a hospital or confined in his own home. The help his Government extended was not too much.

If America gets into this world war we will have 10 times as many of these "forgotten men" when the conflict is concluded. Go back to the cause of the Russian revolution and see if that could not have been avoided had the powers that be not forgot to remember.

And we will have a bankrupt Nation—of that there can be no doubt.

To finance this war we already have seen what the cost would be. America would be economically annihilated.

Of course, I want to defend America. But I do not want to be a party to putting my country into such a position that if England sinks, or any other nation sinks the United States will go down with her.

IS AMERICA VULNERABLE?

I do not believe it is possible for any outside enemy to invade America successfully.

Germany could not invade the United States, with any hope of victory, without enormous numbers of troops. How could she get them actually onto our shores—with our naval and military and aerial might to fend her off?

Could Germany—if she is victorious in the war in Europe—hold many more millions of people than there are Germans under her heel while she is attempting to conquer America? Would all the other nations abroad stand idle, totally helpless, if Germany were so foolish as to move her military machine off the European Continent to undertake a conquest of another continent?

No; my friends, I think military invasion of America by any outside enemy is fantastically impossible.

I fully realize that national defense in its broader sense means more than keeping hostile forces from this continent. It means, insofar as we can, protecting ourselves from other threats to our security. There is not a single doubt but what our interests—financial and economic—are tied in with Britain's victory, but I am not one of those who believes that we are tied in to such an extent that such a victory is essential to our economic existence and to the continuation of our way of life. Regardless of the outcome of this war, a new order is in the making with reference to our domestic economy and our trade with foreign nations. Our whole internal set-up is going to have to be revamped and revised to meet the change in world conditions. . . .

Unless peace can be brought about it is imperative, until we get in better shape to defend ourselves, that we do everything for the democracies that we possibly can within the framework of the Constitution and our laws to enable them to carry on, but I am not prepared to surrender the power of Congress under the Constitution and to jeopardize the future of my country to the point where we are going to populate the cemeteries of Europe again.

A PEACE SEEKER

No, my friends, to me the role for us is clear. It is the role of peace seeker, not war seeker.

A warring world is a sick world. Peace is to the world body politic what health is to an individual.

Individuals rejoice when health is restored—not when they start a sickness.

Nations rejoice when peace is declared—not when they begin a war. . . .

I would feel that I would be untrue to myself, the laws of my country, and my country, were I to support this bill as written.

FOR FURTHER READING

Wayne S. Cole, *Roosevelt and the Isolationists, 1932–1945.* Lincoln: University of Nebraska Press, 1983.

Warren F. Kimball, *The Most Unsordid Act: Lend-Lease, 1939–1941.* Baltimore: Johns Hopkins University Press, 1969.

David Reynolds, *From Munich to Pearl Harbor: Roosevelt's America and the Origins of the Second World War.* Chicago: Ivan R. Dee, 2002.

John E. Wiltz, *From Isolation to War, 1931–1941.* New York: Crowell, 1968.

Viewpoint 23A

The Internment of Japanese Americans Was Justified (1944)

Hugo Black (1886–1971)

INTRODUCTION *The United States declared war on Japan following the Japanese attack on Pearl Harbor, Hawaii, on December 8, 1941. The approximately 110,000 Japanese Americans who resided on the West Coast of the United States quickly became objects of fear and suspicion. Many people expressed worries that they would sabotage America's military effort and assist a possible Japanese invasion. In 1942, under authority of an executive order by President Franklin D. Roosevelt, the U.S. military declared the entire West Coast a vital military area and forcibly evacuated all Japanese American residents from their homes. They detained these people in barbed wire-enclosed "relocation centers" constructed in California, Montana, and other states, holding most of them for the duration of the war.*

The relocation program received several legal challenges. One such case involved Fred Korematsu, a shipyard worker who was arrested and convicted for refusing to obey an evacuation order to leave his home in San Leandro, California. His appeal reached the Supreme Court, which in a 6–3 vote ruled against him in 1944. Writing for the majority was Hugo Black, an associate justice from 1937 to 1971, who is remembered today as a staunch defender of the Bill of Rights. Citing an earlier case, Hirabayashi v. United States, *in which the Supreme Court upheld a curfew regulation on Japanese Americans as a necessary war measure, Black defends the evacuation program. While declaring the civil rights restrictions on the basis of race were "immediately suspect," he ultimately upholds the military evacuation measures as justifiable to protect national security.*

How does war affect civil liberties, according to Black? How does he defend the actions taken against Japanese Americans from charges of racism?

The petitioner, an American citizen of Japanese descent, was convicted in a federal district court for remaining in San Leandro, California, a "Military Area,"

contrary to Civilian Exclusion Order No. 34 of the Commanding General of the Western Command, U.S. Army, which directed that after May 9, 1942, all persons of Japanese ancestry should be excluded from that area. No question was raised as to petitioner's loyalty to the United States. The Circuit Court of Appeals affirmed, and the importance of the constitutional question involved caused us to grant certiorari.

It should be noted, to begin with, that all legal restrictions which curtail the civil rights of a single racial group are immediately suspect. That is not to say that all such restrictions are unconstitutional. It is to say that courts must subject them to the most rigid scrutiny. Pressing public necessity may sometimes justify the existence of such restrictions; racial antagonism never can. . . .

WAR POWERS

The 1942 Act was attacked in the *Hirabayashi* case as an unconstitutional delegation of power; it was contended that the curfew order and other orders on which it rested were beyond the war powers of the Congress, the military authorities and of the President, as Commander in Chief of the Army; and finally that to apply the curfew order against none but citizens of Japanese ancestry amounted to a constitutionally prohibited discrimination solely on account of race. To these questions, we gave the serious consideration which their importance justified. We upheld the curfew order as an exercise of the power of the government to take steps necessary to prevent espionage and sabotage in an area threatened by Japanese attack.

In the light of the principles we announced in the *Hirabayashi* case, we are unable to conclude that it was beyond the war power of Congress and the Executive to exclude those of Japanese ancestry from the West Coast war area at the time they did. True, exclusion from the area in which one's home is located is a far greater deprivation than constant confinement to the home from 8 p.m. to 6 a.m. Nothing short of apprehension by the proper military authorities of the gravest imminent danger to the public safety can constitutionally justify either. But exclusion from a threatened area, no less than curfew, has a definite and close relationship to the prevention of espionage and sabotage. The military authorities, charged with the primary responsibility of defending our shores, concluded that curfew provided inadequate protection and ordered exclusion. They did so, as pointed out in our *Hirabayashi* opinion, in accordance with Congressional authority to the military to say who should, and who should not, remain in the threatened areas.

From the majority opinion of the U.S. Supreme Court in *Korematsu v. United States,* 319 U.S. 624 (1944).

> *When under conditions of modern warfare*
> *our shores are threatened by hostile forces,*
> *the power to protect must be commensurate*
> *with the threatened danger.*

In this case the petitioner challenges the assumptions upon which we rested our conclusions in the *Hirabayashi* case. He also urges that by May 1942, when Order No. 34 was promulgated, all danger of Japanese invasion of the West Coast had disappeared. After careful consideration of these contentions we are compelled to reject them.

Here, as in the *Hirabayashi* case, *supra*, at p. 99, ". . . we cannot reject as unfounded the judgment of the military authorities and of Congress that there were disloyal members of that population, whose number and strength could not be precisely and quickly ascertained. We cannot say that the war-making branches of the Government did not have ground for believing that in a critical hour such persons could not readily be isolated and separately dealt with, and constituted a menace to the national defense and safety, which demanded that prompt and adequate measures be taken to guard against it."

Like curfew, exclusion of those of Japanese origin was deemed necessary because of the presence of an unascertained number of disloyal members of the group, most of whom we have no doubt were loyal to this country. It was because we could not reject the finding of the military authorities that it was impossible to bring about an immediate segregation of the disloyal from the loyal that we sustained the validity of the curfew order as applying to the whole group. In the instant case, temporary exclusion of the entire group was rested by the military on the same ground. The judgment that exclusion of the whole group was for the same reason a military imperative answers the contention that the exclusion was in the nature of group punishment based on antagonism to those of Japanese origin. That there were members of the group who retained loyalties to Japan has been confirmed by investigations made subsequent to the exclusion. Approximately five thousand American citizens of Japanese ancestry refused to swear unqualified allegiance to the United States and to renounce allegiance to the Japanese Emperor, and several thousand evacuees requested repatriation to Japan.

THE BURDENS OF CITIZENSHIP

We uphold the exclusion order as of the time it was made and when the petitioner violated it. . . . In doing so, we are not unmindful of the hardships imposed by it upon a large group of American citizens. . . . But hardships are part of war, and war is an aggregation of hardships. All citizens alike, both in and out of uniform, feel the impact of war in greater or lesser measure. Citizenship has its responsibilities as well as its privileges, and in time of war the burden is always heavier. Compulsory exclusion of large groups of citizens from their homes, except under circumstances of direst emergency and peril, is inconsistent with our basic governmental institutions. But when under conditions of modern warfare our shores are threatened by hostile forces, the power to protect must be commensurate with the threatened danger. . . .

RACIAL PREJUDICE NOT AN ISSUE

It is said that we are dealing here with the case of imprisonment of a citizen in a concentration camp solely because of his ancestry, without evidence or inquiry concerning his loyalty and good disposition towards the United States. Our task would be simple, our duty clear, were this a case involving the imprisonment of a loyal citizen in a concentration camp because of racial prejudice. Regardless of the true nature of the assembly and relocation centers—and we deem it unjustifiable to call them concentration camps with all the ugly connotations that term implies—we are dealing specifically with nothing but an exclusion order. To cast this case into outlines of racial prejudice, without reference to the real military dangers which were presented, merely confuses the issue. Korematsu was not excluded from the Military Area because of hostility to him or his race. He *was* excluded because we are at war with the Japanese Empire, because the properly constituted military authorities feared an invasion of our West Coast and felt constrained to take proper security measures, because they decided that the military urgency of the situation demanded that all citizens of Japanese ancestry be segregated from the West Coast temporarily, and finally, because Congress, reposing its confidence in this time of war in our military leaders—as inevitably it must—determined that they should have the power to do just this. There was evidence of disloyalty on the part of some, the military authorities considered that the need for action was great, and time was short. We cannot—by availing ourselves of the calm perspective of hindsight—now say that at that time these actions were unjustified.

Viewpoint 23B
The Internment of Japanese Americans Was Not Justified (1944)
Frank Murphy (1890–1949)

INTRODUCTION *During World War II, which began for the United States when Japan attacked Pearl Harbor in December 1941, the United States government forcibly removed thousands of Japanese Americans from their homes on the West Coast and detained them in barbed wire-enclosed detention centers. The mass evacuations provoked debate as to whether such curtailment of civil liberties was justified in time of war. The following viewpoint is taken from a dissenting opinion in the 1944 Supreme Court case* Korematsu v. United States, *in which shipyard worker Fred Korematsu challenged his evacuation from his California home. A majority of Supreme Court justices voted to uphold his evacuation as a legitimate war measure (see opposing viewpoint). One of the dissenting justices was Frank Murphy, an associate justice of the Supreme Court from 1940 to 1949. As a Michigan governor, U.S. attorney general who established the first civil liberties unit in the Justice Department, and a Supreme Court justice, Murphy gained a reputation as a strong advocate and defender of civil liberties.*

What deference should be given to the judgment of military authorities, according to Murphy? Which constitutional rights does he believe were being violated by the internment program? What arguments does he make in implicating racism as the reason behind the detentions?

This exclusion of "all persons of Japanese ancestry, both alien and non-alien," from the Pacific Coast area on a plea of military necessity in the absence of martial law ought not to be approved. Such exclusion goes over "the very brink of constitutional power" and falls into the ugly abyss of racism.

In dealing with matters relating to the prosecution and progress of a war, we must accord great respect and consideration to the judgments of the military authorities who are on the scene and who have full knowledge of the military facts. The scope of their discretion must, as a matter of necessity and common sense, be wide. And their judgments ought not to be overruled lightly by those whose training and duties ill-equip them to deal intelligently with matters so vital to the physical security of the nation.

This racial restriction . . . is one of the most sweeping and complete deprivations of constitutional rights in the history of this nation in the absence of martial law.

At the same time, however, it is essential that there be definite limits to military discretion, especially where martial law has not been declared. Individuals must not be left impoverished of their constitutional rights on a plea of military necessity that has neither substance nor support. Thus, like other claims conflicting with the

From the dissenting opinion in *Korematsu v. United States*, 319 U.S. 624 (1944).

asserted constitutional rights of the individual, the military claim must subject itself to the judicial process of having its reasonableness determined and its conflicts with other interests reconciled. "What are the allowable limits of military discretion, and whether or not they have been over-stepped in a particular case, are judicial questions."

VIOLATING CONSTITUTIONAL RIGHTS

The judicial test of whether the Government, on a plea of military necessity, can validly deprive an individual of any of his constitutional rights is whether the deprivation is reasonably related to a public danger that is so "immediate, imminent, and impending" as not to admit of delay and not to permit the intervention of ordinary constitutional processes to alleviate the danger. . . . Civilian Exclusion Order No. 34, banishing from a prescribed area of the Pacific Coast "all persons of Japanese ancestry, both alien and non-alien," clearly does not meet that test. Being an obvious racial discrimination, the order deprives all those within its scope of the equal protection of the laws as guaranteed by the Fifth Amendment. It further deprives these individuals of their constitutional rights to live and work where they will, to establish a home where they choose and to move about freely. In excommunicating them without benefit of hearings, this order also deprives them of all their constitutional rights to procedural due process. Yet no reasonable relation to an "immediate, imminent, and impending" public danger is evident to support this racial restriction which is one of the most sweeping and complete deprivations of constitutional rights in the history of this nation in the absence of martial law.

It must be conceded that the military and naval situation in the spring of 1942 was such as to generate a very real fear of invasion of the Pacific Coast, accompanied by fears of sabotage and espionage in that area. The military command was therefore justified in adopting all reasonable means necessary to combat these dangers. In adjudging the military action taken in light of the then apparent dangers, we must not erect too high or too meticulous standards; it is necessary only that the action have some reasonable relation to the removal of the dangers of invasion, sabotage and espionage. But the exclusion, either temporarily or permanently, of all persons with Japanese blood in their veins has no such reasonable relation. And that relation is lacking because the exclusion order necessarily must rely for its reasonableness upon the assumption that all persons of Japanese ancestry may have a dangerous tendency to commit sabotage and espionage and to aid our Japanese enemy in other ways. It is difficult to believe that reason, logic or experience could be marshalled in support of such an assumption.

That this forced exclusion was the result in good measure of this erroneous assumption of racial guilt rather than bona fide military necessity is evidenced by the Commanding General's Final Report on the evacuation from the Pacific Coast area. In it he refers to all individuals of Japanese descent as "subversive," as belonging to "an enemy race" whose "racial strains are undiluted," and as constituting "over 112,000 potential enemies . . . at large today" along the Pacific Coast. In support of this blanket condemnation of all persons of Japanese descent, however, no reliable evidence is cited to show that such individuals were generally disloyal, or had generally so conducted themselves in this area as to constitute a special menace to defense installations or war industries, or had otherwise by their behavior furnished reasonable ground for their exclusion as a group.

RACIAL PREJUDICE

Justification for the exclusion is sought, instead, mainly upon questionable racial and sociological grounds not ordinarily within the realm of expert military judgment, supplemented by certain semi-military conclusions drawn from an unwarranted use of circumstantial evidence. Individuals of Japanese ancestry are condemned because they are said to be "a large, unassimilated, tightly knit racial group, bound to an enemy nation by strong ties of race, culture, custom and religion." They are claimed to be given to "emperor worshipping ceremonies" and to "dual citizenship." Japanese language schools and allegedly pro-Japanese organizations are cited as evidence of possible group disloyalty, together with facts as to certain persons being educated and residing at length in Japan. It is intimated that many of these individuals deliberately resided "adjacent to strategic points," thus enabling them "to carry into execution a tremendous program of sabotage on a mass scale should any considerable number of them have been inclined to do so." . . . Finally, it is intimated, though not directly charged or proved, that persons of Japanese ancestry were responsible for three minor isolated shellings and bombings of the Pacific Coast area, as well as for unidentified radio transmissions and night signalling.

The main reasons relied upon by those responsible for the forced evacuation, therefore, do not prove a reasonable relation between the group characteristics of Japanese Americans and the dangers of invasion, sabotage and espionage. The reasons appear, instead, to be largely an accumulation of much of the misinformation, half-truths and insinuations that for years have been directed against Japanese Americans by people with racial and economic prejudices—the same people who have been among the foremost advocates of the evacuation. A military judgment based upon such racial and sociological considerations is not entitled to the great weight ordinarily given the judgments based upon strictly military considerations. Especially is this so when every charge relative to race, religion, culture, geographical location, and legal and economic status has been substantially discredited by independent studies made by experts in these matters.

The military necessity which is essential to the validity of the evacuation order thus resolves itself into a few intimations that certain individuals actively aided the enemy, from which it is inferred that the entire group of Japanese Americans could not be trusted to be or remain loyal to the United States. No one denies, of course, that there were some disloyal persons of Japanese descent on the Pacific Coast who did all in their power to aid their ancestral land. Similar disloyal activities have been engaged in by many persons of German, Italian and even more pioneer stock in our country. But to infer that examples of individual disloyalty prove group disloyalty and justify discriminatory action against the entire group is to deny that under our system of law individual guilt is the sole basis for deprivation of rights. Moreover, this inference, which is at the very heart of the evacuation orders, has been used in support of the abhorrent and despicable treatment of minority groups by the dictatorial tyrannies which this nation is now pledged to destroy. To give constitutional sanction to that inference in this case, however well-intentioned may have been the military command on the Pacific Coast, is to adopt one of the cruelest of the rationales used by our enemies to destroy the dignity of the individual and to encourage and open the door to discriminatory actions against other minority groups in the passions of tomorrow.

No adequate reason is given for the failure to treat these Japanese Americans on an individual basis by holding investigations and hearings to separate the loyal from the disloyal, as was done in the case of persons of German and Italian ancestry. . . . It is asserted merely that the loyalties of this group "were unknown and time was of the essence." Yet nearly four months elapsed after Pearl Harbor before the first exclusion order was issued; nearly eight months went by until the last order was issued; and the last of these "subversive" persons was not actually removed until almost eleven months had elapsed. Leisure and deliberation seem to have been more of the essence than speed. And the fact that conditions were not such as to warrant a declaration of martial law adds strength to the belief that the factors of time and military necessity were not as urgent as they have been represented to be.

Moreover, there was no adequate proof that the Federal Bureau of Investigation and the military and naval intelligence services did not have the espionage and sabotage situation well in hand during this long period. Nor is there any denial of the fact that not one person of Japanese ancestry was accused or convicted of espionage or sabotage after Pearl Harbor while they were still free, a fact which is some evidence of the loyalty of the vast majority of these individuals and of the effectiveness of the established methods of combatting these evils. It seems incredible that under these circumstances it would have been impossible to hold loyalty hearings for the mere 112,000 persons involved—or at least for the 70,000 American citizens—especially when a large part of this number represented children and elderly men and women. Any inconvenience that may have accompanied an attempt to conform to procedural due process cannot be said to justify violations of constitutional rights of individuals.

ALL AMERICANS HAVE EQUAL RIGHTS

I dissent, therefore, from this legalization of racism. Racial discrimination in any form and in any degree has no justifiable part whatever in our democratic way of life. It is unattractive in any setting but it is utterly revolting among a free people who have embraced the principles set forth in the Constitution of the United States. All residents of this nation are kin in some way by blood or culture to a foreign land. Yet they are primarily and necessarily a part of the new and distinct civilization of the United States. They must accordingly be treated at all times as the heirs of the American experiment and as entitled to all the rights and freedoms guaranteed by the Constitution.

FOR FURTHER READING

Roger Daniels, *Prisoners Without Trial: Japanese-Americans in World War II*. New York: Hill and Wang, 1993.

John W. Dower, *War Without Mercy: Race and Power in the Pacific War*. New York: Pantheon Books, 1986.

Peter Irons, *Justice at War*. New York: Oxford University Press, 1983.

John Tateishi, *And Justice for All: An Oral History of the Japanese-American Detention Camps*. New York: Random House, 1984.

Viewpoint 24A

Using the Atomic Bomb Against Japan Is Justified (1945)

Harry S. Truman (1884–1972)

INTRODUCTION *In 1942, the United States undertook a secret research effort—the Manhattan Project—to develop a new kind of weapon powered by the splitting of the atom. The original impetus for the Manhattan Project was the fear of Germany's developing such a weapon. However, Germany surrendered in May 1945, a little more than two months before America successfully tested an atomic bomb in New Mexico. The decision facing President Harry S. Truman, who only learned of the atomic bomb's existence when he became* president upon Franklin D. Roosevelt's death on April 12, 1945, was whether to use the weapon against America's other World War II enemy, Japan.

Truman and the other Allied leaders meeting in Potsdam, Germany, had issued an ultimatum on July 26, 1945, for Japan to surrender. The Japanese government failed to respond, and on August 6, the United States dropped an atomic bomb on the Japanese city of Hiroshima, obliterating four square miles of the Japanese city, and instantly killing tens of thousands of people. The following viewpoint is excerpted from Truman's address to the nation that same day, in which most Americans learned of the atomic bomb for the first time. Truman defends the secret project and his decision to use the weapon as a way to compel Japan to surrender and end World War II.

What does Truman emphasize in his description of the atomic bomb and the project that created it? Does he acknowledge any doubt or debate over the morality of using the bomb? What recommendations does he make regarding the future of atomic weapons?

Sixteen hours ago an American airplane dropped one bomb on Hiroshima, an important Japanese Army base. That bomb had more power than 20,000 tons of TNT. It had more than 2,000 times the blast power of the British "Grand Slam," which is the largest bomb ever yet used in the history of warfare.

The Japanese began the war from the air at Pearl Harbor. They have been repaid manyfold. And the end is not yet. With this bomb we have now added a new and revolutionary increase in destruction to supplement the growing power of our armed forces. In their present form these bombs are now in production, and even more powerful forms are in development.

It is an atomic bomb. It is a harnessing of the basic power of the universe. The force from which the sun draws its power has been loosed against those who brought war to the Far East.

THE EFFORT TO BUILD THE BOMB

Before 1939, it was the accepted belief of scientists that it was theoretically possible to release atomic energy. But no one knew any practical method of doing it. By 1942, however, we knew that the Germans were working feverishly to find a way to add atomic energy to the other engines of war with which they hoped to enslave the world. But they failed. We may be grateful to Providence that the Germans got the V-1's and V-2's [missiles] late and in limited quantities and even more grateful that they did not get the atomic bomb at all.

Harry S. Truman, address to the nation, August 6, 1945. From *Public Papers of the Presidents of the United States: Harry S. Truman, Containing the Public Messages, Speeches, and Statements of the President, April 12, to December 31, 1945.* Washington, 1961, pp. 197–200.

The battle of the laboratories held fateful risks for us as well as the battles of the air, land, and sea, and we have now won the battle of the laboratories as we have won the other battles.

Beginning in 1940, before Pearl Harbor, scientific knowledge useful in war was pooled between the United States and Great Britain, and many priceless helps to our victories have come from that arrangement. Under that general policy the research on the atomic bomb was begun. With American and British scientists working together we entered the race of discovery against the Germans....

------------◼------------

We shall completely destroy Japan's power to make war.

------------◼------------

We now have two great plants and many lesser works devoted to the production of atomic power. Employment during peak construction numbered 125,000 and over 65,000 individuals are even now engaged in operating the plants. Many have worked there for two and a half years. Few know what they have been producing. They see great quantities of material going in and they see nothing coming out of these plants, for the physical size of the explosive charge is exceedingly small. We have spent $2 billion on the greatest scientific gamble in history—and won.

But the greatest marvel is not the size of the enterprise, its secrecy, nor its cost, but the achievement of scientific brains in putting together infinitely complex pieces of knowledge held by many men in different fields of science into a workable plan. And hardly less marvelous has been the capacity of industry to design, and of labor to operate, the machines and methods to do things never done before so that the brainchild of many minds came forth in physical shape and performed as it was supposed to do. Both science and industry worked under the direction of the United States Army, which achieved a unique success in managing so diverse a problem in the advancement of knowledge in an amazingly short time. It is doubtful if such another combination could be got together in the world. What has been done is the greatest achievement of organized science in history. It was done under high pressure and without failure.

A MESSAGE FOR JAPAN

We are now prepared to obliterate more rapidly and completely every productive enterprise the Japanese have above ground in any city. We shall destroy their docks, their factories, and their communications. Let

there be no mistake; we shall completely destroy Japan's power to make war.

It was to spare the Japanese people from utter destruction that the ultimatum of July 26 was issued at Potsdam. Their leaders promptly rejected that ultimatum. If they do not now accept our terms they may expect a rain of ruin from the air, the like of which has never been seen on this earth. Behind this air attack will follow sea and land forces in such numbers and power as they have not yet seen and with the fighting skill of which they are already well aware....

A NEW ERA

The fact that we can release atomic energy ushers in a new era in man's understanding of nature's forces. Atomic energy may in the future supplement the power that now comes from coal, oil, and falling water, but at present it cannot be produced on a basis to compete with them commercially. Before that comes there must be a long period of intensive research.

It has never been the habit of the scientists of this country or the policy of this government to withhold from the world scientific knowledge. Normally, therefore, everything about the work with atomic energy would be made public.

But under present circumstances it is not intended to divulge the technical processes of production or all the military applications, pending further examination of possible methods of protecting us and the rest of the world from the danger of sudden destruction.

I shall recommend that the Congress of the United States consider promptly the establishment of an appropriate commission to control the production and use of atomic power within the United States. I shall give further consideration and make further recommendations to the Congress as to how atomic power can become a powerful and forceful influence towards the maintenance of world peace.

Viewpoint 24B
Dropping the Atomic Bomb on Japan Was Immoral (1945)
Christian Century

INTRODUCTION *World War II ended with America dropping two atomic bombs on the Japanese cities of Hiroshima and Nagasaki. President Harry S. Truman's and his advisers' decision to use the newly developed weapons had the desired result—Japan surrendered on September 2, 1945, sparing the United States the necessity of invading the country. However, the joy many Americans felt over the end of World War II was tempered by the realization of the destructiveness of these weapons, which killed or injured hundreds of thousands of people. Some Americans were profoundly disturbed at what they saw as the immoral mass killing of civilians. The following viewpoint is taken from an editorial in the* Christian Century, *a journal with a readership of Protestant religious leaders. The editors of the magazine question both the morality and the military necessity of actually using the atomic bomb, and conclude that its use has marred America's victory in World War II.*

What alternative courses of action to what America did do the writers of the editorial suggest? What predictions do they make on how Japan will react?

Something like a moral earthquake has followed the dropping of atomic bombs on two Japanese cities. Its continued tremors throughout the world have diverted attention even from the military victory itself.... It is our belief that the use made of the atomic bomb has placed our nation in an indefensible moral position.

We do not propose to debate the issue of military necessity, though the facts are clearly on one side of this issue. The atomic bomb was used at a time when Japan's navy was sunk, her airforce virtually destroyed, her homeland surrounded, her supplies cut off, and our forces poised for the final stroke. Recognition of her imminent defeat could be read between the lines of every Japanese communique. Neither do we intend to challenge Mr. Churchill's highly speculative assertion that the use of the bomb saved the lives of more than one million American and 250,000 British soldiers. We believe, however, that these lives could have been saved had our government followed a different course, more honorable and more humane. Our leaders seem not to have weighed the moral considerations involved. No sooner was the bomb ready than it was rushed to the front and dropped on two helpless cities, destroying more lives than the United States has lost in the entire war.

NO WARNING GIVEN

Perhaps it was inevitable that the bomb would ultimately be employed to bring Japan to the point of surrender.... But there was no military advantage in hurling the bomb upon Japan without warning. The least we might have done was to announce to our foe that we possessed the atomic bomb; that its destructive power was beyond anything known in warfare; and that its terrible effectiveness had been experimentally demonstrated in this country. We could thus have warned Japan of what was in store for her unless she surrendered immediately. If she doubted the good faith of our representations, it would have been a simple matter to select a demonstration target in the enemy's own country at a place where the loss of human life would be at a minimum.

From "America's Atomic Atrocity," *Christian Century*, August 29, 1945.

If, despite such warning, Japan had still held out, we would have been in a far less questionable position had we then dropped the bombs on Hiroshima and Nagasaki. At least our record of deliberation and ample warning would have been clear. Instead, with brutal disregard of any principle of humanity we "demonstrated" the bomb on two great cities, utterly extinguishing them. This course has placed the United States in a bad light throughout the world. What the use of poison gas did to the reputation of Germany in World War I, the use of the atomic bomb has done for the reputation of the United States in World War II. Our future security is menaced by our own act, and our influence for justice and humanity in international affairs has been sadly crippled.

EFFECTS ON JAPAN

We have not heard the last of this in Japan itself. There a psychological situation is rapidly developing which will make the pacification of that land by our occupying forces—infinitely delicate and precarious at best—still more difficult and dubious. In these last days before the occupation by American forces, Japanese leaders are using their final hours of freedom of access to the radio to fix in the mind of their countrymen a psychological pattern which they hope will persist into an indefinite future. They reiterate that Japan has won a moral victory by not stooping as low as her enemies, that a lost war is regrettable but not necessarily irreparable, that the United States has been morally defeated because she has been driven to use unconscionable methods of fighting. They denounce the atomic bomb as the climax of barbarity and cite its use to prove how thin the veneer of Christian civilization is. They declare that Japan must bow to the conqueror at the emperor's command, but insist that she must devote all her available energies to scientific research. That of course can mean only one thing—research in methods of scientific destruction. Some officials have openly admonished the people to discipline themselves until the day of their revenge shall come.

Vengeance as a motive suffers from no moral or religious stigma in Japanese life. In the patriotic folklore of that land, no story is more popular than that of the Forty-Seven Ronin. It is a tale of revenge taken at the cost of their lives by the retainers of a feudal lord on an enemy who had treacherously killed their master. Every Japanese child knows that story. Until 1931, when Japan took Manchuria, the sacred obligation of retaliation was directed against the nations which had prevented Japanese expansion in that area and then had expanded their own holdings. After that it was aimed at white imperialism which was held to be the enemy of all people of color in the world, and particularly those in east Asia.

In each case the justification of revenge was found in a real weakness in the moral position of the adversary. Our widespread use of the diabolic flame-thrower in combat, our scattering of millions of pounds of blazing jellied gasoline over wood and paper cities, and finally our employment of the atomic bomb give Japan the only justification she will require for once more seeking what she regards as justified revenge....

The Japanese leaders are now in the act of creating a new myth as the carrier of the spirit of revenge. The myth will have much plausible ground in fact to support it. But its central core will be the story of the atomic bomb, hurled by the nation most reputed for its humanitarianism. Myths are hard to deal with. They lie embedded in the subconscious mind of a people, and reappear with vigor in periods of crisis. The story of the bomb will gather to itself the whole body of remembered and resented inconsistencies and false pretensions of the conquerors. The problem of spiritual rapprochement between the West and the Japanese will thus baffle the most wide and sensitive efforts of our occupying forces to find a solution. Yet our theory of occupation leaves us with no chance ever to let go of our vanquished foe until the roots of revenge have been extirpated. The outlook for the reconciliation of Germany with world civilization is ominous enough, but the outlook for the reconciliation of Japan is far more ominous....

This act which has put the United States on the moral defensive has also put the Christian church on the defensive throughout the world and especially in Japan....

THE SHAME OF THE AMERICAN PEOPLE

The churches of America must dissociate themselves and their faith from this inhuman and reckless act of the American government. There is much that they can do, and it should be done speedily. They can give voice to the shame the American people feel concerning the barbaric methods used in their name in this war. In particular, in pulpits and conventions and other assemblies they can dissociate themselves from the government's use of the atomic bomb as an offensive weapon. They can demonstrate that the American people did not even know of the existence of such a weapon until it had been unleashed against an already beaten foe. By a groundswell of prompt protest expressing their outraged moral sense, the churches may enable the Japanese people, when the record is presented to them, to divorce the Christian community from any responsibility for America's atomic atrocity.

FOR FURTHER READING

Barton J. Bernstein, ed., *The Atomic Bomb: The Critical Issues.* Boston: Little, Brown, 1976.

Herbert Feis, *The Atomic Bomb and the End of World War II.* Princeton, NJ: Princeton University Press, 1966.

Martin Sherman, *A World Destroyed: Hiroshima and the Origins of the Arms Race.* New York: Vintage Books, 1987.

Stephen Walker, *Shockwave: Countdown to Hiroshima.* New York: HarperCollins, 2005.

Part 4

THE COLD WAR ABROAD AND AT HOME (1945–1989)

CHRONOLOGY

1945

April Vice President Harry S Truman becomes president after death of Franklin D. Roosevelt.

September 2 World War II ends.

1947

March 12 Truman Doctrine pledges U.S. aid to countries threatened by communist aggression.

April Major league baseball desegregated with the debut of Jackie Robinson.

1948

November 2 Truman wins presidential election.

1949

September 23 Truman announces that the Soviet Union has tested an atomic bomb.

1950

February 9 Senator Joseph R. McCarthy begins accusations of widespread communist subversion.

June 25 North Korea invades South Korea.

1952

November 1 U.S. explodes hydrogen bomb.

November 4 Dwight D. Eisenhower elected president.

1953

July 27 Armistice ends fighting in the Korean War, with North and South Korea still divided.

August 12 Soviet Union successfully detonates a hydrogen bomb.

1954

May 17 Supreme Court, in *Brown v. Board of Education*, declares segregated schools unconstitutional.

1955

April 12 The Salk vaccine against polio is declared safe and effective.

December Martin Luther King Jr. and others lead a boycott of bus service in Montgomery, Alabama.

1956

November 6 Eisenhower reelected president.

1957

September 24 Eisenhower sends in federal troops to enforce desegregation of Central High School in Little Rock, Arkansas.

October 4 The Soviet Union launches *Sputnik I*, the world's first space satellite.

1959

January 1 Fidel Castro comes to power in Cuba.

January 3 Alaska becomes 49th state.

August 21 Hawaii becomes 50th state.

1960

September 26 John Kennedy and Richard Nixon engage in the first televised presidential election debate.

November 8 Kennedy elected president.

1961

May 5 Alan Shepard becomes the first American in space.

August Berlin Wall constructed.

1962

October 22–November 2 The Cuban missile crisis brings the United States and the Soviet Union to the brink of nuclear conflict.

1963

August 28 March on Washington for civil rights occurs.

October 7 Kennedy signs limited nuclear test ban treaty.

November 22 President Kennedy assassinated in Dallas; Vice President Lyndon Johnson becomes president.

1964

January 11 U.S. Surgeon General Luther Terry issues report on health dangers of smoking.

August Tonkin Gulf Resolution authorizes military action against North Vietnam.

November 3 Lyndon Johnson elected president.

1965

August 11–16 Riots in Watts, Los Angeles, leave 35 dead.

September Medicare and Medicaid created.

October 3 National origins quotas for immigrants are abolished by Immigration Reform Act.

1967

July 23 Race riot in Detroit kills 43.

October 2 Thurgood Marshall sworn in as nation's first black Supreme Court justice.

1968

January 31 The Tet Offensive shakes American confidence in Vietnam.

April 4 Martin Luther King assassinated.

June 5 Robert Kennedy assassinated.

November 5 Richard Nixon elected president.

1969

June 27 Stonewall riots signal start of gay rights movement.

July 20 Neil Armstrong becomes first man on the moon.

1970

April 20 The first Earth Day observations signal growing environmental movement.

May 4 National Guard troops kill 4 students at Kent State University.

June 24 U.S. Senate votes to terminate 1964 Tonkin Gulf Resolution.

1972

February/May Nixon visits China and the Soviet Union.

June 17 The Watergate break-in occurs.

November 7 Nixon reelected president.

1973

January 22 U.S. agrees to withdraw all its troops from Vietnam; Supreme Court, in *Roe v. Wade*, legalizes abortion during the first trimester of pregnancy.

July 16 The Senate committee investigating Watergate learns of the taping system in the Nixon White House.

October 10 Vice President Spiro Agnew pleads no contest to tax evasion and resigns.

October 18 Arab oil embargo begins.

December 6 Gerald Ford sworn in as nation's first non-elected vice president.

1974

July 27 The House Judiciary Committee passes the first of three articles of impeachment against President Nixon.

August 9 Nixon becomes the first president to resign from office; Vice President Gerald Ford becomes president.

1975

April South Vietnam falls to North Vietnam.

November 20 A Senate committee investigation reports FBI and CIA abuses against U.S. citizens and foreign governments.

1976

November 2 Jimmy Carter elected president.

1978

April The U.S. Senate ratifies a treaty turning over the Panama Canal to Panama in 2000.

1979

March 28 Nuclear accident narrowly averted at Three Mile Island, Pennsylvania.

November 4 The U.S. embassy is stormed in Teheran, Iran; 66 Americans are taken hostage.

1980

November 4 Ronald Reagan elected president.

1981

January 20 The American hostages in Iran are released.

June First reports of AIDS cases in the U.S. are published.

September 25 Sandra Day O'Connor sworn in as first woman Supreme Court justice.

1982

October 23 Terrorist truck bomb explosion kills 241 U.S. Marines in Beirut, Lebanon.

October 24 U.S. invades Grenada.

1984

November 6 Reagan reelected president.

1985

November First of four summits between President Reagan and new reformist Soviet leader Mikhail Gorbachev takes place.

1987

October 19 The stock market plunges a record 500 points.

December Reagan and Gorbachev sign INF Treaty.

1988

November George Bush elected president.

1989

November Opening of Berlin Wall signals end of the Cold War.

December U.S. invades Panama to extradite its leader, Manuel Noriega, wanted on drug smuggling charges.

PREFACE

The Cold War provides one of the main unifying themes for post–World War II American history. For more than four decades the conflict between the United States and the Soviet Union (which never escalated into direct military engagement) dominated U.S. foreign policy and overshadowed much of American life. In large part because of the Cold War, the United States reversed its pre–World War II policy of isolationism, entered into several military alliances, sent its soldiers to fight in Korea and Vietnam, and went to great lengths to promote a spirit of patriotism and a sense of conformity at home.

COLD WAR ORIGINS

The basis of the Cold War as it began in the late 1940s had both strategic and ideological dimensions. Actions taken by each nation immediately following World War II were considered threatening by the other. The United States objected to the Soviet Union's establishment of Soviet-controlled communist regimes in Eastern Europe. The Soviet government viewed Eastern Europe as a necessary defensive buffer and perceived U.S. demands for democratic elections in the region as an attempt to surround the Soviet Union with hostile neighbors. The line between Eastern and Western Europe, which ran through Germany itself, thus became the first and central dividing line of the Cold War. Relations between the United States and the Soviet Union were further complicated by the ideological divide between the two nations' respective political and economic systems: capitalist democracy in the United States and communism in the Soviet Union. Both sides believed in the superiority of their respective systems and feared the other. For many Americans the Cold War was as much a struggle against the idea of communism as it was against the Soviet Union and its allies.

Responding to Soviet expansion into Europe and to fears of worldwide communist agitation and revolution, some leading U.S. foreign policy experts, led by George Kennan, formulated the doctrine of containment. America should not risk open war to force the Soviet Union to relinquish its hold on Eastern Europe or change its system of government, they argued, but all further expansion of Soviet influence on other countries should be prevented. The central goal of U.S. Cold War policy, they believed, should be to contain the spread of Soviet control and of communism (which many viewed as one and the same). Because of the broad goals of containment, which guided U.S. policy for four decades, the United States viewed almost all areas of the world as potentially vital national interests.

REPERCUSSIONS OF THE COLD WAR

For more than forty years the two superpowers competed against each other in several different areas. They struggled over the fate of Germany and control of Europe. They sought the allegiances of nations in Asia, Africa, and Central and South America. They raced to develop space vehicles and to be the first to send a person to the moon.

Perhaps most ominously, the two countries competed in a nuclear arms race. By 1949 the Soviet Union had produced its own atomic weapons. Both nations shortly thereafter developed the more powerful hydrogen bomb. The development of rocket missile technology meant that nuclear weapons, once launched, could reach targets thousands of miles away in a matter of minutes instead of hours. Eventually both nations targeted thousands of intercontinental missiles with multiple nuclear warheads at each other's cities and military bases. By doing so, both the United States and the Soviet Union sought to deter the other side from military attack by convincing each other that such an attack would result in massive nuclear retaliation and widespread nuclear destruction. The deterrent factor of nuclear weapons was, in the opinion of some, the main reason full-scale war never erupted between the Cold War adversaries (perhaps the closest brush with nuclear war was in 1962 when the two nations confronted each other over the installation of Soviet missiles in Cuba).

Americans differed over the use of nuclear weapons and the nuclear arms race during the Cold War. Some saw nuclear weapons as useful tools for influencing the Soviet Union's behavior and for possibly waging limited nuclear war. Others were haunted by fears of a "nuclear holocaust" and sought to place nuclear weapons under international control.

The Cold War strongly colored American domestic issues as well as foreign policy. One direct result of the conflict was the fear held by many Americans of communist subversion and betrayal. Beginning in the 1940s government agencies, congressional committees, and private groups investigated thousands of American citizens for suspected communist affiliations and beliefs—investigations that some people criticized as witch hunts. Another consequence of the Cold War was the creation of a large military and foreign policy apparatus—what President Dwight D. Eisenhower in 1961 called the "military-industrial complex." Some Americans viewed this development as a Cold War necessity, but others feared the potential of a professional standing army to influence America's government.

Many of the ongoing debates over American society and government were framed by the Cold War. In their arguments, both critics and defenders of America's social, economic, and political beliefs and institutions compared and contrasted America with the Soviet Union. Supporters of America's freedom of speech and political dissent pointed out that such freedoms were largely absent in the Soviet Union's totalitarian society. Defenders of America's free-market economic system, and its attendant potential to generate wealth, argued that the Soviets' state-controlled system was inefficient and oppressive. On the other hand, critics of American capitalism maintained that the Soviet system was more egalitarian than the U.S. system because it guaranteed jobs, pensions, and other government assistance to Soviet citizens.

A QUARTER CENTURY OF ECONOMIC GROWTH

When World War II ended in 1945 many Americans were afraid that the U.S. economy would slip back into depression. Such fears proved unfounded as the country instead entered the greatest period of sustained economic growth in its history. National income almost doubled in the 1950s and again in the 1960s. Spurred by technology and education, workers' productivity rose steadily, doubling between 1950 and 1970. Such growth brought America's standard of living to new heights. Builders created an unprecedented number of new homes, many in suburban sites away from city centers. By 1960 approximately 60 percent of American families owned their own homes, 75 percent possessed cars (a suburban necessity), and 87 percent had a television set. Comprising only 6 percent of the world's population, Americans consumed about 40 percent of the world's resources.

America's prosperity and dominance in the world economy was founded on several factors. One was the fact that the United States, unlike much of the industrialized world, escaped most of the physical destruction of World War II. Another was the military spending that accompanied the Cold War. Defense spending accounted for nearly 10 percent of America's gross national product (GNP) during the 1950s. Supporters of the military buildup argued that besides stimulating the economy and spurring employment, defense spending also financed a great deal of scientific research and development that helped establish new high-technology industries, especially in aerospace and electronics. Critics accused the United States of creating a "permanent war economy" that was dependent on defense dollars to keep it strong. A third important factor in America's economic growth

was cheap energy, aided by American control of the international oil business. A fourth factor was the "baby boom"—the sharp rise in births between 1946 and 1964—that helped fuel economic growth and in other ways greatly shaped American society.

CIVIL RIGHTS AND THE GREAT SOCIETY

In the early 1950s national debates over social change were relatively limited, as many Americans believed that economic growth and rising incomes could solve most individual and societal needs. Beginning with the black civil rights movement, however, a growing number of Americans began to debate and demonstrate for political change and social reform—a development that peaked in the 1960s.

In 1954 the Supreme Court issued its historic *Brown v. Board of Education* decision declaring racially segregated schools unconstitutional. The decision struck down the judicial foundations of the Jim Crow legal structure, which had instituted racial segregation in the South in the 1890s. Actual school desegregation, however, proved slow in coming, as whites in southern states resisted court orders to integrate their schools. Black civil rights leaders such as Martin Luther King Jr. led marches, boycotts, and other actions of nonviolent resistance against discriminatory laws in the South. Some critics of the civil rights movement tried to discredit King and his followers by linking them to communism; more extreme opponents resorted to violence, intimidation, and even murder of civil rights activists. Despite such opposition, the civil rights movement raised the nation's awareness about racial inequality and helped pave the way for historic national civil rights legislation in 1964 and 1965.

The federal government, both through Supreme Court decisions and congressional legislation, played a key role in effecting progress on civil rights. Partly as a result, an increasing number of Americans began to advocate utilizing the federal government to address problems of poverty, crime, and health. Lyndon B. Johnson, who became president in 1963 following the assassination of John F. Kennedy, sought to expand the welfare functions of the federal government with his calls for a "war on poverty," medical care for the elderly, and numerous social programs aimed at creating what Johnson termed a "Great Society." Johnson's proposals stimulated much debate and controversy within the nation on how best to deal with social problems.

SIXTIES MOVEMENTS

The Civil Rights Acts of 1964 and 1965 all but ended state-supported segregation and helped ensure the right to vote for African Americans, some of whom also benefited from Johnson's Great Society programs. Many blacks, however, still faced significant poverty, prejudice, and discrimination in employment and housing, not only in the South but throughout the nation. King led demonstrations in Chicago and other northern cities to protest residential segregation, but these proved less successful in effecting change than his protests against legal segregation in the South. Some black activists, such as Stokely Carmichael and Malcolm X, questioned King's principle of nonviolence and the goal of racial integration. They called for black separatism and more militant assertions of "black power." Optimism over the progress of civil rights and racial equality faded in the last half of the 1960s, which were marked by urban riots in Los Angeles, Detroit, and other major cities, and the 1968 assassinations of King and Robert Kennedy, brother of the late president.

Despite its internal divisions, the civil rights movement helped to inspire other groups of people to demonstrate and work for social change. The 1960s saw a revival of feminism as women's groups organized against workplace discrimination and restrictions on abortion. In *The Feminine Mystique*, which came to be regarded as the manifesto of the feminist movement, Betty Friedan criticized American society for limiting women to the roles of wives and mothers. To different degrees, Hispanics, American Indians, and gays and lesbians also organized and pressed for equality and redresses for past injustices. A highly visible minority of America's baby boomers became part of a counterculture that explored alternatives to mainstream American society, including communal living arrangements, Eastern religions, and experimentation with drugs. By the late 1960s, however, the dominant political issue in American life was not civil rights, poverty, or youth culture, but the Vietnam War.

THE COLD WAR AND VIETNAM

The Vietnam War was a product of America's Cold War strategy, first voiced by President Harry S Truman in 1947, to aid all nations threatened by communist takeover. Truman administration policy makers took credit for successfully containing communism in Western Europe through economic aid (the Marshall Plan) and a treaty alliance (the North Atlantic Treaty Organization, or NATO), but were bitterly attacked by some critics for "losing" China in 1949, when the American-supported regime of Jiang Jieshi (Chiang Kai-shek) fell after a long war to communist revolutionaries led by Mao Zedong (Mao Tse-tung). In 1950 the United States sent soldiers to fight in Korea to prevent that divided country from being united under North Korean communist rule. During the administration of President Dwight D. Eisenhower (1953–1961), the United States made defense treaties in the Middle East and Southeast Asia and sponsored Central Intelligence Agency (CIA) operations

that helped topple left-wing regimes in Guatemala and Iran.

It was in this Cold War context that a series of U.S. presidents gradually committed American military power to Vietnam. The former French colony in Southeast Asia was divided between communist North Vietnam and noncommunist South Vietnam after France's withdrawal in 1954. The American-supported regime in South Vietnam was threatened by communist rebels within its territory and eventually by forces from North Vietnam itself. In the 1950s President Eisenhower sent several hundred civilian and military advisers to South Vietnam. John F. Kennedy, president from 1961 to 1963, increased the number of advisers to 16,000, including members of the Green Berets, a special counterinsurgency force. Lyndon B. Johnson, president from 1963 to 1969, began to commit regular combat troops to South Vietnam and to initiate massive bombing raids on North Vietnam in 1965. By 1969 the number of U.S. soldiers in Vietnam stood at 543,000.

The Vietnam War drained funds from Johnson's Great Society domestic programs and played a large part in Johnson's 1968 decision not to run for reelection. Richard M. Nixon, elected president that year after promising to carry out a "secret plan" to end the war, pursued the gradual withdrawal of American soldiers from South Vietnam, an increase in bombing raids, and controversial air and ground incursions into neighboring Cambodia and Laos. Nixon also sought improved relations with China and the Soviet Union, in part to encourage those nations to pressure North Vietnam to agree to a peace settlement. The United States and North Vietnam finally signed a peace agreement in January 1973 providing for the removal of American forces. By 1975 South Vietnam had fallen and Vietnam was unified under communist rule.

The Vietnam War was one of the most controversial wars in American history. The nation was bitterly torn in the 1960s between "hawks" who wanted increased military action and immediate victory in Vietnam (a few advocated the use of nuclear weapons) and "doves" who opposed the war and demanded an immediate military withdrawal (even if it meant American defeat). The war shattered the general Cold War consensus that had guided foreign policy of both Republicans and Democrats since World War II.

Those who opposed the war staged numerous antiwar marches and demonstrations. Two of the most notable protests were a march in Washington, D.C., in October 1967, in which fifty thousand people participated, and a demonstration on the campus of Kent State University in Ohio on May 4, 1970, in which National Guardsmen fired into a crowd and killed four students. Many Americans were shocked by the Kent

State incident. Some U.S. citizens, however, directed their anger at the antiwar demonstrators for what they believed to be a lack of patriotism and proper support of the government.

AN ERA OF LIMITS

If the 1960s could be generalized as an era of protests, the 1970s could be called an era of limits. Much of the optimism for the possibilities of social change in America faded. Social problems such as poverty and crime persisted despite government programs. The Vietnam experience seemed to many to demonstrate the limits of American military power. Even technology itself—which many people celebrated for enabling America to land a man on the moon in 1969—was under attack by a growing environmental movement that questioned the ecological costs of America's industrialization.

In many respects the early 1970s marked the end of an economic era for the United States. Two important factors that had helped sustain the nation's phenomenal economic growth and world economic leadership since the end of World War II were gone: cheap, unlimited energy (especially oil) and the lack of foreign competition in the manufacture and trade of goods and services. In 1971 the United States ran its first trade deficit since 1890, as countries such as Germany and Japan threatened American dominance in automobile manufacturing and other key industries. Under three successive presidents, the United States struggled against "stagflation"—the combination of high inflation, high unemployment, and sluggish productivity growth that plagued the United States for much of the 1970s. By the end of the decade income growth had slowed significantly and increasing numbers of American families were depending on two incomes to maintain their standard of living.

The decade also was one in which numerous Americans questioned their faith in their own government. The Vietnam War caused many citizens to doubt America's effectiveness as a world power and led others to question the morality of their government's actions. This distrust was heightened by the Watergate affair, a series of political scandals that forced the 1974 resignation of Richard Nixon (the first such departure by a U.S. president). Investigations in 1973 and 1974 by journalists, Congress, and special federal prosecutors had revealed to the nation that members of Nixon's staff had tried to sabotage the president's Democratic challengers in the 1972 presidential election and that Nixon had actively impeded investigations into their activities and had lied to the American people about his own knowledge of the events. Vice President Gerald Ford became president after Nixon's resignation; one month later Ford pardoned Nixon from all crimes Nixon committed or might have

committed while in office, an act criticized by many Americans disillusioned by Watergate.

CARTER AND REAGAN

Democrat Jimmy Carter, a relative unknown running on a platform of restoring trust in government, defeated Ford in the 1976 presidential election. Carter impressed many Americans with his personal honesty and his strong commitment to human rights, but much of the public came to question his ability to lead America out of its economic difficulties and to preserve American influence abroad. Inflation, spurred by oil price hikes, soared during his term. The Iranian hostage crisis, in which the Islamic government of Iran seized and held fifty-two Americans from November 1979 to January 1981, was for many Americans (especially after a failed April 1980 military rescue mission) a powerful symbol of American impotence and even humiliation. Carter was defeated for reelection by Ronald Reagan in 1980.

A former motion picture actor and conservative governor of California, Ronald Reagan entered the Oval Office pledging to cut taxes, decrease government spending and regulation, reduce inflation, restore America's international prestige, and improve the nation's moral climate. After a severe recession in 1981 and 1982, the U.S. economy did improve, with years of steady growth and little inflation. Reagan became the first president to be reelected and serve two full terms since Eisenhower. However, federal budget deficits during Reagan's presidency added nearly $2 trillion to the national debt, leaving the long-term economic legacy of the "Reagan revolution" an uncertain one. Reagan's budgetary and rhetorical attacks on social programs were a sharp repudiation of Johnson's Great Society, and many believed that cutbacks in social welfare promoted by Reagan unfairly hurt the poor. Americans remained divided on whether such programs should be supported or eliminated.

REVIVAL AND END OF THE COLD WAR

Reagan entered office pledging an intensification of the Cold War against the Soviet Union. Under Presidents Nixon, Ford, and Carter, the United States had sought to ease Cold War tensions by pursuing a policy of diplomatic cooperation, negotiating the SALT I and SALT II nuclear arms accords, and establishing trade agreements. Reagan and other conservatives argued that such an approach had placed the United States in a weak position and had enabled the Soviet Union to expand its influence into Central America, West Africa, and the Middle East. Reagan's Cold War initiatives were in some respects foreshadowed by events in the last year of Carter's presidency following the Soviet invasion of Afghanistan in December 1979. Carter responded to the invasion by dropping the

SALT II nuclear arms treaty, canceling trade agreements with the Soviet Union, increasing military spending, and calling for the placement of intermediate-range nuclear missiles in Europe. Reagan continued and greatly expanded Carter's Cold War policies, especially in the area of defense spending, which increased from $171 billion in 1981 to $360 billion in 1986. He sent military aid to anticommunist forces in Nicaragua and to Afghans fighting Soviet occupation of their country. In 1983 he proposed a "strategic defense initiative" (SDI), or space-based antimissile defense system of orbiting satellites that would detect and intercept incoming Soviet missiles.

Reagan's foreign policy was not without its critics. Many Americans questioned the technical feasibility of SDI; others argued that it was a waste of money and a dangerous escalation of the nuclear arms race. Some called for a "nuclear freeze" on the development and deployment of any new nuclear weapons systems. And while there was relatively little opposition to Reagan's Afghanistan policy, there was much controversy over what critics labeled a U.S.-sponsored covert war in Nicaragua.

During Reagan's second term, the Cold War took a striking new turn. A new Soviet leader, Mikhail Gorbachev, promised major concessions on nuclear arms control, Afghanistan, and other issues and sought to lessen Cold War tensions between the United States and the Soviet Union. Gorbachev also implemented major internal social and economic reforms that seemed to some Americans to narrow the ideological divide between the two nations. Reagan and Gorbachev met four times in four years, and in 1988 they signed a treaty calling for the destruction of all intermediate-range nuclear missiles in Europe.

During the presidency of George H.W. Bush (1989–1993) the Cold War came to an end. In 1989 the people in several nations in Eastern Europe rose up against communist rule; unlike previous instances, the Soviet Union did not militarily intervene to crush such developments. The Berlin Wall, a symbol of Cold War division since its construction in 1961, was dismantled, and East and West Germany were reunited. The Cold War's end was marked by the dissolution of the Soviet Union itself. By the end of 1991 an attempted coup by hard-line Soviet communists had failed, Gorbachev had resigned, the Soviet Communist Party (which had ruled the Soviet Union since 1917) had lost power, and the Soviet Union's republics had become independent nations under noncommunist rule.

The United States experienced no such dramatic internal developments at the end of the Cold War. What it did face was the loss of a constant enemy that had helped define America's place in the world and provide a focus for its energies at home. While many Americans celebrated the Cold War's end as a great triumph for the United Sates, others questioned the relevance of the Soviet Union's collapse to the well-being of most Americans as they continued to grapple with domestic economic and social problems.

RISE OF THE COLD WAR

Viewpoint 25A

America Should Seek Peace with the Soviet Union (1946)

Henry A. Wallace (1888–1960)

INTRODUCTION *Relations between the United States and the Soviet Union, World War II allies who had emerged from the conflict as the world's dominant powers, sharply deteriorated after the war. Despite pledges made by the two superpowers (and Great Britain) at the Yalta and Potsdam conferences during World War II to support postwar democratic elections in Germany and the rest of Europe, after the war the Soviet Union established communist regimes in areas under its military control. Faltering negotiations made the prospect of a permanently divided Germany seem increasingly likely. In addition, disputes between the Soviet Union and the United States briefly threatened to erupt into a military confrontation over oil interests in Iran, and conflict between the two nations derailed a proposed American plan for the international control of atomic weapons under the new United Nations.*

Some historians have wondered how the United States might have responded to such situations had Henry A. Wallace been president. Wallace served as vice president for Franklin D. Roosevelt's third term from 1941 to 1945, having previously been Roosevelt's secretary of agriculture. Replaced as vice president by Harry S Truman after Roosevelt's fourth election in 1944, Wallace became secretary of commerce shortly before Roosevelt's death and Truman's assumption of the presidency in April 1945. Wallace differed with many in the Truman administration over what he saw as confrontational policies toward the Soviet Union. On September 12, 1946, in a speech at Madison Square Garden in New York City, Wallace called for improving relations with the Soviet Union and argued that the United States should not interfere too much within the Soviet Union's "sphere of influence," which he defines to include Eastern Europe. Wallace's address, excerpted here, angered many within the Truman administration and led to Wallace's resignation from Truman's cabinet.

Henry A. Wallace, a speech delivered at Madison Square Garden in New York City. Reprinted in *Vital Speeches of the Day*, October 1, 1946.

What aspects of Russia's history must be understood in order to reach a peaceful understanding with them, according to Wallace? What arguments does he make about the future of communism and capitalism? What future role does Wallace see for the United Nations?

Tonight I want to talk about peace—and how to get peace. Never have the common people of all lands so longed for peace. Yet, never in a time of comparative peace have they feared war so much.

Up till now peace has been negative and unexciting. War has been positive and exciting. Far too often, hatred and fear, intolerance and deceit have had the upper hand over love and confidence, trust and joy. Far too often, the law of nations has been the law of the jungle; and the constructive spiritual forces of the Lord have bowed to the destructive forces of Satan.

ANOTHER WAR WOULD BE DISASTROUS

During the past year or so, the significance of peace has been increased immeasurably by the atom bomb, guided missiles and airplanes which soon will travel as fast as sound. Make no mistake about it—another war would hurt the United States many times as much as the last war. We cannot rest in the assurance that we invented the atom bomb—and therefore that this agent of destruction will work best for us. He who trusts in the atom bomb will sooner or later perish by the atom bomb—or something worse.

I say this as one who steadfastly backed preparedness throughout the Thirties. We have no use for namby-pamby pacifism. But we must realize that modern inventions have now made peace the most exciting thing in the world—and we should be willing to pay a just price for peace. If modern war can cost us $400 billion, we should be willing and happy to pay much more for peace. But certainly, the cost of peace is to be measured not in dollars but in the hearts and minds of men. . . .

I plead for an America vigorously dedicated to peace—just as I plead for opportunities for the next generation throughout the world to enjoy the abundance which now, more than ever before, is the birthright of man.

THE RUSSIAN CHARACTER

To achieve lasting peace, we must study in detail just how the Russian character was formed—by invasions of Tartars, Mongols, Germans, Poles, Swedes, and French; by the czarist rule based on ignorance, fear and force; by the intervention of the British, French and Americans in Russian affairs from 1919 to 1921; by the geography of the huge Russian land mass situated strategically between Europe and Asia; and by the vitality derived

131

from the rich Russian soil and the strenuous Russian climate. Add to all this the tremendous emotional powers which Marxism and Leninism give to the Russian leaders— and then we can realize that we are reckoning with a force which cannot be handled successfully by a "Get tough with Russia" policy. "Getting tough" never bought anything real and lasting—whether for schoolyard bullies or businessmen or world powers. The tougher we get, the tougher the Russians will get.

Throughout the world there are numerous reactionary elements which had hoped for Axis victory—and now profess great friendship for the United States. Yet these enemies of yesterday and false friends of today continually try to provoke war between the United States and Russia. They have no real love of the United States. They long for the day when the United States and Russia will destroy each other.

We must not let our Russian policy be guided or influenced by those inside or outside the United States who want war with Russia. This does not mean appeasement.

The real peace treaty we now need is between the United States and Russia.

PEACE WITH RUSSIA

We must earnestly want peace with Russia—but we want to be met half way. We want cooperation. And I believe that we can get cooperation once Russia understands that our primary objective is neither saving the British Empire nor purchasing oil in the Near East with the lives of American soldiers. We cannot allow national oil rivalries to force us into war. All of the nations producing oil, whether inside or outside of their own boundaries, must fulfill the provisions of the United Nations Charter and encourage the development of world petroleum reserves so as to make the maximum amount of oil available to all nations of the world on an equitable peaceful basis—and not on the basis of fighting the next war.

For her part, Russia can retain our respect by cooperating with the United Nations in a spirit of openminded and flexible give-and-take.

The real peace treaty we now need is between the United States and Russia. On our part, we should recognize that we have no more business in the *political* affairs of Eastern Europe than Russia has in the *political* affairs of Latin America, Western Europe and the United States. We may not like what Russia does in Eastern Europe. Her type of land reform, industrial expropriation, and suppression of basic liberties offends the great majority of the people of the United States. But whether we like

it or not the Russians will try to socialize their sphere of influence just as we try to democratize our sphere of influence. This applies also to Germany and Japan. We are striving to democratize Japan and our area of control in Germany, while Russia strives to socialize eastern Germany.

As for Germany, we all must recognize that an equitable settlement, based on a unified German nation, is absolutely essential to any lasting European settlement. This means that Russia must be assured that never again can German industry be converted into military might to be used against her—and Britain, Western Europe and the United States must be certain that Russia's German policy will not become a tool of Russian design against Western Europe.

The Russians have no more business in stirring up native communists to political activity in Western Europe, Latin America and the United States than we have in interfering in the politics of Eastern Europe and Russia. We know what Russia is up to in Eastern Europe, for example, and Russia knows what we are up to. We cannot permit the door to be closed against our trade in Eastern Europe any more than we can in China. But at the same time we have to recognize that the Balkans are closer to Russia than to us—and that Russia cannot permit either England or the United States to dominate the politics of that area....

A FRIENDLY COOPERATION

Russian ideas of social-economic justice are going to govern nearly a third of the world. Our ideas of free enterprise democracy will govern much of the rest. The two ideas will endeavor to prove which can deliver the most satisfaction to the common man in their respective areas of political dominance. But by mutual agreement, this competition should be put on a friendly basis and the Russians should stop conniving against us in certain areas of the world just as we should stop scheming against them in other parts of the world. Let the results of the two systems speak for themselves.

Meanwhile, the Russians should stop teaching that their form of communism must, by force if necessary, ultimately triumph over democratic capitalism—while we should close our ears to those among us who would have us believe that Russian communism and our free enterprise system cannot live, one with another, in a profitable and productive peace.

Under friendly peaceful competition the Russian world and the American world will gradually become more alike. The Russians will be forced to grant more and more of the personal freedoms; and we shall become more and more absorbed with the problems of social-economic justice.

Russia must be convinced that we are not planning for war against her and we must be certain that Russia is not carrying on territorial expansion or world domination through native communists faithfully following every twist and turn in the Moscow party line. But in this competition, we must insist on an open door for trade throughout the world. There will always be an ideological conflict—but that is no reason why diplomats cannot work out a basis for both systems to live safely in the world side by side.

THE UNITED NATIONS

Once the fears of Russia and the United States Senate have been allayed by practical regional political reservations, I am sure that concern over the veto power would be greatly diminished. Then the United Nations would have a really great power in those areas which are truly international and not regional. In the world-wide, as distinguished from the regional field, the armed might of the United Nations should be so great as to make opposition useless. Only the United Nations should have atomic bombs and its military establishment should give special emphasis to air power. It should have control of the strategically located air bases with which the United States and Britain have encircled the world. And not only should individual nations be prohibited from manufacturing atomic bombs, guided missiles and military aircraft for bombing purposes, but no nation should be allowed to spend on its military establishment more than perhaps 15 per cent of its budget....

ORGANIZING FOR PEACE

In the United States an informed public opinion will be all-powerful. Our people are peace-minded. But they often express themselves too late—for events today move much faster than public opinion. The people here, as everywhere in the world, must be convinced that another war is not inevitable. And through mass meetings such as this, and through persistent pamphleteering, the people can be organized for peace—even though a large segment of our press is propagandizing our people for war in the hope of scaring Russia. And we who look on this war-with-Russia talk as criminal foolishness must carry our message direct to the people—even though we may be called communists because we dare to speak out.

I believe that peace—the kind of peace I have outlined tonight—is the basic issue, both in the Congressional campaign this fall and right on through the Presidential election in 1948. How we meet this issue will determine whether we live not in "one world" or "two worlds"—but whether we live at all.

America Should Contain the Soviet Union (1947)

George F. Kennan (1904–2005)

INTRODUCTION *In July 1947 an article about the Soviet Union attributed to "X" appeared in* Foreign Affairs, *a prestigious political journal. Published at a time of growing tensions between the United States and the Soviet Union, the article became one of the most widely discussed and reprinted articles on foreign policy ever published, and its basic arguments formed a basis for U.S. actions for the next forty years. "X" was eventually revealed to be George F. Kennan, the director of the Policy Planning Staff at the U.S. State Department in Washington. Kennan had recently returned from an embassy position in the Soviet Union and was one of the first U.S. diplomats to express pessimism about continuing the cooperation with the Soviet Union that had begun during World War II.*

In his Foreign Affairs *article, excerpted here, Kennan argues that the ideology and the political interests of the leaders of the Soviet Union compel them to seek international domination and to take an adversarial stance toward the United States. To counter the Soviet threat, Kennan advocates a policy of containment—of preventing Soviet power and communist ideology from spreading to additional countries. He argues that while America should seek to contain the Soviet Union, it should not risk open war by forcing a Soviet withdrawal from Eastern Europe or otherwise directly challenging or provoking Soviet leaders. Kennan's prescriptions were influential in the development of the "Truman Doctrine," in which President Harry S Truman pledged American support to regimes in Greece and Turkey as part of a worldwide struggle against Soviet communism.*

What important ideological factors motivate the behavior of the Kremlin (the Soviet communist leadership), according to Kennan? What predictions does he make concerning the future of the Soviet Union? What positive benefits to America does he foresee from the Cold War?

The political personality of Soviet power as we know it today is the product of ideology and circumstances: ideology inherited by the present Soviet leaders from the movement in which they had their political origin, and circumstances of the power which they now have exercised for nearly three decades in Russia....

It is difficult to summarize the set of ideological concepts with which the Soviet leaders came into power. Marxian ideology, in its Russian-Communist projection,

George F. Kennan, "The Sources of Soviet Conduct," *Foreign Affairs*, Spring 1987, p. 51.

has always been in process of subtle evolution. The materials on which it bases itself are extensive and complex. But the outstanding features of Communist thought as it existed in 1916 may perhaps be summarized as follows: (a) that the central factor in the life of man, the factor which determines the character of public life and the "physiognomy of society," is the system by which material goods are produced and exchanged; (b) that the capitalist system of production is a nefarious one which inevitably leads to the exploitation of the working class by the capital-owning class and is incapable of developing adequately the economic resources of society or of distributing fairly the material goods produced by human labor; (c) that capitalism contains the seeds of its own destruction and must, in view of the inability of the capital-owning class to adjust itself to economic change, result eventually and inescapably in a revolutionary transfer of power to the working class; and (d) that imperialism, the final phase of capitalism, leads directly to war and revolution. . . .

The circumstances of the immediate post-revolution period—the existence in Russia of civil war and foreign intervention, together with the obvious fact that the Communists represented only a tiny minority of the Russian people—made the establishment of dictatorial power a necessity. . . .

Now the outstanding circumstance concerning the Soviet régime is that down to the present day . . . the men in the Kremlin have continued to be predominantly absorbed with the struggle to secure and make absolute the power which they seized in November 1917. They have endeavored to secure it primarily against forces at home, within Soviet society itself. But they have also endeavored to secure it against the outside world. . . .

SOVIET POLICY

So much for the historical background. What does it spell in terms of the political personality of Soviet power as we know it today?

Of the original ideology, nothing has been officially junked. Belief is maintained in the basic badness of capitalism, in the inevitability of its destruction, in the obligation of the proletariat to assist in that destruction and to take power into its own hands. But stress has come to be laid primarily on those concepts which relate most specifically to the Soviet régime itself: to its position as the sole truly Socialist régime in a dark and misguided world, and to the relationships of power within it.

The first of these concepts is that of the innate antagonism between capitalism and Socialism. We have seen how deeply that concept has become imbedded in foundations of Soviet power. It has profound implications for Russia's conduct as a member of international society. It means that there can never be on Moscow's side any

sincere assumption of a community of aims between the Soviet Union and powers which are regarded as capitalist. It must invariably be assumed in Moscow that the aims of the capitalist world are antagonistic to the Soviet régime, and therefore to the interests of the peoples it controls. If the Soviet Government occasionally sets its signature to documents which would indicate the contrary, this is to be regarded as a tactical manœuvre permissible in dealing with the enemy (who is without honor) and should be taken in the spirit of *caveat emptor.* Basically, the antagonism remains. It is postulated. And from it flow many of the phenomena which we find disturbing in the Kremlin's conduct of foreign policy: the secretiveness, the lack of frankness, the duplicity, the wary suspiciousness, and the basic unfriendliness of purpose. These phenomena are there to stay, for the foreseeable future. There can be variations of degree and of emphasis. When there is something the Russians want from us, one or the other of these features of their policy may be thrust temporarily into the background; and when that happens there will always be Americans who will leap forward with gleeful announcements that "the Russians have changed," and some who will even try to take credit for having brought about such "changes." But we should not be misled by tactical manœuvres. These characteristics of Soviet policy, like the postulate from which they flow, are basic to the internal nature of Soviet power, and will be with us, whether in the foreground or the background, until the internal nature of Soviet power is changed.

This means that we are going to continue for a long time to find the Russians difficult to deal with. It does not mean that they should be considered as embarked upon a do-or-die program to overthrow our society by a given date. The theory of the inevitability of the eventual fall of capitalism has the fortunate connotation that there is no hurry about it. The forces of progress can take their time in preparing the final *coup de grâce.* Meanwhile, what is vital is that the "Socialist fatherland"—that oasis of power which has been already won for Socialism in the person of the Soviet Union—should be cherished and defended by all good Communists at home and abroad, its fortunes promoted, its enemies badgered and confounded. The promotion of premature, "adventuristic" revolutionary projects abroad which might embarrass Soviet power in any way would be an inexcusable, even a counter-revolutionary act. The cause of Socialism is the support and promotion of Soviet power, as defined in Moscow.

KREMLIN AUTHORITY

This brings us to the second of the concepts important to contemporary Soviet outlook. That is the infallibility of the Kremlin. The Soviet concept of power, which permits no focal points of organization outside the Party itself, requires that the Party leadership remain in theory the sole repository of truth. For if truth were to be found elsewhere, there would be justification for its expression in organized activity. But it is precisely that which the Kremlin cannot and will not permit. . . .

The main element of any United States policy toward the Soviet Union must be that of a long-term . . . vigilant containment of Russian expansive tendencies.

But we have seen that the Kremlin is under no ideological compulsion to accomplish its purposes in a hurry. Like the Church, it is dealing in ideological concepts which are of long-term validity, and it can afford to be patient. It has no right to risk the existing achievements of the revolution for the sake of vain baubles of the future. The very teachings of Lenin himself require great caution and flexibility in the pursuit of Communist purposes. . . .

These considerations make Soviet diplomacy at once easier and more difficult to deal with than the diplomacy of individual aggressive leaders like Napoleon and Hitler. On the one hand it is more sensitive to contrary force, more ready to yield on individual sectors of the diplomatic front when that force is felt to be too strong, and thus more rational in the logic and rhetoric of power. On the other hand it cannot be easily defeated or discouraged by a single victory on the part of its opponents. And the patient persistence by which it is animated means that it can be effectively countered not by sporadic acts which represent the momentary whims of democratic opinion but only by intelligent long-range policies on the part of Russia's adversaries—policies no less steady in their purpose, and no less variegated and resourceful in their application, than those of the Soviet Union itself.

CONTAINMENT

In these circumstances it is clear that the main element of any United States policy toward the Soviet Union must be that of a long-term, patient but firm and vigilant containment of Russian expansive tendencies. It is important to note, however, that such a policy has nothing to do with outward histrionics: with threats or blustering or superfluous gestures of outward "toughness." While the Kremlin is basically flexible in its reaction to political realities, it is by no means unamenable to considerations of prestige. Like almost any other government, it can be placed by tactless and threatening gestures in a position where it cannot afford to yield even though this might

be dictated by its sense of realism. The Russian leaders are keen judges of human psychology, and as such they are highly conscious that loss of temper and of self-control is never a source of strength in political affairs. They are quick to exploit such evidences of weakness. For these reasons, it is a *sine qua non* of successful dealing with Russia that the foreign government in question should remain at all times cool and collected and that its demands on Russian policy should be put forward in such a manner as to leave the way open for a compliance not too detrimental to Russian prestige.

In light of the above, it will be clearly seen that the Soviet pressure against the free institutions of the western world is something that can be contained by the adroit and vigilant application of counter-force at a series of constantly shifting geographical and political points, corresponding to the shifts and manœuvres of Soviet policy, but which cannot be charmed or talked out of existence. The Russians look forward to a duel of infinite duration, and they see that already they have scored great successes. It must be borne in mind that there was a time when the Communist Party represented far more of a minority in the sphere of Russian national life than Soviet power today represents in the world community.

But if ideology convinces the rulers of Russia that truth is on their side and that they can therefore afford to wait, those of us on whom that ideology has no claim are free to examine objectively the validity of that premise. The Soviet thesis not only implies complete lack of control by the west over its own economic destiny, it likewise assumes Russian unity, discipline and patience over an infinite period. Let us bring this apocalyptic vision down to earth, and suppose that the western world finds the strength and resourcefulness to contain Soviet power over a period of ten to fifteen years. What does that spell for Russia itself? . . .

The future of Soviet power may not be by any means as secure as Russian capacity for self-delusion would make it appear to the men in the Kremlin: That they can keep power themselves, they have demonstrated. That they can quietly and easily turn it over to others remains to be proved. Meanwhile, the hardships of their rule and the vicissitudes of international life have taken a heavy toll of the strength and hopes of the great people on whom their power rests. It is curious to note that the ideological power of Soviet authority is strongest today in areas beyond the frontiers of Russia, beyond the reach of its police power. This phenomenon brings to mind a comparison used by Thomas Mann in his great novel *Buddenbrooks*. Observing that human institutions often show the greatest outward brilliance at a moment when inner decay is in reality farthest advanced, he compared the Buddenbrook family, in the days of its greatest glamour, to one of those stars whose light shines most brightly on this world when in reality it has long since ceased to exist. And who can say with assurance that the strong light still cast by the Kremlin on the dissatisfied peoples of the western world is not the powerful afterglow of a constellation which is in actuality on the wane? This cannot be proved. And it cannot be disproved. But the possibility remains (and in the opinion of this writer it is a strong one) that Soviet power, like the capitalist world of its conception, bears within it the seeds of its own decay, and that the sprouting of these seeds is well advanced.

A RIVAL, NOT A PARTNER

It is clear that the United States cannot expect in the fore-seeable future to enjoy political intimacy with the Soviet régime. It must continue to regard the Soviet Union as a rival, not a partner, in the political arena. It must continue to expect that Soviet policies will reflect no abstract love of peace and stability, no real faith in the possibility of a permanent happy coexistence of the Socialist and capitalist worlds, but rather a cautious, persistent pressure toward the disruption and weakening of all rival influence and rival power.

Balanced against this are the facts that Russia, as opposed to the western world in general, is still by far the weaker party, that Soviet policy is highly flexible, and that Soviet society may well contain deficiencies which will eventually weaken its own total potential. This would of itself warrant the United States entering with reasonable confidence upon a policy of firm containment, designed to confront the Russians with unalterable counter-force at every point where they show signs of encroaching upon the interests of a peaceful and stable world.

But in actuality the possibilities for American policy are by no means limited to holding the line and hoping for the best. It is entirely possible for the United States to influence by its actions the internal developments, both within Russia and throughout the international Communist movement, by which Russian policy is largely determined. This is not only a question of the modest measure of informational activity which this government can conduct in the Soviet Union and elsewhere, although that, too, is important. It is rather a question of the degree to which the United States can create among the peoples of the world generally the impression of a country which knows what it wants, which is coping successfully with the problems of its internal life and with the responsibilities of a World Power, and which has a spiritual vitality capable of holding its own among the major ideological currents of the time. To the extent that such an impression can be created and maintained, the aims of Russian Communism must appear sterile and quixotic, the hopes and enthusiasm of Moscow's supporters must wane, and added strain must be imposed on the Kremlin's foreign

policies. For the palsied decrepitude of the capitalist world is the keystone of Communist philosophy. Even the failure of the United States to experience the early economic depression which the ravens of the Red Square have been predicting with such complacent confidence since hostilities ceased would have deep and important repercussions throughout the Communist world. . . .

It would be an exaggeration to say that American behavior unassisted and alone could exercise a power of life and death over the Communist movement and bring about the early fall of Soviet power in Russia. But the United States has it in its power to increase enormously the strains under which Soviet policy must operate, to force upon the Kremlin a far greater degree of moderation and circumspection than it has had to observe in recent years, and in this way to promote tendencies which must eventually find their outlet in either the break-up or the gradual mellowing of Soviet power. For no mystical, Messianic movement—and particularly not that of the Kremlin—can face frustration indefinitely without eventually adjusting itself in one way or another to the logic of that state of affairs.

Thus the decision will really fall in large measure in this country itself. The issue of Soviet-American relations is in essence a test of the over-all worth of the United States as a nation among nations. To avoid destruction the United States need only measure up to its own best traditions and prove itself worthy of preservation as a great nation.

Surely, there was never a fairer test of national quality than this. In the light of these circumstances, the thoughtful observer of Russian-American relations will find no cause for complaint in the Kremlin's challenge to American society. He will rather experience a certain gratitude to a Providence which, by providing the American people with this implacable challenge, has made their entire security as a nation dependent on their pulling themselves together and accepting the responsibilities of moral and political leadership that history plainly intended them to bear.

FOR FURTHER READING

John C. Culver, *American Dreamer: The Life and Times of Henry A. Wallace*. New York: Norton, 2000.

John Lewis Gaddis, *The Cold War: A New History*. New York: Penguin, 2005.

George F. Kennan, *Memoirs, 1925–1950*. Boston: Little, Brown, 1967.

Melvyn P. Leffler, *A Preponderance of Power: National Security, the Truman Administration, and the Cold War*. Stanford, CA: Stanford University Press, 1992.

David Mayers, *George Kennan and the Dilemma of U.S. Foreign Policy*. New York: Oxford University Press, 1988.

Communist Subversives Threaten America (1950)

Joseph R. McCarthy (1908–1957)

INTRODUCTION *The Cold War had profound effects on America's domestic situation as well as its foreign policy. One of the most spectacular episodes of the early Cold War period was the rise and fall of Joseph R. McCarthy, a Republican senator from Wisconsin who gained notoriety for his hunts for communists within the United States government. McCarthy worked in relative obscurity before gaining national attention with a February 9, 1950, speech in Wheeling, West Virginia. The following viewpoint is excerpted from the text of that speech as entered by McCarthy into the* Congressional Record *several days later. McCarthy claimed in his address that America was denied the fruits of victory from World War II because of treasonous subversives inside the U.S. State Department.*

His source of information was never identified, and no communists were ever found as a direct result of his accusations, but despite the lack of proof, McCarthy gained widespread media attention and public support. Several events probably contributed to this public reaction to McCarthy's charges. China had undergone a communist revolution in 1949, prompting an intense debate over how America "lost" China. The Soviet Union exploded its own atomic bomb the same year, depriving the United States of its nuclear monopoly and raising fears about Soviet espionage. Also that same year, Alger Hiss, a prominent U.S. diplomat, was charged with and found guilty of subversion and treason, convincing many Americans of the possibility of treason in high places.

How is the United States faring in the Cold War, according to McCarthy? Why is the case of Alger Hiss so important, in his view?

Five years after a world war has been won, men's hearts should anticipate a long peace, and men's minds should be free from the heavy weight that comes with war. But this is not such a period—for this is not a period of peace. This is a time of the "cold war." This is a time when all the world is split into two vast, increasingly hostile armed camps—a time of a great armaments race....

Ladies and gentlemen, can there be anyone here tonight who is so blind as to say that the war is not on? Can there be anyone who fails to realize that the Communist world has said, "The time is now"—that this is the time for the show-down between the democratic Christian world and the Communist atheistic world?

Unless we face this fact, we shall pay the price that must be paid by those who wait too long.

Joseph R. McCarthy, *Congressional Record*, 81st Cong., 2nd sess., 1950, pp. 1952–57.

COMMUNIST GAINS

Six years ago...there was within the Soviet orbit 180,000,000 people. Lined up on the antitotalitarian side there were in the world at that time roughly 1,625,000,000 people. Today, only 6 years later, there are 800,000,000 people under the absolute domination of Soviet Russia—an increase of over 400 percent. On our side, the figure has shrunk to around 500,000,000. In other words, in less than 6 years the odds have changed from 9 to 1 in our favor to 8 to 5 against us. This indicates the swiftness of the tempo of Communist victories and American defeats in the cold war. As one of our outstanding historical figures once said, "When a great democracy is destroyed, it will not be because of enemies from without, but rather because of enemies from within."

The truth of this statement is becoming terrifyingly clear as we see this country each day losing on every front.

In my opinion the State Department... is thoroughly infested with Communists.

At war's end we were physically the strongest nation on earth and, at least potentially, the most powerful intellectually and morally. Ours could have been the honor of being a beacon in the desert of destruction, a shining living proof that civilization was not yet ready to destroy itself. Unfortunately, we have failed miserably and tragically to arise to the opportunity.

The reason why we find ourselves in a position of impotency is not because our only powerful potential enemy has sent men to invade our shores, but rather because of the traitorous actions of those who have been treated so well by this Nation. It has not been the less fortunate or members of minority groups who have been selling this Nation out, but rather those who have had all the benefits that the wealthiest nation on earth has had to offer—the finest homes, the finest college education, and the finest jobs in Government we can give.

This is glaringly true in the State Department. There the bright young men who are born with silver spoons in their mouths are the ones who have been worst....

In my opinion the State Department, which is one of the most important government departments, is thoroughly infested with Communists.

I have in my hand 57 cases of individuals who would appear to be either card carrying members or certainly loyal to the Communist Party, but who nevertheless are still helping to shape our foreign policy.

One thing to remember in discussing the Communists in our Government is that we are not dealing with spies who get 30 pieces of silver to steal the blueprints of a new weapon. We are dealing with a far more sinister type of activity because it permits the enemy to guide and shape our policy....

ALGER HISS

This brings us down to the case of one Alger Hiss who is important not as an individual any more, but rather because he is so representative of a group in the State Department. It is unnecessary to go over the sordid events showing how he sold out the Nation which had given him so much. Those are rather fresh in all of our minds.

However, it should be remembered that the facts in regard to his connection with this international Communist spy ring were made known to the then Under Secretary of State [Adolf] Berle 3 days after [Adolf] Hitler and [Joseph] Stalin signed the Russo-German alliance pact. At that time one Whittaker Chambers—who was also part of the spy ring—apparently decided that with Russia on Hitler's side, he could no longer betray our Nation to Russia. He gave Under Secretary of State Berle—and this is all a matter of record—practically all, if not more, of the facts upon which Hiss' conviction was based.

Under Secretary Berle promptly contacted Dean Acheson [then an assistant secretary of state] and received word in return that Acheson (and I quote) "could vouch for Hiss absolutely"—at which time the matter was dropped. And this, you understand, was at a time when Russia was an ally of Germany. This condition existed while Russia and Germany were invading and dismembering Poland, and while the Communist groups here were screaming "warmonger" at the United States for their support of the allied nations.

Again in 1943, the FBI had occasion to investigate the facts surrounding Hiss' contacts with the Russian spy ring. But even after that FBI report was submitted, nothing was done.

Then late in 1948—August 5—when the Un-American Activities Committee called Alger Hiss to give an accounting, President Truman at once issued a Presidential directive ordering all Government agencies to refuse to turn over any information whatsoever in regard to the Communist activities of any Government employee to a congressional committee.

Incidentally, even after Hiss was convicted—it is interesting to note that the President still labeled the exposé of Hiss as a "red herring."...

As you hear this story of high treason, I know that you are saying to yourself, "Well, why doesn't the Congress do something about it?" Actually, ladies and gentlemen, one of the important reasons for the graft, the corruption, the dishonesty, the disloyalty, the treason in high Government positions—one of the most important

reasons why this continues is a lack of moral uprising on the part of the 140,000,000 American people. In the light of history, however, this is not hard to explain.

It is the result of an emotional hang-over and a temporary moral lapse which follows every war. It is the apathy to evil which people who have been subjected to the tremendous evils of war feel. As the people of the world see mass murder, the destruction of defenseless and innocent people, and all of the crime and lack of morals which go with war, they become numb and apathetic. It has always been thus after war.

However, the morals of our people have not been destroyed. They still exist. This cloak of numbness and apathy has only needed a spark to rekindle them. Happily, this spark has finally been supplied.

ATTACKING DEAN ACHESON

As you know, very recently the Secretary of State [Dean Acheson] proclaimed his loyalty to a man guilty of what has always been considered as the most abominable of all crimes—of being a traitor to the people who gave him a position of great trust. The Secretary of State, in attempting to justify his continued devotion to the man who sold out the Christian world to the atheistic world, referred to Christ's Sermon on the Mount as a justification and reason therefor, and the reaction of the American people to this would have made the heart of Abraham Lincoln happy.

When this pompous diplomat in striped pants, with a phony British accent, proclaimed to the American people that Christ on the Mount endorsed communism, high treason, and betrayal of a sacred trust, the blasphemy was so great that it awakened the dormant indignation of the American people.

He has lighted the spark which is resulting in a moral uprising and will end only when the whole sorry mess of twisted, warped thinkers are swept from the national scene so that we may have a new birth of national honesty and decency in Government.

Viewpoint 26B

McCarthyism Threatens America (1950)

The Tydings Committee

INTRODUCTION *Senator Joseph R. McCarthy's charges of communist subversion in the U.S. State Department (see opposing viewpoint) caused a national uproar. On March 8, 1950, a subcommittee of the Senate Foreign Relations Committee, headed by Maryland senator Millard Tydings, a Democrat, was established to investigate McCarthy's accusations. After testimony by McCarthy and those he had accused proved inconclusive, the committee decided to compare McCarthy's accusations with internal State Department loyalty files.*

These files had been kept since President Harry S Truman issued an executive order in 1947 requiring loyalty and background probes of all government employees. The Federal Bureau of Investigation (FBI) conducted investigations on thousands of people, not only for acts of espionage, but for any association with persons or organizations deemed suspect. Truman at first resisted the Tydings committee's request to release the files, but eventually relented. McCarthy argued that the files, which failed to substantiate his charges of widespread subversion, had been "raped" to remove derogatory material. The Tydings committee disagreed, and in its concluding report, excerpted here, sharply criticized McCarthy for making false accusations and leading the country into hysteria.

Senator Tydings lost his reelection bid in 1950. McCarthy continued making news with his charges of communist subversion until December 1954, when he was officially censured by the U.S. Senate. He died in 1957. "McCarthyism" became a term describing personal attacks in the form of indiscriminate allegations unsupported by evidence.

Did the Tydings committee uncover the presence of any communists in the State Department? What tactics of McCarthy does the committee criticize?

We have carefully and conscientiously reviewed each and every one of the loyalty files relative to the individuals charged by Senator McCarthy. In no instance was any one of them now employed in the State Department found to be a "card-carrying Communist," a member of the Communist Party, or "loyal to the Communist Party." Furthermore, in no instance have we found in our considered judgment that the decision to grant loyalty and security clearance has been erroneously or improperly made in the light of existing loyalty standards. Otherwise stated, we do not find basis in any instance for reversing the judgment of the State Department officials charged with responsibility for employee loyalty; or concluding that they have not conscientiously discharged their duties. . . .

What the State Department knows concerning an employee's loyalty is to be found in its loyalty and security files. These files contain all information bearing on loyalty, obtained from any and all sources, including, of course, the reports of full field investigations by the FBI. Interestingly, in this regard, no sooner had the President indicated that the files would be available for review by the subcommittee than Senator McCarthy charged they were being "raped," altered, or otherwise subjected to a "housecleaning." This charge was found to be utterly without foundation in fact. The files were reviewed by

Senate Committee on Foreign Relations, *State Department Loyalty Investigation*, 81st Cong., 2nd sess., July 20, 1950, S. Rept 2108.

representatives of the Department of Justice, and the Department has certified that all information bearing on the employee's loyalty as developed by the FBI appears in the files which were reviewed by the subcommittee. . . .

THE FACTS BEHIND THE CHARGE OF "WHITEWASH"

Seldom, if ever, in the history of congressional investigations has a committee been subjected to an organized campaign of vilification and abuse comparable to that with which we have been confronted throughout this inquiry. This campaign has been so acute and so obviously designed to confuse and confound the American people that an analysis of the factors responsible therefor is indicated.

The first of these factors was the necessity of creating the impression that our inquiry was not thorough and sincere in order to camouflage the fact that the charges made by Senator McCarthy were groundless and that the Senate and the American people had been deceived. No sooner were hearings started than the cry of "whitewash" was raised along with the chant "investigate the charges and not McCarthy." This chant we have heard morning, noon, and night for almost 4 months from certain quarters for readily perceptible motives. Interestingly, had we elected to investigate Senator McCarthy, there would have been ample basis therefor, since we have been reliably informed that at the time he made the charges initially he had no information whatever to support them, and, furthermore, it early appeared that in securing Senate Resolution 231 [passed in February 1950, authorizing a "full and complete study and investigation as to whether persons who are disloyal to the United States are, or have been, employed by the Department of State"] a fraud had been perpetrated upon the Senate of the United States.

From the very outset of our inquiry, Senator McCarthy has sought to leave the impression that the subcommittee has been investigating him and not "disloyalty in the State Department." The reason for the Senator's concern is now apparent. He had no facts to support his wild and baseless charges, and lived in mortal fear that this situation would be exposed.

Few people, cognizant of the truth in even an elementary way, have, in the absence of political partisanship, placed any credence in the hit-and-run tactics of Senator McCarthy. He has stooped to a new low in his cavalier disregard of the facts.

The simple truth is that in making his speech at Wheeling, Senator Mccarthy was talking of a subject and circumstances about which he knew nothing. His extreme and irresponsible statements called for emergency measures. As Senator [Kenneth S.] Wherry told Emmanuel S. Larsen, "Oh, Mac has gone out on a limb and kind of made a fool of himself and we have to back him up now." Starting with nothing, Senator McCarthy plunged headlong forward, desperately seeking to develop some information, which colored with distortion and fanned by a blaze of bias, would forestall a day of reckoning.

Certain elements rallied to his support, particularly those who ostensibly fight communism by adopting the vile methods of the Communists themselves and in so doing actually hinder the fight of all right-minded people who detest and abhor communism in all its manifestations. We cannot, however, destroy one evil by the adoption of another. Senator McCarthy and McCarthyism have been exposed for what they are—and the sight is not a pretty one....

THE BIG LIE

In concluding our report, we are constrained to make observations which we regard as fundamental.

It is, of course, clearly apparent that the charges of Communist infiltration of and influence upon the State Department are false. This knowledge is reassuring to all Americans whose faith has been temporarily shaken in the security of their Government by perhaps the most nefarious campaign of untruth in the history of our Republic.

We believe, however, that this knowledge and assurance, while important, will prove ultimately of secondary significance in contemplating the salutary aspects of our investigation. For, we believe that, inherent in the charges that have been made and the sinister campaign to give them ostensible verity, are lessons from which the American people will find inspiration for a rededication to the principles and ideals that have made this Nation great.

We have seen an effort to inflame the American people with a wave of hysteria and fear on an unbelievable scale.

We have seen the technique of the "Big Lie," elsewhere employed by the totalitarian dictator with devastating success, utilized here for the first time on a sustained basis in our history. We have seen how, through repetition and shifting untruths, it is possible to delude great numbers of people.

We have seen the character of private citizens and of Government employees virtually destroyed by public condemnation on the basis of gossip, distortion, hearsay, and deliberate untruths. By the mere fact of their associations with a few persons of alleged questionable proclivities an effort has been made to place the stigma of disloyalty upon individuals, some of whom are little

people whose only asset is their character and devotion to duty and country. This has been done without the slightest vestige of respect for even the most elementary rules of evidence or fair play or, indeed, common decency. Indeed, we have seen an effort not merely to establish guilt by association but guilt by accusation alone. The spectacle is one we would expect in a totalitarian nation where the rights of the individual are crushed beneath the juggernaut of statism and oppression; it has no place in America where government exists to serve our people, not to destroy them.

CREATING HYSTERIA

We have seen an effort to inflame the American people with a wave of hysteria and fear on an unbelievable scale in this free Nation. Were this campaign founded in truth it would be questionable enough; where it is fraught with falsehood from beginning to end, its reprehensible and contemptible character defies adequate condemnation.

We sincerely believe that charges of the character which have been made in this case seriously impair the efforts of our agencies of Government to combat the problem of subversion. Furthermore, extravagant allegations, which cannot be proved and are not subject to proof, have the inevitable effect of dulling the awareness of all Americans to the true menace of communism....

At a time when American blood is again being shed to preserve our dream of freedom, we are constrained fearlessly and frankly to call the charges, and the methods employed to give them ostensible validity, what they truly are: A fraud and a hoax perpetrated on the Senate of the United States and the American people. They represent perhaps the most nefarious campaign of half-truths and untruths in the history of this Republic. For the first time in our history, we have seen the totalitarian technique of the "big lie" employed on a sustained basis. The result has been to confuse and divide the American people, at a time when they should be strong in their unity, to a degree far beyond the hopes of the Communists themselves whose stock in trade is confusion and division. In such a disillusioning setting, we appreciate as never before our Bill of Rights, a free press, and the heritage of freedom that has made this Nation great.

FOR FURTHER READING

William F. Buckley Jr. and L. Brent Bozell, *McCarthy and His Enemies.* Chicago: H. Regnery Co., 1954.

Richard M. Fried, *Nightmare in Red: The McCarthy Era in Perspective.* New York: Oxford University Press, 1990.

Thomas Reeves, *The Life and Times of Joe McCarthy.* New York: Stein and Day, 1982.

Ellen Schrecker, *The Age of McCarthyism: A Brief History with Documents.* Boston: Bedford/St. Martin's, 1994.

Viewpoint 27A

America Should Send a Man to the Moon (1961)

John F. Kennedy (1917–1963)

INTRODUCTION *The Cold War between the United States and the Soviet Union not only shaped foreign policy and domestic politics of both nations, but also played an integral role in one of the most significant historical developments of the twentieth century— humanity's exploration of outer space. On October 4, 1957, the Soviet Union launched* Sputnik I, *the world's first artificial satellite. The event stunned the American people, who had been largely confident in U.S. technological supremacy over their Cold War rival. In subsequent years, for reasons both of military strategy and international prestige, both superpowers engaged in a "space race." They competed in developing rocket technology and sending satellites and people into space— a competition in which the Soviet Union took an early lead. On April 12, 1961, Soviet Yuri A. Gagarin became the first man in space. Alan B. Shepard became the first American in space a few weeks later on May 5.*

Perhaps the element of the space race that most completely captured the imaginations of Americans was the race to send a person to the moon. The start of America's effort toward this goal can be traced back in part to an address to Congress by President John F. Kennedy, excerpts of which appear here. Speaking a few weeks after Shepard's space flight, Kennedy proposes that America commit itself to a manned lunar expedition. The president, who based his successful 1960 election campaign in part on the argument that America was falling behind the Soviet Union in key areas, placed his idea within the context of a deadly serious competition with the "adversaries of freedom" for world power and influence. Kennedy succeeded in getting Congressional approval for the lunar project; eight years and $24 billion later, American astronaut Neil Armstrong became the first person to set foot on the moon.

How does Kennedy characterize the enemies of America? Why is space exploration so important, according to Kennedy?

Mr. Speaker, Mr. Vice President, my copartners in Government, and ladies and gentlemen: The Constitution imposes upon me the obligation to from time to time give to the Congress information on the state of the Union. While this has traditionally been interpreted as an annual affair, this tradition has been broken in extraordinary times.

These are extraordinary times. We face an extraordinary challenge. But our strength as well as our convictions have imposed upon this Nation the role of leader in

Excerpted from John F. Kennedy's speech to the 87th Congress, May 25, 1961.

freedom's cause. We face opportunities and adversaries that do not wait for annual addresses or fiscal years. This Nation is engaged in a long and exacting test for the future of freedom—a test which may well continue for decades to come.

WE STAND FOR FREEDOM

No role in history could be more difficult or more important. It is not a negative or defensive role—it is a great positive adventure. We stand for freedom. That is our conviction for ourselves, that is our only commitment to others. No friend, no neutral, and no adversary should think otherwise. We are not against any man, or any nation, or any system, except as it is hostile to freedom. Nor am I here to present a new military doctrine bearing any one name or aimed at any one area. I am here to promote the freedom doctrine.

The great battleground for the defense and expansion of freedom today is the whole southern half of the globe—Asia, Latin America, Africa, and the Middle East—the lands of rising peoples. Their revolution, the greatest in human history, is one of peace and hope for freedom and equality, for order and independence. They seek an end, they seek a beginning. And theirs is a revolution which we would support regardless of the cold war, and regardless of which political or economic route they choose to freedom.

ADVERSARIES OF FREEDOM

For the adversaries of freedom did not create this revolution; nor did they create the conditions which compel it. But they are seeking to ride the crest of its wave, to capture it for themselves.

Yet their aggression is more often concealed than open. They have fired no missiles; and their troops are seldom seen. They send arms, agitators, aid, technicians and propaganda to every troubled area. But where the fighting is required, it is usually done by others, by guerrillas striking at night, by assassins striking alone, assassins who have taken the lives of 4,000 civil officers in the last 12 months in Vietnam, by subversives and saboteurs and insurrectionists, who in some cases control whole areas inside of independent nations.

They possess a powerful intercontinental striking force, large forces for conventional war, a well-trained underground in nearly every country, the power to conscript talent and manpower for any purpose, the capacity for quick decisions, a closed society without dissent or free information, and long experience in the techniques of violence and subversion. They make the most of their scientific successes, their economic progress and their pose as a foe of colonialism and friend of popular revolution. They prey on unstable or unpopular governments, unsealed or unknown boundaries, unfilled hopes, convulsive change, massive poverty, illiteracy, unrest and frustration.

With these formidable weapons, the adversaries of freedom plan to consolidate their territory, to exploit, to control, and finally to destroy the hopes of the world's newest nations, and they have ambition to do it before the end of this decade. It is a contest of will and purpose as well as force and violence, a battle for minds and souls as well as lives and territory. In that contest we cannot stand aside. . . .

There is no single simple policy with which to meet this challenge. Experience has taught us that no one nation has the power or the wisdom to solve all the problems of the world or manage all its revolutionary tides; that extending our commitments does not always increase our security; that any initiative carries with it the risk of temporary defeat; that nuclear weapons cannot prevent subversion; that no free peoples can be kept free without will and energy of their own; and that no two nations or situations are exactly alike.

Yet there is much we can do and must do. The proposals I bring before you today are numerous and varied. They arise from the host of special opportunities and dangers which have become increasingly clear in recent months. Taken together, I believe that they mark another step forward in our effort as a people. Taken together they will help advance our own progress, encourage our friends, and strengthen the opportunities for freedom and peace. I am here to ask the help of this Congress and the Nation in approving these necessary measures. . . .

THE IMPORTANCE OF SPACE

If we are to win the battle that is going on around the world between freedom and tyranny, if we are to win the battle for men's minds, the dramatic achievements in space which occurred in recent weeks should have made clear to us all, as did the sputnik in 1957, the impact of this adventure on the minds of men everywhere who are attempting to make a determination of which road they should take. Since early in my term our efforts in space have been under review. With the advice of the Vice President, who is Chairman of the National Space Council, we have examined where we are strong and where we are not, where we may succeed and where we may not. Now it is time to take longer strides—time for a great new American enterprise—time for this Nation to take a clearly leading role in space achievement which in many ways may hold the key to our future on earth.

I believe we possess all the resources and all the talents necessary. But the facts of the matter are that we have never made the national decisions or marshaled

the national resources required for such leadership. We have never specified long-range goals on an urgent time schedule, or managed our resources and our time so as to insure their fulfillment.

I believe that this Nation should commit itself to achieving the goal . . . of landing a man on the moon and returning him safely to earth.

Recognizing the head start obtained by the Soviets with their large rocket engines, which gives them many months of leadtime, and recognizing the likelihood that they will exploit this lead for some time to come in still more impressive successes, we nevertheless are required to make new efforts on our own. For while we cannot guarantee that we shall one day be first, we can guarantee that any failure to make this effort will find us last. We take an additional risk by making it in full view of the world—but as shown by the feat of Astronaut [Alan B.] Shepard, this very risk enhances our stature when we are successful. But this is not merely a race. Space is open to us now; and our eagerness to share its meaning is not governed by the efforts of others. We go into space because whatever mankind must undertake, free-men must fully share.

A MAN ON THE MOON

I therefore ask the Congress, above and beyond the increases I have earlier requested for space activities, to provide the funds which are needed to meet the following national goals:

First, I believe that this Nation should commit itself to achieving the goal, before this decade is out, of landing a man on the moon and returning him safely to earth. No single space project in this period will be more exciting, or more impressive to mankind, or more important for the long-range exploration of space; and none will be so difficult or expensive to accomplish. Including necessary supporting research, this objective will require an additional $531 million this year and still higher sums in the future. We propose to accelerate development of the appropriate lunar spacecraft. We propose to develop alternate liquid and solid fuel boosters much larger than any now being developed, until certain which is superior. We propose additional funds for other engine development and for unmanned explorations—explorations which are particularly important for one purpose which this Nation will never overlook; the survival of the man who first makes this daring flight. But in a very real sense, it will not be one man going to the moon—we make this judgment affirmatively—it will be an entire nation. For all of us must work to put him there.

OTHER SPACE GOALS

Second, an additional $23 million, together with $7 million already available, will accelerate development of the ROVER nuclear rocket. This is a technological enterprise in which we are well on the way to striking progress, and which gives promise of some day providing a means for even more exciting and ambitious exploration of space, perhaps beyond the moon, perhaps to the very ends of the solar system itself.

Third, an additional $50 million will make the most of our present leadership by accelerating the use of space satellites for worldwide communications. When we have put into space a system that will enable people in remote areas of the earth to exchange messages, hold conversations, and eventually see television programs, we will have achieved a success as beneficial as it will be striking.

Fourth, an additional $75 million—of which $53 million is for the Weather Bureau—will help give us at the earliest possible time a satellite system for worldwide weather observation. Such a system will be of inestimable commercial and scientific value; and the information it provides will be made freely available to all the nations of the world.

Let it be clear—and this is a judgment which the Members of the Congress must finally make—let it be clear that I am asking the Congress and the country to accept a firm commitment to a new course of action—a course which will last for many years and carry very heavy costs, $531 million in the fiscal year 1962 and an estimated $7–9 billion additional over the next five years. If we are to go only halfway, or reduce our sights in the face of difficulty, in my judgment it would be better not to go at all. This is a choice which this country must make, and I am confident that under the leadership of the Space committees of the Congress and the appropriations committees you will consider the matter carefully. It is a most important decision that we make as a nation; but all of you have lived though the last 4 years and have seen the significance of space and the adventures in space, and no one can predict with certainty what the ultimate meaning will be of the mastery of space. I believe we should go to the moon. But I think every citizen of this country as well as the Members of the Congress should consider the matter carefully in their judgment, to which we have given attention over many weeks and months, as it is a heavy burden; and there is no sense in agreeing, or desiring, that the United States take an affirmative position in outer space unless we are prepared to do the work and bear the burdens to make it successful. If we are not, we should decide today.

A NATIONAL COMMITMENT

Let me stress also that more money alone will not do the job. This decision demands a major national commitment of scientific and technical manpower, material and facilities, and the possibility of their diversion from other important activities where they are already thinly spread. It means a degree of dedication, organization, and discipline which have not always characterized our research and development efforts. It means we cannot afford undue work stoppages, inflated costs of material or talent, wasteful interagency rivalries, or a high turnover of key personnel.

New objectives and new money cannot solve these problems. They could, in fact, aggravate them further—unless every scientist, every engineer, every serviceman, every technician, contractor, and civil servant involved gives his personal pledge that this Nation will move forward, with the full speed of freedom, in the exciting adventure of space.

Viewpoint 27B

America's Race to the Moon Is Misguided (1962)

Carl Dreher (1896–1976)

INTRODUCTION *Following President John F. Kennedy's 1961 proposal that America send people to the moon within the decade, the National Aeronautics and Space Administration (NASA) began plans for a manned lunar expedition. Annual government appropriations for space exploration rose to $5 billion during the Kennedy administration. Many scientists and others questioned the wisdom of Kennedy's plan. Several concerns are expressed in the following viewpoint, taken from a 1962 article by Carl Dreher, science editor for the* Nation *magazine from 1961 to 1975.*

Why is Dreher skeptical of the "cries of anguish" being made over the Soviet Union's lead in space? What does he estimate the costs of a moon landing to be? In what areas does Dreher believe international space cooperation is most likely to develop?

Before the [Soviet] Vostok III and IV flights, some prominent scientists and politicians were expressing misgivings about the cost of American participation in the race to the moon. The rising volume of protest was drowned out by the cries of anguish over the manifest Soviet lead. Most of this clamor was quite baldly inspired by partisan and commercial considerations, and since the earlier criticism had and still has a solid technological basis, no doubt it will be voiced anew. Those who say what they think, rather than what the Pentagon and the aerospace industry would like them to say, will be helping to safeguard the lives of our astronauts, which are endangered by energetic space promoters like Vice President

Carl Dreher, "Wrong Way to the Moon," *The Nation,* September 15, 1962.

Lyndon Johnson, who incessantly warns us that "our future as a nation is at stake," and that "we dare not lose."

In the first place, we may lose even if we commit everything we have: neither men nor money will necessarily overcome a late start. In the second place, why don't we dare? The moon race has little to do with military power at the present time and, the Air Force and its Congressional reserve generals to the contrary, may never assume decisive military importance. A space war is much more likely to be fought in earth orbit. We cannot, then, be overwhelmed by a Soviet victory in the lunar sweepstakes. Nor has the breakneck effort now in the whooping-up stage anything to do with our industrial and agricultural capacity and our ability to aid other nations; rather, it detracts from these assets. And they are assets in that older race against hunger and disease; the sick and hungry are not interested in the moon, but in food and medicine. As for the things of the spirit, if our national self-respect is on such a shaky basis that it cannot survive one more Russian triumph in space, we are in a bad way indeed. The Russians launched the first satellite and we felt somewhat humiliated, yet here we are, five years later, still grappling with them and causing them as many worries as they cause us.

Aside from the extravagant and juvenile character of these alarums, their authors ignore the fact that a premature moon landing, followed by the death of the astronauts on the moon or subsequently in space, would not enhance national prestige. This is a risk for the Soviets as well as for us. The more sanguine contestant may fail; the more wary one may wait, learn from the other's disasters and succeed. That is, indeed, a likely denouement, for the lunar problem is one of enormous difficulty. Hans Thirring, the noted Austrian physicist, has likened it to the leveling of the Rocky Mountains. If the first attempts succeed, it will be little short of a miracle.

VOICES OF MODERATION

On the side of moderation there are some impressive names and arguments. Already in December, 1960, when plans and budgets were still relatively modest (and they will seem minuscule in another year), Dr. James R. Killian, chairman of the M.I.T. Corporation and President [Dwight] Eisenhower's first scientific adviser in the post-sputnik era, said, "Will several billion dollars a year additional for enhancing the quality of education not do more for the future of the United States and its position in the world than several billions a year additional for man in space?" More recently, General Eisenhower has inveighed against what he called "a mad effort to win a stunt race," which it is, and "a great boondoggle," which is rather an oversimplification. More conversant with the technological realities, Dr. Lee DuBridge,

whose California Institute of Technology manages the Jet Propulsion Laboratory for the National Aeronautics and Space Administration [NASA], has referred to "space idiots" and shown that the arguments for a military crash program in space are fallacious. Dr. George B. Kistiakowsky, another scientific adviser to President Eisenhower, Dr. James van Allen, Dr. Edward U. Condon and Senator William Proxmire have reasoned to much the same effect.

None of these critics can be brushed off, but perhaps the most cogent evaluation has been provided by Dr. Warren Weaver, former president of the American Association for the Advancement of Science and one of the most highly respected of scientists, in the *Saturday Review* of August 4 [1962]. Assuming that it would cost the United States $30 billion to put a man on the moon, Dr. Weaver pointed out that this would give a 10 per cent raise in salary to every teacher in the country over a ten-year period, give $10 million each to 200 of the best small colleges, finance seven-year scholarships (freshman through Ph.D.) for 50,000 new scientists and engineers, contribute $200 million each toward the creation of ten new medical schools, build and largely endow complete universities for all fifty-three of the nations added to the United Nations since its founding, create three more Rockefeller Foundations and still have $100 million left over to popularize science, which bestrides us like a colossus and of whose spirit, principles and procedures probably not one American in a hundred has the faintest conception. . . .

The monetary argument does carry some weight and should continue to be pressed, but it does not follow that because the money could be put to good use here below there will be a popular revulsion against shooting it off into space. The moon race, as Dr. Condon has pointed out, is a kind of lunar Olympic game, exciting to both Russians and Americans and providing a much-needed effervescence for millions of drab lives. The astronauts have largely supplanted movie stars and ordinary athletes as popular heroes.

ENDANGERING LIVES

Instead of talking only about money, therefore, we should be talking of ways to spare as many of these attractive young men as possible, rather than offering them as a human sacrifice on the altar of nationalistic passions. There will be fatalities in any event, but we cannot condemn the moon project on that account. There is nothing particularly admirable about dying in bed. The appeal, if it is to be effective, must be based on the fact that astronauts will die unnecessarily and, by accelerating the moon race, we shall be accessories to a crime. . . .

[A] direction in which the risks of the lunar venture can be reduced is through cooperation between the contestants. Since, no matter what experiments precede the initial attempts to land on and escape from the moon, the odds will be against the early explorers, one would think that the two sides would at least exchange views on rescue techniques and perhaps work out a plan for common utilization of rescue facilities. They could still compete, but must it be a competition to the death? After the Nikolayev-Popovich flights the director of Britain's radio-astronomy and satellite-tracking station at Jodrell Bank, Sir Bernard Lovell, remarked, "More than ever one is appalled by the foolishness of these two countries attempting the moon problem in competition. After all, the common problem is the exploration of space and the manned conquest of the solar system." The common problem, unhappily, is subordinate to the separate problem of the superpowers, which is to do each other in by whatever means come to hand. Space may be infinite, but in the minds of the diplomats and militarists it is compressed into just one more counter in the war game. They brush off advice of the sort offered by Sir Bernard, just as they frustrate the attempts of the neutrals to get them to stop nuclear testing. They are perfectly ready to sacrifice the astronauts, their own lionized fellow countrymen, to national ambition, and in the fullness of their masculinity and patriotism the astronauts are willing and eager to take their chances.

This perhaps paints the situation darker than it actually is—but not much, I am afraid. . . .

PUBLIC OBLIVIOUS TO DANGERS

The sports-minded public has no conception of the difficulties of lunar exploration, and even the heads of governments, with access to expert information but no expertise of their own, tend to be oblivious to the obstacles and disasters that lie ahead. But this will not avert the troubles.

For the present, the prospects of limited cooperation among voluntary bodies, with the sufferance of the governments, are considerably better than for cooperation between the governments themselves. Enlightened scientists and engineers on both sides, as well as their counterparts in the allied and neutral camps, know that the existing status of space research is grossly improvident, that it risks human lives unnecessarily, and that it tends to retard rather than promote progress. Celestial mechanics is the same for Russians and Americans and for all races and nationalities. The two sides are simply duplicating each other's research and in the end arrive at the same techniques and vehicles. Along the way sometimes one will be ahead, sometimes the other, in some particular sector. Just now the Soviets are ahead in boosters and life-support systems, while the United States is ahead in the number and versatility of its unmanned satellites. But, as the race continues, the technological and industrial resources of both will be taxed to the utmost. The

moon flight alone threatens to swallow up a significant proportion of the superpowers' resources and to keep the Soviet people, in particular, in a state of permanent poverty. The military technicians of each look jealously on the funding of quasipeaceful space activity and struggle for a better position at the public trough. To the extent that the superpowers find it possible to cooperate, these dangers and burdens may be mitigated. The scientists see this more clearly than any other group and it is the obligation of the big names among them to call attention to it at opportune times.

AN INTERNATIONAL SPACE EFFORT

The ultimate, sensible answer would be an international consortium of the industrialized powers in which, it should be noted, the Germans would have to be given a prominent place. Before and during World War II they were the leaders not only in military rocketry but in many phases of theoretical space research. But the prerequisite to anything like this is an end to the cold war.

FOR FURTHER READING

William B. Breuer, *Race to the Moon: America's Duel with the Soviets.* Westport, CT: Praeger, 1993.

Amitai Etzioni, *The Moon-Doggle: Domestic and International Implications of the Space Race.* Garden City, NY: Doubleday, 1964.

James N. Giglio, *The Presidency of John F. Kennedy.* Lawrence: University Press of Kansas, 1991.

T.A. Heppenheimer, *Countdown: A History of Space Flight.* New York: John Wiley & Sons, 1997.

THE STRUGGLE FOR CIVIL RIGHTS AND EQUALITY

Viewpoint 28A

Racial Segregation in Public Schools Is Unconstitutional (1954)

Earl Warren (1891–1974)

INTRODUCTION *Earl Warren, a moderate Republican governor of California and presidential contender in 1948 and 1952, was appointed Supreme Court chief justice in 1953 by President Dwight D. Eisenhower. Warren went on to preside over many landmark decisions on social and civil rights issues. Perhaps the most important of these rulings was the first: the 1954 case of* Brown v. Board of Education *in which racially segregated schools were declared unconstitutional.*

The ruling, excerpted here, reversed the "separate but equal" doctrine affirmed by the 1896 Supreme Court decision in Plessy v. Ferguson *(see viewpoints 7A and 7B). Warren wrote the opinion of the Court in* Brown, *making significant use of arguments advanced by*

Thurgood Marshall of the National Association for the Advancement of Colored People (NAACP), the organization that represented the black plaintiffs seeking admission to white-only public schools. Brown was in some respects the culmination of the litigation that the NAACP had conducted on this issue since the 1930s, including Sweatt v. Painter, a 1950 case in which the Supreme Court decided that making black law students go to a segregated law school rather than admit them to the University of Texas deprived them of equal educational opportunities. Sweatt was one of several cases cited by Warren in the Brown decision.

What are the limitations of examining the history of the Fourteenth Amendment for the purposes of deciding this case, according to Warren? On what basis did the Supreme Court justices ascertain that segregation harmed black children? Why did they decide not to immediately implement their decision?

These cases come to us from the States of Kansas, South Carolina, Virginia, and Delaware. They are premised on different facts and different local conditions, but a common legal question justifies their consideration together in this consolidated opinion.

In each of the cases, minors of the Negro race, through their legal representatives, seek the aid of the courts in obtaining admission to the public schools of their community on a nonsegregated basis. In each instance, they had been denied admission to schools attended by white children under laws requiring or permitting segregation according to race. This segregation was alleged to deprive the plaintiffs of the equal protection of the laws under the Fourteenth Amendment. In each of the cases other than the Delaware case, a three-judge federal district court denied relief to the plaintiffs on the so-called "separate but equal" doctrine announced by this Court in *Plessy v. Ferguson*. . . . Under that doctrine, equality of treatment is accorded when the races are provided substantially equal facilities, even though these facilities be separate. In the Delaware case, the Supreme Court of Delaware adhered to that doctrine, but ordered that the plaintiffs be admitted to the white schools because of their superiority to the Negro schools.

The plaintiffs contend that segregated public schools are not "equal" and cannot be made "equal," and that hence they are deprived of the equal protection of the laws. Because of the obvious importance of the question presented, the Court took jurisdiction. Argument was heard in the 1952 Term, and reargument was heard this Term on certain questions propounded by the Court.

From the Supreme Court's unanimous decision in *Brown v. Board of Education*, 347 U.S. 483 (1954).

THE FOURTEENTH AMENDMENT

Reargument was largely devoted to the circumstances surrounding the adoption of the Fourteenth Amendment in 1868. It covered exhaustively consideration of the Amendment in Congress, ratification by the states, then existing practices in racial segregation, and the views of proponents and opponents of the Amendment. This discussion and our own investigation convince us that, although these sources cast some light, it is not enough to resolve the problem with which we are faced. At best, they are inconclusive. The most avid proponents of the post-War Amendments undoubtedly intended them to remove all legal distinctions among "all persons born or naturalized in the United States." Their opponents, just as certainly, were antagonistic to both the letter and the spirit of the Amendments and wished them to have the most limited effect. What others in Congress and the state legislatures had in mind cannot be determined with any degree of certainty.

An additional reason for the inconclusive nature of the Amendment's history, with respect to segregated schools, is the status of public education at that time. In the South, the movement toward free common schools, supported by general taxation, had not yet taken hold. Education of white children was largely in the hands of private groups. Education of Negroes was almost nonexistent, and practically all of the race were illiterate. In fact, any education of Negroes was forbidden by law in some states. Today, in contrast, many Negroes have achieved outstanding success in the arts and sciences as well as in the business and professional world. It is true that public school education at the time of the Amendment had advanced further in the North, but the effect of the Amendment on Northern States was generally ignored in the congressional debates. Even in the North, the conditions of public education did not approximate those existing today. The curriculum was usually rudimentary; ungraded schools were common in rural areas; the school term was but three months a year in many states; and compulsory school attendance was virtually unknown. As a consequence, it is not surprising that there should be so little in the history of the Fourteenth Amendment relating to its intended effect on public education.

In the first cases in this Court construing the Fourteenth Amendment, decided shortly after its adoption, the Court interpreted it as proscribing all state-imposed discriminations against the Negro race. The doctrine of "separate but equal" did not make its appearance in this Court until 1896 in the case of *Plessy v. Ferguson*, . . . involving not education but transportation. American courts have since labored with the doctrines for over half a century. In this Court, there have been six cases involving the "separate but equal" doctrine in the field of public education. In *Cumming v. County Board of Education...* and *Gong Lum v. Rice,...* the validity of the doctrine itself was not challenged. In more recent cases, all on the graduate school level, inequality was found in that specific benefits enjoyed by white students were denied to Negro students of the same educational qualifications.... In none of these cases was it necessary to re-examine the doctrine to grant relief to the Negro plaintiff. And in *Sweatt v. Painter,...* the Court expressly reserved decision on the question whether *Plessy v. Ferguson* should be held inapplicable to public education.

In the instant cases, that question is directly presented. Here, unlike *Sweatt v. Painter*, there are findings below that the Negro and white schools involved have been equalized, or are being equalized, with respect to buildings, curricula, qualifications and salaries of teachers, and other "tangible" factors. Our decision, therefore, cannot turn on merely a comparison of these tangible factors in the Negro and white schools involved in each of the cases. We must look instead to the effect of segregation itself on public education.

SEGREGATION AND EDUCATION

In approaching this problem, we cannot turn the clock back to 1868 when the Amendment was adopted, or even to 1896 when *Plessy v. Ferguson* was written. We must consider public education in the light of its full development and its present place in American life throughout the Nation. Only in this way can it be determined if segregation in public schools deprives these plaintiffs of the equal protection of the laws.

Today, education is perhaps the most important function of state and local governments. Compulsory school attendance laws and the great expenditures for education both demonstrate our recognition of the importance of education to our democratic society. It is required in the performance of our most basic public responsibilities, even service in the armed forces. It is the very foundation of good citizenship. Today it is a principal instrument in awakening the child to cultural values, in preparing him for later professional training, and in helping him to adjust normally to his environment. In these days, it is doubtful that any child may reasonably be expected to succeed in life if he is denied the opportunity of an education. Such an opportunity where the state has undertaken to provide it, is a right which must be made available to all on equal terms.

We come then to the question presented: Does segregation of children in public schools solely on the basis of race, even though the physical facilities and other "tangible" factors may be equal, deprive the children of the minority group of equal educational opportunities? We believe that it does.

■

*Separate educational facilities
are inherently unequal.*

■

In *Sweatt v. Painter,...* in finding that a segregated law school for Negroes could not provide them equal educational opportunities, this Court relied in large part on "those qualities which are incapable of objective measurement but which make for greatness in a law school." In *McLaurin v. Oklahoma State Regents,...* the Court, in requiring that a Negro admitted to a white graduate school be treated like all other students, again resorted to intangible considerations: "... his ability to study, to engage in discussions and exchange views with other students, and, in general, to learn his profession." Such considerations apply with added force to children in grade and high schools. To separate them from others of similar age and qualifications solely because of their race generates a feeling of inferiority as to their status in the community that may affect their hearts and minds in a way unlikely ever to be undone. The effect of this separation on their educational opportunities was well stated by a finding in the Kansas case by a court which nevertheless felt compelled to rule against the Negro plaintiffs:

> Segregation of white and colored children in public schools has a detrimental effect upon the colored children. The impact is greater when it has the sanction of the law; for the policy of separating the races is usually interpreted as denoting the inferiority of the negro group. A sense of inferiority affects the motivation of a child to learn. Segregation with the sanction of law, therefore, has a tendency to [retard] the education and mental development of negro children and to deprive them of some of the benefits they would receive in a racial[ly] integrated school system.

Whatever may have been the extent of psychological knowledge at the time of *Plessy v. Ferguson*, this finding is amply supported by modern authority. Any language in *Plessy v. Ferguson* contrary to this finding is rejected.

SEPARATE AND UNEQUAL

We conclude that in the field of public education the doctrine of "separate but equal" has no place. Separate educational facilities are inherently unequal. Therefore, we hold that the plaintiffs and others similarly situated for whom the actions have been brought are, by reason of the segregation complained of, deprived of the equal protection of the laws guaranteed by the Fourteenth Amendment. This disposition makes unnecessary any discussion whether such segregation also violates the Due Process Clause of the Fourteenth Amendment.

Because these are class actions, because of the wide applicability of this decision, and because of the great variety of local conditions, the formulation of decrees in these cases presents problems of considerable complexity. On reargument, the consideration of appropriate relief was necessarily subordinated to the primary question—the constitutionality of segregation on public education. We have now announced that such segregation is a denial of the equal protection of the laws. In order that we may have the full assistance of the parties in formulating decrees, the cases will be restored to the docket.

Viewpoint 28B

The Supreme Court Should Not Interfere in Southern Racial Practices (1956)

The Southern Manifesto

INTRODUCTION *The U.S. Supreme Court in the landmark case* Brown v. Board of Education *ruled that racially segregated public schools were unconstitutional. The Court made no direct statement on how this ruling was to be implemented; one year later the Court issued an "Enforcement Decree" calling for states to integrate their schools "with all deliberate speed." Despite these pronouncements communities and state governments in the southern states actively resisted school desegregation. In 1956 one hundred members of Congress signed a declaration of opposition to* Brown. *Most of the writing of the declaration, known as the "Southern Manifesto," was the work of North Carolina senator Sam J. Ervin Jr. Other signers included Senators Strom Thurmond, J. William Fullbright, and Richard B. Russell. The declaration, reprinted here, argues that the Supreme Court exceeded its legal authority in outlawing segregation. The signers go on to support all efforts to "resist forced integration by any lawful means."*

What evidence is presented to demonstrate that the Constitution and the Fourteenth Amendment do not require racial integration? How has the Brown *ruling affected race relations in the South, according to the Manifesto?*

The unwarranted decision of the Supreme Court in the public school cases is now bearing the fruit always produced when men substitute naked power for established law.

The Founding Fathers gave us a Constitution of checks and balances because they realized the inescapable lesson of history that no man or group of men can be safely entrusted with unlimited power. They framed this Constitution with its provisions for change by amendment in order to secure the fundamentals of government against the dangers of temporary popular

"The Southern Manifesto: Declaration of Constitutional Principles," *Congressional Record*, 84th Cong., 2nd sess., March 12, 1956.

passion or the personal predilections of public officeholders.

AN ABUSE OF POWER

We regard the decision of the Supreme Court in the school cases as a clear abuse of judicial power. It climaxes a trend in the Federal Judiciary undertaking to legislate, in derogation of the authority of Congress, and to encroach upon the reserved rights of the States and the people.

The original Constitution does not mention education. Neither does the 14th Amendment nor any other amendment. The debates preceding the submission of the 14th Amendment clearly show that there was no intent that it should affect the system of education maintained by the States.

The very Congress which proposed the amendment subsequently provided for segregated schools in the District of Columbia.

When the amendment was adopted in 1868, there were 37 States of the Union. Every one of the 26 States that had any substantial racial differences among its people, either approved the operation of segregated schools already in existence or subsequently established such schools by action of the same law-making body which considered the 14th Amendment.

As admitted by the Supreme Court in the public school case (*Brown* v. *Board of Education*), the doctrine of separate but equal schools "apparently originated in *Roberts* v. *City of Boston* (1849), upholding school segregation against attack as being violative of a State constitutional guarantee of equality." This constitutional doctrine began in the North, not in the South, and it was followed not only in Massachusetts, but in Connecticut, New York, Illinois, Indiana, Michigan, Minnesota, New Jersey, Ohio, Pennsylvania and other northern States until they, exercising their rights as States through the constitutional processes of local self-government, changed their school systems.

■

This unwarranted exercise of power by the Court . . . is creating chaos and confusion in the States principally affected.

■

In the case of *Plessy* v. *Ferguson* in 1896 the Supreme Court expressly declared that under the 14th Amendment no person was denied any of his rights if the States provided separate but equal public facilities. This decision has been followed in many other cases. It is notable that the Supreme Court, speaking through Chief Justice

[William H.] Taft, a former President of the United States, unanimously declared in 1927 in *Lum* v. *Rice* that the "separate but equal" principle is "within the discretion of the State in regulating its public schools and does not conflict with the 14th Amendment."

This interpretation, restated time and again, became a part of the life of the people of many of the States and confirmed their habits, customs, traditions, and way of life. It is founded on elemental humanity and commonsense, for parents should not be deprived by Government of the right to direct the lives and education of their own children.

Though there has been no constitutional amendment or act of Congress changing this established legal principle almost a century old, the Supreme Court of the United States, with no legal basis for such action, undertook to exercise their naked judicial power and substituted their personal political and social ideas for the established law of the land.

This unwarranted exercise of power by the Court, contrary to the Constitution, is creating chaos and confusion in the States principally affected. It is destroying the amicable relations between the white and Negro races that have been created through 90 years of patient effort by the good people of both races. It has planted hatred and suspicion where there has been heretofore friendship and understanding.

Without regard to the consent of the governed, outside agitators are threatening immediate and revolutionary changes in our public-school systems. If done, this is certain to destroy the system of public education in some of the States.

RESPONDING TO OUTSIDE MEDDLERS

With the gravest concern for the explosive and dangerous condition created by this decision and inflamed by outside meddlers:

We reaffirm our reliance on the Constitution as the fundamental law of the land.

We decry the Supreme Court's encroachments on rights reserved to the States and to the people, contrary to established law, and to the Constitution.

We commend the motives of those States which have declared the intention to resist forced integration by any lawful means.

We appeal to the States and people who are not directly affected by these decisions to consider the constitutional principles involved against the time when they too, on issues vital to them, may be the victims of judicial encroachment.

Even though we constitute a minority in the present Congress, we have full faith that a majority of the American people believe in the dual system of government which has enabled us to achieve our greatness and will in time demand that the reserved rights of the States and of the people be made secure against judicial usurpation.

We pledge ourselves to use all lawful means to bring about a reversal of this decision which is contrary to the Constitution and to prevent the use of force in its implementation.

In this trying period, as we all seek to right this wrong, we appeal to our people not to be provoked by the agitators and trouble-makers invading our States and to scrupulously refrain from disorder and lawless acts.

FOR FURTHER READING

Norman V. Bartley, *The Rise of Massive Resistance: Race & Politics in the South During the 1950s.* Baton Rouge: Louisiana State University Press, 1969.

Richard Kluger, *Simple Justice: the History of Brown v. Board of Education and Black America's Struggle for Equality.* New York: Knopf, 1976.

Waldo E. Martin, Jr., ed., *Brown v. Board of Education: A Brief History with Documents.* Boston: Bedford/St. Martin's, 1998.

Mark Whitman, ed., *Removing the Badge of Slavery: The Record of Brown v. Board of Education.* Princeton, NJ: Markus Wiener, 1993.

Viewpoint 29A
Blacks Should Strive to Be Part of the American Dream (1961)
Martin Luther King Jr. (1929–1968)

INTRODUCTION *In December 1955, less than two years after the* Brown v. Board of Education *Supreme Court decision outlawing racial segregation in public schools, African American residents of Montgomery, Alabama, took matters into their own hands against racial segregation and mistreatment of blacks on the city's buses. They organized a boycott that lasted more than one year before the Supreme Court issued a ruling invalidating Alabama's laws upholding segregation in transportation. The successful boycott made its leader—a young Baptist minister named Martin Luther King Jr.—a national figure renowned for his eloquence and his advocacy of nonviolent protests and civil disobedience. King's advocacy of nonviolent resistance is evident in the events of 1960 and 1961. In 1960 black college students in the South initiated "sit-in" demonstrations to desegregate lunch counters, libraries, and other public facilities. In 1961 the Congress of Racial Equality (CORE) sponsored "Freedom Rides," in which interracial groups traveled on previously segregated interstate buses. King himself remained the personification of the civil rights movement in the minds of many Americans.*

The following viewpoint is taken from a college commencement address King gave on June 6, 1961, at Lincoln University, a historically black college in Pennsylvania. It provides a good summary of King's views regarding nonviolence, the place of African Americans in U.S. history, and the progress of the civil rights movement. It is essential, he asserts, for people of all races to embrace the American dream of equality and brotherhood, and to reject notions of both white and black supremacy. The speech's closing is similar to that of a more famous King address—one he made two years later at the March on Washington.

What is the American dream, according to King? What myths about the races and segregation does he criticize? What are the special advantages of nonviolent resistance, in his view?

Today you bid farewell to the friendly security of this academic environment, a setting that will remain dear to you as long as the cords of memory shall lengthen. As you go out today to enter the clamorous highways of life, I should like to discuss with you some aspects of the American dream. For in a real sense, America is essentially a dream, a dream as yet unfulfilled. It is a dream of a land where men of all races, of all nationalities and of all creeds can live together as brothers. The substance of the dream is expressed in these sublime words, words lifted to cosmic proportions: "We hold these truths to be self-evident, that all men are created equal, that they are endowed by their Creator with certain unalienable rights, that among these are life, liberty, and the pursuit of happiness." This is the dream.

One of the first things we notice in this dream is an amazing universalism. It does not say some men, but it says all men. It does not say all white men, but it says all men, which includes black men. It does not say all Gentiles, but it says all men, which includes Jews. It does not say all Protestants, but it says all men, which includes Catholics.

And there is another thing we see in this dream that ultimately distinguishes democracy and our form of government from all of the totalitarian regimes that emerge in history. It says that each individual has certain basic rights that are neither conferred by nor derived from the state. To discover where they came from it is necessary to move back behind the dim mist of eternity, for they are God-given. Very seldom if ever in the history of the world has a sociopolitical document expressed in such profoundly eloquent and unequivocal language the dignity and the worth of human personality. The American dream reminds us that every man is heir to the legacy of worthiness.

Excerpted from Martin Luther King Jr, commencement address, Lincoln University (Pennsylvania), June 6, 1961.

Ever since the Founding Fathers of our nation dreamed this noble dream, America has been something of a schizophrenic personality, tragically divided against herself. On the one hand we have proudly professed the principles of democracy, and on the other hand we have sadly practiced the very antithesis of those principles. Indeed slavery and segregation have been strange paradoxes in a nation founded on the principle that all men are created equal. This is what the Swedish sociologist, Gunnar Myrdal, referred to as the American dilemma.

But the shape of the world today does not permit us the luxury of an anemic democracy. The price America must pay for the continued exploitation of the Negro and other minority groups is the price of its own destruction. The hour is late; the clock of destiny is ticking out. It is trite, but urgently true, that if America is to remain a first-class nation she can no longer have second-class citizens. Now, more than ever before, America is challenged to bring her noble dream into reality, and those who are working to implement the American dream are the true saviors of democracy.

Now may I suggest some of the things we must do if we are to make the American dream a reality. First I think all of us must develop a world perspective if we are to survive. The American dream will not become a reality devoid of the larger dream of a world of brotherhood and peace and good will. The world in which we live is a world of geographical oneness and we are challenged now to make it spiritually one. . . .

We are caught in an inescapable network of mutuality; tied in a single garment of destiny. Whatever affects one directly, affects all indirectly. As long as there is poverty in this world, no man can be totally rich even if he has a billion dollars. As long as diseases are rampant and millions of people cannot expect to live more than twenty or thirty years, no man can be totally healthy, even if he just got a clean bill of health from the finest clinic in America. Strangely enough, I can never be what I ought to be until you are what you ought to be. You can never be what you ought to be until I am what I ought to be. This is the way the world is made. I didn't make it that way, but this is the interrelated structure of reality. John Donne caught it a few centuries ago and could cry out, "No man is an island entire of itself; every man is a piece of the continent, a part of the main . . . any man's death diminishes me, because I am involved in mankind, and therefore never send to know for whom the bell tolls; it tolls for thee." If we are to realize the American dream we must cultivate this world perspective. . . .

NO INFERIOR RACES

Another thing we must do is to get rid of the notion once and for all that there are superior and inferior races. Now we know that this view still lags around in spite of the fact that many great anthropologists, Margaret Mead and Ruth Benedict and Melville Herskovits and others have pointed out and made it clear through scientific evidence that there are no superior races and there are no inferior races. There may be intellectually superior individuals within all races. In spite of all this evidence, however, the view still gets around somehow that there are superior and inferior races. The whole concept of white supremacy rests on this fallacy.

You know, there was a time when some people used to argue the inferiority of the Negro and the colored races generally on the basis of the Bible and religion....

But we don't often hear these arguments today. Segregation is now based on "sociological and cultural" grounds. "The Negro is not culturally ready for integration, and if integration comes into being it will pull the white race back a generation. It will take fifty or seventy-five years to raise these standards." And then we hear that the Negro is a criminal, and there are those who would almost say he is a criminal by nature. But they never point out that these things are environmental and not racial; these problems are problems of urban dislocation. They fail to see that poverty, and disease, and ignorance breed crime whatever the racial group may be. And it is a tortuous logic that views the tragic results of segregation and discrimination as an argument for the continuation of it.

If we are to implement the American dream we must get rid of the notion once and for all that there are superior and inferior races. This means that members of minority groups must make it clear that they can use their resources even under adverse circumstances. We must make full and constructive use of the freedom we already possess. We must not use our oppression as an excuse for mediocrity and laziness.

CREATIVE PROTEST

Finally, if we are to implement the American dream, we must continue to engage in creative protest in order to break down all of those barriers that make it impossible for the dream to be realized. Now I know there are those people who will argue that we must wait on something. They fail to see the necessity for creative protest, but I say to you that I can see no way to break loose from an old order and to move into a new order without standing up and resisting the unjust dogma of the old order.

To do this, we must get rid of two strange illusions that have been held by the so-called moderates in race relations. First is the myth of time advanced by those who say that you must wait on time; if you "just wait and be patient," time will work the situation out. They will say this even about freedom rides. They will say this about sit-ins: that you're pushing things too fast—cool off—time will work these problems out. Well, evolution may

hold in the biological realm, and in that area Darwin was right. But when a Herbert Spencer [nineteenth-century philosopher and formulator of "Social Darwinism"] seeks to apply "evolution" to the whole fabric of society, there is no truth in it. Even a superficial look at history shows that social progress never rolls in on the wheels of inevitability. It comes through the tireless effort and the persistent work of dedicated individuals. Without this hard work, time itself becomes an ally of the primitive forces of irrational emotionalism and social stagnation. And we must get rid of the myth of time.

EDUCATION AND LEGISLATION

There is another myth, that bases itself on a species of educational determinism. It leads one to think that you can't solve this problem through legislation; you can't solve this problem through judicial decree; you can't solve this problem through executive orders on the part of the president of the United States. It must be solved by education. Now I agree that education plays a great role, and it must continue to play a great role in changing attitudes, in getting people ready for the new order. And we must also see the importance of legislation.

It is not a question either of education or of legislation. Both legislation and education are required. Now, people will say, "You can't legislate morals." Well, that may be true. Even though morality may not be legislated, behavior can be regulated. And this is very important. We need religion and education to change attitudes and to change the hearts of men. We need legislation and federal action to control behavior. It may be true that the law can't make a man love me, but it can keep him from lynching me, and I think that's pretty important also.

And so we must get rid of these illusions and move on with determination and with zeal to break down the unjust systems we find in our society, so that it will be possible to realize the American dream. As I have said so often, if we seek to break down discrimination, we must use the proper methods. I am convinced more than ever before that, as the powerful, creative way opens, men and women who are eager to break the barriers of oppression and of segregation and discrimination need not fall down to the levels of violence. They need not sink into the quicksands of hatred. Standing on the high ground of noninjury, love and soul force, they can turn this nation upside down and right side up.

NONVIOLENT RESISTANCE

I believe, more than ever before, in the power of nonviolent resistance. It has a moral aspect tied to it. It makes it possible for the individual to secure moral ends through moral means. This has been one of the great debates of history. People have felt that it is impossible to achieve moral ends through moral means. And so a Machiavelli could come into being and so force a sort of duality within the moral structure of the universe. Even communism could come into being and say that anything justifies the end of a classless society—lying, deceit, hate, violence—anything. And this is where nonviolent resistance breaks with communism and with all of those systems which argue that the end justifies the means, because we realize that the end is preexistent in the means. In the long run of history, destructive means cannot bring about constructive ends.

The practical aspect of nonviolent resistance is that it exposes the moral defenses of the opponent. Not only that, it somehow arouses his conscience at the same time, and it breaks down his morale. He has no answer for it. If he puts you in jail, that's all right; if he lets you out, that's all right too. If he beats you, you accept that; if he doesn't beat you—fine. And so you go on, leaving him with no answer. But if you use violence, he does have an answer. He has the state militia; he has police brutality.

Nonviolent resistance is one of the most magnificent expressions going on today. We see it in the movement taking place among students in the South and their allies who have been willing to come in from the North and other sections. They have taken our deep groans and passionate yearnings, filtered them in their own souls, and fashioned them into the creative protest, which is an epic known all over our nation. They have moved in a uniquely meaningful orbit, imparting light and heat to a distant satellite. And people say, "Does this bring results?" Well, look at the record.

In less than a year, lunch counters have been integrated in more than 142 cities of the Deep South, and this was done without a single court suit; it was done without spending millions and millions of dollars. We think of the freedom rides, and remember that more than sixty people are now in jail in Jackson, Mississippi. What has this done? These people have been beaten; they have suffered to bring to the attention of this nation, the indignities and injustices Negro people still confront in interstate travel. It has, therefore, had an educational value. But not only that—signs have come down from bus stations in Montgomery, Alabama. They've never been down before. Not only that—the attorney general of this nation has called on ICC [Interstate Commerce Commission] to issue new regulations making it positively clear that segregation in interstate travel is illegal and unconstitutional.

And so this method can bring results. Sometimes it can bring quick results. But even when it doesn't bring immediate results, it is constantly working on the conscience; it is at all times using moral means to bring about moral ends. And so I say we must continue on the way of creative protest. I believe also that this method will help us to enter the new age with the proper attitude. . . .

AGAINST RACIAL SEPARATION

I know sometimes we get discouraged and sometimes disappointed with the slow pace of things. At times we begin to talk about racial separation instead of racial integration, feeling that there is no other way out. My only answer is that the problem never will be solved by substituting one tyranny for another. Black supremacy is as dangerous as white supremacy, and God is not interested merely in the freedom of black men and brown men and yellow men. God is interested in the freedom of the whole human race and in the creation of a society where all men can live together as brothers, where every man will respect the dignity and the worth of human personality.

By following this method, we may also be able to teach our world something that it so desperately needs at this hour. In a day when Sputniks and Explorers are dashing through outer space, and guided ballistic missiles are carving highways of death through the stratosphere, no nation can win a war. The choice is no longer between violence and nonviolence; it is either nonviolence or nonexistence. Unless we find some alternative to war, we will destroy ourselves by the misuse of our own instruments. And so, with all of these attitudes and principles working together, I believe we will be able to make a contribution as men of good will to the ongoing structure of our society and toward the realization of the American dream. And so, as you go out today, I call upon you not to be detached spectators, but involved participants, in this great drama that is taking place in our nation and around the world.

Every academic discipline has its technical nomenclature, and modern psychology has a word that is used, probably, more than any other. It is the word *maladjusted*. This word is the ringing cry of modern child psychology. Certainly all of us want to live a well-adjusted life in order to avoid the neurotic personality. But I say to you, there are certain things within our social order to which I am proud to be maladjusted and to which I call upon all men of good will to be maladjusted.

A CALL TO BE MALADJUSTED

If you will allow the preacher in me to come out now, let me say to you that I never did intend to adjust to the evils of segregation and discrimination. I never did intend to adjust myself to religious bigotry. I did intend to adjust myself to economic conditions that will take necessities from the many to give luxuries to the few. I never did intend to adjust myself to the madness of militarism, and the self-defeating effects of physical violence. And I call upon all men of good will to be maladjusted because it may well be that the salvation of our world lies in the hands of the maladjusted.

So let us be maladjusted, as maladjusted as the prophet Amos, who in the midst of the injustices of his day could cry out in words that echo across the centuries, "Let justice run down like waters and righteousness like a mighty stream." Let us be as maladjusted as Abraham Lincoln, who had the vision to see that this nation could not exist half slave and half free. Let us be maladjusted as Jesus of Nazareth, who could look into the eyes of the men and women of his generation and cry out, "Love your enemies. Bless them that curse you. Pray for them that despitefully use you."

I believe that it is through such maladjustment that we will be able to emerge from the bleak and desolate midnight of man's inhumanity to man into the bright and glittering daybreak of freedom and justice. That will be the day when all of God's children, black men and white men, Jews and Gentiles, Catholics and Protestants, will be able to join hands and sing in the words of the old Negro spiritual, "Free at last! Free at last! Thank God almighty, we are free at last!"

Viewpoint 29B

Blacks Can Never Be Part of the American Dream (1963)

Malcolm X (1925–1965)

INTRODUCTION *During the height of the civil rights movement in the 1950s and 1960s, not all blacks were united behind the ideas of Martin Luther King Jr., including the tactics of nonviolent protest and the goal of racial integration. A controversial alternative vision of blacks in America was expressed in the black nationalist speeches and statements by Malcolm X.*

Malcolm Little was in prison for burglary when he became a follower of the Nation of Islam, a religious sect led by Elijah Muhammad that combined Islamic teachings with black nationalist beliefs. Followers were commonly called Black Muslims. Malcolm adopted X—a symbol of his stolen identity as a descendant of slaves brought from Africa—as his surname. After his release from prison he emerged as one of the leading speakers for the Nation of Islam. The following viewpoint is excerpted from a November 10, 1963, speech at a rally at King Solomon Baptist Church in Detroit, Michigan. He argues that blacks are not and never will be Americans but are instead an oppressed population that shares the same white enemy as colonized African and Asian peoples. He further contends that blacks should strive for racial separation and self-sufficiency rather than integration and that they should reserve the right to use violence if necessary.

What is the basis of a successful revolution, according to Malcolm X? What argument does he make about the two different kinds of slaves that existed in the days of slavery?

We want to have just an off-the-cuff chat between you and me, us. We want to talk right down to earth in a language that everybody here can easily understand. We all agree tonight, all of the speakers have agreed, that America has a very serious problem. Not only does America have a very serious problem, but our people have a very serious problem. America's problem is us. We're her problem. The only reason she has a problem is she doesn't want us here. And every time you look at yourself, be you black, brown, red or yellow, a so-called Negro, you represent a person who poses such a serious problem for America because you're not wanted. Once you face this as a fact, then you can start plotting a course that will make you appear intelligent, instead of unintelligent.

What you and I need to do is learn to forget our differences. When we come together, we don't come together as Baptists or Methodists. You don't catch hell because you're a Baptist, and you don't catch hell because you're a Methodist. You don't catch hell because you're a Methodist or Baptist, you don't catch hell because you're a Democrat or a Republican, you don't catch hell because you're a Mason or an Elk, and you sure don't catch hell because you're an American; because if you were an American, you wouldn't catch hell. You catch hell because you're a black man. You catch hell, all of us catch hell, for the same reason.

So we're all black people, so-called Negroes, second-class citizens, ex-slaves. You're nothing but an ex-slave. You don't like to be told that. But what else are you? You are ex-slaves. You didn't come here on the "Mayflower." You came here on a slave ship. In chains, like a horse, or a cow, or a chicken. And you were brought here by the people who came here on the "Mayflower," you were brought here by the so-called Pilgrims, or Founding Fathers. They were the ones who brought you here....

THE BLACK REVOLUTION

I would like to make a few comments concerning the difference between the black revolution and the Negro revolution. Are they both the same? And if they're not, what is the difference? What is the difference between a black revolution and a Negro revolution? First, what is a revolution? Sometimes I'm inclined to believe that many of our people are using this word "revolution" loosely, without taking careful consideration of what this word actually means, and what its historic characteristics are. When you study the historic nature of revolutions, the motive of a revolution, the objective of a revolution, the result of a revolution, and the methods used in a revolution, you may change words. You may devise another program, you may change your goal and you may change your mind.

From Malcolm X, "Message to the Grass Roots," in *Malcolm X Speaks*, edited by George Breitman (New York: Pathfinder Press, 1989).

Look at the American Revolution in 1776. That revolution was for what? For land. Why did they want land? Independence. How was it carried out? Bloodshed. Number one, it was based on land, the basis of independence. And the only way they could get it was bloodshed. The French Revolution—what was it based on? The landless against the landlord. What was it for? Land. How did they get it? Bloodshed. Was no love lost, was no compromise, was no negotiation. I'm telling you—you don't know what a revolution is. Because when you find out what it is, you'll get back in the alley, you'll get out of the way.

The Russian Revolution—what was it based on? Land; the landless against the landlord. How did they bring it about? Bloodshed. You haven't got a revolution that doesn't involve bloodshed. And you're afraid to bleed. I said, you're afraid to bleed.

As long as the white man sent you to Korea, you bled. He sent you to Germany, you bled. He sent you to the South Pacific to fight the Japanese, you bled. You bleed for white people, but when it comes to seeing your own churches being bombed and little black girls murdered, you haven't got any blood. You bleed when the white man says bleed; you bite when the white man says bite; and you bark when the white man says bark. I hate to say this about us, but it's true. How are you going to be nonviolent in Mississippi, as violent as you were in Korea? How can you justify being nonviolent in Mississippi and Alabama, when your churches are being bombed, and your little girls are being murdered, and at the same time you are going to get violent with Hitler, and Tojo, and somebody else you don't even know?

If violence is wrong in America, violence is wrong abroad. If it is wrong to be violent defending black women and black children and black babies and black men, then it is wrong for America to draft us and make us violent abroad in defense of her. And if it is right for America to draft us, and teach us how to be violent in defense of her, then it is right for you and me to do whatever is necessary to defend our own people right here in this country. . . .

Of all our studies, history is best qualified to reward our research. And when you see that you've got problems, all you have to do is examine the historic method used all over the world by others who have problems similar to yours. Once you see how they got theirs straight, then you know how you can get yours straight. There's been a revolution, a black revolution, going on in Africa. In Kenya, the Mau Mau were revolutionary; they were the ones who brought the word "Uhuru" to the fore. The Mau Mau, they were revolutionary, they believed in scorched earth, they knocked everything aside that got in their way, and their revolution also was based on

land, a desire for land. In Algeria, the northern part of Africa, a revolution took place. The Algerians were revolutionists, they wanted land. France offered to let them be integrated into France. They told France, to hell with France, they wanted some land, not some France. And they engaged in a bloody battle.

NONVIOLENCE IS NO REVOLUTION

So I cite these various revolutions, brothers and sisters, to show you that you don't have a peaceful revolution. You don't have a turn-the-other-cheek revolution. There's no such thing as a nonviolent revolution. The only kind of revolution that is nonviolent is the Negro revolution. The only revolution in which the goal is loving your enemy is the Negro revolution. It's the only revolution in which the goal is a desegregated lunch counter, a desegregated theater, a desegregated park, and a desegregated public toilet; you can sit down next to white folks—on the toilet. That's no revolution. Revolution is based on land. Land is the basis of all independence. Land is the basis of freedom, justice, and equality.

The white man knows what a revolution is. He knows that the black revolution is world-wide in scope and in nature. The black revolution is sweeping Asia, is sweeping Africa, is rearing its head in Latin America. The Cuban Revolution—that's a revolution. They overturned the system. Revolution is in Asia, revolution is in Africa, and the white man is screaming because he sees revolution in Latin America. How do you think he'll react to you when you learn what a real revolution is? You don't know what a revolution is. If you did, you wouldn't use that word.

Revolution is bloody, revolution is hostile, revolution knows no compromise, revolution overturns and destroys everything that gets in its way. And you, sitting around here like a knot on the wall, saying, "I'm going to love these folks no matter how much they hate me." No, you need a revolution. Whoever heard of a revolution where they lock arms, as Rev. [Albert B.] Cleage was pointing out beautifully, singing "We Shall Overcome"? You don't do that in a revolution. You don't do any singing, you're too busy swinging. It's based on land. A revolutionary wants land so he can set up his own nation, an independent nation. These Negroes aren't asking for any nation—they're trying to crawl back on the plantation.

When you want a nation, that's called nationalism. When the white man became involved in a revolution in this country against England, what was it for? He wanted this land so he could set up another white nation. That's white nationalism. The American Revolution was white nationalism. The French Revolution was white nationalism. The Russian Revolution too—yes, it was—white nationalism. You don't think so? Why do you think Khrushchev and Mao can't get their heads together?

White nationalism. All the revolutions that are going on in Asia and Africa today are based on what?—black nationalism. A revolutionary is a black nationalist. He wants a nation. I was reading some beautiful words by Rev. Cleage, pointing out why he couldn't get together with someone else in the city because all of them were afraid of being identified with black nationalism. If you're afraid of black nationalism, you're afraid of revolution. And if you love revolution, you love black nationalism.

THE HOUSE SLAVE AND THE FIELD SLAVE

To understand this, you have to go back to what the young brother here referred to as the house Negro and the field Negro back during slavery. There were two kinds of slaves, the house Negro and the field Negro. The house Negroes—they lived in the house with master, they dressed pretty good, they ate good because they ate his food—what he left. They lived in the attic or the basement, but still they lived near the master; and they loved the master more than the master loved himself. They would give their life to save the master's house—quicker than the master would. If the master said, "We got a good house here," the house Negro would say, "Yeah, we got a good house here." Whenever the master said "we," he said "we." That's how you can tell a house Negro.

If the master's house caught on fire, the house Negro would fight harder to put the blaze out than the master would. If the master got sick, the house Negro would say, "What's the matter, boss, *we* sick?" *We* sick! He identified himself with his master, more than his master identified with himself. And if you came to the house Negro and said, "Let's run away, let's escape, let's separate," the house Negro would look at you and say, "Man, you crazy. What you mean, separate? Where is there a better house than this? Where can I wear better clothes than this? Where can I eat better food than this?" That was that house Negro. In those days he was called a "house nigger." And that's what we call them today, because we've still got some house niggers running around here.

This modern house Negro loves his master. He wants to live near him. He'll pay three times as much as the house is worth just to live near his master, and then brag about "I'm the only Negro out here." "I'm the only one on my job." "I'm the only one in this school." You're nothing but a house Negro. And if someone comes to you right now and says, "Let's separate," you say the same thing that the house Negro said on the plantation. "What you mean, separate? From America, this good white man? Where you going to get a better job than you get here?" I mean, this is what you say. "I ain't left nothing in Africa," that's what you say. Why, you left your mind in Africa.

On that same plantation, there was the field Negro. The field Negroes—those were the masses. There were always more Negroes in the field than there were Negroes in the house. The Negro in the field caught hell. He ate leftovers. In the house they ate high up on the hog. The Negro in the field didn't get anything but what was left of the insides of the hog. They call it "chitt'lings" nowadays. In those days they called them what they were—guts. That's what you were—gut-eaters. And some of you are still gut-eaters.

The field Negro was beaten from morning to night; he lived in a shack, in a hut; he wore old, castoff clothes. He hated his master. I say he hated his master. He was intelligent. That house Negro loved his master, but that field Negro—remember, they were in the majority, and they hated the master. When the house caught on fire, he didn't try to put it out; that field Negro prayed for a wind, for a breeze. When the master got sick, the field Negro prayed that he'd die. If someone came to the field Negro and said, "Let's separate, let's run," he didn't say "Where we going?" He'd say, "Any place is better than here." You've got field Negroes in America today. I'm a field Negro. The masses are the field Negroes. When they see this man's house on fire, you don't hear the little Negroes talking about "*our* government is in trouble." They say, "*The* government is in trouble." Imagine a Negro: "*Our* government"! I even heard one say "*our* astronauts." They won't even let him near the plant—and "*our* astronauts"! "*Our* Navy"—that's a Negro that is out of his mind, a Negro that is out of his mind.

Just as the slavemaster of that day used Tom, the house Negro, to keep the field Negroes in check, the same old slavemaster today has Negroes who are nothing but modern Uncle Toms, twentieth-century Uncle Toms, to keep you and me in check, to keep us under control, keep us passive and peaceful and nonviolent. That's Tom making you nonviolent. It's like when you go to the dentist, and the man's going to take your tooth. You're going to fight him when he starts pulling. So he squirts some stuff in your jaw called novocaine, to make you think they're not doing anything to you. So you sit there and because you've got all of that novocaine in your jaw, you suffer—peacefully. Blood running all down your jaw, and you don't know what's happening. Because someone has taught you to suffer—peacefully.

The white man does the same thing to you in the street, when he wants to put knots on your head and take advantage of you and not have to be afraid of your fighting back. To keep you from fighting back, he gets these old religious Uncle Toms to teach you and me, just like novocaine, to suffer peacefully. Don't stop suffering—just suffer peacefully. As Rev. Cleage pointed out, they say you should let your blood flow in the streets. This is a shame. You know he's a Christian preacher. If it's a shame to him, you know what it is to me.

There is nothing in our book, the Koran, that teaches us to suffer peacefully. Our religion teaches us to be intelligent. Be peaceful, be courteous, obey the law, respect everyone; but if someone puts his hand on you, send him to the cemetery. That's a good religion. In fact, that's that old-time religion. That's the one that Ma and Pa used to talk about: an eye for an eye, and a tooth for a tooth, and a head for a head, and a life for a life. That's a good religion. And nobody resents that kind of religion being taught but a wolf, who intends to make you his meal.

This is the way it is with the white man in America. He's a wolf—and you're sheep. Any time a shepherd, a pastor, teaches you and me not to run from the white man and, at the same time, teaches us not to fight the white man, he's a traitor to you and me. Don't lay down a life all by itself. No, preserve your life, it's the best thing you've got. And if you've got to give it up, let it be even-steven.

FOR FURTHER READING

Clayborne Carson, *In Struggle: SNCC and the Black Awakening of the 1960s.* Cambridge, MA: Harvard University Press, 1981.

David J. Garrow, *Bearing the Cross.* New York: Morrow, 1986.

Juan Williams, *Eyes on the Prize: America's Civil Rights Years, 1954–1965.* New York: Viking, 1987.

Malcolm X, with the assistance of Alex Haley, *The Autobiography of Malcolm X.* New York: Grove Press, 1965.

Viewpoint 30A

American Women Need an Equal Rights Amendment (1970)

Margaret M. Heckler (b. 1931)

INTRODUCTION *The movement for civil rights for African Americans affected other groups, including women. In 1966 the National Organization for Women was founded to end sex discrimination in education and the workplace and to liberalize abortion laws. More radical groups also sprouted up to combat what they saw as deep-rooted sexism in American culture. One of the main goals of the women's rights movement during the 1960s and 1970s was to amend the U.S. Constitution to formally enshrine equality of the sexes. The following viewpoint is taken from 1970 testimony before Congress in favor of what became known as the Equal Rights Amendment (ERA) by Margaret M. Heckler, a Republican member of the House of Representatives from Massachusetts. Heckler would later serve as secretary of health and human services and as U.S. ambassador to Ireland.*

What do most American women want, according to Heckler? What evidence of sex discrimination does she present? In her view, why is passage of the Equal Rights Amendment urgent?

It is assumed today by many persons that women were granted equality with the passage of the 14th amendment, ratified in 1868. Only 50 years later, however, was woman suffrage guaranteed by the ratification of the 19th amendment. Half a century of waiting for the vote required a great deal of patience. In the temper of these turbulent times, I do not believe that total equality of opportunity for women can be further postponed.

Thus I speak out in support of the equal rights amendment—a measure that has been before each Congress since 1923. The fast pace of life in the world today fosters impatience. And when much is promised, failure to deliver becomes a matter of critical importance.

THE CRUSADE FOR EQUALITY

I am sure that every woman who has been in the position of "job seeker" identifies in some small measure with the fundamental complaints that have generated the crusade for equality in employment for women. The 42 percent of working women who are heads of household takes a serious economic interest in fair job opportunity, a basic goal in the cause for women's rights. And the women who have contributed their full share to social security, yet who receive the sum allotted widows, certainly have cause for contemplation.

The average woman in America has no seething desire to smoke cigars or to burn the bra—but she does seek equal recognition of her status as a citizen before the courts of law, and she does seek fair and just recognition of her qualifications in the employment market. The American working woman does not want to be limited in advancement by virtue of her sex. She does not want to be prohibited from the job she desires or from the overtime work she needs by "protective" legislation.

These types of discrimination must be stopped, and the forthright means of halting discrimination against women is passage of the equal rights amendment at the earliest possible time. In fact, I have heard it said quite often that the only discrimination that is still fashionable is discrimination against women.

Perhaps, as some say, it is derived from a protective inclination on the part of men. But women seek recognition as individual human beings with abilities useful to society—rather than shelter or protection from the real world....

Legal remedies are clearly in order, and the equal rights amendment is especially timely. Although changes in social attitudes cannot be legislated, they are guided by the formulation of our Federal laws. This constitutional amendment must be passed so that discriminatory legislation will be overturned. That custom and attitude be

Margaret M. Heckler, testimony before the Senate Subcommittee on Constitutional Amendments, Committee on the Judiciary, 91st Cong., 2nd sess., May 5, 1970.

subject to a faster pace of evolution is essential if we are to avoid revolution on the part of qualified women who seek equality in the employment world.

THE STATUS OF AMERICAN WOMEN

Time and again I have heard American men question the fact of discrimination against women in America. "American women," they say, "enjoy greater freedom than women of any other nation." This may be true with regard to freedom from kitchen labor—because the average American housewife enjoys a considerable degree of automation in her kitchen. But once she seeks to fill her leisure time gained from automated kitchen equipment by entering the male world of employment, the picture changes. Many countries we consider "underprivileged" far surpass America in quality and availability of child care available to working mothers, in enlightened attitudes about employment leave for pregnancy, and in guiding women into the professions.

Since World War II, nearly 14 million American women have joined the labor force—double the number of men. Forty percent of our Nation's labor force is now composed of women. Yet less than 3 percent of our Nation's attorneys are women, only about 7 percent of our doctors, and 9 percent of our scientists are women. Only a slightly higher percentage of our graduate students in these fields of study are women, despite the fact that women characteristically score better on entrance examinations. The average woman college graduate's annual earnings ($6,694) exceed by just a fraction the annual earnings of an average male educated only through the eighth grade ($6,580). An average male college graduate, however, may be expected to earn almost twice as much as the female—$11,795. Twenty percent of the women with 4 years of college training can find employment only in clerical, sales, or factory jobs. The equal pay provision [a 1963 amendment] of the Fair Labor Standards Act does not include administrative, executive, or professional positions—a loophole which permits the talents and training of highly qualified women to be obtained more cheaply than those of comparable qualified men.

Of the 7.5 million American college students enrolled in 1968, at least 40 percent were women. American parents are struggling to educate their daughters as well as their sons—and are sending them to the best colleges they can possibly afford. As many of these mothers attend commencement exercises this summer, their hearts will swell with pride as their daughters receive college degrees—and these mothers may realize their daughters will have aspirations far exceeding their own horizons.

Few of the fathers or mothers, enrolling their daughters in college several years ago, were at the time aware of the obstacles to opportunity their daughters would face. But today they are becoming aware that opportunity for their daughters is only half of that available to their sons. And they are justifiably indignant. Young women graduating with degrees in business administration take positions as clerks while their male counterparts become management trainees. Women graduating from law school are often forced to become legal secretaries, while male graduates from the same class survey a panorama of exciting possibilities.

THE NATION'S NEEDS

To frustrate the aspirations of the competent young women graduating from our institutions of higher learning would be a dangerous and foolish thing. The youth of today are inspired with a passion to improve the quality of life around us—an admirable and essential goal, indeed. The job is a mammoth one, however; and it would be ill-advised to assume that the role of women in the crusade of the future will not be a significant one. To the contrary, never before has our Nation and our world cried out for talent and creative energy with greater need. To deny full participation of the resources of women, who compose over half the population of our country, would be a serious form of neglect. The contributions of women have always been intrinsic in our national development. With the increasing complexity of our world, it becomes all the more essential to tap every conceivable resource at our command.

The time is thus ripe for passage of the equal rights amendment. The women of America are demanding full rights and full responsibilities in developing their individual potential as human beings in relationship to the world as well as to the home and in contributing in an active way to the improvement of society.

The equal rights amendment is necessary to establish unequivocally the American commitment to full and equal recognition of the rights of all its citizens.

In this day of the urban crisis, when we seem to be running out of clean air and water, when the quantity of our rubbish defies our current disposal methods, when crime on the streets is rampant, when our world commitments seem at odds with our obligations here at home, when breaking the cycle of ongoing poverty requires new and innovative approaches, when increased lifespan generates a whole new series of gerontological problems—in these complicated and critical times, our Nation needs the fully developed resources of all our citizens—both men and women—in order to meet the demands of society today.

Women are not requesting special privilege—but rather a full measure of responsibility, a fair share of the load in the effort to improve life in America. The upcoming generation is no longer asking for full opportunity to contribute, however—they are demanding this opportunity.

The equal rights amendment is necessary to establish unequivocally the American commitment to full and equal recognition of the rights of all its citizens. Stopgap measures and delays will no longer be acceptable—firm guarantees are now required. The seventies mark an era of great promise if the untapped resource of womanpower is brought forth into the open and allowed to flourish so that women may take their rightful place in the mainstream of American life. Both men and women have a great deal to gain.

Viewpoint 30B

An Equal Rights Amendment Would Be Harmful (1970)

Myra Wolfgang (1914–1976)

INTRODUCTION *In 1972 Congress passed an amendment to the Constitution stating, "Equality of rights under the law shall not be denied or abridged by the United States or any State on the basis of sex." After almost a decade of campaigning, however, supporters of the Equal Rights Amendment (ERA) were unable to attain ratification by the necessary thirty-six state legislatures. Opposition to the amendment came from a number of conservative organizations and leaders, as well as some labor leaders who contended that the proposed amendment might abolish needed protective job legislation for women. Such arguments are included in the following viewpoint by Myra Wolfgang, taken from Senate hearings on the ERA in May 1970. Wolfgang, a union official representing hotel and restaurant workers in Detroit, Michigan, argues that while there is much wrongful discrimination against women, the proposed amendment would do working women more harm than good.*

What specific objections does Wolfgang have to the Equal Rights Amendment? How does she characterize the feminist movement? Why do women sometimes need special protective legislation, according to Wolfgang?

My name is Myra Wolfgang. I reside in the city of Detroit. I am the international vice president of the Hotel and Restaurant Employees Union, AFL-CIO, and also the secretary-treasurer of its Detroit local. I bring to this hearing 35 years of experience in representing the interests of service workers, both organized, and may I hasten to add, unorganized as well. I am a member of the Michigan Minimum Wage Board representing

Myra Wolfgang, testimony before the Senate Subcommittee on Constitutional Amendments, Committee on the Judiciary, 91st Cong., 2nd sess., May 6, 1970.

service employees thereon. I have been a member of the mayor's committee on human relations, and...I am a member of the current Governor's commission on the status of women and was a member of the Governor's commission under the previous two administrations. I am quite proud of the fact that I made the suggestion to Gov. John Swainson that we have a commission on the status of women, and Michigan was the first State to have such a commission.

SERVICE WORKERS

The service industries which I represent comprise more than 5.5 million women workers. There are an additional 5 million women employed in wholesale and retail trades industries. I represent unskilled and untrained women workers, the majority of whom are not organized into trade unions. They also are not burdened with the necessity of holding philosophical discussions on whether women should or should not be in the work force. They are in the work force because of dire, economic necessity and have no choice in the matter.

My concern with the equal rights amendment, Senator, is not an academic one. It embodies the problems that I work with day in and day out, year in and year out. My concern is for the widowed, divorced mothers of children who are the heads of their families and earn less than $3,500 a year working as maids, laundry workers, hospital cleaners, or dishwashers. And there are millions of such women in the work force. Now is as good a time as any to remind you that only 1 out of 10 women in the work force has had 4 or more years of college, so I am not speaking of, or representing, the illusive "bird in the gilded cage." I speak for "Tillie the Toiler."

I am opposed to enactment of the equal rights amendment. I recognize that the impetus for the passage of the equal rights amendment is the result of a growing anger amongst women over job discrimination, social and political discrimination, and many outmoded cultural habits of our way of life.

And the anger is justified, for certainly discrimination against women exists. I do not believe, however, that passage of the equal rights amendment will satisfy, or is the solution to, the problem. The problem of discrimination against women will not be solved by an equal rights amendment to the Constitution; conversely, the amendment will create a whole new series of problems. It will neither bring about equal pay for equal work, nor guarantee job promotion free from discrimination....

The amendment is excessively sweeping in scope, reaching into the work force, into family and social relationships, and other institutions, in which, incidentally, "equality" cannot always be achieved through "identity." Differences in laws are not necessarily discriminatory, nor should all laws containing different provisions for men and women be abolished, as the equal rights amendment would do....

THREAT TO LABOR LEGISLATION

Representing service workers gives me a special concern over the threat that an equal rights amendment would present to minimum labor standards legislation. I am sure you are aware of the influence of such legislation upon working conditions. And I am sure you are aware that many such laws apply to women only.

They are varied and they are in the field of minimum wages, hours of work, rest periods, weight lifting, childbirth legislation, et cetera.

These State laws are outmoded and many of them are discriminatory. They should be amended where they are. They should be strengthened and they should be handled on a case-by-case basis.

It is difficult to unite women against vague philosophies, so the new feminists look for a focus in the law. Thus, the revived interest in the equal rights amendment. The feminist movement in the main is middle class, professional woman, college girl oriented....

DIFFERENCES BETWEEN MEN AND WOMEN

Some feminist groups have concluded that since only females reproduce—and to be a mother is to be a "slave eternal"—that nothing short of the destruction of the family and the end of internal reproduction will do. Having discovered "artificial insemination," all that is missing now, in order to do away with women entirely, is discovering an artificial womb.

You will be hearing, I am sure, from many who will contend that there are no real differences between men and women, other than those enforced by culture. Has culture created the differences in the size of the hands, in muscular mass, in respiratory capacity? Of course not. The differences are physical.

Let me add some more. Women on the average—these are averages, Senator—are 85 percent as heavy as men and have only 60 percent as much physical strength. Therefore, they cannot lift as heavy weights. They cannot direct as much weight or have the same strength for pushing or pulling of loads.

One can take any cell from a human being and determine whether it came from a male or a female. This does not suggest superiority or inferiority among the sexes, it emphasizes differences. Because of the physical—and I emphasize physical—differences between men and women, the question of protective legislation for women must be reviewed. In addition, the dual role of women in our modern society makes protective legislation necessary.

The working mother has no "wife" to care for her or her children. She assumes the role of home maker and worker and must perform both these roles in a 24-hour period. Even in the two-parent households, there is an unequal division of domestic chores. While much could be done to ease the burden of the working woman by men assuming the fair and equal share of domestic chores, they are not prepared to do so. And I am not prepared to become confused with what should be and what is.

If the community does not take action through protective legislation to enable women to work outside the home, then the expressed desire for equal rights is an empty promise and a myth. The equal rights amendment would make it unconstitutional to enact and would repeal legislation embodying this protection for working women. You must ask yourself this question: Should women workers be left without any legislation because of State legislature's failure and unwillingness to enact such legislation for men?

The elimination of laws regulating hours women may work permits employers to force them to work excessive overtime, endangering not only their health and safety, but disrupting the entire family relationship.

The women in the work force who are in the greatest need of the protection of maximum hour legislation are in no position to fight for themselves....

I oppose the equal rights amendment since the equality it may achieve may well be equality of mistreatment.

UNANSWERED QUESTIONS

In this mad whirl toward equality and sameness one question remains unanswered: Who will take care of the children, the home, cleaning, the laundry, and the cooking? Can we extend this equality into the home? Obviously not, since the proponents of the equal rights amendment are quick to point out the amendment would restrict only governmental action and would not apply to purely private action....

You have been reminded in strong and ominous tones, and I was here yesterday and heard it, that women represent the majority of the voters. That is true. But there is no more unanimity of opinion among women than there is amongst men. Indeed, a woman on welfare in Harlem, a unionized laundryworker in California, and an elderly socialite from Philadelphia may be of the same sex and they may be wives and mothers, but they have little in common to cause them to be of one opinion.

Whatever happens to the structure of opportunity, women are increasingly motivated to work—and they want to work short hours on schedules that meet their needs as wives and mothers. They want fewer hours a week because emancipation, while it has released them for work, has not released them from home and family responsibilities.

I oppose the equal rights amendment since the equality it may achieve may well be equality of mistreatment.

FOR FURTHER READING

Flora Davis, *Moving the Mountain: The Women's Movement in America Since 1960.* New York: Simon & Schuster, 1991.

Mary A. Delsman, *Everything You Need to Know About ERA.* Riverside, CA: Meranza Press, 1975.

Jane J. Mansbridge, *Why We Lost the ERA.* Chicago: University of Chicago Press, 1986.

Willliam L. O'Neill, *Feminism in America: A History.* New Brunswick, NJ: Transaction, 1989.

THE TURBULENT SIXTIES

Viewpoint 31A

America Is Fighting for a Just Cause in Vietnam (1965)

Lyndon B. Johnson (1908–1973)

INTRODUCTION *The Vietnam conflict was a central dividing issue during the 1960s. Controversy over Vietnam was largely responsible for the political downfall of Lyndon B. Johnson, president of the United States from 1963 (after John F. Kennedy's assassination) to 1969.*

Johnson had inherited the conflict from his White House predecessors. Vietnam was an Asian nation that had been under French colonial rule. In 1954 Vietnamese rebel forces led by Ho Chi Minh, a longtime nationalist leader, defeated the French and established a communist government in what became North Vietnam. The United States under President Dwight D. Eisenhower, was locked in a Cold War rivalry with the Soviet Union and China. Unwilling to let all of Vietnam fall into the communist orbit, the United States lent its support to a noncommunist regime that became South Vietnam. Eisenhower sent several hundred American soldiers as military advisers and millions of economic aid dollars to South Vietnam. Kennedy increased the number of American troops there to sixteen thousand during his brief presidency. Under Johnson the United States began intensive bombing campaigns against North Vietnam in early 1965 and increased the number of U.S. troops deployed there to 267,000 by 1966 (American troop levels eventually peaked at 543,000 in 1969).

As U.S. involvement escalated, the war became an increasingly divisive issue within the nation. In the following viewpoint, taken from an April 7, 1965, speech delivered at Johns Hopkins University, Johnson defends his actions, arguing that the American war effort was necessary to fight communism in that part of the world.

What American goals and ideals are at stake, according to Johnson? What U.S. objectives does he state?

Tonight Americans and Asians are dying for a world where each people may choose its own path to change.

This is the principle for which our ancestors fought in the valleys of Pennsylvania. It is the principle for which our sons fight tonight in the jungles of Viet-Nam.

Viet-Nam is far away from this quiet campus. We have no territory there, nor do we seek any. The war is dirty and brutal and difficult. And some 400 young men, born into an America that is bursting with opportunity and promise, have ended their lives on Viet-Nam's steaming soil.

Why must we take this painful road?

Why must this Nation hazard its ease, and its interest, and its power for the sake of a people so far away?

WHY WE FIGHT

We fight because we must fight if we are to live in a world where every country can shape its own destiny. And only in such a world will our own freedom be finally secure.

This kind of world will never be built by bombs or bullets. Yet the infirmities of man are such that force must often precede reason, and the waste of war, the works of peace.

We wish that this were not so. But we must deal with the world as it is, if it is ever to be as we wish.

The world as it is in Asia is not a serene or peaceful place.

The first reality is that North Viet-Nam has attacked the independent nation of South Viet-Nam. Its object is total conquest.

Of course, some of the people of South Viet-Nam are participating in attacks on their own government. But trained men and supplies, orders and arms, flow in a constant stream from north to south. This support is the heartbeat of the war.

And it is a war of unparalleled brutality. Simple farmers are the targets of assassination and kidnapping. Women and children are strangled in the night because their men are loyal to their government. And helpless villages are ravaged by sneak attacks. Large-scale raids are conducted on towns, and terror strikes in the heart of cities.

The confused nature of this conflict cannot mask the fact that it is the new face of an old enemy.

Reprinted from *Public Papers of the Presidents: Lyndon B. Johnson, 1965* (Washington, DC: Government Printing Office, 1966).

THE THREAT OF CHINA

Over this war—and all Asia—is another reality: the deepening shadow of Communist China. The rulers in Hanoi [the capital of North Vietnam] are urged on by Peking [Beijing, the capital of China]. This is a regime which has destroyed freedom in Tibet, which has attacked India, and has been condemned by the United Nations for aggression in Korea. It is a nation which is helping the forces of violence in almost every continent. The contest in Viet-Nam is part of a wider pattern of aggressive purposes.

Why are these realities our concern? Why are we in South Viet-Nam?

We are there because we have a promise to keep. Since 1954 every American President has offered support to the people of South Viet-Nam. We have helped to build, and we have helped to defend. Thus, over many years, we have made a national pledge to help South Viet-Nam defend its independence.

And I intend to keep that promise.

To dishonor that pledge, to abandon this small and brave nation to its enemies, and to the terror that must follow, would be an unforgivable wrong.

We're also there to strengthen world order. Around the globe, from Berlin to Thailand, are people whose well-being rests, in part, on the belief that they can count on us if they are attacked. To leave Viet-Nam to its fate would shake the confidence of all these people in the value of an American commitment and in the value of America's word. The result would be increased unrest and instability, and even wider war.

IMPORTANT STAKES

We are also there because there are great stakes in the balance. Let no one think for a moment that retreat from Viet-Nam would bring an end to conflict. The battle would be renewed in one country and then another. The central lesson of our time is that the appetite of aggression is never satisfied. To withdraw from one battlefield means only to prepare for the next. We must say in southeast Asia—as we did in Europe—in the words of the Bible: "Hitherto shalt thou come, but no further."

There are those who say that all our effort there will be futile—that China's power is such that it is bound to dominate all southeast Asia. But there is no end to that argument until all of the nations of Asia are swallowed up.

There are those who wonder why we have a responsibility there. Well, we have it there for the same reason that we have a responsibility for the defense of Europe. World War II was fought in both Europe and Asia, and when it ended we found ourselves with continued responsibility for the defense of freedom.

Our objective is the independence of South Viet-Nam, and its freedom from attack. We want nothing for ourselves—only that the people of South Viet-Nam be allowed to guide their own country in their own way.

We will do everything necessary to reach that objective. And we will do only what is absolutely necessary.

In recent months attacks on South Viet-Nam were stepped up. Thus, it became necessary for us to increase our response and to make attacks by air. This is not a change of purpose. It is a change in what we believe that purpose requires.

We do this in order to slow down an aggression.

We do this to increase the confidence of the brave people of South Viet-Nam who have bravely borne this brutal battle for so many years with so many casualties.

WE WILL NOT LOSE

And we do this to convince the leaders of North Viet-Nam—and all who seek to share their conquest—of a very simple fact:

We will not be defeated.

Because we fight for values and we fight for principles, rather than territory or colonies, our patience and our determination are unending.

We will not grow tired.

We will not withdraw, either openly or under the cloak of a meaningless agreement.

We know that air attacks alone will not accomplish all of these purposes. But it is our best and prayerful judgment that they are a necessary part of the surest road to peace. . . .

Because we fight for values and we fight for principles, rather than territory or colonies, our patience and our determination are unending.

Once this is clear, then it should also be clear that the only path for reasonable men is the path of peaceful settlement.

Such peace demands an independent South Viet-Nam—securely guaranteed and able to shape its own relationships to all others—free from outside interference—tied to no alliance—a military base for no other country.

These are the essentials of any final settlement.

We will never be second in the search for such a peaceful settlement in Viet-Nam.

There may be many ways to this kind of peace: in discussion or negotiation with the governments concerned; in large groups or in small ones; in the reaffirmation of old agreements or the strengthening with new ones.

We have stated this position over and over again, fifty times and more, to friend and foe alike. And we remain ready, with this purpose, for unconditional discussions. . . .

These countries of southeast Asia are homes for millions of impoverished people. Each day these people rise at dawn and struggle through until the night to wrestle existence from the soil. They are often wracked by disease, plagued by hunger, and death comes at the early age of 40.

Stability and peace do not come easily in such a land. Neither independence nor human dignity will ever be won, though, by arms alone. It also requires the work of peace. The American people have helped generously in times past in these works. Now there must be a much more massive effort to improve the life of man in that conflict-torn corner of our world.

ECONOMIC DEVELOPMENT

The first step is for the countries of southeast Asia to associate themselves in a greatly expanded cooperative effort for development. We would hope that North Viet-Nam would take its place in the common effort just as soon as peaceful cooperation is possible.

The United Nations is already actively engaged in development in this area. As far back as 1961 I conferred with our authorities in Viet-Nam in connection with their work there. And I would hope tonight that the Secretary General of the United Nations could use the prestige of his great office, and his deep knowledge of Asia, to initiate, as soon as possible, with the countries of that area, a plan for cooperation in increased development.

For our part I will ask the Congress to join in a billion-dollar American investment in this effort as soon as it is under way.

And I would hope that all other industrialized countries, including the Soviet Union, will join in this effort to replace despair with hope, and terror with progress. . . .

I also intend to expand and speed up a program to make available our farm surpluses to assist in feeding and clothing the needy in Asia. We should not allow people to go hungry and wear rags while our own warehouses overflow with an abundance of wheat and corn, rice and cotton. . . .

In areas that are still ripped by conflict, of course, development will not be easy. Peace will be necessary for final success. But we cannot and must not wait for peace to begin this job.

WE MUST CHOOSE

We may well be living in the time foretold many years ago when it was said: "I call heaven and earth to record this day against you, that I have set before you life and death, blessing and cursing: therefore choose life, that both thou and thy seed may live."

This generation of the world must choose: destroy or build, kill or aid, hate or understand.

We can do all these things on a scale never dreamed of before.

Well, we will choose life. In so doing we will prevail over the enemies within man, and over the natural enemies of all mankind.

Viewpoint 31B
America Is Not Fighting for a Just Cause in Vietnam (1967)
Eugene McCarthy (1916–2005)

INTRODUCTION *Between 1950 and 1975 the conflict in Vietnam cost the United States more than fifty-eight thousand lives and $150 billion. The Vietnam War was fought as part of America's Cold War containment policy of opposing the spread of communism (and the influence of communist China and the Soviet Union). Defenders of American actions argued that the United States must take all necessary actions to defend South Vietnam from falling to the communist North Vietnam. But as military intervention sharply escalated in the 1960s under Presidents John F. Kennedy and Lyndon B. Johnson, peace demonstrations and public debate swept the United States, both over U.S. actions in Vietnam, and the Cold War assumptions behind them.*

On November 30, 1967, political opposition to the Vietnam War took a new turn when Eugene McCarthy, a Democratic senator from Minnesota, announced that he would challenge President Johnson for the Democratic Party's nomination for president in 1968. The following viewpoint is excerpted from a December 2, 1967, address by McCarthy to a gathering of Democratic antiwar activists in Chicago, Illinois. McCarthy argues that the war has become indefensible on both military and moral grounds. McCarthy ultimately did not get the presidential nomination he sought, but his early success in the Democratic primaries—attributable at least in part to the antiwar stance expressed here—is credited by many historians for influencing Johnson's decision to not seek reelection in 1968.

What contrast does McCarthy make between America in 1963 and 1967? To what does he attribute the changes? How does he define what would be an acceptable and peaceful outcome in Vietnam?

In 1952, in this city of Chicago, the Democratic party nominated as its candidate for the presidency Adlai Stevenson.

His promise to his party and to the people of the country then was that he would talk sense to them. And he did in the clearest tones. He did not speak above the people, as his enemies charged, but he raised the hard and difficult questions and proposed the difficult answers. His voice became the voice of America. He lifted the spirit of this land. The country in his language, was purified and given direction.

Before most other men, he recognized the problem of our cities and called for action.

Before other men, he measured the threat of nuclear war and called for a test-ban treaty.

Before other men, he anticipated the problem of conscience which he saw must come with maintaining a peacetime army and a limited draft and urged the political leaders of this country to put their wisdom to the task.

In all of these things he was heard by many but not followed, until under the presidency of John F. Kennedy his ideas were revived in new language and in a new spirit. To the clear sound of the horn was added the beat of a steady and certain drum.

John Kennedy set free the spirit of America. The honest optimism was released. Quiet courage and civility became the mark of American government, and new programs of promise and of dedication were presented: the Peace Corps, the Alliance for Progress, the promise of equal rights for all Americans—and not just the promise, but the beginning of the achievement of that promise.

All the world looked to the United States with new hope, for here was youth and confidence and an openness to the future. Here was a country not being held by the dead hand of the past, nor frightened by the violent hand of the future which was grasping at the world.

This was the spirit of 1963.

THE SPIRIT OF 1967

What is the spirit of 1967? What is the mood of America and of the world toward America today?

It is a joyless spirit—a mood of frustration, of anxiety, of uncertainty.

In place of the enthusiasm of the Peace Corps among the young people of America, we have protests and demonstrations.

In place of the enthusiasm of the Alliance for Progress, we have distrust and disappointment.

Instead of the language of promise and of hope, we have in politics today a new vocabulary in which the

Address by Eugene McCarthy at Conference of Concerned Deomcrats, Chicago, Illinois, December 2, 1967.

critical word is *war*: war on poverty, war on ignorance, war on crime, war on pollution. None of these problems can be solved by war but only by persistent, dedicated, and thoughtful attention.

But we do have one war which is properly called a war—the war in Vietnam, which is central to all of the problems of America.

AN INDEFENSIBLE WAR

A war of questionable legality and questionable constitutionality.

A war which is diplomatically indefensible; the first war in this century in which the United States, which at its founding made an appeal to the decent opinion of mankind in the Declaration of Independence, finds itself without the support of the decent opinion of mankind.

A war which cannot be defended in the context of the judgment of history. It is being presented in the context of an historical judgment of an era which is past. Munich appears to be the starting point of history for the secretary of state [Dean Rusk] and for those who attempt to support his policies. What is necessary is a realization that the United States is a part of the movement of history itself; that it cannot stand apart, attempting to control the world by imposing covenants and treaties and by violent military intervention; that our role is not to police the planet but to use military strength with restraint and within limits, while at the same time we make available to the world the great power of our economy, of our knowledge, and of our good will.

It is no longer possible to prove that the good that may come with what is called victory . . . is proportionate to the loss of life . . . and to other disorders that follow from this war.

A war which is not defensible even in military terms; which runs contrary to the advice of our greatest generals—Eisenhower, Ridgway, Bradley, and MacArthur—all of whom admonished us against becoming involved in a land war in Asia. Events have proved them right, as estimate after estimate as to the time of success and the military commitment necessary to success has had to be revised—always upward: more troops, more extensive bombing, a widening and intensification of the war. Extension and intensification have been the rule, and projection after projection of success have been proved wrong.

With the escalation of our military commitment has come a parallel of overleaping of objectives: from protecting South Vietnam, to nation building in South Vietnam, to protecting all of Southeast Asia, and ultimately to suggesting that the safety and security of the United States itself is at stake.

Finally, it is a war which is morally wrong. The most recent statement of objectives cannot be accepted as an honest judgment as to why we are in Vietnam. It has become increasingly difficult to justify the methods we are using and the instruments of war which we are using as we have moved from limited targets and somewhat restricted weapons to greater variety and more destructive instruments of war, and also have extended the area of operations almost to the heart of North Vietnam.

Even assuming that both objectives and methods can be defended, the war cannot stand the test of proportion and of prudent judgment. It is no longer possible to prove that the good that may come with what is called victory, or projected as victory, is proportionate to the loss of life and property and to other disorders that follow from this war. . . .

THE PRICE OF VICTORY

Those of us who are gathered here tonight are not advocating peace at any price. We are willing to pay a high price for peace—for an honorable, rational, and political solution to this war, a solution which will enhance our world position, which will permit us to give the necessary attention to our other commitments abroad, both military and nonmilitary, and leave us with both human and physical resources and with moral energy to deal effectively with the pressing domestic problems of the United States itself.

I see little evidence that the administration has set any limits on the price which it will pay for a military victory which becomes less and less sure and more hollow and empty in promise.

The scriptural promise of the good life is one in which the old men see visions and the young men dream dreams. In the context of this war and all of its implications, the young men of America do not dream dreams, but many live in the nightmare of moral anxiety, of concern and great apprehension; and the old men, instead of visions which they can offer to the young, are projecting, in the language of the secretary of state, a specter of one billion Chinese threatening the peace and safety of the world—a frightening and intimidating future.

The message from the administration today is a message of apprehension, a message of fear, yes—even a message of fear of fear.

RECLAIMING HOPE

This is not the real spirit of America. I do not believe that it is. This is a time to test the mood and spirit:

To offer in place of doubt—trust.

In place of expediency—right judgment.

In place of ghettos, let us have neighborhoods and communities.

In place of incredibility—integrity.

In place of murmuring, let us have clear speech; let us again hear America singing.

In place of disunity, let us have dedication of purpose.

In place of near despair, let us have hope.

This is the promise of greatness which was stated for us by Adlai Stevenson and which was brought to form and positive action in the words and actions of John Kennedy.

Let us pick up again these lost strands and weave them again into the fabric of America.

Let us sort out the music from the sounds and again respond to the trumpet and the steady drum.

FOR FURTHER READING

Lloyd C. Gardner, *Pay Any Price: Lyndon Johnson and the Wars for Vietnam.* Chicago: Ivan R. Dee, 1997.

George C. Herring, *America's Longest War: The United States and Vietnam, 1950–1975.* New York: McGraw Hill, 1996.

Stanley Karnow, *Vietnam: A History.* New York: Viking, 1991.

David Levy, *The Debate Over Vietnam.* Baltimore: Johns Hopkins University Press, 1991.

Dominic Sandbrook, *Eugene McCarthy: The Rise and Fall of Postwar American Liberalism.* New York: Knopf, 2004.

Herbert Schandler, *The Unmaking of a President: Lyndon Johnson and Vietnam.* Princeton, NJ: Princeton University Press, 1977.

Viewpoint 32A
Riots Are Mob Criminal Acts (1966)
Richard M. Nixon (1913–1994)

INTRODUCTION *Martin Luther King Jr.'s dream of a nonviolent revolution in American race relations (see viewpoint 29A) was shattered by a series of urban riots in the mid-1960s. In Harlem, New York, in 1964; Watts, Los Angeles, in 1965; Chicago and Cleveland in 1966; Detroit and Newark in 1967, and numerous other places, local residents clashed with police, looted stores and businesses, and burned buildings; they in turn were fired upon by police and National Guard troops who were sent to restore order. From 1964 to 1968, riots resulted in almost $200 million in destroyed property, forty thousand arrests, seven thousand injured, and around two hundred deaths.*

Americans differed on the causes of the riots. The National Advisory Commission on Civil Disorders, appointed by President Lyndon B. Johnson, implicated "white racism"

for creating an "explosive mixture" of poverty, police bru-
tality, and poor schools in the nation's cities, and called for
government programs to help the urban poor. But in the
following viewpoint, Richard Nixon provides a different
explanation. In a 1966 article, excerpted here, he argues
that riots are caused by a general societal breakdown in
respect for law, which he attributes in part to the civil
disobedience ideas of the civil rights movement. Nixon,
who lost the 1960 presidential race to John F. Kennedy,
was able to successfully utilize the theme of "law and order"
to make a political comeback and win the presidency
in 1968.

What two "extremist" positions about riots does Nixon
reject? What examples of lawlessness does he describe?
How does he respond to the argument that a person's
conscience should determine whether a law is unjust
and should be disobeyed?

The polls still place the war in Vietnam and the rising cost of living as the major political issues of 1966.
But, from my own trips across the nation, I can affirm
that private conversations and public concern are increasingly focusing upon the issues of disrespect for law and
race turmoil.

The recent riots in Chicago, Cleveland, New York
and Omaha have produced in the public dialogue too
much heat and very little light. The extremists have
held the floor for too long.

---■---

It would be a grave mistake to charge off the
recent riots to unredressed Negro grievances
alone. To do so is to Ignore . . . a major
national problem: the deterioration
of respect for the rule of law.

---■---

One extreme sees a simple remedy for rioting in a
ruthless application of the truncheons and an earlier call
to the National Guard.

The other extremists are more articulate, but their
position is equally simplistic. To them, riots are to be
excused upon the grounds that the participants have legitimate social grievances or seek justifiable social goals.

DECLINING RESPECT FOR LAW

I believe it would be a grave mistake to charge off the recent riots to unredressed Negro grievances alone.

To do so is to ignore a prime reason and a major national problem: the deterioration of respect for the rule of
law all across America.

Richard M. Nixon, "If Mob Rule Takes Hold in the U.S.—A Warning from
Richard Nixon," *U.S. News & World Report*, August 15, 1966.

That deterioration can be traced directly to the
spread of the corrosive doctrine that every citizen possesses an inherent right to decide for himself which laws
to disobey and when to disobey them.

The doctrine has become a contagious national disease, and its symptoms are manifest in more than just racial violence. We see them in the contempt among many
of the young for the agents of the law—the police. We see
them in the public burning of draft cards and the block-
ing of troop trains.

We saw those symptoms when citizens in Chicago
took to the streets to block public commerce to force
the firing of a city official. We saw them on a campus
of the University of California, where students brought
a great university to its knees in protest of the policies
of its administration.

Who is responsible for the breakdown of law and
order in this country? I think it both an injustice and
oversimplification to lay blame at the feet of the sidewalk
demagogues alone. For such a deterioration of respect for
law to occur in so brief a time in so great a nation, we must
look to more important collaborators and auxiliaries.

It is my belief that the seeds of civil anarchy would
never have taken root in this nation had they not been
nurtured by scores of respected Americans: public officials, educators, clergymen and civil rights leaders as well.

When the junior Senator from New York [Robert
Kennedy] publicly declares that "there is no point in telling Negroes to obey the law," because to the Negro "the
law is the enemy," then he has provided a rationale and
justification for every Negro intent upon taking the law
into his own hands. . . .

The agonies and indignities of urban slums are hard
facts of life. Their elimination is properly among our
highest national priorities, but within those slums, political phrases which are inflammatory are as wrong and
dangerous as political promises which are irredeemable.

In this contest, men of intellectual and moral eminence who encourage public disobedience of the law are responsible for the acts of those who inevitably follow their
counsel: the poor, the ignorant and the impressionable.

A CLIMATE OF LAWLESSNESS

Such leaders are most often men of good will who do not
condone violence and, perhaps even now, see no relation
between the civil disobedience which they counsel and the
riots and violence which have erupted. Yet, once the decision is made that laws need not be obeyed—whatever
the rationale—a contribution is made to a climate of
lawlessness.

To the professor objecting to de facto segregation, it
may be crystal clear where civil disobedience may begin
and where it must end. But the boundaries have become

fluid to his students. And today they are all but invisible in the urban slums.

In this nation we raise our young to respect the law and public authority. What becomes of those lessons when teachers and leaders of the young themselves deliberately and publicly violate the laws?

There is a crucial difference between lawful demonstration and protests on the one hand—and illegal demonstrations and "civil disobedience" on the other.

I think it is time the doctrine of civil disobedience was analyzed and rejected as not only wrong but potentially disastrous.

If all have a right to engage in public disobedience to protest real or imagined wrongs, then the example set by the minority today will be followed by the majority tomorrow.

Issues then will no longer be decided upon merit by an impartial judge. Victory will go to the side which can muster the greater number of demonstrations in the streets. The rule of law will be replaced by the rule of the mob. And one may be sure that the majority's mob will prevail.

From mob rule it is but a single step to lynch law and the termination of the rights of the minority. This is why it is so paradoxical today to see minority groups engaging in civil disobedience; their greatest defense is the rule of law. . . .

Civil disobedience creates a climate of disrespect for law. In such a climate the first laws to be ignored will be social legislation that lacks universal public support. In short, if the rule of law goes, the civil-rights laws of recent vintage will be the first casualties.

Historic advances in civil rights have come through court decisions and federal laws in the last dozen years.

Only the acceptances of those laws and the voluntary compliance of the people can transfer those advances from the statute books into the fabric of community life.

If indifference to the rule of law permeates the community, there will be no voluntary acceptance. A law is only as good as the will of the people to obey it. . . .

Continued racial violence and disorders in the cities of the nation will produce growing disenchantment with the cause of civil rights—even among its staunchest supporters.

It will encourage a disregard for civil rights laws and resistance to the legitimate demands of the Negro people.

Does anyone think that progress will be made in the hearts of men by riots and disobedience which trample upon the rights of those same men? But then is it not enough to simply demand that all laws be obeyed?

Edmund Burke once wrote concerning loyalty to a nation that "to make us love our country, our country

ought to be lovely." There is an analogy in a commitment to the rule of law. For a law to be respected, it ought to be worthy of respect. It must be fair and it must be fairly enforced.

It certainly did nothing to prevent a riot when Negroes in Chicago learned that while water hydrants in their own area were being shut down, they were running free in white neighborhoods just blocks away.

BASIC DIGNITY

Respect for the dignity of every individual is absolutely essential if there is to be respect for law.

The most common and justifiable complaint of Negroes and members of other minority groups is not that their constitutional rights have been denied, but that their personal dignity is repeatedly insulted.

As an American citizen, the American Negro is entitled to equality of rights, under the Constitution and the law, with every other citizen in the land. But, as important as this, the Negro has the right to be treated with the basic dignity and respect that belong to him as a human being.

Advocates of civil disobedience contend that a man's conscience should determine which law is to be obeyed and when a law can be ignored. But, to many men, conscience is no more than the enshrinement of their own prejudices. . . . But if every man is to decide for himself which to obey and which to ignore, the end result is anarchy.

The way to make good laws is not to break bad laws, but to change bad laws through legitimate means of protest within the constitutional process.

In the last analysis, the nation simply can no longer tolerate men who are above the law. For, as Lincoln said, "There is no grievance that is a fit object of redress by mob law."

Viewpoint 32B
Riots Are Social Revolutions (1967)
Tom Hayden (b. 1939)

INTRODUCTION *The arrest of a black taxi driver in July 1967 in Newark, New Jersey, set off five days of arson and looting. The violence, in which twenty-five blacks were killed by police, was one of a series of riots that swept many American cities during that time, including Watts, Los Angeles, in 1965 and Detroit in 1967.*

Some people argued that the root cause of the Newark riots and similar incidents was the oppressive living conditions under which America's black urban poor were living. Among those who put forth such an interpretation was Tom Hayden, a political and antiwar activist and former president of Students for a

Democratic Society (SDS). Hayden, one of the principal authors of the 1962 "Port Huron Statement" of SDS (see viewpoint 33A), had been active in Newark since 1964 as part of SDS's Economic Research and Action Project (ERAP), an effort to promote community empowerment and organizing in urban ghettos. He argues in the following viewpoint, excerpted from his 1967 book Rebellion in Newark, *that because ordinary political and economic channels of change have been ineffective for blacks in Newark and similar impoverished areas, ghetto residents are forced to resort to an "American form of guerilla warfare" in order to force necessary social reforms.*

What objections does Hayden make to the idea that blacks need economic "self-help"? What role do the police play in creating urban riots, according to Hayden? What assumption do both liberals and conservatives make about riots, according to Hayden?

This country is experiencing its fourth year of urban revolt, yet the message from Newark is that America has learned almost nothing since Watts.

Of primary importance is the fact that no national program exists to deal with the social and economic questions black people are raising. Despite exhaustive hearings over the last five years on problems of manpower and unemployment, anti-poverty programs and the urban crisis, there is no apparent commitment from national power centers to do something constructive.

During the height of the rioting in Newark and Detroit, Congress discussed gun-control laws, voted down with chuckles a bill for rat extermination, and President [Lyndon] Johnson set up a commission to do more investigating of the crisis. The main emphasis of governmental remedial programs seems likely to be on ending the riots rather than dealing with the racial and economic problem. President Johnson made this clear in his televised July 28 [1967] address on the "deeper questions" about the riots:

> Explanations may be offered, but nothing can excuse what [the rioters] have done. There will be attempts to interpret the events of the past few days, but when violence strikes, then those in public responsibility have an immediate and a very different job: *not to analyze but to end disorder.*

When it moves past riot-control to discussion of social programs, Congress is likely to lament the failure of past civil rights, welfare, and anti-poverty programs, rather than focus on the need for new ones. As with foreign aid, white politicians (and their voters) tend to view aid to Negroes as a form of "charity" to be trimmed wherever possible, or as a means of eliminating surplus food, or a way to enlarge urban patronage roles. Negroes more than likely will be instructed to "help themselves."

From *Rebellion in Newark* by Tom Hayden. New York: Random House, 1967.

But unlike the Italians, Irish, and Jews, black Americans have always faced a shrinking structure of economic opportunity in which to "help themselves." If sheer effort were the answer, the black people who chopped cotton from dawn to sunset would today be millionaire suburban homeowners. Self-help does not build housing, hospitals, and schools. The cost of making cities livable and institutions responsive is greater than any sum this country has ever been willing to spend on domestic reform. In addition, the very act of spending such money would disrupt much of the status quo. Private interests, from the real estate lobby and the construction unions to the social work profession, would be threatened. Urban political machines would have to make space for black political power. Good intentions tend to collapse when faced with the necessity for massive spending and structural change.

This political bankruptcy leads directly to the use of military force. When citizens have no political way to deal with revolution, they become counter-revolutionary. The race issue becomes defined exclusively as one of maintaining white society. Holding this view forces the white community to adopt the "jungle attitudes" that they fear the Negroes hold. "Go kill them niggers," white crowds shouted to Guardsmen at 7 o'clock Friday morning as they rode into Newark. During the riot, a *New York Times* reporter was stopped at 2:30 A.M. in Mayor Addonizio's west side neighborhood by a pipe-smoking gentleman carrying (illegally) a shotgun. He explained that a protection society was formed in case "they" should come into the neighborhood. Rifle stores in white neighborhoods all over the east coast are selling out. In such way, the society becomes militarized.

DECLARING WAR ON NEGROES

A police "takeover" of local government is not necessary to declare war on Negroes. All that is necessary is to instill in the white citizens the idea that only military force stands between them and black savages. The civilians merely turn over the problem to the troops, who define the problem in terms of using arms to maintain the racial status quo. A typical military attitude in the wake of the riots was offered in the July 29th [1967] *[New York] Times* by the commander of the New York State National Guard, who said that a greater commitment of force might have prevented rioting around the country. He recommended the use of heavy weapons including hand grenades, recoilless rifles and bazookas. He blamed indecisive civilian authority for making National Guard units operate "with one hand behind their backs" in riot areas.

This military orientation means that outright killing of people is condoned where those people cannot accept law and order as defined by the majority. The country is not moved by the deaths of twenty-five Negro "rioters."

News of a Negro's death is received at most as a tragedy, the inevitable result of looting and lawlessness. When a picture appears of a policeman over a fallen victim, the typical reaction is framed in the terms set by the majority: the dead man is a sniper, a looter, a burner, a criminal. If history is any guide, it is a foregone conclusion that no white policeman will be punished for murder in Newark.

Even many white sympathizers with the Negro cause, and Negro leaders themselves, believe that disorder must be stopped so that, in [NAACP leader] Roy Wilkins' words, "society can proceed." The question they do not ask is: whose society? They say that Negro rioting will create a backlash suppressing the liberties needed to organize for change. But this accurate prediction overlooks the fact that those very civil liberties have meant little protection for civil rights workers and ordinary black people in the South, and nearly as little for people in the ghettoes of the North. The freedom that middle-class people correctly feel are real to themselves have very little day-to-day meaning in the ghetto, which is more like a concentration camp than an open society for a large number of its residents. But in order to protect these liberties, many civil rights leaders take part in condemning the ghetto to brutal occupation. Even where "excessive force" is deplored, as Roy Wilkins deplored it in Newark, the assumption still remains that there is a "proper" degree of force that should be used to maintain the status quo. Top officials welcome this liberal support, and agree that any "excessive" force is regrettable and will be investigated. Thus most of the society becomes involved in organizing and protecting murder.

However, the use of force can do nothing but create a demand for greater force. The Newark riot shows that troops cannot make a people surrender. The police had several advantages over the community, particularly in firepower and mechanical mobility. Their pent-up racism gave them a certain amount of energy and morale as well. But as events in the riot showed, the troops could not apply their methods to urban conditions. The problem of precision shooting—for example, at a sniper in a building with forty windows and escape routes through rooftop, alley, and doorway—is nearly as difficult in the urban jungle as precision bombing is in Vietnam. There is a lack of safe cover. There is no front line and no rear, no way to cordon an area completely. A block that is quiet when the troops are present can be the scene of an outbreak the moment the troops leave.

At the same time, the morale fueled by racism soon turns into anxiety. Because of racism, the troops are unfamiliar with both the people and structure of the ghetto. Patrol duty after dark becomes a frightening and exhausting experience, especially for men who want to return alive to their families and homes. A psychology of desperation leads to careless and indiscriminate violence toward

the community, including reprisal killing, which inflames the people whom the troops were sent to pacify.

The situation thus contains certain built-in advantages for black people. The community is theirs. They know faces, corners, rooms, alleys. They know whom to trust and whom not to trust. They can switch in seconds from a fighting to a passive posture. It is impressive that state and local officials could not get takers for their offer of money and clemency to anyone turning in a sniper.

This is not a time for radical illusions about "revolution." Stagnancy and conservatism are essential facts of ghetto life. It undoubtedly is true that most Negroes desire the comforts and security that white people possess. There is little revolutionary consciousness or commitment to violence *per se* in the ghetto. Most people in the Newark riot were afraid, unorganized, and helpless when directly facing the automatic weapons. But the actions of white America toward the ghetto are showing black people, especially the young, that they must prepare to fight back.

GUERRILLA WARFARE

The conditions slowly are being created for an American form of guerrilla warfare based in the slums. The riot represents a signal of this fundamental change.

Disobedience, disorder, and even violence must be risked as the only alternative to continuing slavery.

To the conservative mind the riot is essentially revolution against civilization. To the liberal mind it is an expression of helpless frustration. While the conservative is hostile and the liberal generous toward those who riot, both assume that the riot is a form of lawless, mob behavior. The liberal will turn conservative if polite methods fail to stem disorder. Against these two fundamentally similar concepts, a third one must be asserted, the concept that a riot represents people making history.

The riot is certainly an awkward, even primitive, form of history-making. But if people are barred from using the sophisticated instruments of the established order for their ends, they will find another way. Rocks and bottles are only a beginning, but they cause more attention than all the reports in Washington. To the people involved, the riot is far less lawless and far more representative than the system of arbitrary rules and prescribed channels which they confront every day. The riot is not a beautiful and romantic experience, but neither is the day-to-day slum life from which the riot springs. Riots will not go away if ignored, and will not be cordoned off. They will only disappear when their energy is absorbed into a more decisive and effective form of history-making.

Men are now appearing in the ghettoes who might turn the energy of the riot to a more organized and continuous revolutionary direction. Middle-class Negro intellectuals (especially students) and Negroes of the ghetto are joining forces. They have found channels closed, the rules of the game stacked, and American democracy a system that excludes them. They understand that the institutions of the white community are unreliable in the absence of black community power. They recognize that national civil-rights leaders will not secure the kind of change that is needed. They assume that disobedience, disorder, and even violence must be risked as the only alternative to continuing slavery.

The role of organized violence is now being carefully considered. During a riot, for instance, a conscious guerrilla can participate in pulling police away from the path of people engaged in attacking stores. He can create disorder in new areas the police think are secure. He can carry the torch, if not all the people, to white neighborhoods and downtown business districts. If necessary, he can successfully shoot to kill.

The guerrilla can employ violence effectively during times of apparent "peace," too. He can attack, in the suburbs or slums, with paint or bullets, symbols of racial oppression. He can get away with it. If he can force the oppressive power to be passive and defensive at the point where it is administered—by the caseworker, landlord, storeowner, or policeman—he can build people's confidence in their ability to demand change. Persistent, accurately-aimed attacks, which need not be on human life to be effective, might disrupt the administration of the ghetto to a crisis point where a new system would have to be considered.

DEMOCRACY: A REVOLUTIONARY ISSUE

These tactics of disorder will be defined by the authorities as criminal anarchy. But it may be that disruption will create possibilities of meaningful change. This depends on whether the leaders of ghetto struggles can be more successful in building strong organization than they have been so far. Violence can contribute to shattering the status quo, but only politics and organization can transform it. The ghetto still needs the power to decide its destiny on such matters as urban renewal and housing, social services, policing, and taxation. Tenants still need concrete rights against landlords in public and private housing, or a new system of tenant-controlled living conditions. Welfare clients still need a livable income. Consumers still need to control the quality of merchandise

and service in the stores where they shop. Citizens still need effective control over those who police their community. Political structures belonging to the community are needed to bargain for, and maintain control over, funds from government or private sources. In order to build a more decent community while resisting racist power, more than violence is required. People need to create self-government. We are at a point where democracy—the idea and practice of people controlling their lives—is a revolutionary issue in the United States.

FOR FURTHER READING

Michael W. Flamm, *Law and Order: Street Crime, Civil Unrest, and the Crisis of Liberalism in the 1960s.* New York: Columbia University Press, 2005.

Tom Hayden, *Reunion: A Memoir.* New York: Random House, 1988.

National Advisory Commission on Civil Disorders. *The Kerner Report: The 1968 Report of the National Advisory Commission on Civil Disorders.* New York: Pantheon, 1988.

Nathan Wright Jr., *Ready to Riot.* New York: Holt, Rinehart and Winston, 1968.

Viewpoint 33A

America's Youth Must Lead a New Revolution (1962, 1968)

Students for a Democratic Society (SDS)

INTRODUCTION *For much of the 1960s a vocal segment of college students was at the forefront of both political and cultural radicalism among America's youth. One leading radical organization of the era was Students for a Democratic Society (SDS). The following viewpoint consists of two SDS documents from different points in the organization's history. Part I is taken from a political platform created at a 1962 meeting in Port Huron, Michigan. The "Port Huron Statement" called on college students to organize against racism, the nuclear arms race, and other perceived injustices of American society. It was widely distributed on college campuses. Due in part to the Vietnam War and the end of automatic student deferments from the military draft, by the end of 1967 SDS claimed about three hundred campus chapters.*

Part II consists of a resolution passed by some members of SDS in its December 1968 National Council meeting. The document reflects the tumultuous events of that year, during which SDS members organized numerous antiwar demonstrations, including an uprising at Columbia University in New York City that shut down the school's operations. Members of SDS were also involved in a violent confrontation with Chicago riot police during the Democratic National Convention that August. The resolution argues for the need for a "revolutionary youth movement" that would transform society. Shortly after the December meeting, SDS split into various factions, some of which became involved in riots, bombings, and other violent activities. It never regained its former prominence.

What faults does SDS see in American society? What events during the generation's coming-of-age account for feelings of discontentment, according to SDS? What differences in tone and content do you see between the 1962 and 1968 statements?

I

We are people of this generation, bred in at least modest comfort, housed now in universities, looking uncomfortably to the world we inherit.

When we were kids the United States was the wealthiest and strongest country in the world; the only one with the atom bomb, the least scarred by modern war, an initiator of the United Nations that we thought would distribute Western influence throughout the world. Freedom and equality for each individual, government of, by, and for the people—these American values we found good, principles by which we could live as men. Many of us began maturing in complacency.

As we grew, however, our comfort was penetrated by events too troubling to dismiss. First, the permeating and victimizing fact of human degradation, symbolized by the Southern struggle against racial bigotry, compelled most of us from silence to activism. Second, the enclosing fact of the Cold War, symbolized by the presence of the Bomb, brought awareness that we ourselves, and our friends, and millions of abstract "others" we knew more directly because of our common peril, might die at any time. We might deliberately ignore, or avoid, or fail to feel all other human problems, but not these two, for these were too immediate and crushing in their impact, too challenging in the demand that we as individuals take the responsibility for encounter and resolution.

PARADOXES OF AMERICA

While these and other problems either directly oppressed us or rankled our consciences and became our own subjective concerns, we began to see complicated and disturbing paradoxes in our surrounding America. The declaration "all men are created equal . . ." rang hollow before the facts of Negro life in the South and the big cities of the North. The proclaimed peaceful intentions of the United States contradicted its economic and military investments in the Cold War status quo.

We witnessed, and continue to witness, other paradoxes. With nuclear energy whole cities can easily be powered, yet the dominant nation-states seem more likely to unleash destruction greater than that incurred in all wars of human history. Although our own technology is destroying old and creating new forms of social organization, men still tolerate meaningless work and idleness. While two-thirds of mankind suffers undernourishment, our own upper classes revel amidst superfluous abundance. Although world population is expected to double in forty years, the nations still tolerate anarchy as a major principle of international conduct and uncontrolled exploitation governs the sapping of the earth's physical resources. Although mankind desperately needs revolutionary leadership, America rests in national stalemate, its goals ambiguous and tradition-bound instead of informed and clear, its democratic system apathetic and manipulated rather than "of, by, and for the people."

Not only did tarnish appear on our image of American virtue, not only did disillusion occur when the hypocrisy of American ideals was discovered, but we began to sense that what we had originally seen as the American Golden Age was actually the decline of an era. The worldwide outbreak of revolution against colonialism and imperialism, the entrenchment of totalitarian states, the menace of war, overpopulation, international disorder, supertechnology—these trends were testing the tenacity of our own commitment to democracy and freedom and our abilities to visualize their application to a world in upheaval. . . .

Some would have us believe that Americans feel contentment amidst prosperity—but might it not better be called a glaze above deeply-felt anxieties about their role in the new world? And if these anxieties produce a developed indifference to human affairs, do they not as well produce a yearning to believe there *is* an alternative to the present, that something *can* be done to change circumstances in the schools, the workplaces, the bureaucracies, the government? It is to this latter yearning, at once the spark and engine of change, that we direct our present appeal. The search for truly democratic alternatives to the present, and a commitment to social experimentation with them, is a worthy and fulfilling human enterprise, one which moves us and, we hope, others today. On such a basis do we offer this document of our convictions and analysis: as an effort in understanding and changing the conditions of humanity in the late twentieth century, an effort rooted in the ancient, still unfulfilled conception of man attaining determining influence over his circumstances of life.

II

At this point in history, SDS is faced with its most crucial ideological decision, that of determining its direction with regards to the working class. At this time there

---

"Port Huron Statement of the Students for a Democratic Society," 1962. Reprinted in *Anatomy of a Student Movement* of the U.S. House of Representatives Committee on Internal Security, 91st Cong., 2nd sess., October 6, 1970. "Toward a Revolutionary Youth Movement," a 1968 resolution of the Students for a Democratic Society.

must be a realization on the part of many in our movement that students alone cannot and will not be able to bring about the downfall of capitalism, the system which is at the root of man's oppression. Many of us are going to have to go through important changes, personally. As students, we have been indoctrinated with many racist and anti-working-class notions that in turn have produced racism and class-chauvinism in SDS and were responsible largely for the student-power focus which our movement has had for many years. Student power at this stage of our movement has to be seen as economism: that is, organizing people around a narrow definition of self-interest as opposed to class-interest. We are moving beyond this now, but that movement must be planned carefully and understood by all.

The fact that we saw ourselves as students as well as radicals, and accepted that classification of ourselves and many of the false privileges that went along with it (2-S deferment [the draft deferment for students], promise of the "good life" upon graduation, etc.) was primarily responsible for the reactionary tendencies in SDS.

Youth around the world have the potential to become a critical force. A youth movement raises the issues about a society in which it will be forced to live.

The main task now is to begin moving beyond the limitations of struggle placed upon a student movement. We must realize our potential to reach out to new constituencies both on and off campus and build SDS into a youth movement that is revolutionary.

The notion that we must remain simply "an anti-imperialist student organization" is no longer viable. The nature of our struggle is such that it necessitates an organization that is made up of youth and not just students, and that these youth become class-conscious. This means that our struggles must be integrated into the struggles of working people.

One thing should be clear. This perspective doesn't see youth as a class or say that youth will make the revolution by itself. Neither does it say that youth are necessarily more oppressed than older people, simply that they are oppressed in different ways. There are contradictions that touch youth specifically. To understand why there is a need for a youth movement, first we must come to see how youth are oppressed.

OPPRESSION OF YOUTH

Youth around the world have the potential to become a critical force. A youth movement raises the issues about

a society in which it will be forced to live. It takes issues to the working class. They do this because, in America, there exists an enormous contradiction around the integration of youth into the system. The period of pre-employment has been greatly extended due to the affluence of this highly industrialized society and the lack of jobs.

Institutions like the schools, the military, the courts and the police all act to oppress youth in specific ways, as does the work place. The propaganda and socialization processes focused at youth act to channel young people into desired areas of the labor market as well as to socialize them to accept without rebellion the miserable quality of life in America both on and off the job.

The ruling class recognizes the critical potential of young people. This is why they developed so many organizational forms to contain them. Many young people have rejected the integration process that the schools are supposed to serve and have broken with and begun to struggle against the "establishment." This phenomenon has taken many forms, ranging from youth dropping out as a response to a dying capitalist culture, to young workers being forced out by industry that no longer has any room for the untrained, unskilled, and unorganized. Both the dropout and the forced-out youth face the repressive nature of America's police, courts, and military, which act to physically and materially oppress them. The response from various strata of youth has been rebellion, from the buildings at Columbia to the movement in the streets of Chicago to Haight-Ashbury [a famous San Francisco "hippie" area] to the Watts uprising [a 1965 Los Angeles riot].

REVOLUTIONARY YOUTH

We must also understand what role a youth movement would have in the context of building a revolution. An organized class-conscious youth movement would serve basically four functions in building revolutionary struggle:

1. An organized revolutionary youth movement is itself a powerful force for revolutionary struggle. In other words, our struggle is the class struggle, as is the Vietnamese and the black liberation struggle. To call youth or even the student movement a section of the bourgeoisie which must simply support any struggle fought by working people is economism. The struggle of youth is as much a part of the class struggle as a union strike. We ally with workers by waging struggle against a common enemy, not by subjugating our movement patronizingly to every trade union battle. We also ally with the liberation struggle of those fighting against imperialism, recognizing that this is the true expression of the working class at its most conscious level.

2. Youth is a critical force which—through struggle—can expose war, racism, the exploitation of labor and the oppression of youth. We do this by putting forth our class analysis of capitalist institutions via propaganda and sharp actions. Exemplary actions of the youth movement lead to higher consciousness and struggle among other people.

3. Because we can organize—as a student movement—around those contradictions which affect youth specifically, we can organize young working people into our class-conscious anti-capitalist movement. These young workers will (a) strengthen the anti-capitalist movement among the work force, (b) provide an organic link between the student movement and the movement of working people, and (c) add to the effect that we will have as a critical force on older working people today.

4. The expansion of the base of the youth movement to include young working people changes the character of our movement importantly: because it fights the tendency of our student movement to define itself in terms of "student interest" rather than class interest.

Because we see a revolutionary youth movement as an important part of building a full revolutionary working-class movement we must shape our own strategy self-consciously now with a view to that youth movement. This means that, in addition to expanding our base to include more young working people, we must insure the class-consciousness of our movement now, and we must attack the class nature of the schools we are organizing against.

Viewpoint 33B

Student Rebellion Leaders Are a Disgrace (1969)

K. Ross Toole (1920–1981)

INTRODUCTION *During the 1960s the activities of America's youth attracted much media and public attention. This was in part due to baby-boom demographics; by 1970 people under the age of thirty constituted more than half of America's population. But in addition to sheer numbers, many (not all) young Americans gained notoriety by rebelling against the values and institutions of mainstream American society. They experimented with drugs, participated in civil rights demonstrations and antiwar marches, and reexamined traditional American beliefs on sex, work, and family.*

Social unrest sparked by youth protests peaked in the late 1960s. In the spring of 1968 at least forty thousand students on one hundred campuses took part in demonstrations against war and racism—protests that sometimes turned violent. University buildings were seized, American flags and draft cards were burned, and universities were closed. Similar demonstrations continued in 1969, when the article reprinted here was

first published. The writer was K. Ross Toole, a history professor at the University of Montana. The essay, critical of the direction student movements were taking, was widely reprinted in newspapers and magazines across the country.

How does Toole defend his own generation? How do his views on American society differ from those expressed in the opposing viewpoint? How should police and college authorities respond to radicals, according to Toole?

I am forty-nine years old. It took me years of considerable anguish to get where I am, which isn't much of any place except exurbia. I was nurtured in the Depression; I lost four years to war; I have had one coronary; I am a "liberal," a square and a professor of history.

As such, I am supposed to have "liaison" with the young. But the fact is that I am fed up with hippies, Yippies, militants and nonsense.

I am also the father of seven children, ranging in age from seven to twenty-three. And I am beginning to wonder what the hell I am incubating as a "permissive" parent. Maybe, indeed, *I* am the fellow who is producing the "campus rebel," whose bearded visage, dirty hair, body odor and "tactics" are childish but brutal, naive but dangerous, and the essence of arrogant tyranny—the tyranny of spoiled brats. Maybe all of this begins with me and my kind.

Wherever and however it begins, it is time to call a halt, time to live in an adult world where we belong and time to put these "children" in their places. We have come by what we have and become what we are through work, sweat, anguish and time. We owe the "younger generation" what all "older generations" have owed younger generations—love, protection to a point and respect when they deserve it. We do not owe them our souls, our privacy, our whole lives; and, above all, we do not owe them immunity from our mistakes or their own.

MY GENERATION

Every generation makes mistakes, always has and always will. We have made our share. But my generation has made America the most affluent country on earth; it has tackled, head-on, a racial problem which no nation on earth in the history of mankind had dared to do. It has publicly declared war on poverty and it has gone to the moon; it has desegregated schools and abolished polio; it has presided over the beginning of what is probably the greatest social and economic revolution in man's history. It has *begun* these things, not finished them. It has declared itself and committed itself and taxed itself and damn near run itself into the ground in the cause of social justice and reform.

From K. Ross Toole, *An Angry Man Talks Up to Youth.* (New York: Award Books, 1970).

Its mistakes are fewer than my father's generation, or his father's, or his father's. Its greatest mistake is *not* Viet Nam; it is the abdication of its first responsibility, its pusillanimous capitulation to its youth and its sick preoccupation with the problems, the minds, and the psyches, the *raison d'être* of the young.

Since when have children ruled this country? By virtue of what right or what accomplishment should thousands of teenagers, wet behind the ears and utterly without the benefit of having lived long enough to have either judgment or wisdom, become the sages of our time?

Well, say the psychologists, the educators and preachers, the young are rebelling against our archaic mores and morals, our materialistic approach to life, our failures in diplomacy, our terrible ineptitude in racial matters, our narrowness as parents, our blindness to the root ills of society. Balderdash!

Too many 'youngsters' are egocentric boors.

Society hangs together by the stitching of many threads. No eighteen-year-old is simply the product of his eighteen years; he is the product of three thousand years of the development of mankind. And throughout those years, injustice has existed and has been fought; rules have grown outmoded and been changed; doom has hung over the heads of men and been avoided; unjust wars have occurred; pain has been the cost of progress. But man has persevered. Society is obviously an imperfect production, but each generation changes its direction just a little, and most of the time it works.

As a professor and father of seven, I have watched this new generation and concluded that *most* of them are fine. A minority are not. The trouble is that that minority genuinely threatens to tyrannize the majority and take over. I dislike that minority; I am aghast that the majority "takes" it and allows itself to be used; I am appalled that I have participated thus far in condoning it. I speak partly as a historian, partly as a father and partly as one fed up, middle-aged and angry member of the so-called "Establishment"—which, by the way, is nothing but a euphemism for "society."

EGOCENTRIC BOORS

Common courtesy and a regard for the opinions of others is not merely a decoration on the pie crust of society, it is the heart of the pie. Too many "youngsters" are egocentric boors. They will not listen, they will only shout down. They will not discuss but, like four-year-olds, they throw rocks and shout.

Wisdom is not precocity; it is an amalgam of experience, reading, thought and the slow development of perception. While age is no guarantor of wisdom, whatever else the young are, they are not wise, precisely because they are young. Too many of them mistake glibness for wisdom and emotion for thought.

Arrogance is obnoxious; it is also destructive. Society has classically ostracized arrogance when it is without the backing of demonstrable accomplishment. Why, then, do we tolerate arrogant slobs who occupy our homes, our administration buildings, our streets and parks, urinating on our beliefs and defiling our premises? It is not the police we need, it is an expression of our disgust and disdain. Yet we do more than permit it, we dignify it with introspective flagellation. Somehow it is *our* fault. Balderdash again!

Sensitivity is not the property of the young, nor was it invented in 1960. The young of any generation have felt the same impulse to grow, to reach out, to touch stars, to live freely and to let the mind loose along unexplored corridors. Young men and young women have always stood on the same hill and felt the same vague sense of restraint that separated them from the ultimate experience, the sudden and complete expansion of the mind and the final fulfillment. It is one of the oldest, sweetest and most bitter experiences of mankind.

Today's young people did not invent it; they do not own it. And what they seek to attain all mankind has sought to attain throughout the ages. Shall we, therefore, approve the presumed attainment of it through violence, heroin, speed, LSD and other drugs? And shall we, permissively, let them poison themselves simply because we brought them into this world? Again, it is not police raids and tougher laws that we need; it is merely strength. The strength to explain, in our potty, middle-aged way, that what they seek, we sought; that it is somewhere but sure as hell not in drugs; that, in the meanwhile, they will goddam well cease and desist. And this we must explain early and hard—and then police it ourselves.

Society, "the Establishment," is not a foreign thing we seek to impose on the young. *We* know it is far from perfect. We did not make it; we have only sought to change it. The fact that we have been only minimally successful is the story of *all* generations, as it will be the story of the generation coming up. Yet we *have* worked a number of wonders with it. We *have* changed it. We are deeply concerned about our failures. We have not solved the racial problem, but we have at least faced it; we are terribly worried about the degradation of our environment, about injustices, inequities, the military-industrial complex and bureaucracy. But we *have* attacked these things. All our lives we have taken arms against our sea of troubles—and fought effectively. But we also have fought with a *rational* knowledge of the strength of our adversary; and, above all, we have known that the war is one of attrition in which the "unconditional surrender" of the forces of evil is not about to occur tomorrow. We win, if we win at all, slowly and painfully. That is the kind of war society has always fought because man and society are what they are.

Knowing this, why do we listen subserviently to the violent tacticians of the new generation? Either they have total victory by Wednesday next or burn down our carefully built barricades in adolescent pique; either they win now or flee off to a commune and quit; either they solve all problems this week or join a wrecking crew of paranoids.

Youth has always been characterized by impatient idealism. If it were not, there would be *no* change. But impatient idealism does not extend to guns, fire bombs, riots, vicious arrogance and instant gratification. That is not idealism; it is childish tyranny. And the worst of it is that we (professors and faculties in particular), go along in a paroxysm of self-abnegation and apology, abdicate, apologize as if we had personally created the ills of the world and thus lend ourselves to chaos. We are the led, not the leaders. And we are fools. . . .

I assert that we are trouble with this younger generation not because we have failed our country, not because of affluence or stupidity, not because we are antediluvian, not because we are middle-class materialists, but simply because we have failed to keep that generation in its place and have failed to put them back there when they got out of it. We have the power, we do not have the will; we have the right, we have not exercised it.

To the extent that we now rely on the police, mace, the National Guard, tear gas, steel fences and a wringing of hands, we will fail. What we need is a reappraisal of our own middle-class selves, our worth and our hard-won progress. We need to use disdain, not mace; we need to reassess a weapon we came by the hard way—firm authority as parents, teachers, businessmen, workers and politicians.

The vast majority of our children from one to twenty are fine kids. We need to back up this majority with authority and with the firm conviction that we owe it to them and to ourselves. Enough of apology, enough of analysis, enough of our abdication of our responsibility, enough of the denial of our own maturity and good sense.

UNIVERSITY REFORMS

The best place to start is at home. But the most practical and effective place, right now, is our campuses. This does not mean a flood of angry edicts, a sudden clampdown, a "new" policy. It simply means that faculties should stop playing chicken, that demonstrators should be met not with police but with expulsions. The power to expell (strangely unused) has been the legitimate recourse of universities since 1209.

More importantly, it means that at freshman orientation, whatever form it takes, the administration should set forth the ground rules—not belligerently but forthrightly.

A university is the microcosm of society itself. It cannot function without rules for conduct. It cannot, as society cannot, legislate morals. It is dealing with young men and women of eighteen to twenty-two. But it can and *must* promulgate rules. It cannot function without order; therefore, those who disrupt order must leave. It cannot permit the students to determine when, what and where they shall be taught; it cannot permit the occupation of its premises, in violation both of the law and its regulations, by "militants."

There is room within the university complex for basic student participation, but there is *no* room for slobs, disruption and violence. Therefore, the first obligation of the administration is to lay down the rules, early in the game, clearly and positively, and to attach to this statement the penalty for violation. It is profoundly simple, and the failure to state it in advance is the salient failure of university administrators in this age. . . .

This is a country full of decent, worried people like myself. It is also a country full of people fed up with nonsense. Those of us over thirty, tax-ridden, harried, confused, weary, need to reassert our hard-won prerogatives. It is our country too. We have fought for it, bled for it, dreamed for it, and we love it. It is time to reclaim it.

FOR FURTHER READING

John A. Andrew, *The Other Side of the Sixties: Young Americans for Freedom and the Rise of Conservative Politics.* New Brunswick, NJ: Rutgers University Press, 1997.

Peter Collier and David Horowitz, *Destructive Generation: Second Thoughts About the Sixties.* New York: Summit Books, 1989.

Todd Gitlin, *The Sixties: Years of Hope, Days of Rage.* New York: Bantam Books, 1987.

James Kunen, *The Strawberry Statement: Notes of a College Revolutionary.* New York: Random House, 1969.

Irwin Unger, *The Movement: History of America's New Left, 1959–1972.* New York: Dodd, Mead, 1974.

FROM NIXON TO REAGAN
Viewpoint 34A

Executive Privilege Protects a President's Private Communications (1973)

Richard M. Nixon (1913–1994)

INTRODUCTION *In the 1970s a series of political scandals involving President Richard M. Nixon caused a national crisis. The focal point of the scandals was a burglary at the Democratic Party National Headquarters at the Watergate building complex in Washington, D.C., on June 17, 1972. Although the seven burglars captured included two former White House aides and a member of Nixon's reelection committee, the president denied any administration involvement, and coasted to reelection victory in November 1972. But questions persisted, and in May 1973 a special Senate committee began televised hearings over what became known as the Watergate scandal. Over the next several months the American public heard numerous disclosures by presidential aides about Nixon's use of government agencies to harass political opponents—and evidence of White House involvement in covering up the Watergate burglary and hindering investigations. One of the key revelations of the hearings was the existence of a White House taping system that had secretly recorded conversations made in the president's Oval Office. Nixon, citing "executive privilege," refused to turn over the tapes to the committee or to the special federal prosecutor he had appointed to investigate Watergate.*

The following viewpoint is excerpted from a speech Nixon made on national television on August 15, 1973. In his speech Nixon reiterates his previous denials of personal involvement in a Watergate cover-up. He also explains why he is resisting turning over the White House tapes, arguing that releasing them would hamper the presidency and prevent him and future presidents from receiving honest and frank advice.

What comments does Nixon make about the Senate Watergate committee? What important principle does he say he is defending with regard to the tapes?

Now that most of the major witnesses in the Watergate phase of the Senate committee hearings on campaign practices have been heard, the time has come for me to speak out about the charges made and to provide a perspective on the issue for the American people.

For over four months Watergate has dominated the news media. During the past three months the three major networks have devoted an average of over 22 hours of television time each week to this subject. The Senate committee has heard over two million words of testimony.

This investigation began as an effort to discover the facts about the break-in and bugging at the Democratic national headquarters and other campaign abuses.

But as the weeks have gone by, it has become clear that both the hearings themselves and some of the commentaries on them have become increasingly absorbed in an effort to implicate the President personally in the illegal activities that took place.

Because the abuses occurred during my Administration, and in the campaign for my re-election, I accept full responsibility for them. I regret that these events

Excerpted from Richard M. Nixon's speech to the American people on nationwide television, August 15, 1973.

took place. And I do not question the right of a Senate committee to investigate charges made against the President to the extent that this is relevant to legislative duties.

DEFENDING THE PRESIDENCY

However, it is my Constitutional responsibility to defend the integrity of this great office against false charges. . . .

From the time when the break-in occurred, I pressed repeatedly to know the facts, and particularly whether there was any involvement of anyone at the White House. I considered two things essential:

First, that the investigation should be thorough and above-board; and second, that if there were any higher involvement, we should get the facts out first. As I said at my August 29 press conference last year, "What really hurts in matters of this sort is not the fact that they occur, because overzealous people in campaigns do things that are wrong. What really hurts is if you try to cover it up." . . .

Far from trying to hide the facts, my effort throughout has been to discover the facts—and to lay those facts before the appropriate law-enforcement authorities so that justice could be done and the guilty dealt with.

I relied on the best law-enforcement agencies in the country to find and report the truth. I believed they had done so—just as they believed they had done so.

THE WHITE HOUSE TAPES

Many have urged that in order to help prove the truth of what I have said, I should turn over to the special prosecutor and the Senate committee recordings of conversations that I held in my office or my telephone.

However, a much more important principle is involved in this question than what the tapes might prove about Watergate.

Each day a President of the United States is required to make difficult decisions on grave issues. It is absolutely necessary, if the President is to be able to do his job as the country expects, that he be able to talk openly and candidly with his advisers about issues and individuals. This kind of frank discussion is only possible when those who take part in it know that what they say is in strictest confidence.

The Presidency is not the only office that requires confidentiality. A member of Congress must be able to talk in confidence with his assistants. Judges must be able to confer in confidence with their law clerks and with each other. For very good reasons, no branch of government has ever compelled disclosure of confidential conversations between officers of other branches of government and their advisers about government business.

This need for confidence is not confined to Government officials. The law has long recognized that there are kinds of conversations that are entitled to be kept confidential, even at the cost of doing without critical evidence in a legal proceeding. This rule applies, for example, to conversations between a lawyer and a client, between a priest and a penitent, and between a husband and a wife. In each case it is thought so important that the parties be able to talk freely to each other that for hundreds of years the law has said that these conversations are "privileged" and that their disclosure cannot be compelled in a court.

This principle of confidentiality of Presidential conversations is at stake in the question of these tapes.

THE NEED FOR CONFIDENTIALITY

It is even more important that the confidentiality of conversations between a President and his advisers be protected. This is no mere luxury, to be dispensed with whenever a particular issue raises sufficient uproar. It is absolutely essential to the conduct of the Presidency, in this and in all future Administrations.

If I were to make public these tapes, containing as they do blunt and candid remarks on many different subjects, the confidentiality of the Office of the President would always be suspect from now on. It would make no difference whether it was to serve the interests of a court, of a Senate committee or the President himself— the same damage would be done to the principle, and that damage would be irreparable. Persons talking with the President would never again be sure that recordings or notes of what they said would not suddenly be made public. No one would want to advance tentative ideas that might later seem unsound. No diplomat would want to speak candidly in those sensitive negotiations which could bring peace or avoid war. No Senator or Congressman would want to talk frankly about the Congressional horse-trading that might get a vital bill passed. No one would want to speak bluntly about public figures, here and abroad.

That is why I shall continue to oppose efforts which would set a precedent that would cripple all future Presidents by inhibiting conversations between them and those they look to for advice. This principle of confidentiality of Presidential conversations is at stake in the question of these tapes. I must and I shall oppose any efforts to destroy this principle, which is so vital to the conduct of this great office.

INTRODUCTION *Warren Burger was chief justice of the United States from 1969 to 1986. In 1974 he authored a key decision against the man who appointed him— President Richard M. Nixon. The case involved the fate of secretly recorded tapes the president made in the Oval Office. The Nixon administration was then being investigated by Congress and by a special prosecutor for scandalous activities related to a burglary episode in 1972 (see viewpoint 34A). In response to subpoenas and requests, Nixon released edited transcriptions of the tapes, but not the tapes themselves, citing executive privilege. However, in an 8–0 decision, excerpted here, Burger and his colleagues ruled that a president's executive privilege was not absolute and that the president must turn over the tapes themselves to Judge John J. Sirica, the presiding judge at the criminal trial of several of Nixon's aides. Nixon ultimately gave in; the public release of the tapes revealed that, contrary to past assertions, the president was directly involved in covering up the Watergate burglary. The House Judiciary Committee passed three articles of impeachment, but before Congress could complete the impeachment process, Nixon became in August 1974 the nation's first president to resign.*

What impediments would absolute executive privilege create for the workings of the federal government, according to Burger and the other Supreme Court Justices? What competing claims on justice are measured in this decision?

[W]e turn to the claim that the subpoena should be quashed because it demands "confidential conversations between a President and his close advisors that it would be inconsistent with the public interest to produce." The first contention is a broad claim that the separation of powers doctrine precludes judicial review of a President's claim of privilege. The second contention is that if he does not prevail on the claim of absolute privilege, the court should hold as a matter of constitutional law that privilege prevails over the subpoena *duces tecum*.

In the performance of assigned constitutional duties each branch of the Government must initially interpret the Constitution, and the interpretation of its powers by any branch is due great respect from the others. The President's counsel, as we have noted, reads the Constitution as providing the absolute privilege of confidentiality for all presidential communications. Many decisions of this court, however, have unequivocally reaffirmed the

United States v. Nixon, 418 U.S. 683 (1974).

holding of *Marbury v. Madison* (1803), that "it is emphatically the province and duty of the judicial department to say what the law is." . . .

In support of his claim of absolute privilege, the President's counsel urges two grounds, one of which is common to all governments and one of which is peculiar to our system of separation of powers. The first ground is the valid need for protection of communications between high government officials and those who advise and assist them in the performance of their manifold duties; the importance of this confidentiality is too plain to require further discussion. Human experience teaches that those who expect public dissemination of their remarks may well temper candor with a concern for appearances and for their own interests to the detriment of the decision-making process. Whatever the nature of the privilege of confidentiality of presidential communications in the exercise of Art. II powers the privilege can be said to derive from the supremacy of each branch within its own assigned area of constitutional duties. Certain powers and privileges flow from the nature of enumerated powers; the protection of the confidentiality of presidential communications has similar constitutional underpinnings.

The second ground asserted by the President's counsel in support of the claim of absolute privilege rests on the doctrine of separation of powers. Here it is argued that the independence of the Executive Branch within its own sphere, *Humphrey's Executor v. United States, Kilbourn v. Thompson* (1880), insulates a president from a judicial subpoena in an ongoing criminal prosecution, and thereby protects confidential presidential communications.

However, neither the doctrine of separation of powers, nor the need for confidentiality of high level communications, without more, can sustain an absolute, unqualified presidential privilege of immunity from judicial process under all circumstances. The President's need for complete candor and objectivity from advisers calls for great deference from the courts. However, when the privilege depends solely on the broad undifferentiated claim of public interest in the confidentiality of such conversations, a confrontation with other values arises. Absent a claim of need to protect military, diplomatic or sensitive national security secrets, we find it difficult to accept the argument that even the very important interest in confidentiality of presidential communications is significantly diminished by production of such material for *in camera* inspection with all the protection that a district court will be obliged to provide.

The impediment that an absolute, unqualified privilege would place in the way of the primary constitutional duty of the Judicial Branch to do justice in criminal prosecutions would plainly conflict with the function of the courts under Art. III. In designing the structure of our Government and dividing and allocating the sovereign power among three coequal branches, the Framers of the Constitution sought to provide a comprehensive system, but the separate powers were not intended to operate with absolute independence. . . .

To read Art. II powers of the President as providing an absolute privilege as against a subpoena essential to enforcement of criminal statutes on no more than a generalized claim of the public interest in confidentiality of nonmilitary and nondiplomatic discussions would upset the constitutional balance of "a workable government" and gravely impair the role of the courts under Art. III. . . .

The expectation of a President to the confidentiality of his conversations and correspondence, like the claim of confidentiality of judicial deliberations, for example, has all the values to which we accord deference for the privacy of all citizens and added to those values the necessity for protection of the public interest in candid, objective, and even blunt or harsh opinions in presidential decisionmaking. A President and those who assist him must be free to explore alternatives in the process of shaping policies and making decisions and to do so in a way many would be unwilling to express except privately. These are the considerations justifying a presumptive privilege for presidential communications. The privilege is fundamental to the operation of government and inextricably rooted in the separation of powers under the Constitution. In *Nixon v. Sirica* (1973), the Court of Appeals held that such presidential communications are "presumptively privileged," and this position is accepted by both parties in the present litigation. . . .

But this presumptive privilege must be considered in light of our historic commitment to the rule of law. This is nowhere more profoundly manifest than in our view that "the twofold aim [of criminal justice] is that guilt shall not escape or innocence suffer." *Berger v. United States* (1935). We have elected to employ an adversary system of criminal justice in which the parties contest all issues before a court of law. The need to develop all relevant facts in the adversary system is both fundamental and comprehensive. The ends of criminal justice would be defeated if judgments were to be founded on a partial or speculative presentation of the facts. The very integrity of the judicial system and public confidence in the system depend on full disclosure of all the facts, within the framework of the rules of evidence. To ensure that justice is done, it is imperative to the function of courts that compulsory process be available for the production of evidence needed either by the prosecution or by the defense. . . .

In this case the President challenges a subpoena served on him as a third party requiring the production of materials for use in a criminal prosecution on the claim that he has a privilege against disclosure of confidential communications. He does not place his claim of privilege on the ground they are military or diplomatic secrets. As to these areas of Art. II duties the courts have traditionally shown the utmost deference to presidential responsibilities. . . .

---■---

Asserting privilege . . . cannot prevail over the fundamental demands of due process of law in the fair administration of criminal justice.

---■---

In this case we must weigh the importance of the general privilege of confidentiality of presidential communications in performance of his responsibilities against the inroads of such a privilege on the fair administration of criminal justice. The interest in preserving confidentiality is weighty indeed and entitled to great respect. However we cannot conclude that advisers will be moved to temper the candor of their remarks by the infrequent occasions of disclosure because of the possibility that such conversations will be called for in the context of criminal prosecution.

On the other hand, the allowance of the privilege to withhold evidence that is demonstrably relevant in a criminal trial would cut deeply into the guarantee of due process of law and gravely impair the basic function of the courts. A President's acknowledged need for confidentiality in the communications of his office is general in nature, whereas the constitutional need for production of relevant evidence in a criminal proceeding is specific and central to the fair adjudication of a particular criminal case in the administration of justice. Without access to specific facts a criminal prosecution may be totally frustrated. The President's broad interest in confidentiality of communications will not be vitiated by disclosure of a limited number of conversations preliminarily shown to have some bearing on the pending criminal cases.

We conclude that when the ground for asserting privilege as to subpoenaed materials sought for use in a criminal trial is based only on the generalized interest in confidentiality, it cannot prevail over the fundamental demands of due process of law in the fair administration of criminal justice. The generalized assertion of privilege must yield to the demonstrated, specific need for evidence in a pending criminal trial.

FOR FURTHER READING

Howard Ball, *"We Have a Duty": The Supreme Court and the Watergate Tapes Litigation.* Westport, CT: Greenwood Press, 1990.

Fred Emery, *Watergate: The Corruption of American Politics and the Fall of Richard Nixon.* New York: Touchstone, 1995.

Michael A. Genovese, *The Watergate Crisis.* Westport, CT: Greenwood Press, 1999.

Stanley L. Kutler, *The Wars of Watergate: The Last Crisis of Richard Nixon.* New York: Knopf, 1990.

Keith W. Olson, *Watergate: The Presidential Scandal that Shook America.* Lawrence: University Press of Kansas, 2003.

America Is Facing a Crisis of Confidence (1979)
Jimmy Carter (b. 1924)

INTRODUCTION *Jimmy Carter, a former governor of Georgia, won election as U.S. president in 1976, following a post-Watergate campaign in which he pledged to restore trust and honesty in government. His popularity waned during his presidency, however, as America struggled with a variety of domestic and international problems. One major area of concern was energy. America in 1978 imported 40 percent of its oil, buying much of it from countries in the turbulent Middle East. In 1979 gasoline shortages developed after the American-supported government of Iran fell to Islamic revolutionaries, who then cut off oil exports to the United States.*

The following viewpoint is taken from a televised speech Carter delivered to the nation on July 15, 1979. Carter argues that the energy crisis is part of a deeper problem—a national "crisis of confidence" in a country struggling to regain trust in its institutions and to adapt to a new era of natural resource limits. He argues that the Vietnam War, Watergate, and other developments have disillusioned many people about the legitimacy and ability of the American government. Carter concludes by listing several recommendations for reducing the nation's dependence on foreign energy suppliers, which he argues will also help renew America's confidence and sense of purpose.

What does Carter mean by "crisis of confidence"? What in his view are the causes of the crisis? Between what two paths must America choose, according to Carter?

Good evening.

This is a special night for me. Exactly 3 years ago, on July 15, 1976, I accepted the nomination of my party to run for President of the United States. I promised you a President who is not isolated from the people, who feels your pain, and who shares your dreams and who draws his strength and his wisdom from you.

During the past 3 years I've spoken to you on many occasions about national concerns, the energy crisis, reorganizing the Government, our Nation's economy, and issues of war and especially peace. But over those years the subjects of the speeches, the talks, and the press conferences have become increasingly narrow, focused more and more on what the isolated world of Washington

From *Public Papers of the Presidents of the United States: Jimmy Carter, 1979,* vol. 2 (Washington DC: National Archives and Records Service, 1980).

thinks is important. Gradually, you've heard more and more about what the Government thinks or what the Government should be doing and less and less about our Nation's hopes, our dreams, and our vision of the future.

Ten days ago I had planned to speak to you again about a very important subject—energy. For the fifth time I would have described the urgency of the problem and laid out a series of legislative recommendations to the Congress. But as I was preparing to speak, I began to ask myself the same question that I now know has been troubling many of you. Why have we not been able to get together as a nation to resolve our serious energy problem? . . .

The erosion of our confidence in the future is threatening to destroy the social and the political fabric of America.

I know, of course, being President, that government actions and legislation can be very important. That's why I've worked hard to put my campaign promises into law—and I have to admit, with just mixed success. But after listening to the American people I have been reminded again that all the legislation in the world can't fix what's wrong with America. So, I want to speak to you first tonight about a subject even more serious than energy or inflation. I want to talk to you right now about a fundamental threat to American democracy.

I do not mean our political and civil liberties. They will endure. And I do not refer to the outward strength of America, a nation that is at peace tonight everywhere in the world, with unmatched economic power and military might.

A CRISIS OF CONFIDENCE

The threat is nearly invisible in ordinary ways. It is a crisis of confidence. It is a crisis that strikes at the very heart and soul and spirit of our national will. We can see this crisis in the growing doubt about the meaning of our own lives and in the loss of a unity of purpose for our Nation.

The erosion of our confidence in the future is threatening to destroy the social and the political fabric of America.

The confidence that we have always had as a people is not simply some romantic dream or a proverb in a dusty book that we read just on the Fourth of July. It is the idea which founded our Nation and has guided our development as a people. Confidence in the future has supported everything else—public institutions and private enterprise,

our own families, and the very Constitution of the United States. Confidence has defined our course and has served as a link between generations. We've always believed in something called progress. We've always had a faith that the days of our children would be better than our own.

Our people are losing that faith, not only in government itself but in the ability as citizens to serve as the ultimate rulers and shapers of our democracy. As a people we know our past and we are proud of it. Our progress has been part of the living history of America, even the world. We always believed that we were part of a great movement of humanity itself called democracy, involved in the search for freedom, and that belief has always strengthened us in our purpose. But just as we are losing our confidence in the future, we are also beginning to close the door on our past.

In a nation that was proud of hard work, strong families, close-knit communities, and our faith in God, too many of us now tend to worship self-indulgence and consumption. Human identity is no longer defined by what one does, but by what one owns. But we've discovered that owning things and consuming things does not satisfy our longing for meaning. We've learned that piling up material goods cannot fill the emptiness of lives which have no confidence or purpose.

The symptoms of this crisis of the American spirit are all around us. For the first time in the history of our country a majority of our people believe that the next 5 years will be worse than the past 5 years. Two-thirds of our people do not even vote. The productivity of American workers is actually dropping, and the willingness of Americans to save for the future has fallen below that of all other people in the Western world.

As you know, there is a growing disrespect for government and for churches and for schools, the news media, and other institutions. This is not a message of happiness or reassurance, but it is the truth and it is a warning.

AMERICA'S WOUNDS

These changes did not happen overnight. They've come upon us gradually over the last generation, years that were filled with shocks and tragedy.

We were sure that ours was a nation of the ballot, not the bullet, until the murders of John Kennedy and Robert Kennedy and Martin Luther King, Jr. We were taught that our armies were always invincible and our causes were always just, only to suffer the agony of Vietnam. We respected the Presidency as a place of honor until the shock of Watergate.

We remember when the phrase "sound as a dollar" was an expression of absolute dependability, until 10 years of inflation began to shrink our dollar and our savings. We believed that our Nation's resources were limitless until 1973, when we had to face a growing dependence on foreign oil.

These wounds are still very deep. They have never been healed.

Looking for a way out of this crisis, our people have turned to the Federal Government and found it isolated from the mainstream of our Nation's life. Washington, D.C., has become an island. The gap between our citizens and our Government has never been so wide. The people are looking for honest answers, not easy answers; clear leadership, not false claims and evasiveness and politics as usual.

What you see too often in Washington and elsewhere around the country is a system of government that seems incapable of action. You see a Congress twisted and pulled in every direction by hundreds of well-financed and powerful special interests. You see every extreme position defended to the last vote, almost to the last breath by one unyielding group or another. You often see a balanced and a fair approach that demands sacrifice, a little sacrifice from everyone, abandoned like an orphan without support and without friends.

Often you see paralysis and stagnation and drift. You don't like it, and neither do I. What can we do?

First of all, we must face the truth, and then we can change our course. We simply must have faith in each other, faith in our ability to govern ourselves, and faith in the future of this Nation. Restoring that faith and that confidence to America is now the most important task we face. It is a true challenge of this generation of Americans....

TWO PATHS

We are at a turning point in our history. There are two paths to choose. One is a path I've warned about tonight, the path that leads to fragmentation and self-interest. Down that road lies a mistaken idea of freedom, the right to grasp for ourselves some advantage over others. That path would be one of constant conflict between narrow interests ending in chaos and immobility. It is a certain route to failure.

All the traditions of our past, all the lessons of our heritage, all the promises of our future point to another path, the path of common purpose and the restoration of American values. That path leads to true freedom for our Nation and ourselves. We can take the first steps down that path as we begin to solve our energy problem. Energy will be the immediate test of our ability to unite this Nation and it can also be the standard around which we rally.

In little more than two decades we have gone from a position of energy independence to one in which almost half the oil we use comes from foreign countries, at prices that are going through the roof. Our excessive dependence on OPEC (Organization of the Petroleum Exporting Countries) has already taken a tremendous toll on our economy and our people.

This is the direct cause of the long lines which have made millions of you spend aggravating hours waiting for gasoline. It is a cause of the increased inflation and unemployment that we now face. This intolerable dependence on foreign oil threatens our economic independence and the very security of our Nation.

A NEW ENERGY POLICY

Point one: I am tonight setting a clear goal for the energy policy of the United States. Beginning this moment, this Nation will never use more foreign oil than we did in 1977—never. From now on, every new addition to our demand for energy will be met from our own production and our own conservation....

Point two: To ensure that we meet these targets, I will use my Presidential authority to set import quotas. I am announcing tonight that for 1979 and 1980, I will forbid the entry into this country of one drop of foreign oil more than these goals allow....

Point three: To give us energy security, I am asking for the most massive peacetime commitment of funds and resources in our nation's history to develop America's own alternative sources of fuel—from coal, from oil shale, from plant products for gasohol, from unconventional gas, from the sun....

Point four: I am asking Congress to mandate, to require as a matter of law, that our Nation's utility companies cut their massive use of oil by 50 percent within the next decade and switch to other fuels, especially coal, our most abundant energy source.

Point five: To make absolutely certain that nothing stands in the way of achieving these goals, I will urge Congress to create an Energy Mobilization Board which, like the War Production Board in World War II, will have the responsibility and authority to cut through the red tape, the delays, and the endless roadblocks to completing key energy projects.

We will protect our environment. But when this Nation critically needs a refinery or a pipeline, we will build it.

Point six: I am proposing a bold conservation program to involve every state, county and city and every average American in our energy battle. This effort will permit you to build conservation into your home and your lives at a cost you can afford.

I ask Congress to give me authority for mandatory conservation and for standby gasoline rationing. To further conserve energy, I am proposing tonight an extra

$10 billion over the next decade to strengthen our public transportation systems, and I am asking you for your good and for your Nation's security to take no unnecessary trips, to use car pools or public transportation whenever you can, to park your car one extra day per week, to obey the speed limit and to set your thermostats to save fuel....

Every gallon of oil each one of us saves is a new form of production. It gives us more freedom, more confidence, that much more control over our own lives.

So the solution of our energy crisis can also help us to conquer the crisis of the spirit in our country. It can rekindle our sense of unity, our confidence in the future, and give our nation and all of us individually a new sense of purpose.

Viewpoint 35B

The American Spirit Remains Strong (1980)
Ronald Reagan (1911–2004)

INTRODUCTION *The 1980 presidential election featured as its two major candidates Jimmy Carter, the incumbent, and Ronald Reagan, a former motion picture actor and governor of California. Reagan, who had sought the Republican nomination in 1968 and 1976 before succeeding on his third attempt, was a leading figure of the conservative wing of the Republican Party. In the following viewpoint, excerpted from his acceptance speech at the 1980 Republican National Convention, Reagan expounds on conservative themes that would help him win both the 1980 and 1984 presidential elections.*

Reagan argues in his 1980 speech that the source of many of America's problems is the federal government itself, which he claims has burdened the American people with high taxes and cumbersome regulations. He advocates cutting both taxes and government programs. The solution to the nation's chronic energy shortages, he asserts as one example, is to reduce government regulation and encourage the increased domestic production of oil, coal, and other energy sources. Reagan attacks his opponent, Carter, both directly, on his policies, and indirectly, on his failure to appreciate and inspire American confidence.

How do Reagan's views of the fundamental problems facing America differ from those of Jimmy Carter, author of the opposing viewpoint? Do you think Reagan and Carter have opposing views on whether the "American spirit" is strong? Why or why not? After reading both viewpoints, tell why you think Reagan won a decisive victory over Carter in 1980?

More than anything else, I want my candidacy to unify our country, to renew the American spirit and

From Ronald Reagan's acceptance speech at the Republican National Convention, Detroit, Michigan, July 17, 1980 (Reprinted in Vital Speeches of the Day, August 15, 1980).

sense of purpose. I want to carry our message to every American, regardless of party affiliation, who is a member of this community, of shared values.

Never before in our history have Americans been called upon to face three grave threats to our very existence, any one of which could destroy us. We face a disintegrating economy, a weakened defense, and an energy policy based on the sharing of scarcity.

A FAILURE OF LEADERSHIP

The major issue of this campaign is the direct political, personal, and moral responsibility of Democratic Party leadership—in the White House and in Congress—for this unprecedented calamity which has befallen us. They tell us they have done the most that could humanly be done. They say that the United States has had its days in the sun, that our nation has passed its zenith. They expect you to tell your children that the American people no longer have the will to cope with their problems, that the future will be one of sacrifice and few opportunities.

My fellow citizens, I utterly reject that view. The American people, the most generous on earth, who created the highest standard of living, are not going to accept the notion that we can only make a better world for others by moving backward ourselves. Those who believe we can have no business leading the nation.

I will not stand by and watch this great country destroy itself under mediocre leadership that drifts from one crisis to the next, eroding our national will and purpose. We have come together here because the American people deserve better from those to whom they entrust our nation's highest office, and we stand united in our resolve to do something about it....

[In 1863] Abraham Lincoln called upon the people of all America to renew their dedication and their commitment to a government of, for, and by the people.

Isn't it time once again to renew our compact of freedom, to pledge to each other all that is best in our lives, all that gives meaning to them—for the sake of this, our beloved and blessed land?

A NEW BEGINNING

Together, let us make this a new beginning. Let us make a commitment to care for the needy, to teach our children the values and the virtues handed down to us by our families, to have the courage to defend those values and the willingness to sacrifice for them.

Let us pledge to restore, in our time, the American spirit of voluntary service, of cooperation, of private and community initiative, a spirit that flows like a deep and mighty river through the history of our nation.

As your nominee, I pledge to restore to the federal government the capacity to do the people's work without dominating their lives. I pledge to you a government that will not only work well, but wisely, its ability to act tempered by prudence, and its willingness to do good balanced by the knowledge that government is never more dangerous than when our desire to have it help us blinds us to its great power to harm us....

THE ENERGY CRISIS

Those who preside over the worst energy shortage in our history tell us to use less, so that we will run out of oil, gasoline, and natural gas a little more slowly. Conservation is desirable, of course, for we must not waste energy. But conservation is not the sole answer to our energy needs.

America must get to work producing more energy. The Republican program for solving economic problems is based on growth and productivity.

Large amounts of oil and natural gas lie beneath our land and off our shores, untouched because the present Administration seems to believe the American people would rather see more regulation, taxes, and controls than more energy.

Coal offers great potential. So does nuclear energy produced under rigorous safety standards. It could supply electricity for thousands of industries and millions of jobs and homes. It must not be thwarted by a tiny minority opposed to economic growth, which often finds friendly ears in regulatory agencies for its obstructionist campaigns.

Make no mistake. We will not permit the safety of our people or our environmental heritage to be jeopardized. But we are going to reaffirm that the economic prosperity of our people is a fundamental part of our environment.

Our problems are both acute and chronic, yet all we hear from those in positions of leadership are the same tired proposals for more government tinkering, more meddling, and more control—all of which led us to this state in the first place....

REDUCING GOVERNMENT

We Republicans believe it is essential that we maintain both the forward momentum of economic growth and the strength of the safety net beneath those in society who need help. We also believe it is essential that the integrity of all aspects of Social Security be preserved.

Beyond these essentials, I believe it is clear our federal government is overgrown and overweight. Indeed, it is time for our government to go on a diet. Therefore, my first act as Chief Executive will be to impose an immediate and thorough freeze on federal hiring. Then, we are going to enlist the very best minds from business, labor, and whatever quarter we can to conduct a detailed review of every department, bureau, and agency that lives by

federal appropriation. We are also going to enlist the help and ideas of many dedicated and hard-working government employees at all levels who want a more efficient government as much as the rest of us do. I know that many are demoralized by the confusion and waste they confront in their work as a result of failed and failing policies.

Our instructions to the groups we enlist will be simple and direct. We will remind them that government programs exist at the sufferance of the American taxpayer and are paid for with money earned by working men and women. Any program that represents a waste of their money—a theft from their pocketbooks—must have that waste eliminated, or the program must go: by Executive Order where possible, by Congressional action where necessary. Everything that can be run more effectively by state and local government, we shall turn over to state and local government, along with the funding sources to pay for it. We are going to put an end to the money merry-go-round where our money becomes Washington's money, to be spent by the states and cities only if they spend it exactly the way the federal bureaucrats tell them to.

I will not accept the excuse that the federal government has grown so big and powerful that it is beyond the control of any President, any Administration or Congress. We are going to put an end to the notion that the American taxpayer exists to fund the federal government. The federal government exists to serve the American people and to be accountable to the American people. On January 20th [1981], we are going to reestablish that truth.

Also on that date we are going to initiate action to get substantial relief for our taxpaying citizens and action to put people back to work. None of this will be based on any new form of monetary tinkering or fiscal sleight of hand. We will simply apply to government the common sense we all use in our daily lives.

Work and family are at the center of our lives, the foundation of our dignity as a free people. When we deprive people of what they have earned, or take away their jobs, we destroy their dignity and undermine their families. We cannot support our families unless there are jobs, and we cannot have jobs unless people have both money to invest and the faith to invest it.

These are concepts that stem from the foundation of an economic system that for more than two hundred years has helped us master a continent, create a previously undreamed-of prosperity for our people, and feed millions of others around the globe. That system will continue to serve us in the future, if our government will stop ignoring the basic values on which it was built and stop betraying the trust and goodwill of the American workers who keep it going.

THE TAX BURDEN

The American people are carrying the heaviest peacetime tax burden in our nation's history—and it will grow even heavier, under present law, next January. This burden is crushing our ability and incentive to save, invest and produce. We are taxing ourselves into economic exhaustion and stagnation.

This must stop. We must halt this fiscal self-destruction and restore sanity to our economic system.

I have long advocated a 30 percent reduction in income tax rates over a period of three years. This phased tax reduction would begin with a 10 percent "down payment" tax cut in 1981, which the Republicans in Congress and I have already proposed.

A phased reduction of tax rates would go a long way toward easing the heavy burden on the American people....

Thanks to the economic policies of the Democratic Party, millions of Americans find themselves out of work. Millions more have never even had a fair chance to learn new skills, hold a decent job, seize the opportunity to climb the ladder and secure for themselves and their families a share in the prosperity of his nation.

---

*The American spirit is still there,
ready to blaze into life.*

It is time to put America back to work, to make our cities and towns resound with the confident voices of men and women of all races, nationalities, and faiths bringing home to their families a decent paycheck they can cash for honest money.

For those who have abandoned hope, we'll restore hope, and we'll welcome them into a great national crusade to make America great again!...

THE AMERICAN SPIRIT

Tonight, let us dedicate ourselves to renewing the American Compact. I ask you not simply to "Trust me," but to trust your values—our values—and to hold me responsible for living up to them. I ask you to trust the American spirit which knows no ethnic, religious, social, political, regional, or economic boundaries, the spirit that burned with zeal in the hearts of millions of immigrants from every corner of the earth who came here in search of freedom.

Some say that spirit no longer exists. But I have seen it—I have felt it—all across the land, in the big cities, in the small towns, in rural America. The American spirit is still there, ready to blaze into life if you and I are willing to do what has to be done, the practical, down-to-earth

things that will stimulate our economy; increase productivity, and put America back to work.

The time is now to limit federal spending, to insist on a stable monetary reform, and to free ourselves from imported oil.

The time is now to resolve that the basis of a firm and principled foreign policy is one that takes the world as it is and seeks to change it by leadership and example, not by lecture and harangue.

The time is now to say that while we shall seek new friendships and expand and improve others, we shall not do so by breaking our word or casting aside old friends and allies.

And the time is now to redeem promises once made to the American people by another candidate, in another time and place. He said:

"For three long years I have been going up and down this country preaching that government—federal, state, and local—costs too much. I shall not stop that preaching. As an immediate program of action, we must abolish useless offices. We must eliminate unnecessary functions of government....

"We must consolidate subdivisions of government and, like the private citizen, give up luxuries which we can no longer afford.

"I propose to you, my friends, and through you, that government of all kinds, big and little, be made solvent, and that an example be set by the President of the United States and his cabinet."

So said Franklin Delano Roosevelt in his acceptance speech to the Democratic National Convention in July 1932.

The time is now, my fellow Americans, to recapture our destiny, to take it into our own hands. But to do this will take many of us, working together. I ask you tonight to volunteer your help in this cause, so we can carry our message throughout the land.

Yes, isn't now the time that we, the people, carry out these unkept promises? Let us pledge to each other and to all America on this July day forty-eight years later that we intend to do just that.

I've thought of something that is not part of my speech, and I'm worried about whether I should do it.

Can we doubt that only a Divine Providence placed this land, this island of freedom, here as a refuge for all those people in the world who yearn to breathe freely: Jews and Christians enduring persecution behind the Iron Curtain, the boat people of Southeast Asia, of Cuba and Haiti, the victims of the drought in Africa, the freedom fighters of Afghanistan, and our own countrymen held in savage captivity?

I'll confess that I've been a little afraid to suggest what I'm going to suggest—I'm more afraid not to: that we begin our crusade joined together in a moment of silent prayer. God bless America.

FOR FURTHER READING

Andrew E. Busch, *Reagan's Victory: The Presidential Election of 1980 and the Rise of the Right.* Lawrence: University Press of Kansas, 2005.

Barry Commoner, *The Politics of Energy.* New York: Knopf, 1979.

Garland C. Haas, *Jimmy Carter and the Politics of Frustration.* Jefferson, NC: McFarland & Co., 1992.

Gil Troy, *Morning in America: How Ronald Reagan Invented the 1980's.* Princeton, NJ: Princeton University Press, 2005.

Garry Wills, *Reagan's America: Innocents at Home.* New York: Penguin, 1988.

THE END OF THE COLD WAR

Viewpoint 36A

The Cold War Was a Great Victory for the United States (1992)

John Lewis Gaddis (b. 1941)

INTRODUCTION *More than four decades since its start following World War II, the Cold War between the United States and Soviet Union ended with the dismantling of the Berlin Wall in Germany in 1989 and the collapse of the Soviet Union in 1991. The lasting repercussions of the Cold War in American history continue to be debated by historians. The following viewpoint is excerpted from a 1992 article by John Lewis Gaddis, a professor of history at Yale University and the author of numerous books on the Cold War, including* Strategies of Containment *and* The Long Peace. *In his article, Gaddis notes that the Cold War was a period of relative peace compared to the conflicts that had preceded it. He disagrees with the claim that the Cold War was a simple struggle between two great powers or an example of American militarism. The Cold War was an ideological confrontation between the democracy of the United States and the communism of the Soviet Union, Gaddis states. It ended as a vindication of American values when the ideological underpinnings of the Soviet Union collapsed.*

What defense does Gaddis make of President Harry S. Truman's decisions at the beginning of the Cold War? How have many scholars been mistaken in their analysis of the Cold War, according to Gaddis? How, in his opinion, did nuclear weapons affect the course of the Cold War?

The Cold War was many things to many people. It was a division of the world into two hostile camps. It was a polarization of Europe in general, and of Germany in particular, into antagonistic spheres of influence. It was an ideological contest, some said between capitalism and communism, others said between democracy and authoritarianism. It was a competition for the allegiance of, and for influence over, the so-called Third World. It was a game of wits played out by massive intelligence organizations behind the scenes. It was a struggle that took place within each of its major adversaries as supporters and opponents of confrontation confronted one another. It was a contest that shaped culture, the social and natural sciences, and the writing of history. It was an arms race that held out the possibility—because it generated the capability—of ending civilization altogether. And it was a rivalry that even extended, at one point, beyond the bounds of earth itself, as human beings for the first time left their planet, but for a set of reasons that are likely to seem as parochial to future generations as those that impelled Ferdinand and Isabella to finance Columbus when he first set out for the New World five hundred years ago. . . .

When President Harry S. Truman told the Congress of the United States on 12 March 1947 that the world faced a struggle between two ways of life, one based on the will of the majority and the other based on the will of a minority forcibly imposed upon the majority, he had more than one purpose in mind. The immediate aim, of course, was to prod parsimonious legislators into approving economic and military assistance to Greece and Turkey, and a certain amount of rhetorical dramatization served that end. But President Truman also probably believed what he said, and most Americans and Europeans, at the time, probably agreed with him. Otherwise, the United States would hardly have been able to abandon its historic policy of peacetime isolationism and commit itself, not only to the Truman Doctrine, but to the much more ambitious Marshall Plan and eventually the North Atlantic Treaty Organization as well. Those plans worked, in turn, because most Europeans wanted them to. The danger at the time seemed to be real, and few people at the time had any difficulty in explaining what it was: freedom was under attack, and authoritarianism was threatening it.

In the years that followed, though, it became fashionable in academic circles to discount this argument. The Cold War, for many scholars, was not about ideology at all, but rather balances of power and spheres of influence; hence it differed little from other Great Power rivalries in modern and even ancient history. Others saw the Cold War as reflecting the demands of an unprecedentedly powerful American military-industrial complex that had set out to impose its hegemony over the rest of the earth. Students of Cold War origins never entirely

John Lewis Gaddis, "The Cold War, the Long Peace, and the Future," *Diplomatic History* 16 (Spring 1992).

neglected issues of ideology and principle, but few of them were prepared to say, as Truman had, that that conflict was *primarily* about the difference between freedom and its absence. Such a view seemed too naïve, too simplistic, and, above all, too self-righteous: politicians might say that kind of thing from public platforms, but professors in the classroom and in their scholarly monographs should not.

WHAT THE COLD WAR WAS ABOUT

As a result, it was left to the people of Eastern Europe and now the Soviet Union itself—through their own spontaneous but collective actions over the past three years—to remind us of a fact that many of us had become too sophisticated to see, which is that the Cold War really was about the imposition of autocracy and the denial of freedom. That conflict came to an end only when it became clear that authoritarianism could no longer be imposed and freedom could no longer be denied. That fact ought to make us look more seriously at how ideology contributed to the coming of the Cold War in the first place.

Much of twentieth-century history has revolved around the testing of a single idea: that one could transform the conduct of politics, government, and even human behavior itself into a "science" which would allow not only predicting the future but even, within certain limits, determining it. This search for a "science" of politics grew out of the revolution that had long since occurred in physics and biology: if scientific laws worked so well in predicting motions of the planets, the argument ran, why should similar laws not govern history, economics, and politics? Karl Marx certainly had such an approach in mind in the 1840s when he worked out his theory of dialectical materialism, which explicitly linked political and social consciousness to irreversible processes of economic development; his collaborator Friedrich Engels insisted in 1880 that the progression from feudalism through capitalism to socialism and ultimately communism was as certain as was the Darwinian process of natural selection.

This movement to transform politics into a science began, it is important to emphasize, with the best of intentions: its goal was to improve the human condition by making human behavior rational, enlightened, and predictable. And it arose as a direct response to abuses, excesses, and inequities that had grown out of the concept of freedom itself, as manifested in the mid-nineteenth century *laissez-faire* capitalism Marx had so strongly condemned.

But the idea of a "science" of politics was flawed from the beginning for the simple reason that human beings do not behave like the objects science studies. People are not laboratory mice; it is impossible to isolate them from the environment that surrounds them. They make judgments, whether rational or irrational, about the probable consequences of their actions, and they can change these actions accordingly. They learn from experience: the inheritance of acquired characteristics may not work in biology, the historian E. H. Carr once pointed out, but it does in history. As a result, people rarely act with the predictability of molecules combining in test tubes, or ball bearings rolling down inclined planes, or even the "dependent variables" that figure so prominently in the writings—and, increasingly, the equations—of our contemporary social scientists.

It was precisely frustration with this irritating unpredictability of human beings that led Lenin at the beginning of this century to invert Marx and make the state the instrument that was supposed to secure human freedom, rather than the obstacle that stood in the way of it. But that same problem of human intractability in turn caused Stalin to invert Lenin and make the state, its survival, and its total control of all its surroundings an end in itself, with a consequent denial of freedom that was as absolute as any autocrat has ever managed to achieve. A movement that had set out in 1848 to free the workers of the world from their chains had wound up, by 1948 and through the logic of its "scientific" approach to politics, insisting that the condition of being in chains was one of perfect freedom.

Anyone contemplating the situation in Europe at the end of World War II would have had good reason, therefore, to regard the very nature of Stalin's regime as a threat, and to fear its possible expansion. That expansion had already taken place in Eastern Europe and the Balkans, not so much because of Stalinism's accomplishments in and of themselves, but rather because of the opportunity created for it by the foolish behavior of the Europeans in allowing another flight from freedom—fascism—to take root among them. In one of history's many paradoxes, a successful, necessary, and wholly legitimate war against fascism created conditions more favorable to the spread of communism than that ideology could ever have managed on its own.

A REAL DANGER

The dangers Truman warned against in 1947, hence, were real enough. There is such a thing as bending before what one mistakenly believes to be the "wave of the future": fascism had gained its foothold in Europe by just these means. Many Europeans saw communism as such a wave following Hitler's defeat, not because they approved of that ideology, and not because they really expected the Red Army to drive all the way to the English Channel and the Pyrenees; the problem rather was that Europe had fallen into a demoralization so deep and so pervasive that Communists might have found paths to power there by constitutional means, much as the Nazis had done in Germany in 1933. Had that happened there is little reason to believe that constitutional procedures would have survived, any more than they did under Hitler; certainly the experiences of Poland, Romania, Hungary, and, after February 1948, Czechoslovakia do not suggest otherwise. Stalin's system could have spread throughout Europe without Stalin having to lift a finger: that was the threat. The actions the United States took, through the Truman Doctrine, the Marshall Plan, and NATO (North Atlantic Treaty Organization), were seen at the time and I think will be seen by future historians as having restored self-confidence among the Europeans, as having preserved the idea of freedom in Europe by a narrow and precarious margin at a time when Europeans themselves, reeling from the effects of two world wars, had almost given up on it.

---■---

The idea of freedom proved more durable than the practice of authoritarianism, and as a consequence, the Cold War ended.

---■---

To be sure, some historians have claimed that Europe might have saved itself even if the Americans had done nothing. There is no way now to prove that they are wrong. But few Europeans saw things this way at the time, and that brings us to one of the most important distinctions that has to be made if we are to understand the origins, evolution, and subsequent end of the Cold War: it is that the expansion of American and Soviet influence into Europe—the processes that really began that conflict—did not take place in the same way and with the same results. The Soviet Union, acting from primarily defensive motives, imposed its sphere of influence directly on Eastern Europe and the Balkans, against the will of the people who lived there. The United States, also acting for defensive reasons, responded to invitations from desperate governments in Western Europe, the Mediterranean, and even the Middle East to create countervailing spheres of influence in those regions. Compared to the alternative, American hegemony—for there is no denying that such a thing did develop—definitely seemed the lesser of two evils.

This distinction between imposition and invitation—too easily lost sight of in too much of the writing that has been done about Cold War history—proved to be critical in determining not only the shape but also the ultimate outcome of the Cold War. The system the United States built in Western Europe quickly won legitimacy in the form of widespread popular support. The Warsaw Pact and the other instruments of Soviet control in Eastern Europe never did. This happened because Europeans

at the time understood the difference between authoritarianism and its absence, just as more recent Europeans and now citizens of the former Soviet Union itself have come to understand it. Survivors of World War II had no more desire to embrace the Stalinist model of "scientific" politics than their children and grandchildren have had to remain under it. Moscow's authority in Eastern Europe turned out to be a hollow shell, kept in place only by the sheer weight of Soviet military power. Once it became apparent, in the late 1980s, that Mikhail Gorbachev's government was no longer willing (or able) to prop it up, the system Stalin had imposed upon half of Europe almost half a century earlier collapsed like a house of cards.

The way the Cold War ended, therefore, was directly related to the way in which it had begun. Perhaps Harry Truman had it right after all: the struggle really was, ultimately, about two ways of life, one that abandoned freedom in its effort to rationalize politics, and another that was content to leave politics as the irrational process that it normally is, thereby preserving freedom. The idea of freedom proved more durable than the practice of authoritarianism, and as a consequence, the Cold War ended.

The Cold War did, however, go on for an extraordinarily long period of time, during which the world confronted extraordinary perils. . . . How close we came to not surviving we will probably never know; but few people who lived through the Cold War took survival for granted during most of its history. The vision of a future filled with smoking, radiating ruins was hardly confined to writers of science fiction and makers of doomsday films; it was a constant presence in the consciousness of several generations after 1945, and the fact that that vision has now receded is of the utmost importance. . . .

Nuclear weapons have for so long been the subject of our nightmares—but sometimes also of our delusions of power—that it is difficult to answer this question dispassionately. We have tended to want to see these devices either as a Good Thing or a Bad Thing, and hence we have talked past one another most of the time. But the role of nuclear weapons in Cold War history was neither wholly good nor bad, which is to say, it was more interesting than either the supporters or the critics of these weapons have made it out to be.

THE BENEFITS OF NUCLEAR WEAPONS

Nuclear weapons were, of course, a very bad thing for the people of Hiroshima and Nagasaki; but those Americans and Japanese spared the necessity of additional killing as a result of their use might be pardoned for seeing some good in them. Nuclear weapons were a bad thing in that they greatly intensified the fears the principal Cold

War adversaries had of one another, and that much of the rest of the world had of both of them. But they were a good thing in that they induced caution on the part of these two Great Powers, discouraging irresponsible behavior of the kind that almost all Great Powers in the past have sooner or later engaged in. Nuclear weapons were a bad thing in that they held the world hostage to what now seems the absurd concept of mutual assured destruction, but they were a good thing in that they probably perpetuated the reputations of the United States and the Soviet Union as superpowers, thereby allowing them to "manage" a world that might have been less predictable and more dangerous had Washington and Moscow not performed that function. Nuclear weapons were a bad thing in that they stretched out the length of the Cold War by making the costs of being a superpower bearable on both sides and for both alliances: if the contest had had to be conducted only with more expensive conventional forces, it might have ended long ago. But nuclear weapons were a good thing in that they allowed for the passage of time, and hence for the education of two competitors who eventually came to see that they did not have all that much to compete about in the first place.

It is important to remember, though, that the peaceful end to the Cold War we have just witnessed is not the *only* conceivable way the Cold War could have ended. In adding up that conflict's costs, we would do well to recognize that the time it took to conclude the struggle was not time entirely wasted. That time—and those costs—appear to us excessive in retrospect, but future historians may see those expenditures as long-term investments in ensuring that the Cold War ended peacefully. For what we wound up doing with nuclear weapons was buying time—the time necessary for the authoritarian approach to politics to defeat itself by nonmilitary means. And the passage of time, even if purchased at an exorbitant price has at last begun to pay dividends.

Viewpoint 36B

The Cold War Was Not a Great Victory for the United States (1993)

Wade Huntley

INTRODUCTION *The collapse of the Soviet Union in 1991 was hailed by many observers as a triumph for the United States and a vindication of its Cold War policies following World War II. A somewhat different perspective on the end of the Cold War is taken in the following viewpoint by Wade Huntley, then a professor of politics at Whitman College in Washington. Huntley examines the origins and development of the Cold War, including the writings of George Kennan (see viewpoint 25B), and concludes that Americans were taking too much credit for the Soviet Union's demise. Government*

actions during the Cold War—especially the massive military spending, CIA-sponsored coups against other nations, wars in Vietnam and other places, and nuclear arms development—compromised American ideals, spiritual values, and democratic institutions, he argues.

What were the three unique features of the Cold War, according to Huntley? What lessons does he derive from the writings of George Kennan? In what ways is America the loser of the Cold War, in his view?

Who won the Cold War? The answer is not as obvious as public debate would make it seem. The question itself hides a deeper one: why did the Cold War end? this latter question is best addressed by reflecting briefly on why the Cold War began.

The Cold War emerged from the smoke and ashes of World War II, which left the United States and the Soviet Union as the two superpowers. Allies but never friends, tensions between the two countries soon congealed, the Iron Curtain fell, and the basic parameters of the next era of world politics were established.

COLD WAR FEATURES

Three features distinguished the Cold War from previous Great Power structures. First, the shift from a multipolar to a bipolar world centering on the U.S. and the U.S.S.R. altered the dynamics of great power behavior by hardening alliances and intensifying the rivalry. Secondly, the introduction of nuclear weapons focused the attention of the superpowers; in retrospect, the prospect of global nuclear war induced great caution by the leadership of both countries, perhaps also preventing a large-scale conventional war between them.

Finally, the U.S. and the U.S.S.R. were set apart not only by their competition for power, but by an unprecedented degree of ideological divisiveness. The two states differed on the most basic aspirations of the human experience and the political principles necessary to pursue them. It is this feature of the Cold War that is most crucial in explicating why and how the Cold War ended.

KENNAN'S FORESIGHT

The importance of this ideological divergence was apparent to sensitive observers from the beginning. We need look no further than George F. Kennan, the Department of State official who in 1947 originated the idea of "containment" of the Soviet Union that became a touchstone of U.S. policy throughout the Cold War. Mr. Kennan stressed the importance of Communist ideology in anticipating Soviet behavior: because its principles were "of long-term validity," the U.S.S.R. could "afford to be patient." Thus, Mr. Kennan expected Soviet leaders, unlike

Wade Huntley, "Who Won the Cold War?" *Chronicle of Higher Education*, March 31, 1993.

Napoleon or [Adolf] Hitler before them, to be willing to yield in particular encounters, but to be less likely to be discouraged by such passing defeats. The contest would be decided not by a key victory at some juncture, but by endurance of will over time.

If the United States could muster such will and sustain it over the long run, ultimately it would prevail. The reason was not simply U.S. military superiority over the U.S.S.R., but differences in the organizing principles of the two societies—the very differences in ideology that formed the core of the Cold War rivalry. Though World War II was but a few years past, already Mr. Kennan perceived the Soviet Union, unlike the United States, to be a nation at war with itself. Communist power and authority had been purchased only, he wrote, "at a terrible cost in human life and human hopes and energies." The Soviet people were "physically and spiritually tired," at the limits of their endurance. Thus, he concluded, "Soviet power bears within it the seeds of its own decay."

It is well to remember Mr. Kennan's foresight in considering current explanations of the demise of the Soviet Union. Many scholars, seemingly more concerned with anticipating future great power configurations, take the end of the Cold War itself for granted. Perhaps more importantly, little of what scholarly attention has been paid to this question has filtered into public forums. There are (at least) four possible explanations for the end of the Cold War, only two of which have found their way into mainstream discourse in the U.S.

EXPLANATIONS FOR VICTORY

The first explanation is that the collapse of Soviet power is directly attributable to the confrontational policies pursued by the [Ronald] Reagan and [George H.W.] Bush Administrations. In other words, the Republicans won the Cold War. According to this story, the massive increases in defense spending and uncompromising stances toward the "evil empire" inaugurated in the early 1980s pressed the Soviet Union to the wall, beyond its material capacity to respond in kind.

The second popular explanation, mostly propounded by Democrats, is best termed the "me too" explanation. It holds that Presidents Reagan and Bush were not the first to confront the Soviets, and trots out hard-line rhetoric and policies from the [Harry S.] Truman to [John F.] Kennedy to [Jimmy] Carter Administrations. Adherents of this view want to insure that history remembers that both parties' leaders had fine moments of hard-headed intransigence.

Lost in this feeding frenzy of credit-taking have been two other possible explanations. The first is that the hard-line postures adopted by the U.S. throughout the Cold War actually did more harm than good. This view, though normally associated in the popular media with out-of-touch liberals and pacifists, has received respectable scholarly attention. According to this view, had it not been for a tendency toward wild-eyed anti-communism on the American side, the Soviet Union may have collapsed under its own weight much sooner than it did. The stridence and belligerency emanating from Washington, from the 1950 adoption of "NSC-68" onward, had little effect but to strengthen comparable hard-line views in the Kremlin.

George Kennan himself endorsed this view in a [1992] *New York Times* opinion piece. According to Mr. Kennan, the "greatest damage" was done not by the military policies themselves, but by the tone of those policies, which produced a "braking effect on all liberalizing tendencies in the regime." As Mr. Kennan concludes, "For this, both Democrats and Republicans have a share of the blame."

A final explanation concerning the end of the Cold War is that the policies of the United States, in substance as well as tone, were not really all that important in the course of Soviet events. This idea has rarely surfaced in public discussion, nor has it received much scholarly attention apart from Soviet specialists who have long stressed the importance of the Soviet Union's own domestic politics.

Kennan himself suggests this point, remarking, "The suggestion that any Administration had the power to influence decisively the course of a tremendous domestic political upheaval in another great country on another side of the globe is simply childish."

From this viewpoint, the only role which the United States had was indirect, in the alternative it presented to communism merely by its existence. The success of American political institutions themselves, rather than the particular policies promulgated through them, set the standard the Soviet Union could not match.

Let us push the ramifications of this final hypothesis a bit further. If Soviet-style communism truly was consumed by the poverty of its own principles, independent of U.S. policies, how should those policies be judged? Perhaps it was not only belligerent rhetoric which was extraneous to the downfall of the U.S.S.R. The U.S. may have needlessly spent billions of dollars on high-technology weapons systems, and tragically sacrificed tens of thousands of American lives in faraway jungles. Perhaps, in setting out to break the back of Soviet Communism, the U.S. simply broke its own bank instead.

SPIRITUAL COSTS

The cost of the Cold War to the United States may have been even steeper spiritually than materially. In 1947 Kennan singled out one standard above military prowess or economic muscle which the Cold War would test: "To avoid destruction the United States need only measure up to its own best traditions and prove itself worthy of preservation as a great nation."

Considering what might have been, the United States was a loser in the Cold War, not its winner.

Now, with the Cold War behind us, can it truly be said that we passed this test? The paranoid red-baiting of Joseph McCarthy, the cynicism of secret CIA-sponsored coups overturning elected regimes, the breached trust of Watergate, the duplicity of the Iran-Contra affair, all add up to a weighty and depressing litany of failures.... Too often both leaders and the public were willing to compromise American principles and ideals (not to mention law) in the name of fighting communism.

The United States emerged from the Cold War overarmed, burdened by debt and poverty, and carrying numerous scars from self-inflicted wounds to cherished institutions—all for the sake of the superpower competition. In forging itself into a hard-line Cold War warrior, the U.S. ultimately undermined its "best traditions" more than it measured up to them. Had its leaders and citizens demonstrated greater faith in the strength of the nation's founding principles, the U.S. might have emerged from the Cold War contest economically leaner, brighter of spirit, and with its democratic institutions and values far stronger. And, to the extent that its course also diminished the potency of the alternative it posed to Soviet totalitarianism, the U.S. might have emerged from the Cold War sooner as well.

Who, then, really won the Cold War? Not the Republicans, nor the Democrats. Considering what might have been, the United States was a loser in the Cold War, not its winner.

LESSONS FOR THE FUTURE

If this conclusion is valid, it suggests some crucial lessons for the future. The United States now shoulders a burden of world leadership perhaps unprecedented in its history. Realists are right in suggesting that, despite the most benign intentions, this new preeminence could generate more new enemies than friends. Minimizing this tendency requires reinforcing what has always been the most important American task in the world: to hold out, chiefly by its own example, a beacon illuminating the path to freedom.

To meet the added challenges of the new era, the United States has simply to follow the sage council of Polonius: above all, to thine own self be true. Should Americans fail to learn this, perhaps the deepest lesson of the Cold War's end, the U.S. may come to lose the post-Cold War as well.

FOR FURTHER READING

John Lewis Gaddis, *The Cold War: A New History*. New York: Penguin, 2005.

Walter Lafeber, *America, Russia, and the Cold War, 1945–2002*. New York: McGraw Hill, 2002.

Don Oberdorfer, *The Turn: From the Cold War to a New Era*. New York: Poseidon, 1991.

Ronald Steel, *Temptations of a Superpower*. Cambridge, MA: Harvard University Press, 1995.

Martin Walker, *The Cold War: A History*. New York: Henry Holt, 1994.

Part 5

NEW CHALLENGES AFTER THE COLD WAR (1991–PRESENT)

CHRONOLOGY

1991

January 16–April 3 Persian Gulf War occurs as U.S. leads multinational force to rout Iraqi army and liberate Kuwait.

July 1 The Warsaw Pact is dissolved.

October 15 Clarence Thomas is confirmed by the Senate for the Supreme Court after controversial hearings in which he was accused of sexual harassment.

December Mikhail Gorbachev resigns; Soviet Union dissolves.

1992

April 29 A police brutality incident in Los Angeles results in riots.

June 29 Supreme Court reaffirms right to abortion in *Planned Parenthood v. Casey.*

November 3 Bill Clinton elected president.

November 24 U.S. military forces withdraw from the Philippines.

December 17 North American Free Trade Agreement (NAFTA) signed by leaders of United States, Canada, and Mexico.

1993

February First popular Internet browser developed.

January 25 First Lady Hillary Clinton appointed Chair of Health Reform Task Force.

January 29 U.S. military adopts "Don't Ask, Don't Tell" policy toward gays in the armed forces.

March American troops leave Somalia; a car bomb explodes in World Trade Center in New York City.

April 19 Federal agents end standoff with Branch Davidian religious cult with raid; subsequent fire kills 72.

1994

April 5 Rock star Kurt Cobain kills himself.

May 6 Clinton formally accused of sexual harassment when he was governor of Arkansas.

November 8 Republicans win control of Congress.

1995

January 24–October 3 Football star O.J. Simpson is acquitted of murder charges after a heavily-covered criminal trial.

April 19 A truck bomb destroys Federal Office Building in Oklahoma City, killing 168; two Americans are arrested.

1996

August Congress passes welfare reform that sets limits on payments to single mothers.

November 5 Clinton reelected president.

1997

January The first cloned mammal, Dolly the sheep, is announced.

March 27 Members of the Heaven's Gate religious cult commit mass suicide.

1998

December Federal government achieves a budget surplus for the first time in two decades.

December House of Representatives impeaches Clinton; Clinton orders air strikes on Iraq after the nation expels UN weapons inspectors.

1999

January Number of Internet users in the United States reaches 75 million.

February Clinton's Senate impeachment trial results in his acquittal.

March–June America acting with NATO launches air strikes to halt Yugoslavian government's ethnic cleansing in Kosovo.

April 20 Fourteen students and one teacher are killed by two students at Columbine High School in Colorado.

2000

October 12 Terrorists attack U.S. Navy ship USS *Cole* in Yemen.

November 8 George W. Bush is initially declared winner of the 2000 election, but legal challenges regarding vote recounts in the state of Florida leave the presidential race essentially tied.

December 19 In *Bush v. Gore* Supreme Court ruling halts vote recounts in Florida and ensures George W. Bush will become the nation's next president.

2001

June 7 Bush signs largest federal tax cut since 1981.

August Bush announces federal government funding restrictions on human cloning and stem cell research.

September 11 Terrorists hijack three planes, which they use as weapons. Attack results in the destruction to the World Trade Center, killing three thousand, and damages the Pentagon.

October Letters containing anthrax alarm nation; Congress passes USA Patriot Act, giving federal government greater powers to investigate and prevent terrorist plots.

October 7–December 9 U.S. military assault on Afghanistan topples Taliban regime and drives September 11 terrorist leader Osama bin Laden into hiding.

November Bush signs a directive to try suspected terrorists in military tribunals rather than civilian courts.

December Energy company Enron declares bankruptcy in the wake of a massive accounting scandal.

2002

January Bush declares Iran, Iraq, and North Korea an "Axis of Evil"—nations bent on threatening the world with weapons of mass destruction.

November Department of Homeland Security created; UN weapons inspectors return to Iraq after Security Council passes resolution calling on Iraq to disarm.

2003

February 1 Breakup of *Columbia* space shuttle on reentry kills all seven astronauts aboard.

March Bush orders U.S.-led invasion of Iraq.

May U.S. forces topple regime of Saddam Hussein; Bush declares "mission accomplished."

2004

May Released photographs of Iraqi prisoner abuse at the hands of U.S. soldiers at Abu Ghraib prison shock many; Massachusetts court legalizes gay marriage in that state.

June 28 United States hands political authority in Iraq over to Iraqi interim government.

September 16 U.S. final report on Iraq's weapons of mass destruction concludes that Iraq had none.

November 2 Bush reelected president.

2005

August 25–30 Hurricane Katrina submerges the city of New Orleans and kills hundreds.

December 15 Journalists expose a secret National Security Agency program to spy on American phone calls without judicial warrants.

2006

March The USA Patriot Act is renewed by Congress.

April–May Millions of demonstrators march in support of immigrants.

June Senate debates anti-gay marriage constitutional amendment.

PREFACE

In the late twentieth and early twenty-first centuries, global conflict and instability dominated U.S. politics and plagued U.S.-international relations. Present-day global conflict has reached such great proportions, in fact, that many would look back on the Cold War years as a period of relative calm. While the collapse of the Soviet Union in 1991 ended the Cold War and left the United States the world's lone superpower, it also brought to a head many long-suppressed ethnic and civil conflicts in Europe, Africa, and the Middle East. What many Americans viewed as distant, regional strife hit home hard when terrorists attacked the United States on September 11, 2001, leading some to conclude that the United States faced a new enemy that respected no borders—terrorists motivated by Islamic fundamentalism. U.S. presidents George H.W. Bush, Bill Clinton, and George W. Bush have had to decide time and again whether and how to intervene in these post–Cold War conflicts.

THE FIRST WAR AGAINST IRAQ

The 1991 Persian Gulf War was the first major conflict involving the United States outside the Cold War framework. The crisis began in August 1990 when Iraq, a Middle East power led by longtime dictator Saddam Hussein, invaded and occupied its small, oil-rich, pro-Western neighbor, Kuwait. Republican president George H.W. Bush responded to the Kuwait invasion by organizing a broad international alliance including Cold War rivals such as the Soviet Union as well as Cold War allies such as Japan and Great Britain. These nations united in support of a clearly articulated goal—Iraq's unconditional withdrawal from Kuwait. In his speeches to the American people in the months following August 1990, Bush stressed America's moral obligation to intervene in the conflict, arguing that letting Iraq's conquest stand would set a bad precedent. He marshaled support in Congress and in the United Nations (UN), which imposed economic sanctions against Iraq and established a January 15, 1991, deadline for Iraqi withdrawal from Kuwait. He ordered U.S. troops to Saudi Arabia and other countries in the region, ultimately putting a half-million soldiers in position for military action. Bush also established an international coalition prepared to lend its own troops and/or financial support in the effort to put additional economic, military, and diplomatic pressure on Hussein.

One day after Hussein failed to meet the UN deadline for withdrawal, U.S.-led forces began an aerial attack against Iraq.

The Persian Gulf War consisted of six weeks of bombing followed by four days of massive ground fighting that destroyed much of Hussein's army. Kuwait was liberated, Bush's approval rating rose to 91 percent, and his articulated dream of a "new world order" of American-led UN-approved actions against aggression seemed within reach. However, the hope that Hussein himself would be ousted proved futile. Hussein remained in power in Iraq, brutally putting down internal rebellions and defying or evading UN commitments to account for chemical, biological, and nuclear weapons of mass destruction (WMDs).

In the postwar analysis, some critics of the Bush administration argued that in cutting short a military drive to Baghdad, Iraq, the president missed a golden opportunity to depose Hussein (a goal that was finally achieved twelve years later when his son was president). Critics also charged that the United Nations proved ineffectual in confronting various crises that followed the Persian Gulf War, including conflicts in Somalia, Serbia, and Rwanda, in part blaming a lack of leadership comparable to that of Bush prior to the 1991 Gulf War.

THE CLINTON ERA

Bill Clinton's presidency (1992–2000) was also challenged by world conflict, and his decisions regarding when and where to involve the United States provoked intense controversy. Clinton, a Democrat, responded to conflicts in Somalia, Haiti, and Kosovo by ordering U.S. military peacekeeping and humanitarian missions to the troubled regions. The rationale behind these interventions was what came to be called the Clinton Doctrine—the idea that the United States and its allies should intervene militarily to prevent genocide and other humanitarian disasters. However, the Clinton Doctrine stopped short of full-scale military intervention. Military actions under Clinton were small compared to the Persian Gulf War; they either relied solely on airpower or involved very limited numbers of ground troops. In some cases—notably the horrific 1994 genocide in Rwanda—the Clinton Doctrine apparently did not apply at all, as the United States abstained from military intervention in that African nation. Clinton's foreign policy, many argued, was based on political calculations that recognized that the American people had little appetite for sending soldiers to die in battle in conflicts that did not directly affect them. For example, Clinton withdrew U.S. troops from Somalia, where they had been sent to maintain order amid civil war and sectarian violence, shortly after images of the bodies of American soldiers being dragged down the streets of Mogadishu were widely televised.

One notable exception to the pattern of American peacekeeping missions came in the military strikes Clinton ordered in Sudan and Afghanistan in 1998. These were authorized in response to terrorist bombings of American embassies in Africa that intelligence sources identified as the work of an Islamic terrorist network—known as al Qaeda—led by Saudi-born Osama bin Laden. Clinton ordered the bombing of a drug-manufacturing factory in Sudan that was a suspected source of chemical weapons for Bin Laden's group. He also authorized cruise missile strikes against bases in Afghanistan described as terrorist training camps. Clinton defended the actions as a necessary response to terrorists. Critics contended, however, that the bombing strikes were ineffective, some also questioned the timing of the military strikes, announced at the same time a federal prosecutor was releasing a report detailing the president's extramarital affair and his efforts to cover up the politically damaging personal scandal.

If the military strikes against Bin Laden were an attempt to divert attention from scandal at home, they failed, as Congress went on in 1998 to impeach Clinton for misleading federal prosecutors. Public support for his presidential performance remained high, however, and Clinton was ultimately acquitted of his impeachment charges and served the remainder of his second term.

SEPTEMBER 11

Clinton's Republican successor, George W. Bush (son of the former president), was faced with perhaps the most cataclysmic event in the history of the nation, one that would have far-reaching effects on Americans' civil liberties, national identity, and sense of national security. On September 11, 2001, terrorists (later determined to be part of al Qaeda) hijacked four commercial jet airliners. Two planes were flown into the Twin Towers of the World Trade Center (WTC) in New York City, causing both skyscrapers to collapse. Terrorists crashed the third hijacked aircraft into the Pentagon in Washington, D.C., and the fourth plane, apparently intended to strike another Washington target, crashed in a Pennsylvania field, the hijackers foiled by a courageous passenger revolt. Approximately three thousand people were killed in the four attacks.

The September 11 attacks were not the first time Americans were victimized by terrorists, and this was not even the first terrorist incident on American soil. Foreign terrorists had detonated bombs in the World Trade Center in 1993, and right-wing extremists blew up a federal office building in Oklahoma in 1995. But it was the spectacular and devastating attacks of September 11 that drew comparisons with Japan's surprise attack on Pearl Harbor nearly six decades before, and which led many people to wonder whether this was the start of a new era of war—the enemy not German Nazis or Soviet Communists, but fanatics from the Middle East and Asia professing a radical Islamic ideology.

GEORGE BUSH AND THE DOCTRINE OF PREEMPTIVE WAR

Americans' and the world's eyes were on President Bush and his response. Defining the parameters of the reprisals to come, Bush declared that the United States would make no distinction between terrorists and nations that harbor terrorists. In October 2001 the United States began military operations against the Taliban in Afghanistan, a totalitarian fundamentalist regime that had provided safe harbor for al Qaeda, the terrorist organization Clinton had attacked with cruise missiles in 1998. The Taliban regime was officially toppled within a few weeks, and foreign and American troops established an occupation in Afghanistan aimed at building a new, democratic government there. Al Qaeda operatives were killed or caught, although Bin Laden himself managed to avoid capture. The decision to go to war in 2001 in Afghanistan received nearly unanimous support in Congress and the widespread support of the American public.

However, Bush clearly indicated that the direct response in Afghanistan would be only part of America's war on terrorism. He eventually articulated a national security strategy that differed sharply from what America had pursued in previous conflicts, including the Cold War. In that long conflict, America did not directly confront or seek to invade the Soviet Union, but sought rather to deter the Soviets through arms buildup and indirectly fight communism in Korea and Vietnam. However, Bush argued that deterrence could not guarantee protection against shadowy and suicidal terrorist groups such as al Qaeda, or "rogue states" including Iraq and Iran that defied diplomatic pressure to stop programs producing weapons of mass destruction. Bush maintained that in some cases, the best way to defend America was to take the offensive—to wage preemptive war against potential terrorist threats before another September 11 attack (or worse) could materialize. Bush has also forcefully argued at various times that the United States should directly challenge certain ideologies, such as the brand of Islamic fundamentalism behind the September 11 attacks, by promoting American-style ideas and democracy in other nations of the world. Both notions have been identified as part of the so-called Bush Doctrine.

THE SECOND WAR AGAINST IRAQ

Bush's ideas regarding the war on terror have been most fully expressed in his decision in March 2003 to wage war against Iraq, a little more than twelve years after his father had made a similar decision. In 1991 the defeated Iraqi leader Saddam Hussein had agreed to drop all of Iraq's programs to develop weapons of mass destruction, but in subsequent years the regime was less than cooperative with international inspections, leading many to suspect that Iraq was conducting secret weapons programs. The possibility that Iraq had chemical, biological, or nuclear weapons at its disposal, and might share them with terrorist groups, was simply unacceptable to the United States in a post–September 11 world, Bush argued, and the threat should be dealt with preemptively.

The war on Iraq that began in March 2003 was in some ways similar to the 1991 Gulf War. Like the elder Bush, George W. Bush sought and received congressional authorization to use military force in Iraq (although neither asked for or received a formal declaration of war), and sought international cooperation with other nations via the United Nations. In 2003, much as in 1991, the Iraqi military was overwhelmed by a technologically superior U.S. fighting force. As in 1991, the opening weeks of the 2003 war were a resounding military victory for the United States; by May 2003 Saddam Hussein's regime had fallen and Bush had declared "mission accomplished."

But important differences soon emerged, differences that became greater with time. In both conflicts the United States led international coalitions, but whereas the 1991 Persian Gulf War was a broad coalition and has been seen as primarily a UN operation, the 2003 attack had a smaller coalition of partners and never received formal UN approval. Much of the world saw the action as evidence that the United States was less willing to work within international agreements and institutions such as the United Nations, and more willing to unilaterally use military force, including preemptive attacks, to defend itself.

The aftermath of the war has heightened this criticism of the United States. Whereas the Persian Gulf War was over in a matter of weeks, the second Iraq war left the United States as an occupying force in Iraq to the present day, as hundreds of thousands of U.S. soldiers face a persistent insurgency that has cost the United States thousands of lives, hundreds of billions of dollars, and a significant degree of respect and stature among other nations. As the war continues, many people have compared it to America's long conflict in Vietnam during the Cold War. Bush, unlike his father, was able to win reelection in 2004, but in subsequent years found the war on Iraq a persistent drag on his public approval ratings.

ONGOING CHALLENGES OF THE WAR ON TERROR

Bush also responded to the September 11 attacks by asking for and asserting broad executive powers. Bush sought and won passage of the USA Patriot Act in late 2001, a law that broadly expanded the investigative powers of law-enforcement agencies. In 2002 he signed legislation creating the Department of Homeland Security, a broad reorganization of government agencies charged with protecting the American people from terrorism and other threats. Under Bush's authority, hundreds of terrorist suspects and enemy combatants captured in Afghanistan have been detained in a U.S. naval facility in Guantánamo Bay, Cuba, for years without legal redress. Certain actions and decisions Bush made in secrecy have proved extremely controversial when revealed to the public through investigative journalism. These actions included the establishment of secret prisoner bases around the world (in addition to Guantánamo); reports of severe mistreatment and torture of terrorist suspects in Iraq, Guantánamo, and elsewhere; and the establishment of domestic surveillance systems including wiretaps on American telephone calls and tracked financial transactions, programs created without full congressional or judicial authorization and with little congressional or public oversight. Revelations about the existence of these secret programs have raised questions about Bush exceeding his executive and constitutional authority—and threatening Americans' civil liberties—in the name of protecting national security.

The decisions and actions taken by Bush since September 11, 2001, can be seen as an experiment in whether America's unmatched military power can be effectively channeled to impose order in world conflicts and protect the American people. America's military has achieved notable successes, including the overthrow of the Taliban and the deposing of Saddam Hussein, but whether these will count as victories in an overarching "war on terror" remains to be seen. Afghanistan remains embroiled in conflict and has seen a resurgence of the Taliban in some areas. Iraq, the site of numerous insurgent and terrorist attacks, has become increasingly divided along religious and ethnic lines; the future of its American-supported elected government remains in doubt. Countries such as Iran and North Korea have refused to dismantle their nuclear weapons programs in the face of criticism from the United States and other nations. The Middle East has remained a problem area where U.S. military might and influence has not prevented further outbreaks of instability and war, including conflict between Israel and Lebanon in 2006, and, some critics charge, has aggravated instability. Whether or not the United States can actually utilize its military personnel to promote global stability and peace, rather than aggravate instability, may be the central question facing Americans in the post–September 11 era.

DOMESTIC CHALLENGES

Viewpoint 37A

America Must Reform Its Health Care System (1994)

Bill Clinton (b. 1946)

INTRODUCTION *Bill Clinton served as president of the United States from 1993 to 2001. The former Arkansas governor had become only the second successful Democratic Party presidential candidate in a quarter century in part by promising voters increased attention to domestic issues. During the first two years of his first term he sought a major expansion in the federal government by leading the nation to a major overhaul of its health care system. He appointed his wife, Hillary Rodham Clinton, to head a health care task force, introduced legislation in which everyone would be guaranteed health coverage, and made national television addresses and numerous speeches promoting his health care proposals. He reiterated some of his main arguments for health care reform in his 1994 State of the Union message to Congress, excerpted here. Clinton argues that many Americans face a health care crisis because they do not have a job that provides health insurance, or face the prospect of no coverage for preexisting health conditions. He also argues that the system is riddled with abuse and inefficiencies, and that federal government reforms can save money and apply it directly to health care needs.*

Clinton's proposals met with strong and ultimately successful opposition from Republicans, business and health care industry groups, and Americans who feared a government takeover of America's health care system. The Republican Party's seizure of Congress in the 1994 elections is attributed in part to public reaction to Clinton's health care plan.

What anecdotes and statistics does Clinton provide to argue that the country is in crisis? Who is "in charge" of America's health care system, according to Clinton?

This year [1994] we will make history by reforming the health care system. And I would say to you, all of you my fellow public servants, this is another issue where the people are way ahead of the politicians.

That may not be popular with either party, but it happens to be the truth.

Bill Clinton, State of the Union Address, January 25, 1994.

A HEALTH INSURANCE CRISIS

You know, the first lady [Hillary Clinton] has received now almost a million letters from people all across America and from all walks of life. I'd like to share just one of them with you. Richard Anderson of Reno, Nevada, lost his job and, with it, his health insurance. Two weeks later, his wife, Judy, suffered a cerebral aneurysm. He rushed her to the hospital, where she stayed in intensive care for 21 days. The Andersons' bills were over $120,000. Although Judy recovered and Richard went back to work at $8 an hour, the bills were too much for them and they were literally forced into bankruptcy.

"Mrs. Clinton," he wrote to Hillary, "no one in the United States of America should have to lose everything they've worked for all their lives because they were unfortunate enough to become ill." It was to help the Richard and Judy Andersons of America that the first lady and so many others have worked so hard and so long on this health care reform issue. We owe them our thanks and our action.

I know there are people here who say there's no health care crisis. Tell it to Richard and Judy Anderson. Tell it to the 58 million Americans who have no coverage at all for some time each year. Tell it to the 81 million Americans with those preexisting conditions; those folks are paying more or they can't get insurance at all or they can't ever change their jobs because they or someone in their family has one of those preexisting conditions. Tell it to the small businesses burdened by skyrocketing costs of insurance. Most small businesses cover their employers, and they pay on average 35 percent more in premiums than big businesses or government. Or tell it to the 76 percent of insured Americans, three out of four whose policies have lifetime limits, and that means they can find themselves without any coverage at all just when they need it the most.

So, if any of you believe there's no crisis, you tell it to those people, because I can't.

There are some people who literally do not understand the impact of this problem on people's lives, but all you have to do is go out and listen to them. Just go talk to them anywhere, in any congressional district in this country. They're Republicans and Democrats and independents. It doesn't have a lick to do with party. They think we don't get it, and it's time we show that we do get it.

If we just let the health care system continue to drift, our country will have people with less care, fewer choices, and higher bills.

195

AN INEFFICIENT HEALTH CARE SYSTEM

From the day we began, our health care initiative has been designed to strengthen what is good about our health care system—the world's best health care professionals, cutting edge research, and wonderful research institutions, Medicare for older Americans. None of this—none of it should be put at risk. But we're paying more and more money for less and less care. Every year, fewer and fewer Americans even get to choose their doctors. Every year, doctors and nurses spend more time on paperwork and less time with patients because of the absolute bureaucratic nightmare the present system has become.

This system is riddled with inefficiency, with abuse, with fraud, and everybody knows it. In today's health care system, insurance companies call the shots. They pick whom they cover and how they cover them. They can cut off your benefits when you need your coverage the most. They are in charge.

What does it mean? It means every night millions of well-insured Americans go to bed just an illness, an accident, or a pink slip away from having no coverage or financial ruin. It means every morning millions of Americans go to work without any health insurance at all—something the workers in no other advanced country in the world do. It means that every year more and more hard working people are told to pick a new doctor because their boss has had to pick a new plan. And countless others turn down better jobs because they know, if they take the better job, they'll lose their health insurance.

If we just let the health care system continue to drift, our country will have people with less care, fewer choices, and higher bills.

PROMOTING PRIVATE INSURANCE

Now, our approach protects the quality of care and people's choices. It builds on what works today in the private sector, to expand employer-based coverage, to guarantee private insurance for every American. And I might say, employer-based private insurance for every American was proposed 20 years ago by President Richard Nixon to the United States Congress. It was a good idea then, and it's a better idea today.

Why do we want guaranteed private insurance? Because right now, nine out of ten people who have insurance get it through their employers—and that should continue. And if your employer is providing good benefits at reasonable prices, that should continue too. And that ought to make the Congress and the president feel better. Our goal is health insurance everybody can depend on—comprehensive benefits that cover preventive care and prescription drugs, health premiums that don't

just explode when you get sick or you get older, the power—no matter how small your business is—to choose dependable insurance at the same competitive rates that governments and big business get today, one simple form for people who are sick, and most of all, the freedom to choose a plan and the right to choose your own doctor....

To those who would cut Medicare without protecting seniors, I say the solution to today's squeeze on middle class working people's health care is not to put the squeeze on middle class retired people's health care. We can do better than that. When it's all said and done, it's pretty simple to me. Insurance ought to mean what it used to mean. You pay a fair price for security, and when you get sick, health care is always there—no matter what.

Along with the guarantee of health security, we all have to admit, too, there must be more responsibility on the part of all of us in how we use this system. People have to take their kids to get immunized. We should all take advantage of preventive care. We must all work together to stop the violence that explodes our emergency rooms. We have to practice better health habits, and we can't abuse the system. And those who don't have insurance under our approach will get coverage, but they will have to pay something for it, too. The minority of businesses that provide no insurance at all, and in so doing, shift the cost of the care of their employees to others, should contribute something. People who smoke should pay more for a pack of cigarettes. Everybody can contribute something if we want to solve the health care crisis. There can't be anymore something for nothing. It will not be easy, but it can be done. Now in the coming months I hope very much to work with both Democrats and Republicans to reform a health care system by using the market to bring down costs and to achieve lasting health security. But if you look at history, we see that for 60 years this country has tried to reform health care. President [Franklin Delano] Roosevelt tried, President [Harry S.] Truman tried, President Nixon tried, President [Jimmy] Carter tried. Every time the special interests were powerful enough to defeat them, but not this time.

Viewpoint 37B

America's Health Care System Does Not Need Government Reform (1993)
Fred Barnes (b. 1943)

INTRODUCTION *President Bill Clinton prompted a national debate in the first years of his presidency (1993–2001) over whether to overhaul America's system of health care. Most Americans get private health care insurance through their employers, but Clinton argued that this system left millions of Americans lacking access* *to health care. He called for increased federal government regulation and involvement to make health care a guaranteed right. But opponents of Clinton's proposals objected to their cost (an estimated $42 billion) and the perceived harms of federal government regulation of America's private health care industry. They also argued that America's health care system was not, in fact, in crisis—an argument made in the following viewpoint, excerpted from a 1993 article by journalist Fred Barnes. Barnes, a writer for the* New Republic, Weekly Standard, *and other political journals, argues here that, contrary to claims made by the president and his wife, Hillary Rodham Clinton, the United States has the world's best health care system, that government regulations and price controls suggested by the president would be harmful, and that the health problems Americans faced were more attributable to lifestyle choices (such as drug abuse) rather than America's health care system.*

Barnes and other opponents of Clinton's proposals were successful in derailing Clinton's plan. However, health care has continued to be a recurring political issue for Americans in the twenty-first century.

Why do so many Americans believe there is a health care crisis, according to Barnes? What rival systems does Barnes use to compare with America's health care delivery? What criticism does he make about liberal advocates of health care reform?

Bill and Hillary Clinton have contributed heavily to a national myth. Mrs. Clinton, as boss of the administration task force plotting to overhaul America's health-care system, refers routinely to "the health-care crisis." Her husband uses the same phrase ("Our government will never again be fully solvent until we tackle the health-care crisis," Clinton declared in his State of the Union address on February 17 [1993]). And he goes one step further. "A lot of Americans don't have health insurance," he told a group of schoolkids February 20 during a nationally televised children's town meeting at the White House. "You know that, don't you? A lot of Americans don't have health care."

The press also trumpets the crisis theme. . . . The result is that the American people, despite their personal experience, now believe there actually is a health-care crisis. Most opinion polls show roughly three-quarters of Americans are satisfied with the availability and quality of the health-care they receive. Yet, in most polls, 60 to 70 percent feel the health-care system is failing and needs significant, if not radical, reform.

There is no health-care crisis. It's a myth. If millions of seriously ill Americans were being denied medical care,

Fred Barnes, "What Health-Care Crisis?" *American Spectator*, May 1993, vol. 26, no. 5, p. 20 (4).

that would be a crisis. But that's not happening. Everyone gets health care in this country—the poor, the uninsured, everyone. No, our health-care system isn't perfect. There isn't enough primary care—regular doctor's visits—for many Americans. Emergency rooms are often swamped. The way hospitals and doctors are financed is sometimes bizarre. Health care may (or may not) be too costly. But it's the best health care system in the world—not arguably the best, but the best. Its shortcomings can be remedied by tinkering, or at least by less-than-comprehensive changes. An overhaul of the sort Hillary Clinton envisions is not only unnecessary, it's certain to reduce, not expand, the amount of health care Americans receive (price controls always lead to less of the controlled commodity). Then we really will have a health-care crisis.

You don't have to take my word that there's no crisis now and that health care here is the world's best. There's solid evidence. Let's examine four key aspects of the health-care debate: access, false measures of quality health care, true measures, and how America's system compares with those of other industrialized democracies (Canada, Germany, Japan, Great Britain).

ACCESS

Will someone please tell Bill Clinton that having no health insurance is not the same as having no health care? The uninsured get health care, only less of it than the insured. Being uninsured means "one is more likely to use emergency-room care and less likely to use office, clinic, or regular inpatient care," said Richard Darman, President [George H.W.] Bush's budget director, in congressional testimony in 1991. "This is not to suggest that this is desirable. It is not." But it is high-quality health care.

Doctors in emergency rooms are specialists. In fact, they have a professional organization, the American College of Emergency Physicians. Its motto is: "Our specialty is devoted to treating everyone in need, no questions asked." Turning away patients isn't an option. Federal law (section 9121 of the Consolidated Omnibus Budget Reconciliation Act of 1985) requires medical screening of everyone requesting care at a hospital emergency room. If treatment is needed, it must be provided. What this adds up to is "universal access" to health care in America, as one head of a hospital board told me. . . .

FALSE TESTS

Judging by the two most common measures of health, life expectancy at birth and the infant mortality rate, health care in the United States is not the best or even among the best. In 1990, life expectancy in America was 72 years for males, 78.8 for women. This put the U.S. behind Canada, France, Germany, Italy, Japan, and Great Britain, among others. On infant mortality, the U.S.

fared still worse, ranking nineteenth in 1989 with a rate of 9.7. (The infant mortality rate is the number of deaths of children under one year of age, divided by the number of births in a given year, multiplied by 1,000.) . . .

What's wrong with these measures? Just this: they're a reflection of health, not the health-care system. Life expectancy is determined by much more than the quality of a nation's health care. Social factors affect life expectancy, and this is where the U.S. runs into trouble. "Exacerbated social problems . . . adversely affect U.S. health outcomes," noted three Department of Health and Human Services officials in the fall 1992 issue of Health Care Financing Review. "The 20,000 annual U.S. homicides result in per capita homicide rates 10 times those of Great Britain and 4 times those of Canada. There are 100 assaults reported by U.S. emergency rooms for every homicide. About 25 percent of spinal cord injuries result from assaults." And so on. The incidence of AIDS is even more telling. Through June 1992, there were 230,179 reported AIDS cases here, two-thirds of whom have died. Japan, where life expectancy is four years longer for men than in the U.S. and three years longer for women, has had fewer than 300 AIDS cases. Once social factors have played out, the U.S. ranks at the top in life expectancy. At age 80, when most people are highly dependent on the health-care system, Americans have the longest life expectancy (7.1 years for men, 9.0 for women) in the world.

The infant mortality rate (IMR) is also "reflective of health and socioeconomic status and not just health care," wrote four Urban Institute scholars in the summer 1992 issue of *Health Care Financing Review*. And there are measurement problems. Many countries make no effort to save very-low-birth-weight infants. They aren't recorded as "live born" and aren't counted in infant mortality statistics. In contrast, American hospitals make heroic efforts in neonatal intensive care, saving some infants, losing others, and driving up the IMR. "The more resources a country's health-care system places on saving high-risk newborns, the more likely its registration will report a higher IMR," according to the Urban Institute scholars. . . .

Not only that. The entire medical system bears the brunt of social and behavioral problems that are far worse in the U.S. than in other industrialized democracies. "We have a large number of people who indulge in high-risk behavior," says Leroy L. Schwartz, M.D., of Health Policy International, a non-profit research group in Princeton, New Jersey. Behavioral problems become health problems: AIDS, drug abuse, assaults and violence, sexually transmitted diseases, etc. "The problem is not the health-care system," says Dr. Schwartz. "The problem is the people. Every year the pool of pathology in this country is getting bigger and bigger. We think we can take care of everything by calling it a health problem." But we can't.

REAL TESTS

While primary and preventive care are important, the best measure of a health-care system is how well it treats the seriously ill. What if you've got an enlarged prostate? Your chances of survival are better if you're treated here. The U.S. death rate from prostate trouble is one-seventh the rate in Sweden, one-fourth that in Great Britain, one-third that in Germany. Sweden, Great Britain, and Germany may have higher incidences of prostate illness, but not high enough to account for the wide disparity in death rates.

An ulcer of the stomach or intestine? The death rate per 100,000 persons is 2.7 in the U.S., compared to 2.8 in the Netherlands, 3.1 in Canada, 4.9 in Germany, 7.6 in Sweden, and 8 in Great Britain. A hernia or intestinal obstruction? The American death rate is 1.7. It's 2 in Canada, 2.7 in Germany, 3 in the Netherlands, 3.1 in Great Britain, and 3.2 in Sweden. Can these be attributed solely to varying incidences of ulcers and obstructions? Nope. . . .

Another measure that's important is the proliferation of new technology. "Major medical technology has had a profound impact on modern medicine and promises even greater impact in the future," wrote Dale A. Rublee, an expert in cross-national health policy comparisons for the AMA's [American Medical Association] Center for Health Policy Research, in Health Affairs. He compared the availability of six technologies—open-heart surgery, cardiac catheterization, organ transplantation, radiation therapy, extracorporeal shock wave lithotripsy, and magnetic resonance imaging [MRI]—in the U.S., Canada, and Germany in 1987. "Canada and Germany were selected because their overall health-care resources are fairly comparable to the United States," Rublee wrote. The U.S. came out ahead in every category, way ahead in several. In MRI's, the U.S. had 3.69 per one million people, Germany 0.94, Canada 0.46. For open-heart surgery, the U.S. had 3.26, Canada 1.23, Germany 0.74. For radiation therapy, the U.S. had 3.97, Germany 3.13, Canada 0.54. Small wonder that, as Rublee put it, "American physicians, with a universe of modern technology at their fingertips, are the envy of the world's physicians."

RIVAL SYSTEMS

Canadian politicians get special health care privileges, moving to the head of waiting lists or getting treatment at the elite National Defence Medical Centre. But that wasn't sufficient for Robert Bourassa, the premier of Quebec. He came to the National Cancer Institute in Bethesda, Maryland, for diagnosis, then returned to the U.S. for surgery, all at his own expense.

The Canadian health-care system has many nice attributes, but speedy treatment isn't one of them. Ian R. Munro, M.D., a Canadian doctor who emigrated to the U.S., wrote in *Reader's Digest* last September of a young boy in Canada who needed open-heart surgery to free the blood flow to his lungs. He was put on a waiting list. He got a surgery date only after news reports embarrassed health officials. After waiting two months, he died four hours before surgery. This was an extreme case, but waiting is common in the Canadian system, in which the government pays all costs, including set fees for private doctors. A study by the Fraser Institute in 1992 found that 250,000 people are awaiting medical care at any given time. "It is not uncommon for patients to wait months or even years for treatments such as cataract operations, hip replacements, tonsillectomies, gallbladder surgery, hysterectomies, heart operations, and major oral surgery," according to Edmund F. Haislmaier, the Heritage Foundation's health-care expert. Canada has other problems: health costs are rising faster than in the U.S., hospital beds and surgical rooms are dwindling, and doctors are fleeing (8,263 were practicing in the U.S. in 1990).

The Japanese model isn't any better. When Louis Sullivan, M.D., President Bush's secretary of health and human services, visited Japan, he was surprised to find medical care matched that of the U.S.—the U.S. of the 1950s. Japan has universal access and emphasizes primary care at clinics, financed mostly through quasi-public insurance companies. The problem is price controls. "Providers seek to maximize their revenue by seeing more patients," wrote Naoki Ikegami, professor of health at Keio University in Tokyo. "This dilutes the services provided." . . .

In truth, the U.S. has little but painful lessons to learn from the health-care experience of other countries. There's practically nothing to emulate. On the contrary, foreign health officials, Germans especially, now look at the incentives in the American medical system as a way to remedy problems in their health-care systems. Hillary Clinton and health policy wonks should stop apologizing for our system.

They won't. The existence of a few health-care problems, chiefly the lack of proper primary care for several million Americans, allows them to declare a crisis and go on wartime footing. Liberals love this. . . . The program that emerges is sure to dwarf the problem. If enacted, it will make the problem worse. This is a common phenomenon in Washington. Some people never learn.

FOR FURTHER READING

Colin Gordon, *Dead on Arrival: The Politics of Health Care in Twentieth Century America*. Princeton, NJ: Princeton University Press, 2003.

Jacob S. Hacker, *The Road to Nowhere: The Genesis of President Clinton's Plan for Health Security*. Princeton, NJ: Princeton University Press, 1999.

Lawrence J. O'Brien, *Bad Medicine: How the American Medical Establishment Is Ruining Our Healthcare System*. Amherst, NY: Prometheus, 1999.

Theda Skocpol, *Boomerang: Health Care Reform and the Turn Against Government*. New York: W.W. Norton, 1997.

President Bill Clinton Should Be Impeached (1998)

House Judiciary Committee

INTRODUCTION *In November 1996 President Bill Clinton became the first Democrat since Franklin D. Roosevelt to win reelection as president. However, two years later, In December 1998 Bill Clinton made a different sort of history by becoming only the second president in U.S. history to be impeached. The impeachment stemmed from an affair the president had with an intern, Monica Lewinsky. In September 1998 Kenneth Starr, an Independent Counsel who had been appointed in 1994 to investigate allegations of wrongdoing by Clinton, submitted a report to Congress and the public that concluded that Clinton had lied under oath when asked if he and Lewinsky were having a sexual affair, and had obstructed justice by lying about his conduct in public (the questions were related to an ongoing sexual harassment lawsuit against Clinton).*

On December 11 and 12, 1998, the House Judiciary Committee, voting on party lines, approved four articles of impeachment against Clinton. The following viewpoint is taken from the official statement of the committee. The members accuse Clinton of perjury and obstruction of justice, and that he hereby failed to uphold his presidential oath to "preserve, protect, and defend the Constitution of the United States." The full House of Representatives approved two articles of impeachment a week later December 19, declaring that he had committed impeachable offenses and should be removed from office.

What important principle of the U.S. government is the committee attempting to uphold, according to its report? What actions of Clinton does the committee argue warrant his removal from office?

Equal Justice Under Law. That principle so embodies the American constitutional order that we have carved it in stone on the front of our Supreme Court. The carving shines like a beacon from the highest sanctum of the Judicial Branch across to the Capitol, the home of the Legislative Branch, and down Pennsylvania Avenue to

"The Case Against President Clinton," *Congressional Digest*, February 1999, originally from the House Judiciary Committee Report 105-830, *The Impeachment of William Jefferson Clinton, President of the United States*, December 15, 1998.

the White House, the home of the Executive Branch. It illuminates our national life and reminds those other branches that despite the tumbling tides of politics, ours is a government of laws and not of men. It was the inspired vision of our Founders and Framers that the Judicial, Legislative, and Executive Branches would work together to preserve the rule of law.

CONSEQUENCES FOR AVERAGE CITIZENS

But "Equal Justice Under Law" amounts to much more than a stone carving. Although we cannot see or hear it, this living breathing force has real consequences in the lives of average citizens every day. Ultimately, it protects us from the knock on the door in the middle of the night. More commonly, it allows us to claim the assistance of the government when someone has wronged us—even if that person is stronger or wealthier or more popular than we are. In America, unlike other countries, when the average citizen sues the Chief Executive of our Nation, they stand equal before the bar of justice. The Constitution requires the Judicial Branch of our government to apply the law equally to both. That is the living consequence of "Equal Justice Under Law."

The President of the United States must work with the Judicial and Legislative Branches to sustain that force. The temporary trustee of that office, William Jefferson Clinton, worked to defeat it. When he stood before the bar of justice, he acted without authority to award himself the special privileges of lying and obstructing to gain an advantage in a Federal civil rights action in the U.S. District Court for the Eastern District of Arkansas, in a Federal grand jury investigation in the U.S. District Court for the District of Columbia, and in an impeachment inquiry in the U.S. House of Representatives. His resistance brings us to this most unfortunate juncture.

So "Equal Justice Under Law" lies at the heart of this matter. It rests on three essential pillars: an impartial judiciary, an ethical bar, and a sacred oath. If litigants profane the sanctity of the oath, "Equal Justice Under Law" loses its protective force. Against that backdrop, consider the actions of President Clinton.

On May 27, 1997, the nine justices of the Supreme Court of the United States unanimously ruled that Paula Corbin Jones could pursue her Federal civil rights actions against William Jefferson Clinton. On December 11, 1997, U.S. District Judge Susan Webber Wright ordered President Clinton to provide Ms. Jones with answers to certain routine questions relevant to the [sexual harassment] lawsuit. Acting under the authority of these court orders, Ms. Jones exercised her rights—rights that every litigant has under our system of justice. She sought answers from President Clinton to help her prove her case against him—just as President Clinton sought and

received answers from her. President Clinton used numerous means to prevent her from getting truthful answers.

On December 17, 1997, he encouraged a witness [Monica Lewinsky], whose truthful testimony would have helped Ms. Jones, to file a false affidavit in the case and to testify falsely if she were called to testify in the case. On December 23, 1997, he provided, under oath, false written answers to Ms. Jones's questions. On December 28, 1997, he began an effort to get the witness to conceal evidence that would have helped Ms. Jones. Throughout this period, he intensified efforts to provide the witness with help in getting a job to ensure that she carried out his designs.

On January 17, 1998, President Clinton provided, under oath, numerous false answers to Ms. Jones's questions during his deposition. In the days immediately following the deposition, he provided a false and misleading account to another witness, Betty Currie, in hopes that she would substantiate the false testimony he gave in the deposition. These actions denied Ms. Jones her rights as a litigant, subverted the fundamental truth-seeking function of the U.S. District Court for the Eastern District of Arkansas, and violated President Clinton's constitutional oath to "preserve, protect, and defend the Constitution of the United States" and his constitutional duty to "take care that the laws be faithfully executed."

[Clinton's] high crimes and misdemeanors undermine our Constitution.

Beginning shortly after his deposition, President Clinton became aware that a Federal grand jury empaneled by the U.S. District Court for the District of Columbia was investigating his actions before and during his civil deposition. President Clinton made numerous false statements to potential grand jury witnesses in hopes that they would repeat these statements to the grand jury. On August 17, 1998, President Clinton appeared before the grand jury by video and, under oath, provided numerous false answers to the questions asked. These actions impeded the grand jury's investigation, subverted the fundamental truth-seeking function of the U.S. District Court for the District of Columbia, and violated President Clinton's constitutional oath to "preserve, protect, and defend the Constitution of the United States" and his constitutional duty to "take care that the laws be faithfully executed."

President Clinton's actions then led to this inquiry. On October 8, 1998, the U.S. House of Representatives passed H.Res. 581, directing the Committee on the judiciary to begin an inquiry to determine whether President

Clinton should be impeached. As part of that inquiry, the Committee sent written requests for admissions to him. On November 27, 1998, President Clinton provided, under oath, numerous false statements to this committee in response to the requests for admission. These actions impeded the committee's inquiry, subverted the fundamental truth-seeking function of the U.S. House of Representatives in exercising the sole power of impeachment, and violated President Clinton's constitutional oath to "preserve, protect, and defend the Constitution of the United States" and his constitutional duty to "take care that the laws be faithfully executed."

HIGH CRIMES AND MISDEMEANORS

By these actions, President Clinton violated the sanctity of the oath without which "Equal Justice Under Law" cannot survive. Rather than work with the Judicial and Legislative Branches to uphold the rule of law, he directly attacked their fundamental truth-seeking function. He has disgraced himself and the high office he holds. His high crimes and misdemeanors undermine our Constitution. They warrant his impeachment, his removal from office, and his disqualification from holding further office.

Viewpoint 38B

Clinton's Impeachment Is Not Justified (1998)

Jerrold Nadler (b. 1947)

INTRODUCTION *Political and sexual scandals dominated American political discourse in the late 1990s, culminating in President Bill Clinton's impeachment by the House of Representatives in December 1998 for offenses related to covering up a sexual affair. The vote, which sent the case to the Senate for trial, was largely on party lines, with Republicans voting to impeach the Democratic president. The following viewpoint is excerpted from a statement by Jerrold Nadler, a Democratic member of Congress representing New York and a member of the House Judiciary Committee (see viewpoint 38A), who opposed impeachment. He argues in his statement that not enough evidence has been presented by special independent prosecutor Kenneth Starr to support the accusations of perjury and obstruction of justice. He further argues that impeachment itself was designed to remove government officials whose actions seriously threatened the U.S. government and nation. Attempting to hide a sexual affair does not rise to that level, Nadler maintains, and does not justify either a lengthy Senate trial or the removal of Clinton from office. The Senate ultimately acquitted Clinton of the impeachment articles in February 1999, leaving the president to serve out the remainder of his second term.*

What historic importance does Nadler attach to the impeachment debates? What response does he have to the argument that the president cannot be above the law?

For only the second time in our Nation's history, this House meets to consider articles of impeachment against a President of the United States. This is a momentous occasion, and I would hope that, despite the sharp partisan tone which has marked this debate, we can approach it with a sober sense of the historic importance of this matter.

The history of the language is also clear. At the Constitutional Convention, the Committee on Style, which was not authorized to make any substantive changes, dropped the words "against the United States" after the words "high crimes and misdemeanors" because it was understood that only high crimes and misdemeanors against the system of government would be impeachable—that the words "against the United States" were redundant and unnecessary.

History and the precedents alike show that impeachment is not a punishment for crimes but a means to protect the constitutional system, and it was certainly not meant to be a means to punish a President for personal wrongdoing not related to his office. Some of our Republican colleagues have made much of the fact that some of the Democrats on this committee in 1974 voted in favor of an article of impeachment relating to President [Richard] Nixon's alleged perjury on his tax returns, but the plain fact is that a bipartisan vote of that Committee—something we have not yet had in this process on any substantive question—rejected that article.

That's the historical record, and it was largely based on the belief that an impeachable offense must be an abuse of Presidential power, a "great and dangerous offense against the Nation," not perjury on a private matter.

We are told that perjury is as serious an offense as bribery, a per se impeachable offense. But bribery goes to the heart of the President's conduct of his constitutional duties. It converts his loyalties and efforts from promoting the welfare of the Republic to promoting some other interest.

Perjury is a serious crime—and, if provable, should be prosecuted in a court of law. But it may, or may not, involve the President's duties and performance in office. Perjury on a private matter—perjury regarding sex—is not a "great and dangerous offense against the Nation." It is not an abuse of uniquely Presidential power. It does not threaten our form of government. It is not an impeachable offense.

The effect of impeachment is to overturn the popular will of the voters as expressed in a national election. We must not overturn an election and remove a President from office except to defend our very system of government

Excerpted from Jerrold Nadler's arguments during the House of Representatives floor debate of December 19, 1998, concerning impeachment of President Clinton, as reprinted in the *Congressional Digest*, February 1999.

and our constitutional liberties against a dire threat. And we must not do so without an overwhelming consensus of the American people and of their Representatives in Congress on its absolute necessity.

There must never be a narrowly voted impeachment, or an impeachment substantially supported by one of our major political parties and largely opposed by the other. Such an impeachment will lack legitimacy, will produce divisiveness and bitterness in our politics for years to come, and will call into question the legitimacy of our political institutions.

The American people have heard all the allegations against the President and they overwhelmingly oppose impeaching him. The people elected President Clinton. They still support him. We have no right to overturn the considered judgment of the American people....

A WEAK CASE

Mr. [Kenneth] Starr has stated in his referral to Congress that his own "star witness" [Monica Lewinsky] is not credible, except when her uncorroborated testimony conflicts with the President's, and then it proves his perjury.

We have received sanctimonious lectures from the other side about the "rule of law," but the law does not permit perjury to be proved by the uncorroborated testimony of one witness. Nor does the law recognize as corroboration the fact that the witness made the same statement to several different people. You may choose to believe that the President was disingenuous, that he was not particularly helpful to Paula Jones' lawyers when they asked him intentionally vague questions, or that he is a bum, but that does not make him guilty of perjury.

This House is not a grand jury. To impeach the President would subject the country to the trauma of a trial in the Senate. It would paralyze the government for many months while the problems of Social Security, Medicare, a deteriorating world economy, and all our foreign concerns festered without proper attention.

We cannot simply punt the duty to judge the facts to the Senate if we find mere "probable cause" that an impeachable offense may have been committed. To do so would be a derogation of our constitutional duty. The proponents of impeachment have provided no direct evidence of impeachable offenses. They rely solely on the findings of an "independent" counsel [Starr] who has repeatedly mischaracterized evidence, failed to include exculpatory evidence, and consistently misstated the law.

We must not be a rubber stamp for Kenneth Starr. We have been entrusted with this grave and dangerous duty by the American people, by the Constitution, and by history. We must exercise that duty responsibly.

At a bare minimum, that means the President's accusers must go beyond hearsay and innuendo, and beyond demands that the President prove his innocence of vague and changing charges. They must provide clear and convincing evidence of specific impeachable conduct. This they have failed to do.

If you believe the President's admission to the grand jury and to the Nation of an inappropriate sexual relationship with Ms. Lewinsky, and his apologies to the Nation, were not abject enough, that is not a reason for impeachment. Contrition is a remedy for sin, and is certainly appropriate here. But while insufficiency of contrition may leave the soul still scarred, unexpiated sin proves no crimes and justifies no impeachment.

IS THE PRESIDENT ABOVE THE LAW?

Some say that if we do not impeach the President, we treat him as if he is above the law.

The allegations, even if proven, do not rise to the level of impeachable offenses.

Is the President above the law? Certainly not. He is subject to the criminal law—to indictment and prosecution when he leaves office—like any other citizen, whether or not he is impeached. And if the Republican leadership allows a vote, he would likely be the third President in U.S. history, and the first since 1848, to be censured by the Congress.

But impeachment is intended as a remedy to protect the Nation, not as a punishment for a President.

The case is not there. There is far from sufficient evidence to support the allegations, and the allegations, even if proven, do not rise to the level of impeachable offenses. We should not dignify these articles of impeachment by sending them to the Senate. To do so would be an affront to the Constitution and would consign this House to the condemnation of history for generations to come.

FOR FURTHER READING

Bill Clinton, *My Life*. New York: Knopf, 2004.

Joe Conason and Gene Lyons, *The Hunting of the President: The Ten-Year Campaign to Destroy Bill and Hillary Clinton*. New York: St. Martin's, 2000.

Michael Isokoff, *Uncovering Clinton: A Reporter's Story*. New York: Crown, 1999.

Nicol C. Rae, *Impeaching Clinton: Partisan Strife on Capital Hill*. Lawrence: University Press of Kansas, 2004.

Mark Rozell and Clyde Wilcox, eds., *The Clinton Scandal and the Future of American Government*. Washington, DC: Georgetown University Press, 2000.

Gay Marriage Must Be Banned (2003)

First Things

INTRODUCTION *In the ongoing debates over what should be done to protect the civil rights and social equality of previously marginalized groups in America such as African Americans and women, the rights of gays and lesbians have taken center stage. One of the civil rights many gay activists have sought is the right to marry—a right granted to same-sex couples in the neighboring country of Canada in 2003. The prospect that state judges or legislatures might legalize gay marriage has in turn sparked political resistance from conservative politicians and religious organizations, many of whom have called for a constitutional amendment to explicitly ban same-sex marriage. The following viewpoint is taken from an editorial published in the conservative religious publication* First Things*. The writers argue that most Americans oppose gay marriage and that their values should not be usurped by those of radical gay activists and unelected judges.*

How do the authors characterize the homosexual movement? What distinction do they make between "gay" and "homosexual"? What do the authors mean when they assert the Constitution will be amended "one way or another"?

Marriage in the United States shall consist only of the union of a man and a woman. Neither this Constitution or the constitution of any state, nor state or federal law, shall be construed to require that marital status or the legal incidents thereof be conferred on unmarried couples or groups.

That is the proposed amendment to the Constitution that is now gathering powerful support in the Congress and in several states. Prudent citizens are reluctant to amend the Constitution unless persuaded that it is necessary. What would become the twenty-eighth amendment is necessary because the courts are moving toward a de facto amendment of the Constitution that mandates the radical redefinition of marriage and family. The question before us is how the Constitution will be amended: by judicial fiat or by "We the People of the United States" employing the means established by the Constitution. Entailed in that question is whether change will serve to advance a social revolution unsought and unwanted by the American people or will serve to secure an institution essential to the well-being of our society. The Constitution will be amended, either by constitutional means or by activist judges practicing what is aptly described as the judicial usurpation of politics. . . .

First Things, "The Marriage Amendment," October 2003, vol. 136, pp. 23–26.

THE HOMOSEXUAL MOVEMENT

We have been brought to the present circumstance by the astonishing success of the homosexual movement over the past three decades. Traditionally, sodomy was viewed as an act, and was condemned as unnatural and deviant. A hundred years ago, homosexuality was viewed as a condition afflicting people who are prone to engaging in such unnatural and deviant acts. Today [2003] "gay" signifies not so much an act or condition as the identity of people who say that they most essentially are what they do and want to do sexually. The rhetorical and conceptual movement has been from act to condition to identity, bringing us to the demand for same-sex marriage. About two percent of the combined teenage and adult male population, and considerably less of the female, are said to be a minority deprived of their rights. In particular, they claim to be discriminated against in that they are "excluded" from the institution of marriage. They are not asking for tolerance of their private sexual practices and of the gay subculture constituted by such practices. They are demanding, rather, public acceptance and approval. That is the whole point of focusing on the status of marriage, which is a quintessentially public institution. . . .

REDEFINING MARRIAGE

There are a few gays who express admiration for traditional marriage and say they simply want to be included in its benefits. They claim they are now excluded. And they are right. They are not excluded by others; they are excluded by their identity as gays. To be homosexual is a condition; to be gay is a decision. Some say no other decision is available to them, but that is not true. Sexual temptations, like other temptations, can be resisted. In many cases, sexual orientation can be changed. Human frailties notwithstanding, chastity is a possibility for all. Yet we are faced with a not-insignificant number of people who say that gay is who they are, whether by choice or by fate, and that they are unfairly excluded from the companionship, stability, and other goods of marriage. Were the Supreme Court to do their bidding tomorrow, however, they would still be excluded from marriage. Throughout history and in all major cultures, marriage is a union between a man and a woman. That is what marriage is. A man and a man or a woman and a woman may have an intense but chaste friendship, including shared living arrangements. It is not the business of the state to certify or regulate friendships. As for those who choose a sexual relationship, we may well understand their yearning for public approval of their choice. But same-sex marriage is not marriage. It is at most a simulacrum of marriage, a poignant attempt to create a semblance of some features of marriage, a pretending to be something like the relationship between husband and wife that is marriage. The reality is not changed if the state collaborates in the pretense and calls it marriage. . . .

■

Concern about the legal establishment and normalization of sexual deviance is fully warranted.

■

PROTECTING THE CHILDREN

Marriage and family law is, above all, about children. Same-sex couples cannot from their sexual acts procreate children. Gay activists contend that that only makes their circumstance identical with that of a marriage in which the woman is beyond the child-bearing years. But that, too, is not true. A marriage between an older man and woman does not contradict the definition of marriage as a union between a man and a woman. In addition, such a marriage aims at preventing the man from having children by other women, which is, obviously, not a consideration in same-sex relations. The activists respond that gays can adopt children, which is legal in some jurisdictions. Here again the concern for children becomes paramount. After decades of experiments with single-parent families, "open marriages," and easy divorce, the evidence is in and there is today near-unanimous agreement on what should always have been obvious: judged by every index of well-being, there is no more important factor in the lives of children than having a mother and father in the home. Lesbians and gays in same-sex unions cannot be mothers and fathers, except in the poignant simulacrum of pretended sex roles. . . .

Many oppose same-sex unions and the consequent revolution in marriage and family law because they believe homosexuality is a disorder and homosexual acts are morally wrong. That is not a private prejudice. It is not, as the Supreme Court has claimed, an "irrational animus." It is a considered and very public moral judgment grounded in clear reason and historical experience, and supported by the authority of the biblical tradition. Nobody should apologize for publicly advocating a position informed by the foundational moral truths of Western Civilization. Of course, those who do so will be accused of "homophobia." Homophobia is a term of recent coinage intended to serve as a conversation stopper. Its power to intimidate is rapidly diminishing. Support for the civilizational tradition in this regard is not a phobia; it is not an irrational fear. Concern about the legal establishment and normalization of sexual deviance is fully warranted. What is called homophobia is more accurately understood as a positive judgment regarding the common good and, most particularly, the well-being of children. It should not be, but it still is, necessary to add that hatred of gays or denial of their human or civil rights is evil and must be unequivocally condemned. Moreover, it must be candidly acknowledged that gay demands and agitations today are not unrelated to patterns of sexual hedonism in the general culture.

The debate is now underway as to whether civil rights include the right of gays to have their relationships legally designated as marriage. There are many factors in the debate not addressed here. It is claimed, for instance, that a gay right to marriage is on a moral and legal continuum with extending rights to blacks and women. That convenient but simplistic comparison does not bear close examination. Discrimination against blacks and women was recognized, albeit too slowly, as contradicting the foundational values and institutions of our society. Those values were vindicated and those institutions strengthened by including people who had been unjustly excluded. The just demand of blacks and women was for full participation in the opportunities and responsibilities of the social order. The demand for gay marriage, by way of sharpest contrast, is premised upon the recognition that gays cannot participate in that order's most basic institution, and it is therefore aimed not at their inclusion but at the institution's deconstruction by redefinition. The humpty-dumpty logic is that, if you cannot do something you want to do, you redefine that something, turning it into something you can do. When such word games are translated into law, the public meaning of the something that most people can and want to do is radically changed. The public meaning of marriage and family—in law, and more gradually, in social customs and expectations—is changed for everybody. Gay activists can try but we do not think they will succeed in persuading most Americans that their marriages and families are the same thing that gays can and want to do. . . .

Without the marriage amendment, the debate that is now underway may well be short-circuited by the courts. One way or another, the Constitution will be amended. If it is amended by the judiciary, as the Supreme Court did in its 1973 invention of an unlimited abortion license, we will almost certainly enter upon a severe intensification of what is rightfully called the culture war. Lincoln forcefully stated in his first inaugural address that the American people are not prepared to surrender their right to self-government to even the most eminent tribunal. Whether that is still true of the American people is once again being put to the test.

Just government is derived from the consent of the governed, says the Declaration of Independence. In this democracy, consent means popular deliberation, debate, and decision through the representative polity established by the Constitution. . . .

It appears that the Supreme Court has quite forgotten the purpose and source of authority set forth by the Constitution. That purpose and source of authority is clearly stated in the Preamble: "We the people of the United States, in order to form a more perfect union, establish justice, insure domestic tranquility, provide for the common defense, promote the general welfare, and secure the blessings of liberty to ourselves and our posterity, do ordain and establish this Constitution for the United States of America."

A GREAT DEBATE

We are now engaged in a great debate about whether same-sex marriage and the criminalizing of opposition to homosexuality and the gay agenda will serve to establish justice, ensure domestic tranquility, and promote the general welfare.... Of crucial importance is the securing of liberty understood as what the Founders called the "ordered liberty" of a blessing bestowed, as distinct from the unbridled license of expressive individualism and the quest for the satisfaction of insatiable desire.

The marriage amendment might finally fail, but its passage by Congress and submission to the states for ratification can ensure that "We the People" will not be excluded from the deliberation and decisions that will determine the future of marriage and family, the most necessary of institutions in the right ordering of this or any society.

Viewpoint 39B

Gay Marriage Should Not Be Banned (2006)

Jamie Raskin (b. 1962)

INTRODUCTION *In 2006 a Maryland judge ruled that a state law defining marriage between one man and one woman violated the state constitution. The state legislature of Maryland responded by debating whether to amend that constitution to explicitly ban same-sex marriage. The state debate in some respects replicated an ongoing national debate over whether same-sex couples had the right under the federal constitution to marry—and whether the national constitution should be amended to address the gay marriage issue.*

The following viewpoint is taken from testimony before the Maryland State Senate by Jamie Raskin, a professor of constitutional law at American University's Washington College of Law. Raskin, who was then campaigning for election to the Maryland State Senate, strongly criticizes the proposed constitutional amendment banning gay marriage. He argues that it violates the separation of church and state, deprives a vulnerable minority of the fundamental right to marry, and is based on outmoded views on sexuality. The amendment in question failed to pass.

What response does Haskin make to those who argue that gay marriage violates their religious beliefs? What constitutional principles can be used to invalidate same-sex marriage bans, according to Haskin?

Jamie Raskin, testimony before the Maryland State Senate Judicial Proceedings Committee, March 1, 2006.

Tom Paine taught us that a Constitution is not an act of government, but of "the people *constituting* a government."

So this is no ordinary legislative proposal before you but an effort to redefine our social contract [by amending the State Constitution to ban gay marriage]. You have been offered the chance to become the first Legislature in Maryland history to subtract and exclude liberty and rights from our Constitution.

COMPARISON TO PROHIBITION

It reminds me of the 18th Amendment, Prohibition, which we adopted at the national level in 1919. The outburst of self-righteous moralism which produced this amendment eventually subsided and Prohibition was repealed after fourteen bloody and disastrous years.

However, as misguided and doomed as Prohibition was, it at least had a public policy rationale, which was to get rid of the social ills associated with drinking, and it applied to everyone equally.

This proposed Amendment has no public policy rationale other than prejudice and it falls exclusively on a vulnerable minority.

As far as I can tell, the argument for writing marriage discrimination into our Constitution rests on essentially theological premises: God forbids gay marriage; my church opposes it; it violates natural law; and so on. But these arguments reflect a basic confusion about the American Constitution and our framework of liberty.

SEPARATION OF CHURCH AND STATE

Under our First Amendment, the State may never dictate to a church who it must marry. If the government wants to force a church to marry inter-faith couples or interracial couples or a couple of people who had been divorced or a gay couple, but the church does not want to marry these people for its own theological reasons, the government loses and the church wins. Under the Free Exercise Clause, a church may marry only those people it wants to marry and reject the rest even for reasons that other people may consider narrow-minded, stupid or prejudiced or indeed for no reason at all.

But, at the same time, individual churches or even coalitions of churches may never dictate to the State who it may marry. Even if a group of large churches decides that it is irreligious or sacrilegious or just plain evil for people to marry outside of their faiths or across racial lines and the churches mobilize their members to lobby the state legislature to unanimously pass a law against miscegenation or inter-faith marriage, these laws will be struck down. They violate Due Process, Equal Protection and the Establishment Clause.

In 1967 the Supreme Court in *Loving v. Virginia* struck down Virginia's law against whites marrying African-Americans, Asian-Americans and Hispanics despite the fact that it was overwhelmingly popular and its champions invoked Biblical authority for its legitimacy. The Court found that Equal Protection and the Due Process right to marry are supreme in America; they control and displace discriminatory state marriage laws, even ones based on religious ideas that majorities passionately endorse.

Thus, when I hear testimony from my fellow Marylanders about how ending statewide marriage discrimination would collide with their church beliefs, my response is simple and, I hope, reassuring: Your church will never have to perform a marriage ceremony of any gay couple or indeed any couple of any kind that it disapproves of. If the state tries to force your church to marry anyone, I will gladly represent your church pro bono to stop the state from imposing its orthodoxy on you and interfering with your freedom to discriminate as a religion.

But the irony here is that the State today is stopping many churches and temples from marrying gay couples that the churches want to marry. That is, the State today is violating the rights of many churches—including Unitarian, Episcopal, Presbeterian and Jewish congregations, among many others—who seek to perform lawful weddings for their parishioners but may not simply because other groups of citizens think it would be wrong for them to do it.

Because America is for all its citizens regardless of religion and because so many churches have so many different belief systems, we are governed here not by religious law but by secular law. The rules of civil marriage—the license that the State grants you to marry—must be determined with respect to the federal and state Constitutions, not particular religious claims, no matter how fervently held.

CONSTITUTIONAL PRINCIPLES

And the constitutional principles are clear. First, Due Process protects the fundamental right of all consenting adults to marry. This is a right so sweeping that it covers even people who marry multiple times like Elizabeth Taylor, people who get married on television game shows like *Who Wants to Marry A Millionaire*, deadbeat dads who seek to remarry . . . , and convicted prisoners, . . . including murderers on death row, many of whom have married people they have met by mail. The fundamental right to marry actually includes even gay and lesbian citizens, who have been able to marry for centuries so long as they would consent to marry people they could never have a successful marriage with—that is, straight people of the opposite sex. And who knows how many thousands

of unhappy marriages of this kind there have been? In any event, the Supreme Court has said that the right to marry is fundamental for all citizens.

Second, Equal Protection gives people the right to be married without discrimination based on race, ethnicity, nationality and other arbitrary factors, such as animosity towards a minority group.

Third, in Maryland we have an Equal Rights Amendment which the Circuit Court has interpreted to forbid marriage discrimination. The theory essentially is that a state cannot allow a lesbian to marry a man but forbid her to marry a woman. This policy is not only irrational and cruel but unconstitutional.

Now, a court could choose—and courts have chosen—to invalidate marriage discrimination on the basis of any and all of these constitutional principles. We can argue about the particular doctrinal basis for doing it, but marriage discrimination has no rational basis; it is rooted in fear of the unknown, animus, and anxiety about other things, like the relentless sexual images purveyed towards our children by the commercial mass media, very high heterosexual divorce rates and the difficulties that people have keeping families together in times of great economic stress and geographic dislocation.

The decision to rope off marriage . . . from certain groups of people based on their sexual orientation can be described as nothing more than cruel and irrational discrimination.

AN OBSOLETE VIEW OF SEXUALITY

But it seems to me that the advocates of this amendment want to cement not only a particular religious doctrine or moral judgment into our Constitution but an obsolete view of human sexuality. The supposition seems to be that gay and lesbian Americans, unlike the rest of us, have chosen their sexuality and have chosen wrong. But all of the gathering scientific evidence suggests very strongly that our sexual orientation has a hereditary and biological basis. Think of the gay people you know in your families or friends; now think of the straight people. Do you really think they have freely chosen their sexual orientation?

Doctors don't even know how to keep grown heterosexual men, like our State Comptroller, from ogling young women in public. Do you really think they can turn millions of gay men and women into straight people?

When all of the scientific and anecdotal evidence we have suggests that our sexual orientation is simply part of us, like our hair color, the decision to rope off marriage—an institution that carries hundreds and hundreds of legal and governmental benefits and privileges—from certain groups of people based on their sexual orientation can be described as nothing more than cruel and irrational discrimination.

Our Constitution should not be an historical record of our prejudices and follies but, as much as possible, a covenant reflecting our devotion to expanding liberty and equality for all of our citizens.

FOR FURTHER READING

Robert M. Baird and Stuart Rosenbaum, eds., *Same-Sex Marriage: The Moral and Legal Debate*. Amherst, NY: Prometheus, 2004.

Jennefer M. Lehmann, ed., *The Gay & Lesbian Marriage & Family Reader*. Lincoln: University of Nebraska Press, 2001.

David Moats, *Civil Wars: A Battle for Gay Marriage*. Orlando, FL: Harcourt, 2004.

Kathy Pories, ed., *The M Word: Writers on Same-Sex Marriage*. Chapel Hill, NC: Algonquin Books, 2004.

Mark Strasser, *On Same-Sex Marriage, Civil Unions, and the Rule of Law: Constitutional Interpretation at the Crossroads*. Westport, CT: Praeger, 2002.

NATIONAL SECURITY, TERRORISM, AND IRAQ

Viewpoint 40A

America Must Use Military Force Against Iraq to Liberate Kuwait (1991)

George H.W. Bush (b. 1924)

INTRODUCTION *George H.W. Bush served one term as U.S. president from 1989 to 1992, having previously served two terms as Ronald Reagan's vice president. Arguably his most momentous foreign policy decision was his response to Iraq's invasion of the small oil-rich kingdom of Kuwait in August 1990. Bush seized the opportunity to create a "new world order" in a Post–Cold War world in which aggressive military actions such as Iraq's would be met with collective military action by the world's nations. He deployed a half million U.S. troops to the Middle East, assembled an international United Nations to demand the immediate withdrawal of Iraqi troops, instituted economic sanctions against Iraq, and got Congressional authorization to use military force. On January 16, one day after a UN-imposed deadline for Iraqi withdrawal, the United States began a massive aerial bombing campaign against Iraqi targets in Iraq and Kuwait. The following viewpoint is excerpted from President Bush's address to*

the nation that same day announcing the commencement of military action, in which he provides Americans his reasons for his decision.

Why could the United States not wait to see whether economic sanctions were working, according to Bush? What does he describe as America's goals in this military action? What similarities and/or differences do you see between the justifications for this war and for the Iraq War begun in 2003?

Just 2 hours ago, allied air forces began an attack on military targets in Iraq and Kuwait. These attacks continue as I speak. Ground forces are not engaged.

This conflict started August 2d when the dictator of Iraq invaded a small and helpless neighbor. Kuwait—a member of the Arab League and a member of the United Nations—was crushed; its people, brutalized. Five months ago, Saddam Hussein started this cruel war against Kuwait. Tonight, the battle has been joined.

This military action, taken in accord with United Nations resolutions and with the consent of the United States Congress, follows months of constant and virtually endless diplomatic activity on the part of the United Nations, the United States, and many, many other countries. Arab leaders sought what became known as an Arab solution, only to conclude that Saddam Hussein was unwilling to leave Kuwait. Others traveled to Baghdad [Iraq] in a variety of efforts to restore peace and justice. Our Secretary of State, James Baker, held an historic meeting in Geneva, only to be totally rebuffed. This past weekend, in a last-ditch effort, the Secretary-General of the United Nations went to the Middle East with peace in his heart—his second such mission. And he came back from Baghdad with no progress at all in getting Saddam Hussein to withdraw from Kuwait.

Now the 28 countries with forces in the Gulf area have exhausted all reasonable efforts to reach a peaceful resolution—have no choice but to drive Saddam from Kuwait by force. We will not fail. . . .

Our objectives are clear: Saddam Hussein's forces will leave Kuwait. The legitimate government of Kuwait will be restored to its rightful place, and Kuwait will once again be free. Iraq will eventually comply with all relevant United Nations resolutions, and then, when peace is restored, it is our hope that Iraq will live as a peaceful and cooperative member of the family of nations, thus enhancing the security and stability of the Gulf.

Some may ask: Why act now? Why not wait? The answer is clear: The world could wait no longer. Sanctions, though having some effect, showed no signs of accomplishing their objective. Sanctions were tried for well

George H.W. Bush's January 16, 1991, address to the nation announcing military action in the Persian Gulf. From *Public Papers of the President: George Bush*, January 16, 1991: 42–45.

over 5 months, and we and our allies concluded that sanctions alone would not force Saddam from Kuwait.

While the world waited, Saddam Hussein systematically raped, pillaged, and plundered a tiny nation, no threat to his own. He subjected the people of Kuwait to unspeakable atrocities—and among those maimed and murdered, innocent children.

While the world waited, Saddam sought to add to the chemical weapons arsenal he now possesses, an infinitely more dangerous weapon of mass destruction—a nuclear weapon. And while the world waited, while the world talked peace and withdrawal, Saddam Hussein dug in and moved massive forces into Kuwait.

While the world waited, while Saddam stalled, more damage was being done to the fragile economies of the Third World, emerging democracies of Eastern Europe, to the entire world, including to our own economy.

The United States, together with the United Nations, exhausted every means at our disposal to bring this crisis to a peaceful end. However, Saddam clearly felt that by stalling and threatening and defying the United Nations, he could weaken the forces arrayed against him.

While the world waited, Saddam Hussein met every overture of peace with open contempt. While the world prayed for peace, Saddam prepared for war.

I had hoped that when the United States Congress, in historic debate, took its resolute action, Saddam would realize he could not prevail and would move out of Kuwait in accord with the United Nations resolutions. He did not do that. Instead, he remained intransigent, certain that time was on his side.

We have before us the opportunity to forge . . . a new world order, a world where the rule of law, not the law of the jungle, governs the conduct of nations.

Saddam was warned over and over again to comply with the will of the United Nations: Leave Kuwait, or be driven out. Saddam has arrogantly rejected all warnings. Instead, he tried to make this a dispute between Iraq and the United States of America.

Well, he failed. Tonight, 28 nations—countries from 5 continents, Europe and Asia, Africa, and the Arab League—have forces in the Gulf area standing shoulder to shoulder against Saddam Hussein. These countries had hoped the use of force could be avoided. Regrettably, we now believe that only force will make him leave. . . .

AMERICA'S GOALS

This is an historic moment. We have in this past year made great progress in ending the long era of conflict and Cold War. We have before us the opportunity to forge for ourselves and for future generations a new world order, a world where the rule of law, not the law of the jungle, governs the conduct of nations.

When we are successful, and we will be, we have a real chance at this new world order, an order in which a credible United Nations can use its peacekeeping role to fulfill the promise and vision of the U.N.'s founders. We have no argument with the people of Iraq. Indeed, for the innocents caught in this conflict, I pray for their safety.

Our goal is not the conquest of Iraq. It is the liberation of Kuwait. It is my hope that somehow the Iraqi people can, even now, convince their dictator that he must lay down his arms, leave Kuwait, and let Iraq itself rejoin the family of peace-loving nations.

Thomas Paine wrote many years ago: "These are the times that try men's souls." Those well-known words are so very true today. But even as planes of the multinational forces attack Iraq, I prefer to think of peace, not war. I am convinced not only that we will prevail, but that out of the horror of combat will come the recognition that no nation can stand against a world united. No nation will be permitted to brutally assault its neighbor.

Viewpoint 40B
War Against Iraq Is Unnecessary (1991)
Arthur Schlesinger Jr. (b. 1917)

INTRODUCTION *Arthur Schlesinger Jr. is a prominent historian and liberal intellectual. His books include* A Thousand Days, *based on his experiences as Special Assistant to President John F. Kennedy,* Cycles of American History *and* War and the American Presidency. *The following viewpoint is taken from an article published in January 1991 when the United States was confronting Iraq over that country's invasion of neighboring Kuwait. President George H.W. Bush had created an international coalition to exert economic sanctions and diplomatic pressures on Iraqi leader Saddam Hussein. Schlesinger argues that Hussein must be dealt with, but urges caution in resorting to military action, arguing that it is not necessary to secure the vital interests of the United States and may bring about harmful consequences to the region. War in Iraq may also detract attention from pressing problems in Europe and within the United States itself.*

Despite the concerns of Schlesinger and others, the United States since 1991 has twice made the decision to invade Iraq. President George H.W. Bush used military force to liberate Kuwait in 1991, but left Hussein in place as Iraqi leader. In 2003 his son, President George W. Bush, ordered U.S. forces into Iraq in a successful effort to oust Hussein.

What distinction does Schlesinger make between vital and peripheral interests? What lessons does Schlesinger discern from the actions and words of previous presidents? Do you think his arguments apply to the debate over George W. Bush's decision to go to war in Iraq in 2003?

President [George H.W.] Bush's gamble in the Gulf may yet pay off. Let us pray that it does—that the combination of international economic sanctions, political pressure, and military buildup will force Saddam Hussein to repent and retreat. Let us pray that the tough talk from Washington is designed primarily as psychological warfare—and that it will work.

But tough talk creates its own momentum and may seize control of policy. If the gamble fails, the president will be hard put to avoid war. Is this a war Americans really want to fight? Senator Robert Dole said the other day that Americans are not yet committed to this war, and he is surely right. And is it a war Americans are wrong in not wanting to fight?

Among our stated objectives are the defense of Saudi Arabia, the liberation of Kuwait and restoration of the royal family, and the establishment, in the president's phrase, of a "stable and secure Gulf." Presumably these generous-hearted goals should win the cooperation, respect, and gratitude of the locals. Indications are, to the contrary, that our involvement is increasing Arab contempt for the U.S.

WHITE SLAVES FROM AMERICA

In *The Wall Street Journal* a few days ago Geraldine Brooks and Tony Horwitz described the reluctance of the Arabs to fight in their own defense. The Gulf states have a population almost as large as Iraq's but no serious armies and limited inclination to raise them. Why should they? The *Journal* quotes a senior Gulf official: "You think I want to send my teen-aged son to die for Kuwait?" He chuckles and adds, "We have our white slaves from America to do that."

At the recent meeting of the Gulf Cooperation Council, the Arab states congratulated themselves on their verbal condemnation of Iraqi aggression but spoke not one word of thanks to the American troops who had crossed half the world to fight for them. A Yemeni diplomat explained this curious omission to Judith Miller of *The New York Times*: "A lot of the Gulf rulers simply do not feel that they have to thank the people they've hired to do their fighting for them."

Arthur Schlesinger, Jr., "White Slaves in the Persian Gulf," *Wall Street Journal,* January 7, 1991.

James LeMoyne reported in *The New York Times* last October [1990] in a dispatch from Saudi Arabia, "There is no mass mobilization for war in the markets and streets. The scenes of cheerful American families saying goodbye to their sons and daughters are being repeated in few Saudi homes." Mr. LeMoyne continued, "Some Saudis' attitude toward the American troops verges on treating them as a sort of contracted superpower enforcer...." He quoted a Saudi teacher: "The American soldiers are a new kind of foreign worker here. We have Pakistanis driving taxis and now we have Americans defending us."

I know that the object of foreign policy is not to win gratitude. It is to produce real effects in the real world. It is conceivable that we should simply swallow the Arab insults and soldier on as their "white slaves" because vital interests of our own are involved. But, as Mr. Dole implied, the case that U.S. vital interests are at stake has simply not been made to the satisfaction of Congress and the American people.

Of course we have interests in the Gulf. But it is essential to distinguish between peripheral interests and vital interests. Vital interests exist when our national security is truly at risk. Vital interests are those you kill and die for. I write as one who has no problem about the use of force to defend our vital interests and who had no doubt that vital interests were involved in preventing the domination of Europe by [Adolf] Hitler and later by [Joseph] Stalin.

PRETEXTS FOR WAR

In defining our vital interests in the Gulf, the administration's trumpet gives an awfully uncertain sound. It has offered a rolling series of peripheral justifications—oil, jobs, regional stability, the menace of a nuclear Iraq, the creation of a new world order. These pretexts for war grow increasingly thin.

If oil is the issue, nothing will more certainly increase oil prices than war, with long-term interruption of supply and widespread destruction of oil fields. Every whisper of peace has brought oil prices down. And the idea of spending American lives in order to save American jobs is despicable—quite unworthy of our intelligent secretary of state.

As for the stabilization of the Middle East, this is a goal that has never been attained for long in history. Stability is not a likely prospect for a region characterized from time immemorial by artificial frontiers, tribal antagonism, religious fanaticisms and desperate inequalities. I doubt that the U.S. has the capacity or the desire to replace the Ottoman empire, and our efforts thus far have won us not the respect of the Arab rulers but their contempt.

What about nuclear weapons? The preventive-war argument is no more valid against Iraq than it was when nuts proposed it against the Soviet Union during the Cold War. In any case, Secretary of State [James] Baker has in effect offered a no-invasion pledge if Iraq withdraws from Kuwait—a pledge that would leave Saddam Hussein in power and his nuclear facilities intact.

As for the new world order, the United Nations will be far stronger if it succeeds through resolute application of economic sanctions than if it only provides a multilateral façade for a unilateral U.S. war. Nor would we strengthen the U.N. by wreaking mass destruction that will appall the world and discredit collective security for years to come.

No one likes the loathsome Saddam Hussein. Other countries would rejoice in his overthrow—and are fully prepared to fight to the last American to bring it about. But, since the threat he poses to the U.S. is far less than the threat to the Gulf states, why are we Americans the fall guys, expected to do ninety percent of the fighting and to take ninety percent of the casualties? Only Britain, loyal as usual, has made any serious military contribution to the impending war—10,000 more troops than Egypt. If we go to war, let not the posse fade away, as befell the unfortunate marshal in *High Noon....*

No one ever supposed that an economic embargo would bring Iraq to its knees in a short five months. Why not give sanctions time to work? The Central Intelligence Agency already reports shortages in Iraq's military spare parts. If we must fight, why not fight a weaker rather than a stronger Iraq? What is the big rush? There is a phrase of President [Dwight] Eisenhower's that comes to mind: "the courage of patience."

I also recall words of President [John F.] Kennedy that seem relevant during these dark days: "Don't push your opponent against a locked door." What is so terribly wrong with a negotiated settlement? Iraq must absolutely withdraw from Kuwait, but the grievances that explain, though not excuse, the invasion might well be adjudicated. As for the nuclear threat, that can be taken care of by a combination of arms embargo, international inspection throughout the Middle East and great-power deterrence. Such measures would do far more than war to strengthen collective security and build a new world order.

WAR'S NEGATIVE CONSEQUENCES

One has the abiding fear that the administration has not thought out the consequences of war. Fighting Iraq will not be like fighting Grenada or Panama. The war will most likely be bloody and protracted. Victory might well entangle us in Middle Eastern chaos for years—all for interests that, so far as the U.S. is concerned, are at best peripheral.

> *War against Iraq will be the most unnecessary war in American history.*

Worst of all, the Iraq sideshow is enfeebling us in areas where vital interests are truly at stake. While we concentrate energies and resources in the Middle East, Eastern Europe is in travail and the Soviet Union is falling apart. We cannot single-handedly rescue democracy in the ex-Communist states, but at least we ought to be thinking hard about ways we could help on the margin. Europe is far more essential to our national security than the Middle East.

And we confront urgent problems here at home—deepening recession, decaying infrastructure, deteriorating race relations, a shaky banking system, crime-ridden cities on the edge of bankruptcy, states in financial crisis, increasing public and private debt, low productivity, diminishing competitiveness in world markets. The crisis of our national community demands major attention and resources too. While we fiddle away in the Middle East, the American economy will continue to decline, and Japan and Germany will seize the world's commanding economic heights.

War against Iraq will be the most unnecessary war in American history, and it well may cause the gravest damage to the vital interests of the republic.

FOR FURTHER READING

Leslie H. Brune, *America and the Iraqi Crisis, 1990–1992; Origins and Aftermath.* Claremont, CA: Regina, 1993.

Majid Khadduri, *War in the Gulf, 1990–1991.* New York: Oxford University Press, 1997.

Micah L. Sifry and Christopher Cerf, eds., *The Gulf War Reader.* New York: Times Books, 1991.

Martin Yant, *Desert Mirage: The True Story of the Gulf War.* Buffalo, NY: Prometheus, 1991.

Steven A. Yetiv, *Explaining Foreign Policy; U.S. Decision-Making and the Persian Gulf War.* Baltimore: Johns Hopkins University Press, 2004.

Viewpoint 41A

America Must Wage War Against Terrorists (2001)
George W. Bush (b. 1946)

INTRODUCTION *The United States entered a new era in its history, many believe, when on September 11, 2001, it found itself under attack from terrorists. Four hijacked planes crashed into the World Trade Center skyscrapers in New York, the Pentagon in Washington, D.C., and the Pennsylvania countryside. Three days later, Congress authorized the president to use military force to find and retaliate against those responsible for the attack.*

The president, George W. Bush, had just been elected in 2000—the second time in American history that a son of an American president reached that office himself (Bush's father was the former president George H.W. Bush). The following viewpoint is excerpted from a nationally televised address by Bush before Congress on September 20, 2001, in which he declared the United States to be in a "war on terror" against "every terrorist group of global reach." Bush called for Americans and for other nations to support the campaign against terrorism and issued an ultimatum against Afghanistan which was then harboring al Qaeda, the terrorist group believed responsible for the attacks. A few weeks later, America launched a military campaign that toppled the Taliban regime in Afghanistan and captured many al Qaeda leaders.

What is America's war on terror directed against, according to Bush? What predictions does he make about America's response to the September 11 attacks?

On September the 11th, enemies of freedom committed an act of war against our country. Americans have known wars—but for the past 136 years, they have been wars on foreign soil, except for one Sunday in 1941. Americans have known the casualties of war—but not at the center of a great city on a peaceful morning. Americans have known surprise attacks—but never before on thousands of civilians. All of this was brought upon us in a single day—and night fell on a different world, a world where freedom itself is under attack.

Americans have many questions tonight. Americans are asking: Who attacked our country? The evidence we have gathered all points to a collection of loosely affiliated terrorist organizations known as al Qaeda. They are the same murderers indicted for bombing American embassies in Tanzania and Kenya, and responsible for bombing the USS Cole.

Al Qaeda is to terror what the mafia is to crime. But its goal is not making money; its goal is remaking the world—and imposing its radical beliefs on people everywhere.

The terrorists practice a fringe form of Islamic extremism that has been rejected by Muslim scholars and the vast majority of Muslim clerics—a fringe movement that perverts the peaceful teachings of Islam. The terrorists' directive commands them to kill Christians and Jews, to kill all Americans, and make no distinction among military and civilians, including women and children.

This group and its leader—a person named Osama bin Laden—are linked to many other organizations in

Excerpted from George W. Bush's "Address to a Joint Session of Congress and the American People," September 20, 2001.

different countries, including the Egyptian Islamic Jihad and the Islamic Movement of Uzbekistan. There are thousands of these terrorists in more than 60 countries. They are recruited from their own nations and neighborhoods and brought to camps in places like Afghanistan, where they are trained in the tactics of terror. They are sent back to their homes or sent to hide in countries around the world to plot evil and destruction.

AL QAEDA AND AFGHANISTAN

The leadership of al Qaeda has great influence in Afghanistan and supports the Taliban regime in controlling most of that country. In Afghanistan, we see al Qaeda's vision for the world.

Afghanistan's people have been brutalized—many are starving and many have fled. Women are not allowed to attend school. You can be jailed for owning a television. Religion can be practiced only as their leaders dictate. A man can be jailed in Afghanistan if his beard is not long enough.

The United States respects the people of Afghanistan—after all, we are currently its largest source of humanitarian aid—but we condemn the Taliban regime. It is not only repressing its own people, it is threatening people everywhere by sponsoring and sheltering and supplying terrorists. By aiding and abetting murder, the Taliban regime is committing murder.

And tonight, the United States of America makes the following demands on the Taliban: Deliver to United States authorities all the leaders of al Qaeda who hide in your land. Release all foreign nationals, including American citizens, you have unjustly imprisoned. Protect foreign journalists, diplomats and aid workers in your country. Close immediately and permanently every terrorist training camp in Afghanistan, and hand over every terrorist, and every person in their support structure, to appropriate authorities. Give the United States full access to terrorist training camps, so we can make sure they are no longer operating.

These demands are not open to negotiation or discussion. The Taliban must act, and act immediately. They will hand over the terrorists, or they will share in their fate. . . .

WHY TERRORISTS HATE AMERICA

Our war on terror begins with al Qaeda, but it does not end there. It will not end until every terrorist group of global reach has been found, stopped and defeated.

Americans are asking, why do they hate us? They hate what we see right here in this chamber—a democratically elected government. Their leaders are self-appointed. They hate our freedoms—our freedom of religion, our freedom of speech, our freedom to vote and assemble and disagree with each other.

They want to overthrow existing governments in many Muslim countries, such as Egypt, Saudi Arabia, and Jordan. They want to drive Israel out of the Middle East. They want to drive Christians and Jews out of vast regions of Asia and Africa.

These terrorists kill not merely to end lives, but to disrupt and end a way of life. With every atrocity, they hope that America grows fearful, retreating from the world and forsaking our friends. They stand against us, because we stand in their way.

We are not deceived by their pretenses to piety. We have seen their kind before. They are the heirs of all the murderous ideologies of the 20th century. By sacrificing human life to serve their radical visions—by abandoning every value except the will to power—they follow in the path of fascism, and Nazism, and totalitarianism. And they will follow that path all the way, to where it ends: in history's unmarked grave of discarded lies.

THE COMING WAR

Americans are asking: How will we fight and win this war? We will direct every resource at our command—every means of diplomacy, every tool of intelligence, every instrument of law enforcement, every financial influence, and every necessary weapon of war—to the disruption and to the defeat of the global terror network.

This war will not be like the war against Iraq a decade ago, with a decisive liberation of territory and a swift conclusion. It will not look like the air war above Kosovo two years ago, where no ground troops were used and not a single American was lost in combat.

Our response involves far more than instant retaliation and isolated strikes. Americans should not expect one battle, but a lengthy campaign, unlike any other we have ever seen. It may include dramatic strikes, visible on TV, and covert operations, secret even in success. We will starve terrorists of funding, turn them one against another, drive them from place to place, until there is no refuge or no rest. And we will pursue nations that provide aid or safe haven to terrorism. Every nation, in every region, now has a decision to make. Either you are with us, or you are with the terrorists. From this day forward, any nation that continues to harbor or support terrorism will be regarded by the United States as a hostile regime....

CIVILIZATION'S FIGHT

This is not, however, just America's fight. And what is at stake is not just America's freedom. This is the world's fight. This is civilization's fight. This is the fight of all who believe in progress and pluralism, tolerance and freedom.

We ask every nation to join us. We will ask, and we will need, the help of police forces, intelligence services, and banking systems around the world. The United States

is grateful that many nations and many international organizations have already responded—with sympathy and with support. Nations from Latin America, to Asia, to Africa, to Europe, to the Islamic world. Perhaps the NATO Charter reflects best the attitude of the world: An attack on one is an attack on all.

The civilized world is rallying to America's side. They understand that if this terror goes unpunished, their own cities, their own citizens may be next. Terror, unanswered, can not only bring down buildings, it can threaten the stability of legitimate governments. And you know what—we're not going to allow it....

AMERICA'S FUTURE

After all that has just passed—all the lives taken, and all the possibilities and hopes that died with them—it is natural to wonder if America's future is one of fear. Some speak of an age of terror. I know there are struggles ahead, and dangers to face. But this country will define our times, not be defined by them. As long as the United States of America is determined and strong, this will not be an age of terror; this will be an age of liberty, here and across the world.

Great harm has been done to us. We have suffered great loss. And in our grief and anger we have found our mission and our moment. Freedom and fear are at war. The advance of human freedom—the great achievement of our time, and the great hope of every time—now depends on us. Our nation—this generation—will lift a dark threat of violence from our people and our future. We will rally the world to this cause by our efforts, by our courage. We will not tire, we will not falter, and we will not fail.

It is my hope that in the months and years ahead, life will return almost to normal. We'll go back to our lives and routines, and that is good. Even grief recedes with time and grace. But our resolve must not pass. Each of us will remember what happened that day, and to whom it happened. We'll remember the moment the news came—where we were and what we were doing. Some will remember an image of a fire, or a story of rescue. Some will carry memories of a face and a voice gone forever.

And I will carry this: It is the police shield of a man named George Howard, who died at the World Trade Center trying to save others. It was given to me by his mom, Arlene, as a proud memorial to her son. This is my reminder of lives that ended, and a task that does not end.

I will not forget this wound to our country or those who inflicted it. I will not yield; I will not rest; I will not relent in waging this struggle for freedom and security for the American people.

The course of this conflict is not known, yet its outcome is certain. Freedom and fear, justice and cruelty, have always been at war, and we know that God is not neutral between them.

Fellow citizens, we'll meet violence with patient justice—assured of the rightness of our cause, and confident of the victories to come. In all that lies before us, may God grant us wisdom, and may He watch over the United States of America.

Viewpoint 41B

America Must Seek Alternatives to a Military Response to Terrorism (2001)

Joyce Neu (b. 1950)

INTRODUCTION *The September 11, 2001, terrorist attacks on America left three thousand people dead and led President George W. Bush to state that America was entering a "war on terror." However, there remained dissent within America on whether a military response to the terrorist attacks was the right one. The following viewpoint is taken from an article written a few weeks after the September 11 attacks by Joyce Neu, then executive director of the Joan B. Kroc Institute for Peace and Justice at the University of San Diego. She contends that while Americans are understandably and justifiably angry at the terrorists behind the attacks, their support of military reprisals is misguided. The United States should seek alternatives to war, which inevitably kills innocent bystanders and civilians, in seeking to bring the September 11 terrorists to justice, she contends. She concludes that a restrained and magnanimous response by the United States could help build a better and more tolerant world and reduce terrorism. President Bush ultimately decided in October 2001 to use military action against Afghanistan, a country that was harboring the leaders of the terrorist network. More controversially, Bush also ordered military action against Iraq in March 2003, arguing that such action was necessary to forestall the possibility of other terrorist attacks.*

What argument does Neu make about the deterrent potential of military action as it relates to terrorism? What messages should Americans be thinking about sending to the rest of the world, according to Neu? What prediction does she make about the results of military action against Afghanistan and Iraq?

In the last decade [the 1990s], I have seen firsthand the consequences of armed conflict in Bosnia, Congo, Georgia, Rwanda, Sudan and Uganda. As a professional in the field of conflict resolution, I have met with government and rebel leaders who argued eloquently, in the words of Bob Dylan's famous sixties song, that "God was on their side."

Joyce Neu, "Extracting Vengeance or Building a Lasting Peace," *San Diego Union-Tribune,* September 27, 2001.

While each conflict may be different in its history and causes, each conflict is the same in causing the deaths of innocents. Of the several million people who have been killed in wars in the last decade [1990s], estimates are that 80 percent to 90 percent of these are civilians. No matter how just the cause, these people did not deserve to die.

HOLDING AMERICA TO A HIGHER STANDARD

As a result of the tragic events of Sept. 11, our government is examining possible responses, including military action. Polls show that most Americans favor military action; but there are those of us who believe the United States is capable of being held to a higher standard. If we believe, like the terrorists who struck the World Trade Center, the Pentagon, and a field in Pennsylvania, that our cause is just, and that innocent lives may have to be lost to extract "justice," then we become moral cowards, defining justice in terms of retribution and revenge and we perpetuate a cycle of violence all too familiar to those who perpetrated the brutal actions of Sept. 11.

The tragic loss of life of Sept. 11 has torn the mask of civility off many of our faces. We are justifiably angry and frustrated at our inability to have predicted or prevented the deaths on our soil of so many good people, Americans and others from around the world.

What kind of response can we have that will demonstrate to the world that we mean business in fighting this campaign against terrorism? Rather than look to military might as our answer, we might seek more creative, sustainable ways to ensure justice is done and that the causes for such violence are extinguished. As patriotic Americans, we may want to demonstrate to the world the power of a free society by acting internationally the way we see firefighters, police officers, and volunteers acting in response to the World Trade Center destruction—with perseverance, generosity and concern.

Why would we choose to respond magnanimously instead of militarily? Would this be seen as weakness? While military power serves as a deterrent to the threat of war between nations, it clearly has not served as a deterrent to terrorism.

Children growing up in the developing world look to the developed world, particularly the United States, as a model. Will Afghan and Iraqi children, having been subjected to hunger, disease and oppression, look at the United States as a model of what they want for their country or as the enemy on whom to seek revenge? This is within our power to decide. Responding magnanimously will sow the seeds of friendship; striking their homelands will give rise to a new generation of terrorists.

Perhaps just as importantly, if we respond militarily, what does it say about us as a people? Does it say that because we have the power to destroy, we must do so? That faced with an attack against us, we have no recourse but to respond in similar fashion? Wouldn't restraint reveal our true nature better?

That our ability to develop sophisticated weaponry does not mean that we are eager to use it? We should be clear that no matter how powerful our military is, it cannot guarantee that we can go into Afghanistan or Iraq without incurring the deaths of our own troops and those of innocent civilians.

Americans should demonstrate that we are not like the terrorists and do not take the lives of innocents.

DIFFICULT CHOICES

We are a nation of the people and by the people, and we are facing difficult choices: do we rationalize the deaths of innocents abroad as the cost of fighting terrorism? Do we make clear to the world that we hold human life sacred only if it is American life? Or do we find ways to safeguard our lives and property in a way that honors the foundations of our society: rule of law, human rights, and the dignity of each person?

The reactions of families whose loved ones were killed or are still missing seems to be that they do not want a military action taken in the name of their loved ones. They do not see that violence will get anything but more families torn apart in grief.

Americans should demonstrate that we are not like the terrorists and do not take the lives of innocents. We need the strength of character and moral authority to pursue a campaign to eradicate the causes of terrorism. While it may involve determining those responsible, routing them out and seeing that they are brought to justice, the campaign against terrorism must seek to pull out the roots that spread the hatred, fear and desperation that give rise to suicide and destruction.

We must begin a campaign of inoculating people against despair by taking on the economic and social disparities that give rise to hopelessness and frustration, whether in our country or outside. Americans are a generous people. The TV images of the work of firefighters, police officers and volunteers in New York City make us all proud to be Americans. We need to take this selflessness to those in need in our own country as well as outside our country.

Just as we export goods, so should we export our know-how, our decency, and our conviction that working together, we can make a difference. One part of our covert campaign against terrorism therefore should consist of rebuilding schools and hospitals, providing training and skills for responsible leadership, and in the short-term, making sure that there are refugee camps ready with food and shelter to accept people fleeing from the feared U.S. military attacks.

Another part of the campaign is to make clear the distinction between religion and fanaticism. Just as many wars are supposedly waged in the name of religion, there are usually other, more material reasons for the violence. Islam is not the enemy just as Arab countries are not the enemy. These acts were the acts of terrorists. Not Islamic terrorists, not Arab terrorists—just terrorists. Our leaders have started to make this clear and we need to continue to emphasize that these acts had nothing to do with any religion or belief system. God was not on their side just as God is not on the side of anyone who perpetrates the killing and destruction of innocent people.

ESTABLISH AN INTERNATIONAL CRIMINAL COURT

The United States should also re-engage in the dialogue to establish a permanent International Criminal Court. Although discussions in the United Nations and other international arenas often take positions that the U.S. government believes are antithetical to ours, if we are not part of the debate, then we cannot complain when we do not like the outcome....

Without an International Criminal Court, we will have to create ad hoc tribunals for people like Osama bin Laden. The world deserves a permanent, standing court where terrorists and war criminals, regardless of country or conflict, can be tried.

Finally, we need to take time to mourn the dead and the missing. Before we react in a manner that undermines our character as a strong and proud people who believe in the rule of law and justice, our leaders should take the time to remember the lessons of U.S. involvement in Japan and Germany post–World War II.

By helping those countries and peoples rebuild and develop, we gained loyal allies that are still with us today. Let us create new allies out of enemies so that our children and grandchildren will remember Sept. 11, 2001 and its victims as giving rise to new understandings and tolerance, not to more violence and death.

FOR FURTHER READING

Mary Buckley and Robert Singh, eds., *The Bush Doctrine and the War on Terrorism.* New York: Routledge, 2006.

Richard A. Clarke, *Against All Enemies: Inside America's War on Terror.* New York: Free Press, 2004.

Robert Jervis, *American Foreign Policy and a New Era.* New York: Routledge, 2005.

John B. Judis, *The Folly of Empire: What George W. Bush Could Learn from Theodore Roosevelt and Woodrow Wilson.* New York: Scribner, 2004.

President George W. Bush Is Abusing the War Powers of His Office (2006)

Elizabeth Holtzman (b. 1941)

INTRODUCTION *Elizabeth Holtzman is an attorney who served four terms in the House of Representatives, from 1973–81. As part of her tenure in Congress, she sat on the House Judiciary Committee during the impeachment proceedings against President Richard Nixon.*

The following viewpoint is from a 2006 article by Holtzman published in The Nation. *Revelations of the existence of a secret electronic eavesdropping operation by the National Security Administration (NSA) that may have violated federal laws against domestic spying without a warrant, have added to violations by the Bush administration that Holtzman equates to high crimes and misdemeanor. She argues that wiretappping is but one example of what she views as a dangerous trend to expand the executive powers of the presidency—a concentration of power and disregard for the rule of law that Holtzman cites as grounds for impeachment.*

Why, does Holtzman argue, should President Bush be impeached? How does Holtzman refute the Bush's legal circumventing of the Foreign Intelligence Surveillance Act (FISA)?

Like many others, I have been deeply troubled by Bush's breathtaking scorn for our international treaty obligations under the United Nations Charter and the Geneva Conventions. I have also been disturbed by the torture scandals and the violations of US criminal laws at the highest levels of our government they may entail. These concerns have been compounded by growing evidence that the President deliberately misled the country into the war in Iraq. But it wasn't until the most recent revelations that President Bush directed the wiretapping of hundreds, possibly thousands, of Americans, in violation of the Foreign Intelligence Surveillance Act (FISA)—and argued that, as Commander in Chief, he had the right in the interests of national security to override our country's laws—that I felt the same sinking feeling in my stomach as I did during Watergate.

As a matter of constitutional law, these and other misdeeds constitute grounds for the impeachment of President Bush. A President, any President, who maintains that he is above the law—and repeatedly violates the law—thereby commits high crimes and misdemeanors, the constitutional standard for impeachment and removal from office. A high crime or misdemeanor is an archaic term that means a serious abuse of power, whether

Elizabeth Holtzman, "The Impeachment of George W. Bush," *The Nation*, January 30, 2006.

or not it is also a crime, that endangers our constitutional system of government.

WARRANTLESS WIRETAPS

On December 17 President Bush acknowledged that he repeatedly authorized wiretaps, without obtaining a warrant, of American citizens engaged in international calls. On the face of it, these warrantless wiretaps violate FISA, which requires court approval for national security wiretaps and sets up a special procedure for obtaining it. Violation of the law is a felony.

While many facts about these wiretaps are unknown, it now appears that thousands of calls were monitored and that the information obtained may have been widely circulated among federal agencies. It also appears that a number of government officials considered the warrantless wiretaps of dubious legality. Reportedly, several people in the National Security Agency refused to participate in them, and a deputy attorney general even declined to sign off on some aspects of these wiretaps. The special FISA court has raised concerns as well, and a judge on that court has resigned, apparently in protest.

FISA was enacted in 1978, against the backdrop of Watergate, to prevent the widespread abuses in domestic surveillance that were disclosed in Congressional hearings. Among his other abuses of power, President Nixon ordered the FBI to conduct warrantless wiretaps of seventeen journalists and White House staffers. Although Nixon claimed the wiretaps were done for national security purposes, they were undertaken for political purposes and were illegal. Just as Bush's warrantless wiretaps grew out of the 9/11 attacks, Nixon's illegal wiretaps grew out of the Vietnam War and the opposition to it. In fact, the first illegal Nixon wiretap was of a reporter who, in 1969, revealed the secret bombing of Cambodia, a program that President Nixon wanted to hide from the American people and Congress. Nixon's illegal wiretaps formed one of the many grounds for the articles of impeachment voted against him by a bipartisan majority of the House Judiciary Committee.

Congress explicitly intended FISA to strike a balance between the legitimate requirements of national security on the one hand and the need both to protect against presidential abuses and to safeguard personal privacy on the other. From Watergate, Congress knew that a President was fully capable of wiretapping under a false claim of national security. That is why the law requires court review of national security wiretaps. Congress understood that because of the huge invasion of privacy involved in wiretaps, there should be checks in place on the executive branch to protect against overzealous and unnecessary wiretapping. At the same time, Congress created special procedures to facilitate obtaining these warrants when justified. Congress also recognized the need for emergency action: The President was given the power to start a wiretap without a warrant as long as court permission was obtained within three days.

FISA can scarcely be claimed to create any obstacle to justified national security wiretaps. Since 1978, when the law was enacted, more than 10,000 national security warrants have been approved by the FISA court; only four have been turned down.

----■----

It is impossible to find in the Constitution unilateral presidential authority to act against US citizens in a way that violates US laws, even in wartime.

----■----

Two legal arguments have been offered for the President's right to violate the law, both of which have been seriously questioned by members of Congress of both parties and by the nonpartisan Congressional Research Service in a recent analysis. The first—highly dangerous in its sweep and implications—is that the President has the constitutional right as Commander in Chief to break any US law on the grounds of national security. As the CRS analysis points out, the Supreme Court has never upheld the President's right to do this in the area of wiretapping, nor has it ever granted the President a "monopoly over war-powers" or recognized him as "Commander in Chief of the country" as opposed to Commander in Chief of the Army and Navy. If the President is permitted to break the law on wiretapping on his own say-so, then a President can break any other law on his own say-so—a formula for dictatorship. This is not a theoretical danger: President Bush has recently claimed the right as Commander in Chief to violate the McCain amendment banning torture and degrading treatment of detainees. Nor is the requirement that national security be at stake any safeguard. We saw in Watergate how President Nixon falsely and cynically used that argument to cover up ordinary crimes and political misdeeds.

Ours is a government of limited power. We learn in elementary school the concept of checks and balances. Those checks do not vanish in wartime; the President's role as Commander in Chief does not swallow up Congress's powers or the Bill of Rights. Given the framers' skepticism about executive power and warmaking— there was no functional standing army at the beginning of the nation, so the President's powers as Commander in Chief depended on Congress's willingness to create and expand an army—it is impossible to find in the Constitution unilateral presidential authority to act against US citizens in a way that violates US laws, even in wartime. As Justice Sandra Day O'Connor recently wrote,

"A state of war is not a blank check for the President when it comes to the rights of the nation's citizens."

The second legal argument in defense of Bush's warrantless wiretaps rests on an erroneous statutory interpretation. According to this argument, Congress authorized the Administration to place wiretaps without court approval when it adopted the 2001 resolution authorizing military force against the Taliban and al Qaeda for the 9/11 attacks. In the first place, the force resolution doesn't mention wiretaps. And given that Congress has traditionally placed so many restrictions on wiretapping because of its extremely intrusive qualities, there would undoubtedly have been vigorous debate if anyone thought the force resolution would roll back FISA. In fact, the legislative history of the force resolution shows that Congress had no intention of broadening the scope of presidential warmaking powers to cover activity in the United States. According to Senator Tom Daschle, the former Senate majority leader who negotiated the resolution with the White House, the Administration wanted to include language explicitly enlarging the President's warmaking powers to include domestic activity. That language was rejected. Obviously, if the Administration felt it already had the power, it would not have tried to insert the language into the resolution.

Indeed, the claim that to protect Americans the President needs to be able to avoid court review of his wiretap applications rings hollow. It is unclear why or in what way the existing law, requiring court approval, is not satisfactory. And, if the law is too cumbersome or inapplicable to modern technology, then it is unclear why the President did not seek to revise it instead of disregarding it and thus jeopardizing many otherwise legitimate antiterrorism prosecutions. His defenders' claim that changing the law would have given away secrets is unacceptable. There are procedures for considering classified information in Congress.

TORTURE AND OTHER ABUSES OF POWER

President Bush recently proclaimed, "We do not torture." In view of the revelations of the CIA's secret jails and practice of rendition, not to mention the Abu Ghraib scandal, the statement borders on the absurd, recalling Nixon's famous claim, "I am not a crook." It has been well documented that abuse (including torture) of detainees by US personnel in connection with the wars in Afghanistan and Iraq has been systemic and widespread. Under the War Crimes Act of 1996 it is a crime for any US national to order or engage in the murder, torture or inhuman treatment of a detainee. (When a detainee death results, the act imposes the death penalty.) In addition, anyone in the chain of command who condones the abuse rather than stopping it could also be in violation of the act. The act simply implements the Geneva Conventions, which are the law of the land.

The evidence before us now suggests that the President himself may have authorized detainee abuse. In January 2002, after the Afghanistan war had begun, White House Counsel Alberto Gonzales advised President Bush in writing that US mistreatment of detainees might be criminally prosecutable under the War Crimes Act. Rather than order the possibly criminal behavior to stop, which under the Geneva Conventions and the War Crimes Act the President was obligated to do, Bush authorized an "opt-out" of the Geneva Conventions to try to shield the Americans who were abusing detainees from prosecution. In other words, the President's response to reports of detainee abuse was to prevent prosecution of the abusers, thereby implicitly condoning the abuse and authorizing its continuation. If torture or inhuman treatment of prisoners took place as a result of the President's conduct, then he himself may have violated the War Crimes Act, along with those who actually inflicted the abuse.

There are many other indications that the President has knowingly condoned detainee abuse. For example, he never removed Defense Secretary Rumsfeld from office or disciplined him, even though Rumsfeld accepted responsibility for the abuse scandal at Abu Ghraib, admitted hiding a detainee from the Red Cross—a violation of the Geneva Conventions and possibly the War Crimes Act, if the detainee was being abused—and issued orders (later withdrawn) for Guantánamo interrogations that violated the Geneva Conventions and possibly the War Crimes Act.

More recently, the President opposed the McCain Amendment barring torture when it was first proposed, and he tacitly supported Vice President Cheney's efforts to get language into the bill that would allow the CIA to torture or degrade detainees. Now, in his signing statement, the President announced that he has the right to violate the new law, claiming once again the right as Commander in Chief to break laws when it suits him.

Furthermore, despite the horrors of the Abu Ghraib scandal, no higher-ups have been held accountable. Only one officer of any significant rank has been punished.... President Bush has made no serious effort to insure that the full scope of the scandal is uncovered or to hold any higher-ups responsible, perhaps because responsibility goes right to the White House.

Viewpoint 42B

The President Needs Broad Wartime Powers to Protect the Nation (2006)

John Yoo (b. 1967)

INTRODUCTION *John Yoo is a law professor at the University of California at Berkeley. From 2001 to 2003 he served in the Office of Legal Counsel under President George W. Bush. Bush has been criticized by some for abusing the powers of his office in prosecuting America's post–September 11, 2001, war on terror, and in launching a war on Iraq without a formal Congressional declaration of war. In the following viewpoint, Yoo argues that these criticisms are misguided, and that the president does and should have broad powers to conduct foreign policy and defend the nation from attack, including waging pre-emptive war. He questions whether greater Congressional involvement in war decisions would yield positive results.*

How many times has the United States conducted military action without a Congressional declaration of war, according to Yoo? In what historical context does he place the creation of the Constitution and its divisions of power?

Iraq is beginning to sound like a rerun of the Vietnam War, and not just because presidential critics again are crying out that the United States has fallen into a quagmire. War opponents also again argue that a wartime president has overstepped the Constitution and that, if Congress' constitutional role in deciding on war had only been respected, the United States could have avoided trouble or at least entered the war with broader popular support.

Opponents of the [George W.] Bush administration make similar arguments against the war on terrorism. The Guantánamo Bay base would never have been created, terrorists never interrogated, and the National Security Agency never would have expanded its surveillance powers, if only President Bush had looked to Congress in setting war policy.

But these critics misread the Constitution's allocation of warmaking powers between the executive and legislative branches. As commander in chief and chief executive, the president has the constitutional authority and the responsibility to protect the nation from foreign attack. Indeed, the framers of the Constitution designed the presidency to wield power quickly and decisively for this very reason.

"Energy in the executive," Alexander Hamilton argued in the Federalist Papers, "is a leading character in the definition of good government. It is essential to the protection of the community against foreign attacks." And, he continued, "the direction of war most peculiarly demands those qualities which distinguish the exercise of power by a single hand."

WHO DECIDES WHEN WAR BEGINS

This is nowhere more true than where the critics' case should be its strongest: who decides when war begins.

During the last two centuries, neither presidents nor Congress have ever acted under the belief that the

John Yoo, "Wartime, Constitution, Empower Presidents," *San Diego Union-Tribune*, January 15, 2006.

Constitution requires a declaration of war before the U.S. can engage in military hostilities abroad. Although this nation has used force abroad more than 100 times, it has declared war only five times: the War of 1812, the Mexican-American and Spanish-American Wars, and World Wars I and II. Without declarations of war or any other congressional authorization, presidents have sent troops to oppose the Russian Revolution, intervene in Mexico, fight Chinese Communists in Korea, remove Manuel Noriega from power in Panama, and prevent human rights disasters in the Balkans. Other conflicts, such as both Persian Gulf Wars, received "authorization" from Congress but not declarations of war.

Bush administration opponents want to toss out this long practice by appeals to an "original understanding" of the Constitution. But the text and structure of the Constitution, as well as its application over the last two centuries, confirm that the president can begin military hostilities without the approval of Congress. The Constitution does not establish a strict war-making process because the framers understood that war would require the speed, decisiveness and secrecy that only the presidency could bring.

Presidential critics appeal to an understanding of declaring war probably taught in most high school civics classes. It is perhaps a commonsense notion to equate the power to "declare" war with the power to "begin" or "commence" war. This view comports with a popular imagery of declarations of war as marking American entry into the most significant conflicts of the twentieth century, the two World Wars.

The Constitution's Declare War Clause, however, should not be considered in isolation. In fact, the Constitution does not consistently use the word "declare" to mean "initiate" or "make," even when referring to war. Moreover, an earlier draft of the Constitution had given Congress the power to "make" war, but the delegates subsequently changed the power to the lesser power to "declare" it. The Constitution usually makes very clear when it requires a specific process before the government can act, particularly when the executive and legislative branches share a power. For example, the Constitution sets out detailed procedures that the president and Congress must follow to enact laws or enter into treaties.

In contrast, the Constitution does not define a process for warmaking. This suggests that the framers gave the executive and legislative branches substantial flexibility to shape the decisionmaking process.

THE BRITISH CONTEXT

Historically, the Framers understood the distribution of war powers between the executive and legislative branches in the context of the British system. As commander in chief, the British king had complete control over war.

A declaration of war was not needed either to begin or to wage a war. Rather, declarations of war served to formally invoke the protections of international law, so that, for example, citizens of the contending nations could lawfully keep captured vessels without fear of being accused of piracy.

It was Parliament's control over funding that provided the check on executive warmaking. Indeed, in the century before the Constitution, Britain engaged in eight significant military conflicts, but only once "declared" war at the start. But Parliament retained the power of the purse, and without parliamentary consent, soldiers would not be paid, armies would not be properly equipped, and the king's war power would be rendered largely illusory. This was not an accident—rather, the distinction between the war power and the powers to fund and legislate was a core element of the separation of powers and the rise of parliamentary democracy.

But suppose the Constitution did not provide a clear answer to the question of which branch of government controls the decision for war. If the Congress and president had to agree on initiating hostilities, it is by no means clear that the fortunes of war would improve for the United States.

First, congressional deliberation does not necessarily ensure consensus. Take the Vietnam War. Though initially approved by Congress, the war did not meet with a consensus over the long term but instead provoked some of the most divisive politics in American history. Much the same goes for the 2002 congressional authorization to use force in Iraq.

It is also not clear that the absence of congressional approval has led the nation into wars that it should not have waged. During the Cold War, for example, the United States fought against Soviet proxies around the globe. Yet the only war arguably authorized by Congress—and this point is debatable—was the Vietnam War. Aside from Vietnam, the strategy of containing the Soviet Union succeeded thanks to the steady leadership of several presidents of both parties and the consistent financial support of Congress.

On the other hand, congressional action can produce poor decisions. Congress led us into two "bad" wars, the 1798 quasi-war with France and the War of 1812. And most would agree now that congressional isolationism before World War II harmed U.S. interests. The United States and the world would have been far better off if President Franklin Roosevelt could have brought the United States into the conflict much earlier.

THE NEED FOR PRE-EMPTIVE ACTION

Critics of presidential war powers exaggerate the benefits of declarations or authorizations of war, and they also fail to examine the potential costs of congressional participation:

delay, inflexibility, and lack of secrecy. Legislative deliberation may breed consensus in the best of cases, but it also may inhibit speed and decisiveness. In the post-Cold War era, the United States confronts several new threats to its national security: proliferation of weapons of mass destruction, the emergence of rogue nations, and the rise of international terrorism. Each of these threats may require preemptive action best undertaken by the president and approved by Congress only afterward.

Take the threat posed by the al-Qaeda terrorist organization. Despite the fact that terrorists generally have no territory or regular armed forces from which to detect signs of an impending attack, WMDs [weapons of mass destruction] allow them to inflict devastation that once only laid in the hands of a nation-state.

The Constitution creates a presidency that can respond forcefully and independently to pre-empt serious threats to our national security.

In order to forestall another 9/11 attack, or to take advantage of a window of opportunity to strike a terrorist cell, the executive branch needs flexibility to act quickly, possibly in situations where congressional consent cannot be obtained in time to act on the intelligence. By pre-empting a terrorist attack, the president might also be able to engage in a more limited, more precisely targeted, use of force.

Similarly, the least dangerous way to prevent rogue nations from acquiring WMDs may depend on secret intelligence gathering and covert action, rather than open military intervention. Delay for a congressional debate could render useless any time-critical intelligence or windows of opportunity. If Congress wants to prevent military adventurism, it can simply do nothing—presidents can wage no war without the troops and weapons funded by Congress.

The Constitution creates a presidency that can respond forcefully and independently to pre-empt serious threats to our national security. Instead of demanding a legalistic process to begin war, the framers left war to politics. Presidents can take the initiative and Congress would use their funding power to check him. As we confront terrorism, rogue nations, and WMD proliferation, now is not the time to engage in a radical change in the way our government has waged war for decades.

FOR FURTHER READING

Glenn Greenwald, *How Would a Patriot Act: Defending American Values from a President Run Amok.* San Francisco: Working Assets Publishing, 2006.

Gary C. Jacobsen and Samuel Kernell, *The Logic of American Politics in Wartime: Lessons from the Bush Administration.* Washington, DC: CQ Press, 2004.

James Risen, *State of War: The Secret History of the CIA and the Bush Administration.* New York: Free Press, 2006.

Bill Sammon, *Strategery: How George W. Bush Is Defeating Terrorists, Outwitting Democrats, and Confounding the Mainstream Media.* Washington, DC: Regnery, 2006.

Index